PEACEBUILDING IN THE AFRI(

CU00689476

Particularly in the context of internal conflicts, international law is frequently unable to create and sustain frameworks for peace in Africa. In *Peacebuilding in the African Union*, Abou Jeng explores the factors which have prevented such steps forward in the interaction between the international legal order and postcolonial Africa. In the first work of its kind, Jeng considers whether these limitations necessitate recasting the existing conceptual structure, and whether the Constitutive Act of the African Union provides exactly this opportunity through its integrated peace and security framework. Using the case studies of Burundi and Somalia, Jeng examines the structures and philosophy of the African Union and assesses the capacity of its practices in peacemaking. In so doing, this book will be of great practical value to scholars and legal . practitioners alike.

DR ABOU JENG is a human rights lawyer and Research Fellow at the Centre for Human Rights in Practice, University of Warwick. His current research focuses on human rights and disaster risk management, constitutional governance, globalisation and refugee law.

PEACEBUILDING IN THE AFRICAN UNION

Law, Philosophy and Practice

ABOU JENG

CAMBRIDGE
UNIVERSITY PRESS

CAMBRIDGE
UNIVERSITY PRESS

University Printing House, Cambridge CB2 8BS, United Kingdom

Cambridge University Press is part of the University of Cambridge.

It furthers the University's mission by disseminating knowledge in the pursuit of education, learning and research at the highest international levels of excellence.

www.cambridge.org
Information on this title: www.cambridge.org/9781107538351

© Abou Jeng 2012

First published 2012
First paperback edition 2015

A catalogue record for this publication is available from the British Library

Library of Congress Cataloguing in Publication data

Jeng, Abou.
Peacebuilding in the African Union : law, philosophy and practice / Abou Jeng.
pages cm
Includes bibliographical references and index.
ISBN 978-1-107-01521-0
1. Peace-building–Africa. 2. African Union. I. Title.
JZ5584.A35J45 2012
341.7´3096–dc23
2012015671

ISBN 978-1-107-01521-0 Hardback
ISBN 978-1-107-53835-1 Paperback

This book is dedicated, in no particular order, to the following formidable women:

Awa (Ndoye) Chow, for being remarkably stoical and hopeful in the face of her adversities in Kuntaya

Kathryn Williams, for investing faith in my line of work when others doubted

Mama Adama Khan, for living a fulfilling and extraordinarily simple life that inspired many

Mam Awa Camara, for leading by manifesting values of virtuous exemplification

Mary F. Touray, for her endless determination to improve the social conditions of those she encountered

CONTENTS

ACKNOWLEDGEMENTS

It is generally presumed that any academic exercise, especially one as relatively challenging as writing a book, would almost inevitably benefit from the services and munificence of people and institutions. The gestation of this book is no exception. The work that formulates it has been a culmination of personal struggles, experiences and excitement, during which I accumulated a considerable debt of gratitude to an ensemble of people without whose support and goodwill this book would have been only a distant possibility. First to whom I owe such gratitude is Dr Andrew T. Williams of the Centre for Human Rights in Practice, University of Warwick. Andrew's encouragement, relentless support and guidance – going well beyond his call of duty – bespeak of hallmarks rare amongst his contemporaries. His acumen, advice, direction, continuous probing and attention to detail accorded me the intellectual resources, personal drive and discipline to overcome the many challenges I faced whilst completing this book. He had also gone to extraordinary lengths in helping ameliorate some of the personal difficulties I endured during the course of my Ph.D., which he so assiduously supervised.

Gratitude is also due to some wonderful people at the Warwick Law School who, during the course of my research and teaching stint, were magnanimous in their support. Professor Abdul Hussein Paliwala and Emeritus Professor Upendra Baxi have been particularly inspiring in their numerous personal and academic engagements with me. Dr Jayan Nayar offered solidarity and encouragement, whilst also provoking thoughts and lines of critical thinking that shaped aspects of this book. Solange Mouthaan, perhaps the most considerate person I have ever met, has been exceptionally helpful, comforting in friendship and reassuring in her goodwill. Similarly, Dr George Meszaros' amiable personality and open-door policy meant that I was always eager to drop by for a chat or a bit of bother. Professor Istvan Pogany deserves special mention for his willingness in taking me on board for teaching activities on the international law programme, from where pleasant encounters with some of the students enhanced my interest in looking at international law from rare perspectives. Istvan's affable, unassuming personality and sometimes self-deprecating sense of humour made possible a mutual dialogical engagement from which I have benefitted most enormously. I am also grateful to Professor Franklyn Lisk at the Centre for the Study of Globalisation and Regionalisation, University of Warwick, for his support, encouragement and goodwill over the years.

Writing the book also involved months of 'residency' at the Wolfson Research Exchange, University of Warwick. The welcoming ambience and interactive nature of the facility made a profound difference. I am therefore thankful to Fiona Colligan, manager of the Exchange, and her wonderful support staff – Peter Murphy, Anna Sloan, Santiago Oyarzabal, Ana Magalhaes and Laura Rattigan – for their dedication to the ethos of the Exchange as well as for making me comfortable and well looked after. Particular gratitude is owed to Allen Newton, who generously offered me his storage space at some great inconvenience to himself. Helen Riley, the Law Librarian – whose remarkable work, sense of support and meticulous qualities are often taken for granted by academics and researchers at Warwick – exemplifies reliability, dependability and congeniality. I am indebted to her for much assistance over the years, especially in helping retrieve valuable archival materials.

Beyond Warwick, I am indebted to many others whose services had positive impact towards the final accomplishment of this book. I am especially grateful to Professor Matthew Craven of the School for Oriental and African Studies (SOAS), University of London, for providing valuable comments and drawing my attention to useful literature and lines of argument. Although the work that anchors this book is the culmination of my research endeavours and interests, I have however greatly benefitted from, and been considerably influenced by, the scholarship of Emeritus Professor Upendra Baxi, formerly of the University of Warwick, Professor Balakrishnan Rajagopal of the Massachusetts Institute of Technology (MIT), Professor B. S. Chimni of the Centre for International Legal Studies at Jawaharlal Nehru University and Professor Obiora Chinedu Okafor of the Osgoode Hall Law School, York University (Toronto). Their efforts in resuscitating interest in, and expanding the intellectual scope of, the patterns and habitats of Third World Approaches to International Law (TWAIL) have culminated in the excavation of numerous research streams previously overlooked.

The intensity and emotional strain of writing a book can sometimes be overwhelming. When it was, support from family and friends was crucial. I am indebted to my family – especially my parents – for their encouragement, prayers and boundless support. By the same token, I am also sorry for heightening anxieties when some of their enquiring messages on my wellbeing remained unanswered during some of the difficult times of writing this book. Especial thanks go to Essa Jallow for being exceptionally supportive and inspirational, whilst also holding the fort in my absence. Conversations with Amie Jeng (Aja) provided much-needed inspiration and strength.

I am similarly grateful to a wonderful group of friends, including Akemi Masuda Hirono, Papa Yusupha Njie, Eleri Davies, Selina Moutia, Rhiannon Owen, Ahmad Alkhamees, Tianyu Qiu (David), Liviu Damsa, Sharon Johnson, Shrey Pathak and Zhaoyang Yue. Their encouragement kept me going for the most part. Naffie Barry's frequent emails, which were often documentary expressions of the sacred and profane happenings around the world, helped lighten up some of my intensely demanding moments. In her, I have a wonderful friend – caring, helpful and accommodating. Gratitude is also owed to Professor Abdoulaye Saine of Miami University (Ohio, USA), Dr Jeggan C. Senghor, Senior Research Fellow at the Institute of Commonwealth Studies, University of London and Dr Ebrima Ceesay for their encouragement and continued support. I should also like to thank Njaimeh Sosseh, whose kindness in sharing her culinary excellence – a distinctly Gambian kindness – could not have come at a better time.

But rarely have I encountered two people who have had such a defining impact on my life as Mary F. Touray and Baboucarr Mbye Touray. Their pastoral support and deep-seated affection, for which I shall be forever grateful, guided me through a path of progressive ambition and personal accomplishments. Yusupha Touray and Jerreh Touray made things lively whilst also making possible some cherished memories.

There are others, too, who offered considerable support during my formative years, the foundation of which, in some ways, makes this book possible. Dr Mangum Mukhtar Ceesay made his time, hospitable home and intellectual resources accessible to me at a time of great need, whilst the tutelage and congenial encounters with Mrs Priscilla Johnson, Gabriel J. Roberts, Mark Hallem Collier and Jonas Ajay elevated my epistemological curiosity and searching enquiries. Uncle Sainey Touray, Sarjo 'Kono' Touray, Gallow Saidy, Bola Carrol, Imam Mass Mbye, Aji Olie Njie-Ceesay, Alasan Jagne, Amadou Sanneh (Debeh), Basiru Njai,

Momodou Amigo Jeng, Alhagi A. F. Conteh, Abdoulie Jobe, Sirra Wally Ndow-Njai, Kathryn Williams and Collin Morgan rendered services and support in various forms. I cannot thank them enough!

And finally, but by no means least, at Cambridge University Press I could not have asked for a more diligent and committed team. Nienke van Schaverbeke, the Commissioning Editor for Law, has been instrumental and profoundly helpful from the conception stages of this book onwards. Her patience, professionalism and encouragement provided both assurance and guidance. Similarly, I would like to thank Sarah Roberts and Elizabeth Spicer, who most diligently handled the editorial process. In particular, Elizabeth's devotion and abilities to navigate around challenges added impetus to the editorial and pre-production stages. I would additionally like to thank Andrew Dawes, whose editorial inputs helped in enhancing clarity. I am also grateful to the anonymous reviewers for their critical and very helpful comments and suggestions. Of course, all errors and inadequacies are mine alone.

ABOU JENG

TABLE OF CASES

TABLE OF RESOLUTIONS AND DECLARATIONS

ABBREVIATIONS

ACHPR	African Charter on Human and Peoples' Rights
ACtHPR	African Court on Human and Peoples' Rights
AEC	African Economic Community
ALF	African Leadership Forum
AMIB	African Union Mission in Burundi
AMISOM	African Union Mission in Somalia
ANC	African National Congress
APRM	Africa Peer Review Mechanism
AU	African Union
AUCIL	African Union Commission on International Law
CENAP	Centre for the Prevention of Conflict
CLS	Critical Legal Studies
CNDD-FDD	Conseil National Pour le Défense de la Démocratie
CSSDCA	Conference on Security, Stability, Development and Cooperation in Africa
DDR	disarmament, demobilisation and reintegration
DPKO	Department of Peacekeeping Operations
DRC	Democratic Republic of Congo
ECA	United Nations Economic Commission for Africa
ECOWAS	Economic Community of West African States
EU	European Union
FRODEBU	Front pour la Démocratie au Burundi
ICIB	International Commission of Inquiry for Burundi
ICISS	International Commission on Intervention and State Sovereignty
ICJ	International Court of Justice
ICRC	International Committee of the Red Cross
IFI	International Financial Institution
IGAD	Intergovernmental Authority on Development
IHL	International Humanitarian Law
IMF	International Monetary Fund
JRR	Jeunnesses Révolutionnaires Rwagasore
MCPMR	Mechanism for Conflict Prevention, Management and Resolution
NAIL	New Approaches to International Law

NATO	North Atlantic Treaty Organisation
NEPAD	New Partnership for Africa's Development
NIEO	New International Economic Order
NSI	North-South Institute
OAU	Organisation of African Unity
OCSE	Organisation for Cooperation and Security in Europe
ONUB	United Nations Operation in Burundi
PALIPEHUTU	Parti pour la libération du peuple Hutu
PCIJ	Permanent Court of International Justice
PDC	Christian Democratic Party
PSC	Peace and Security Council
REC	Regional Economic Communities
RPF	Rwandan Patriotic Front
SACB	Somalia Aid Coordination Body
SAPSD	South African Protection Support Detachment
SNM	Somali National Movement
SOMA	Status of Mission Agreement
SSDF	Somali Salvation Democratic Front
SYL	Somali Youth League
TFG	Transitional Federal Government
TNG	Transitional National Government
TWAIL	Third World Approaches to International Law
UDHR	Universal Declaration of Human Rights
UIC	Union of Islamic Courts
UN	United Nations
UNCTAD	United Nations Conference on Trade and Development
UNDOS	United Nations Development Office for Somalia
UNDP	United Nations Development Programme
UNITAF	Unified Task Force
UNOSOM	United Nations Operation in Somalia
UPRONA	Union pour le Progrès National
USC	United Somali Congress
VCLT	Vienna Convention on the Law of Treaties
WB	World Bank

1

Towards an introduction

Whose peace are we talking about? Peace on what terms? Peace in whose interests? And peace negotiated by which individuals or groups? In one sense, everybody wants peace; it is just that they want their own version of peace.

David Keen[1]

International law and postcolonial peace

A perception prevails that no matter the vast expanse of international legal transformations in the past century or so, international law, as a discipline and operative mechanism, remains largely entrapped in layers of normative and institutional inadequacies.[2] For the most part, the inadequacies have been manifested in a crisis of method and dispute about the basis, legitimacy and relevance of international law to Third World struggles, particularly aspects of those struggles preoccupied with the searching enquiries on the quest for peace and progressive social transformations.[3] The traditional narrative of international law had long been perceived to have an inclination for the dominance and consolidation of values shaped by a certain mindset, one which assumes that those values are neutral, just and universal. The claim to universalism and impartiality often tends to feed into the proposition that international law is invisible to, and isolated from, the dynamics of power in the interfaces between hegemonic and subaltern elements in international society.

---

[1] D. Keen, 'War and Peace: What's the Difference?' in A. Adebajo and C. L. Sriram (eds.), *Managing Armed Conflicts in the 21st Century* (London: Frank Cass, 2001), p. 18.

[2] See M. Koskenniemi, *From Apology to Utopia: The Structure of International Legal Argument* (Cambridge University Press, 2005); B. S. Chimni, *International Law and World Order: A Critique of Contemporary Approaches* (Delhi: SAGE Publications Ltd, 1993).

[3] See A. Carty, *The Decay of International Law: A Reappraisal of the Limits of Legal Imagination in International Affairs* (Manchester University Press, 1986), p. 1.

These assumptions, though, and the rationale upon which they are framed, continue to be contested. After all, law as an instrument for social change is often a mirror image of the very society that determines its content, praxis and operational hierarchy. Contemporary international law is no exception. Its history suggests that as a discipline, it duly initiates the reproduction of norms and values, conceptualised from the viewpoint of Western civilisation and political culture, which in its relation with non-European societies often arrogates a sense of dominance with a tincture of abrasive quality. The narrative of dominance underpinning some of international law's foundational values conditions a sense of universalism, seen by some as a kind of departure point which limits the scope for alternative thinking. As Edwin Burrows observes,

> We generally assume that we know, from ... observation, what is universally human. But a little scrutiny will show that such conclusions are based only on experience with one culture, our own. We assume that what is familiar, unless obviously shaped by special conditions, is universal.[4]

For some, though, international law's foundational precepts and claims to universalism seem too presumptuous to provide solutions to the needs and concerns of the Third World. The challenges to dominant inclinations of international law have been construed on the premise that the history of international law has been a struggle, most of which conjures an imagination of disempowerment of institutions and cultures of non-European societies, ultimately reducing them to what Upendra Baxi calls 'geographies of injustice'.[5] The scale and scope of these disjunctures are such that a renewal of international law on terms sensitive to, and reflective of, Third World struggles and settings would appear sensible. Yet, despite significant progress, not much has been achieved on this front, partly because the advocacy and advocates of international law are frozen in what Peter Goodrich calls 'a tenuous twilight zone between academic homelessness and practical professional insecurity' and often 'peddling a variant form of positive law where it is plausible, most needed and most unwelcome'.[6] The neglect of both the practitioner

---

[4] E. Burrows, *Flower in My Ear: Arts and Ethos on Ifaluk Atoll* (Seattle: University of Washington Press, 1963), p. 421.
[5] U. Baxi, 'Geographies of Injustice: Human Rights at the Altar of Convenience' in C. Scot (ed.), *Torture as Tort: Comparative Perspectives on the Development of Transnational Human Rights Litigation* (Oxford: Hart Publishing, 2001), p. 197.
[6] P. Goodrich, 'On the Relational Aesthetics of International Law: Philosophy of International Law', *Journal of the History of International Law*, 10 (2008), 321–341 at 322.

and what ought to be practised has culminated in 'the inclusion of international law within the identity of the self, so that it merely serves as a boundary of the self and as a weapon against the other'.[7] The implication has been to deny voice and obscure the other view, that 'there are practical alternatives to the current status quo of which, however, we rarely take notice, simply because such alternatives are not visible or credible to our ways of thinking'.[8]

Some of the disjunctures in the orientation of international law have the tendency to reproduce patterns of behaviour with some far-reaching implications, as experiences in postcolonial Africa have shown. Ever since decolonisation crystallised into self-rule, there has emerged what is referred to as 'postcolonial statehood'. The period facilitated closer encounters between international law and Africa through the concepts of sovereign equality, non-interference and territorial integrity. But these encounters and their trappings appear to have brought little to celebrate. Sovereignty occupies a contradictory position in the dynamics of these encounters. As the brainchild of the Treaty of Westphalia and configured through the European model of the nation state, it is the framework upon which international society is built. It is the source of legitimacy and the guarantor for the protection of the common interest of states. Moreover, sovereignty had also historically been seen as an antidote to interference in the domestic affairs of states. Whilst the benefit of this Westphalian ethos is essential, its related obligations are far more nuanced. They require strength to impose presence, legitimacy and conformity.

The postcolonial African state has, however, largely struggled to fulfil its most basic of obligations. In fact, the majority of its recent history has been a story of distress and contrasting ironies. It has been riddled with upheavals ranging from economic collapse and political turbulence to armed conflicts. Some of its defining futures have emerged from the rocky exercise of nation-building, whilst others emanated from the consequences and fissures of the immediate aftermath of decolonisation struggles. Yet in spite of all these, the postcolonial state and its formal apparatuses continue to be the primary mediums through which

---

[7] A. Carty, 'The Implosion of the Legal Subject and the Unravelling of the Law on the Use of Force: American Identity and New American Doctrines of Collective Security' in H. Kochler (ed.), *The Use of Force in International Relations: Challenges to Collective Security* (Vienna: International Progress Organization, 2006), p. 106.

[8] B. S. Santos, 'Epistemologies of the South: Reinventing Social Imagination'. Paper presented at the Staff-Student Seminar, School of Law, University of Warwick, 12 April 2010, 1–51 at 1.

international law's approaches to conflicts and peacebuilding are conceived. Andrew Linklater has suggested that the failure of theorising the world outside the state makes the 'modern political imagination profoundly impoverished'.[9] This impoverished imagination implies that the recurrent attributes of violence and conflicts have posed considerable challenges on the structures and instruments of international law. The actuality of these consequences remains a reference point for the quest for international and endogenous mechanisms for approaches to conflict and peacebuilding.

The traditional focus and ambition of international law in its encounters with postcolonial Africa have been the provision of normative and institutional frameworks through which international order could be maintained and interstate relations conducted. But the core of the framework mainly regulated states' behaviour on the international stage through sets of responsibilities, entitlements and reciprocal obligations. The focus has meant that violence of a type that erupted within the domestic affairs of states was largely outside the remits of international regulatory structures. It was assumed, however, that once states were at ease and in peace with each other, the cross-cultural dialogue arising from such mutual conviviality and encounters would encourage the promotion of peace within domestic boundaries. Perhaps two factors helped shape this assumption. The first was the idea that strong interstate relations could provide an incentive for the promotion of peace within the respective internal jurisdictions. The second factor had to do with the privilege and benefit accruing from sovereign equality. States' claim to sovereign statehood was consolidated by their ability to exercise effective control of internal borders. But despite these efforts, the frequency and intensity of violence and conflicts continue unabated, culminating in considerable human suffering.

There is, then, a strong basis for alternative thinking – that considers and engages propositions from Third World perspectives on international law and their relevance to the need for conceptual recasting of approaches to violence and conflicts. This is particularly compelling given that a significant part of postcolonial African statehood has been characterised by the eruption and reoccurrence of violence and conflicts. And for the most part, too, the encounters between international law and

---

[9] A. Linklater, 'Community' in A. Danchev (ed.), *Fin de Siecle: The Meaning of the Twentieth Century* (London: I. B. Tauris, 1995), p. 178.

postcolonial African statehood have provided little respite, especially in offering viable approaches to confronting these conflicts. It is perhaps due to this bifurcation between international law and African postcoloniality that achieving peace through viable peacebuilding frameworks has become a challenge and an aspiration worthy of vigorous pursuit. What then are the alternatives? Is wholesome recasting of contemporary international law approaches to internal conflicts necessary? Are any such efforts bound for Albert Camus' supposition of an 'interminable tension resigned to only proposing to diminish suffering' given that the 'injustice and the suffering of the world will remain'?[10] Or is this perhaps the basis for the quest for the searching enquiries for alternatives?

The quest for alternative approaches to conflicts

Ever since the emergence of the post-war international legal order, the social, political and legal structures of Third Word states have been framed by and subject to the normative and philosophical underpinning of this order. The nature of this existence has been defining both in methods and outcome. Perhaps nowhere is this more manifestly visible than in the encounters between international law's approaches to peace and the social conditions of African postcoloniality. This is most evident in the context of internal conflicts in Africa where the approaches have been largely unable to engender appropriate frameworks for the achievement of durable peace. And for decades there was little scope for optimism on this front, particularly in that the ethos and institutions of postcolonial Africa remained for the most part conditioned by the dynamics of the contemporary international legal order. The implication of the dominance of contemporary approaches to conflicts has been that the advancement of alternative non-European approaches has been either circumscribed to irrelevance or considered incongruent with the institutional and normative configuration of international law. Its origin, though, lies also in the very vocabulary of colonial legitimation which was, as Ali Mazrui notes, replete with 'references to the "order", "law" and "peace" which the imperial umbrella had [presumed to have] afforded the areas it covered'.[11]

---

[10] A. Camus, *The Rebel* (London: Penguin Books Ltd, 1978), pp. 266–7.
[11] A. A. Mazrui, *Towards a Pax Africana: A Study of Ideology and Ambition* (London: Weidenfeld and Nicolson, 1967), p. 147.

Joseph Chamberlain made this central to the articulation of the idea of Pax Britannica in 1897:

> In carrying out this work of civilization we are fulfilling what I believe to be our national mission, and we are finding scope for the exercise of those faculties and qualities which have made us a great governing race ... In almost every instance in which the rule of the Queen has been established and the great Pax Britannica has been enforced, there has come with it greater security to life and property, and a material improvement in the condition of the bulk of the population.[12]

Over a hundred years later, Tony Blair, the former British Prime Minister, came close to reinforcing Chamberlain. The 'best defence of our security', he said, 'lies in the spread of our [liberal international law] values. But we cannot advance these values except within a framework that recognises their universality.'[13]

Thus, dominant peace advocacy had generally conceptualised peace and peacebuilding in the context of Eurocentric thinking. The imperative to challenge the dominance of international law approaches to conflicts and interpretations of peace has become increasingly palpable. Indian political theorist Vrajenda Raj Mehta has, for instance, argued against the adoption of neo-liberal democracy as a model for development, peacebuilding and a prescription for social stability in India and the Third World.[14] He locates the model's shortcoming in its unidimensional view of human life and society. According to Mehta, the antidote to this non-representative ascription to universalism is for non-European communities to rediscover their own path to self-fulfilment, given that their 'broken mosaic cannot be recreated in the image of the west'.[15] Mehta goes on to advocate for an indigenous process of social transformation which he describes as 'a process towards increasing self-awareness in terms of certain normatively defined goals ... largely defined by [a] society's own distinct history and way of life'.[16]

From an African viewpoint, a similar work of significance is Emmanuel Hansen's edited volume on African perspectives on peace and development.[17]

---

[12] J. Chamberlain, cited by Mazrui, *Towards a Pax Africana*, p. 148.

[13] See 'PM Warns of Continuing Global Terror Threat, 5 March 2004', cited in P. Sands, *Lawless World: The Whistle-blowing Account of How Bush and Blair are Taking the Law into their Own Hands* (London: Penguin Books, 2006), p. 1.

[14] V. R. Mehta, *Beyond Marxism: Towards an Alternative Perspective* (New Delhi: Manohar Publications, 1978).

[15] *Ibid.*, p. 92.   [16] *Ibid.*, p. 104.

[17] E. Hansen (ed.), *Africa: Perspectives on Peace and Development* (London: Zed Books, 1987).

Covering a spectrum of postcolonial security dilemmas, the volume's contributors variously tease out the imperatives of an African perspective to a peace paradigm. The formulations, which range from development-related peace to regional economic integration, centre on certain visions that attempt to depart from dominant international law peacebuilding conceptions and methodologies. Hansen's departure point is that although the notion of peace is acclaimed as a universal desideratum, perspectives on its attainment are varied and contingent on a social group's history and material conditions.[18] In whatever perspective the quest for peace is articulated, Hansen argues, it must encompass the primacy of physical security, material prosperity, political efficacy and the satisfaction of human existence.[19] According to Hansen, the approach that actually prevails is what he calls the 'establishment perspective' consolidated through a kind of Western European thinking that 'sees minimalist conflict management as a sufficient condition, or the only sufficient condition of peace'.[20]

Since the volume's publication, there have been significant transformations which have exacerbated the challenges of postcolonial peace on the one hand, whilst on the other, reignited interest in the quest for alternatives. Although these transformations have not entirely restructured the conceptual and methodological approaches to violence and conflicts in Africa, they nonetheless presented some space and possibilities for the quest for alternative thinking on three fronts. First, the Cold War, a system that legitimised and institutionalised armed conflicts as means of addressing political and ideological grievances, has ceased to exist. This had the double effect of exposing many African states that relied on the patronage of superpower rivalry, and providing the opportunity for the beginning of some form of transformation in countries caught up in violence and proxy wars. It is this enduring, and in some ways defining, character of the Cold War that led some to suggest that it was for Africa more than just a Cold War.[21] Second, the Organisation of African Unity (OAU), which epitomised both post-independence African political order and a frame of reference for continental legal order, has been replaced by a new organisation, the African Union (AU).

---

[18] E. Hansen, 'Introduction' in E. Hansen (ed.), *Africa: Perspectives*, p. 1.   [19] *Ibid.*

[20] *Ibid.*, p. 5.

[21] John Paul Lederach holds the view that whilst the Cold War provided a means of survival for some African states, it was far from 'cold' given that a significant portion of conflicts during that time were proxy wars. See J. P. Lederach, *Building Peace: Sustainable Peace in Divided Societies* (Washington, DC: United States Institute of Peace, 1997), p. 9.

Throughout its existence the OAU's approaches to conflicts were embedded in a framework conceptualised through the prevailing international legal architecture, which shielded possibilities for viable alternatives outside of that order. Soon, the OAU was overcome by rapidly shifting developments in Africa and collapsed thereafter; this collapse provided an opportunity for reform. Third, there has been considerable consolidation of instruments of power with the diffusion of the traditional role of the state through the abrasive embodiments of globalisation. These changes have triggered the need for a renewal in the approaches to, and perception of, peace and peacebuilding in Africa.

But for this normative and institutional renewal to happen there is a need to fashion an approach that is inclusive in its orientation for the construction of appropriate peacebuilding models. The imperative to do so is accentuated by the fact that in the realm of peacebuilding the 'critical task ahead cannot be limited to [merely] generating alternatives', but requires, in effect, 'an alternative thinking of alternatives'.[22] The alternatives are especially poignant given that in much of international law's early encounters with non-European nations, a 'sociology of absences'[23] emerged in which Africa was 'constituted as an intrinsically disqualified being'.[24] The plausibility of this alternative thinking is conditional to moving beyond what Boaventura de Sousa Santos calls 'abyssal thinking'. By this he implies a knowledge system which comprises 'visible and invisible distinctions, the invisible ones being the foundation of the visible ones'. The distinctions generate radical lines with two realms: 'this side of the line' and 'the other side of the line'. According to Santos, the resulting divisions are such that the other side of the line 'vanishes as reality, becomes nonexistent, and is indeed produced as nonexistent'.[25]

Thus the calls for alternative approaches and thinking are motivated by the understanding that dominance and universalism are not ideal departure points, yet both have been strongly associated with, and the

---

[22] B. Sousa Santos, 'Beyond Abyssal Thinking: From Global Lines to Ecologies of Knowledges', *Review*, XXX(1) (2007), 45–89 at 63.

[23] B. Sousa Santos, 'A Critique of Lazy Reason: Against the Waste of Experience' in I. Wallerstein (ed.), *The Modern World-System in the Longue Durée* (Boulder, Colo.: Paradigm Publishers, 2004), p. 158.

[24] B. Sousa Santos, J. A. Nunes and M. P. Meneses, 'Introduction: Opening Up the Canon of Knowledge and Recognition of Difference' in B. Sousa Santos (ed.), *Another Knowledge is Possible: Beyond Northern Epistemologies* (London: Verso, 2008), p. xxxv.

[25] Sousa Santos, 'Beyond Abyssal Thinking', 45.

operating dynamics of, the historical determinants of international law. This culminated in the beginning of a paradigmatic shift. Whilst the shift was not entirely totalising in its bearing, it nonetheless produced certain social conditions that facilitated a renewed engagement with internal conflicts in postcolonial Africa. One such potential alternative proposition is the normative framework underpinning the institutions of the African Union and its Constitutive Act. Formally launched in 2002, this framework has been perceived as representing a milestone in the evolution of a particular kind of legal and philosophical peacebuilding disposition, and the beginning of a narrative of Africa's norms formulation agenda. Such optimism springs from the perceived potential of the Constitutive Act in providing avenues for recasting approaches to internal conflicts in Africa. This book explores this potential and its meaning for Africa's quest for a peaceful and progressive social order. Although the inspiration for the African Union's transformation comes from a number of dimensions, it is in part an admission that conventional international law approaches to conflicts have had little or no impact in postcolonial Africa. The reasons for this owe as much to the particularity and configuration of the international order as to the complex attributes of internal conflicts in Africa.

Argument and focus of the book

This book explores the encounters between international law and postcolonial internal conflicts in Africa, and gauges the extent to which an alternative approach to conflict and peacebuilding can be conceptualised from the Constitutive Act of the African Union. It examines the perceived limitations in the philosophy and structural configuration of international law, and from this synthesis draws its principal claim that international law's treatment of internal conflicts and the postcolonial peace problematic in Africa not only exposes a multitude of dilemmas, but equally raises critical questions as regards the utility of its approaches. The incongruence and the questions this generates partly hover around the relevance and capabilities of current approaches conceptualised through the normative frame and institutional ordering of international law. This necessitates a conceptual recasting, one that may potentially be done through the emerging integrated normative and institutional framework embedded in the Constitutive Act of the African Union. In this instrument, there appears to emerge a window of opportunity through which such recasting of the approaches to African postcolonial peace and conflict problematics could be conceived and articulated.

The relevance of the Constitutive Act as a potential outlet for alternative propositions is located in its three-tier integrated approach to conflicts. These are Article 4 non-indifference, norms formulation and localisation and the binary of social integration and interdependence. Of course, this is not to suggest that the Constitutive Act personifies, in its totality, a robust challenge to the dominance of neo-liberal international approaches to peace, but that it was conceived in the backdrop of the loss of faith in some of the principles and institutional settings of international law, opening in effect, an opportunity for the possibility of an alternative. Although there are still limitations and patterns of tension in the emerging African Union's legal architecture, the Constitutive Act provides, nonetheless, a narrative and conceptual essence that attempts a departure from, and alteration of, aspects of international law's foundational ethos which for long conditioned postcolonial African legal orders, especially in relation to the practices and ideals of peacebuilding. The perceived departure, it is argued, represents a kind of reorientation that may potentially constitute parameters of what could be an African-induced recharacterisation of international law approaches to internal conflicts.

But, of course, as this normative and legal architectural vision variously remains *entrapped* in the evolving norms of the African Union, it is at risk of being overburdened by neo-liberal international law, thereby remaining unrealised. The book suggests that the capacity of the African Union to fulfil the Constitutive Act's philosophy and evolving practices in peacebuilding would hinge on its ability to appropriate a life of its own, one that constructs its frame of reference from Pan-African principles and matters of social justice and integration. The benefits of doing so are many. Besides the possibility of avoiding the pitfalls of the OAU, such approach will avail the African Union considerable scope in shaping a genuine endogenous legal space capable of constructing an inclusionary approach to durable and sustainable peace. Research on this, though, is thin, despite the increasing international engagement with, and academic interest in, the structures, institutions and legal instruments of the African Union. Moreover, most of the emerging studies and perspectives hinge largely on the implementation of the African Union's interventionist mechanism, with an almost disproportionate emphasis on a particular dimension of intervention. The dearth of research beyond this is lamentable, providing, however, space for this book to articulate perspectives on what it claims to be a window of opportunity embedded in the African Union's institutional and normative order. In so doing, the book poses a number of questions and frames of enquiry.

The first is to establish the nature and limitations of international law approaches, and the second is to determine the extent to which these approaches, and the body of international law in general, are applicable to internal conflicts. A related line of questioning is how much are the fissures inherent in neo-liberal international law approaches responsible for the recurrence of internal conflicts in Africa? These preliminary questions lead to a more substantive enquiry into the possibilities and potentials of theorising alternatives in the Constitutive Act. This is the thrust of the book. What is it about this new African dispensation that appears distinct from the old order in respect of normative philosophy and institutional capabilities? Fundamentally, the book sketches and synthesises the Constitutive Act's philosophy and integrated approaches to internal conflicts. It is hoped that the depths of such an interrogation will help gauge as well as contextualise the potential of the Constitutive Act's normative order and the extent to which it demonstrates differentials with international law's rendition of violence and conflicts.

Approach of the book

The principal approach deployed in completing this book has been a mixture of library and selective field research. This included identifying and utilising relevant literature such as monographs, primary materials and instruments. The difficulties in accessing primary materials on certain Africa-specific research areas have been constantly lamented by contemporary researchers on African-related studies. And even where materials are available, accessing them can prove to be daunting. Where this has been the case, the book navigated around it by adopting a measured reliance on secondary materials, some of which came from a multitude of sources including electronic archives, interviews and monograph papers. Although this book is largely a work of international law seeking to interrogate the latter's encounters with internal conflicts in Africa, it is not by any stretch fanatical about legal processes or formalism. There are three reasons for this.

First, social upheavals that result in violence and conflicts are, at least in the context of African postcoloniality, driven by a complex mix of predatory segments of the state and the interplay of non-static elements. Also, the dynamics of internal conflicts in Africa are suffused in layers of historical factors that are as defining as they are instructive. Legalities alone cannot provide a comprehensive frame of understanding, nor are they able to proffer transformative solutions to these conflicts. So where necessary, a socio-legal approach is incorporated to complement legal methodologies and epistemologies. This is vital, for as Siba N'zatioula Grovogui notes, the general principles of law as instruments of social change are for the most part in conformity with their assigned objects and subjectively constituted teleos.[26] Where the hegemonic dimension of international law is concerned this subjectivity may render the treatment of postcolonial internal conflicts and the quest for spaces of peace in certain perspectives that are neither representative nor adequately constituted to reflect particularities outside its historiography.

Second, international law developed out of a cultural system and mindset that initially expanded outwards through largely coercive, non-consensual methods. In the process, civilisations were conquered, societies subjugated and indigenous values compromised. Most of these occurred with the complicity or validation of some of the foundational precepts of international law through treaties, doctrines and institutions aligned to them. Anthony Anghie has elaborately untangled the acquiescence and coercive role of international law in authoring some of the enduring colonial and postcolonial legacies. From this perspective, international law's presumed emancipatory capabilities are not only increasingly contested, but approaches to problems that its structures and normative frame have partly brought about cannot be entirely conceived within them. Doing so would miscue and obscure the scale and nuances of the binaries of Africa's struggles.

Third, the issues of the approaches to conflict and peacebuilding that anchor this book are in many ways rooted in the encounters between international law and postcolonial Africa. The extent to which international law is part of the problem is increasingly becoming both recognised and engaged. So, embracing other approaches and epistemologies is perhaps motivated by what Anne-Marie Slaughter characterises elsewhere as the 'pragmatic recognition of the relative merits of formal rule-oriented solutions versus [others] designed to address particular

---

[26] S. N. Grovogui, *Sovereignty, Quasi Sovereigns and Africans* (Minneapolis: University of Minnesota Press, 1996), p. 55.

problems in particular contexts'.[27] The suggestion here, then, is that the search for solutions to the postcolonial African peace and conflict problematic cannot be solely framed within the boundaries of law. It must reach out in an interdisciplinary manner with the view to benefitting from other epistemological outposts. In that way, it would be possible to not only interrogate international law, but also highlight its 'ambivalences, contradictions ... and the tragedies and ironies that attend it'.[28]

The book does not, of course, offer comprehensive answers to peace-building in Africa, neither are the approaches advocated viewed as definitive. They merely constitute part of the devotion to undertake what may be called an inspective assessment of a prospective alternative. In addition, the case studies, whilst encouraging in their seeming support of the claim of the book and the theoretical framework that underpins it, are still evolving in nature and therefore straddled between what may well be perceived as patterns of hope and promise. It is also worth emphasising too, that the primary focus of the book is on internal conflicts in Africa. Interstate conflicts are only brought into the frame to highlight the imbalances in the international regulatory regime between the two typologies of conflicts.

There are varying interpretations as to what the exact definition or elements of internal conflicts entail. Unless otherwise indicated, the book applies a broad formulation of internal conflicts. By this it is generally meant situations of violence and disorder which not only disturb conditions of peace but also the conduct of daily life in a predictable fashion. This can either be direct physical violence or violence and disorder through other manifestations. Also, the historical determinants of international law and its continuing vestiges in Africa are vast and varied. Whilst an attempt has been made to trace aspects of this genesis, it is brief and concise, and so only intended to provide a synopsis and reinforce context. For the most part, some of the more pronounced natures of these encounters are assumed. Also, the book does not examine the merits or shortfalls of the numerous conceptual

---

[27] A. Slaughter, 'Pushing the Limits of the Liberal Peace: Ethnic Conflicts and the "Ideal Polity"' in D. Wippman (ed.), *International Law and Ethnic Conflict* (Ithaca: Cornell University Press, 1998), p. 135.

[28] D. Chakrabarty, 'Postcoloniality and the Artifice of History: Who Speaks for "Indian" Pasts?', *Representations*, 37 (1992), 1, reprinted in B. Aschcroft, G. Griffiths and H. Tiffin (eds.), *The Postcolonial Studies Reader* (London: Routledge, 1995), p. 386.

approaches to conflicts. A selective approach is adopted here, and so only those conceptualised through the frame of international law are considered.

It is worth pointing out that discussions and analyses on peace, violence and conflict, as for other discourses on Africa, almost inevitably involve some degree of assumption and generalisation. This is not to suggest that Africa's social, economic and political entities are sufficiently homogeneous to generate a sense of uniformity of the universal. The diversity of the continent is obvious; its ecological layout, linguistic diversity, sociological variations, ethnic composition, political structures and even wealth distribution, whether by mineral deposits or development endeavours, are considerably different and distinct. And as Christopher Clapham warns, 'generalized explanations rarely capture what is distinctive about each case'.[29] But in the same vein, there are incredible similarities in the midst of this diversity, sufficient to provide a common thread of lived experiences. This common denominator is quite often significant enough to make acceptable a certain amount of assumptions and generalisations. Where possible, however, generalisations are avoided and qualifiers introduced. Also, there are numerous references to, and usages of, the term 'postcolonial African state'. Of course the nature and capacity of the state in Africa vary, and sometimes significantly. Yet due to similar historical constructions and post-independence travails, there are patterns of commonalities that bind them. It is often these commonalities that informed the use of the term and ought to be the context upon which it is read and understood in this book.

The theoretical framework of the book is mediated through Third World Approaches to International Law (TWAIL), an intellectual, political and ideological methodology which raises questions of legitimacy, relevance, coherence and competence vis-à-vis international law's encounters with the Third World. With its intellectual outreach growing, TWAIL inscribes powerful keynotes and footnotes to the reclamation and recreation of an international law that appeals to the needs and sensibilities of the Third World peoples. In the context of peacebuilding, the claim of the book is that there are potentials for the reclamation to be conceived through regional international law instruments. To test the claims of the book, two case studies – Somalia and Burundi – are utilised to gauge the extent to which the Constitutive Act and the institutions that it formulates

---

[29] C. Clapham (ed.), *African Guerrillas* (London: James Currey, 1998), p. 5.

represent an evolving functional duality capable of confronting violence and conflicts in Africa. Burundi and Somalia are chosen due to their relevance to the Constitutive Act's peacebuilding disposition. Burundi was the first country where the African Union invoked provisions of its peace and security conception, whilst Somalia, on the other hand, represents the first 'collapsed state' to have been subject to the Constitutive Act's peacebuilding mandate. The African Union intervention in the Comoros Islands in 2008 is not engaged here as it was primarily to dislodge an unconstitutional government; neither is the AU/UN operation in Darfur examined given that as a hybrid mission, it provides little insight into the Constitutive Act's peacebuilding framework. The case studies attempt to provide valuable insights into the potential of the Constitutive Act in providing a tabula rasa, a clean slate upon which a reorientation of approaches to conflicts can be drawn up.

Structure of the book

In order to elaborate its principal argument and lines of enquiry, the book is organised around three main themes: Africa and the International Legal Order; Genesis, Structures and Philosophy of the African Union; and the African Union's Practices in Peacebuilding. Subsequent to this introduction there are eight chapters that examine a number of issues underpinning the legal, philosophical and practical peacebuilding initiatives in the African Union. Constituting the theoretical framework of the book, Chapter 2 examines the encounters between international law and the Third World. The objective is as much to establish the architectural configuration of this order as it is to undertake analyses and enquiries into its impact and mechanisms, particularly in relation to Africa's historical and contingent struggles. The frames and ethos that undergird these encounters are assessed and the extent to which they have conditioned the anatomy of African postcoloniality is gauged. Key questions are considered. For instance, to what extent are the historical origins of international law culpable in the imposition of normative limits on Africa? And how much of this has shaped international law's approaches to peacebuilding? The chapter utilises TWAIL to expose some of the nuances and broader fissures that animate the legitimacy and universality of international law, whilst also providing a platform for the conceptualisation of alternative approaches to conflicts in Africa.

As international law's normative and institutional frameworks are constantly challenged by internal conflicts, the character and dynamics of these conflicts continue to remain invincible to the regulatory regimes of international legal structures and instruments. The reoccurrences of these conflicts often confine and freeze the ability of the affected states to actively participate in the conduct and affairs of international society, and even where they attempt to do so, they are dismissed with indifference or even subject to patrimonial ridicule. The impact of these disjunctures needs to be analysed and contextualised. So in Chapter 3, the character and dynamics of internal conflicts in Africa are explored. A line of enquiry particularly engaged here pertains to their attributes, and reasons for their recurrence and continued resilience to international law's peacebuilding approaches. Questions raised include: could the prevalence of conflicts be situated in the inherited particularities of international law and its transplantation of certain pathologies into the institutional and legal order of Africa? What is the role of the African postcolonial state in this? And could a TWAIL understanding and interpretation of violence and conflicts provide perspectives that transcend conventional analytic approaches to internal conflicts?

The scope, frequency and enormous impact of internal conflicts in Africa often trigger international and endogenous initiatives to confronting them. Chapter 4 considers some of these institutional responses by offering an overview of international legal responses to conflicts. At the regional international level, the Organisation of African Unity (OAU) embodied some of these initiatives. As an institution that emerged in the post-war international order, its structures and philosophy also replicated, to some considerable degree, the ethos of international law. Given its relationship with international law a question engaged here is, how much of this burden of inheritance did influence the OAU's approaches to internal conflicts? Three aspects that defined both the OAU's relation with international law and its treatment of internal conflicts are examined. First, the background and principles of the OAU are revisited to establish the genetic link between the organisation and international law. Second, an assessment of the structures of the OAU's conflict management approaches is made. This is to establish not only the influence of international law, but also to show how the limitations in mandate condemned the OAU to long spells of inactivity. Third, examples of the OAU's responses to internal conflicts are outlined and analysed.

With internal violence, unconstitutional governments and human rights abuses abounding in Africa for the most part of the 1980s and 90s, it was increasingly becoming clear that the initial flame that inspired the creation of the OAU had run out of steam, or nearly so. Further transformational changes in international society coupled with the compelling internal circumstances in Africa finally culminated in the collapse of the OAU, and the emergence of the African Union. Chapter 5 traces the genesis of the latter and evaluates some of the transformational epochs that led to its creation. But could these origins also owe much to the ideals and potentials inherent in the revival of Pan-Africanism, given that its impact as a norm-engendering discourse lies in its perceived ability to self-transformation? And could this possible Pan-African transformation be said to embody a particular project of African institution-building? These issues are explored to determine the true ideological and historical basis of the African Union, and by so doing make sense of the motivations outside the politics and conveniences of international global transformations, some of which paved the way for the Constitutive Act.

The adoption of the Constitutive Act of the African Union was seen as a milestone in the historical evolution of the continent's security architecture and the beginning of a particular kind of narrative of Africa's norms. This stems from the perceived potential of the Constitutive Act in providing a window of opportunity in confronting internal conflicts. Chapter 6 examines the underlying rationale and potentialities of the Constitutive Act in the quest for alternative approaches to peacebuilding. In particular, what ways could its normative framework enunciate viable approaches to internal conflicts beyond current international law inadequacies? Could this constitute parameters of an African-induced reinvention of international law? The book confronts these questions by examining the three distinct but interrelated peace paradigms which it claims constitute the African Union's peace and security framework. These are: first, the 'non-indifference' conception; second, norms formulation; and third, social integration and interdependence. It then considers whether this integrated peacebuilding disposition provides sufficient ground for optimism.

Although consensus is yet to emerge on the actual impact of the Constitutive Act, its potentialities in helping fashion alternative approaches to peacebuilding remain plausible. It is these potentialities that provided the framework through which the African Union initiated engagement with the violence and conflict in both Burundi and Somalia. In Chapter 7, the first of the two case studies is formulated and analysed. Focusing on Burundi, its objective is to test the potential of the Constitutive Act's peacebuilding framework and enquires whether it is capable of confronting conflicts beyond the limitations of international law. Burundi's relevance points to the fact that it was the first country where the African

Union attempted to invoke aspects of its peace and security framework. The aim was to utilise the Constitutive Act's Article 4 emergency stabilisation mechanism in the wake of international dithering and abdication of collective responsibility. This provided an opportunity for the creation of the African Union Mission in Burundi (AMIB). Thus an assessment of AMIB provides an understanding of the potentials and challenges of the African Union's practices in peacebuilding.

Focusing on Somalia, Chapter 8 constitutes the second case study. Like Burundi, Somalia has had a long sequence of political and social disorder, most of which continues to pose challenges to international legal structures. This pathway was triggered by a series of events in 1991, resulting in the incumbent president vacating the seat of power, plunging Somalia into violence with 'warlords' quickly replacing state authority. Numerous attempts by the UN to restore order failed. The African Union, buoyed by its peacebuilding initiatives in Burundi, entered the Somali security fray through the African Union Mission in Somalia (AMISOM). A key objective of the chapter is to further interrogate the viability of the Constitutive Act's integrated framework. Given that Somalia has lacked a functioning government for many years, despite efforts in recent years, the chapter considers the extent to which these approaches constitute evolving functional dualities capable of confronting not only 'orthodox' types of internal conflicts, but also those that emerge from situations where there is virtual collapse of state institutional apparatuses. Also examined are the differences in the conditions of peace between southern Somalia and the self-declared state of Somaliland, and it is specifically asked, what has been responsible for the restoration of peaceful order in Somaliland, whilst southern Somalia, which had considerable international engagement, has remained in chaos for well over two decades?

Chapter 9 concludes by harmonising some of the key issues raised in this book. The individual and collective significance of the findings of the two case studies are summarised and their benefits to the book restated. The chapter then draws conclusions on the importance of the findings and their implications not only to the transformative approaches enunciated in the Constitutive Act, but also in the broader context of the development of regional international law. A series of questions is engaged here. From an international law perspective, does the AU framework constitute a departure from the tepid responses to and reception of conflicts, and the modes of approaches to their transformation in Africa? And from an African standpoint, does it usher a new dawn in the functional dynamics of endogenous institutions driven by an Africa which cannot afford to wait until tomorrow to have its problems resolved? Could this constitute an African-induced paradigm of approaches to internal conflicts? And what, if any, may current international approaches learn from these peacebuilding travails?

2

International law and the Third World

If Third World scholars are serious about bringing about real and effective changes, they must look from outside the existing framework with its inherent biases ... To carry out emancipation projects in international law, there is a need to challenge more seriously the categories that now construct international legal discourse and the way they frame issues of resolution.

Joel Ngugi[1]

Introduction

Rarely, perhaps, have the encounters between an operative mechanism and a geographic appellation produced so much contestation and consternation as those of international law and the Third World. Implicit in the encounters is the proactive inclination of international law to consolidate particular values, processes and mindsets. But the means and mediums through which these have historically unfolded reveal both the aspired and uninspiring dimension of international law. Whilst this owes as much to the outlook of international law and its burden of ambition, a significant part may well be a progeny of the nature of its outgrowth and history. Nowhere is this more evident than in the Third World. As a constituent of the Third World, Africa largely embodies some of the more proximate and defining reflexes of the historical impact and determinants of international law.

The encounters between international law and the Third World are central to the genesis and oscillation of violence and conflicts in Africa. The nature and fissures of these encounters provide part of the analytic framework that undergirds this book. The framework is premised on the

---

[1] J. Ngugi, 'Making New Wine for Old Wineskins: Can the Reform of International Law Emancipate the Third World in the Age of Globalisation?', *UC Davies Journal of International Law and Policy*, 8 (2002), 73–80 at 73.

claim that international law in its normative and institutional configuration is largely incapable of advancing innovative approaches to confronting specificities and complexities of internal conflicts in postcolonial Africa. One possible reason is that despite the rhetorical claims and emancipatory dispositions of international law, it is still overwhelmingly entrapped in dialogues of historical contradictions and controversies. In so far as approaches to postcolonial internal conflicts and peacebuilding are concerned, the contradictions have been manifested in a crisis of method and dispute about the contextual basis, legitimacy and relevance of international law. Integral to this is the nature and source of the development of international law and the particular ethos that has emerged from it over different historical timeframes. Although Antonio Cassese has warned that periodisation is almost always arbitrary,[2] the historical development of international law is worth exploring for two primary reasons. First, it provides the frame upon which approaches to peacebuilding conceived through international law can be contextualised. Second, the context provides a prism through which a postmodern critique of the identity and identification of international law can be understood.

Development of international law

Unlike other disciplines, the development and purpose of international law have been as organically interrelated as they are dependent on each other, more perhaps than international scholars would or are ready to acknowledge. Yet little is known of this. The reason for the inadequate exploration could be attributed to the dearth of scholarship on the history of international law, which has only fairly recently begun to be seriously remedied.[3] A fair amount of the accounts and affirmation of international law's history often spring from a particular dominant narrative, one that perceives its development and outlook from Western European influences and culture. J. H. W. Verzijl has, for instance, asserted that:

> the actual body of international law, as it stands today, is not only the
> product of the conscious activity of the European mind, but has also

---

[2] A. Cassese, *International Law* (Oxford University Press, 2005), p. 22.
[3] S. C. Neff, 'A Short History of International Law' in M. D. Evans (ed.), *International Law* (Oxford University Press, 2006), p. 29.

> drawn its vital essence from a common source of European beliefs, and in
> both these aspects is mainly of Western European origin.[4]

The nature of this influence has been aligned with the emergence of a political order through the nation state and notion of sovereignty. This development, it is said, demanded a mechanism that could mediate interstate relations in 'accordance with commonly accepted standards of behaviour', a role which international law appeared to have provided.[5] But of course, what was associated with, and interpreted as, international law has also been ascribed a much earlier heritage predating modern European influences. There are suggestions that aspects of this history could be traced from the cultural patterns and practices across civilisations. Arthur Nussbaum's *Concise History of the Law of Nations* offers a version which he claims 'is coterminous with the documentary history of mankind'.[6] Nussbaum situates this in four periodic timeframes.

The first periodisation relates to antiquity, a period Charles de Montesquieu describes in his *Esprit des Lois* as comprising communities whose acts and practices, though antithetical to modern values, nonetheless constituted patterns of law-making akin to international law.[7] Yet organised structures and coherence in value systems hardly existed, although there was evidence, according to Nussbaum, of the practice of receiving and sending envoys. This was also complemented to a limited extent by the existence of treaties relating to specific aspects of social cooperation. For instance, in 3100 BC a treaty was concluded between two rival Mesopotamian cities following a bitter war.[8] The treaty addressed a wide range of issues including norms framing diplomatic reciprocity. In ancient Egypt, China and India, treaties of varying scope and focus were entered into with fairly advanced diplomatic engagement regulating matters from the trivial to the sophisticated. From this period, however, the Greeks were perceived to have acquired a multidimensional cultural set-up which 'became an inexhaustible source of inspiration for later generations', the highlight of which was the outline of an effective arbitration system.[9] Like the Greeks,

---

[4] J. H. W. Verzijl, cited in M. Bedjaoui, 'General Introduction' in M. Bedjaoui, *International Law: Achievements and Prospects* (Boston: Martinus Nijhoff, 1991), p. 9.

[5] M. N. Shaw, *International Law* (Cambridge University Press, 2008), p. 14.

[6] A. Nussbaum, *A Concise History of the Law of Nations* (New York: Macmillan & Co Ltd, 1947), p. 2.

[7] *Ibid.*, p. 7.   [8] *Ibid.*, p. 8.   [9] *Ibid.*, p. 11.

the Romans made a huge leap, credited with what is regarded as the most sophisticated institutional legal system, particularly in regulating circumstances leading to warfare.[10]

The Middle Ages, as the second periodic history, saw a remarkable change in the perception of law. For the first time, the ambits of particular norms were made applicable to 'foreigners', whose earlier exclusion had been one of the defining hallmarks of antiquity. The change could be attributed to the influence of religious values shaped by Christianity and to some extent Islamic jurisprudence and expansionism. Although the period was influential on a number of levels, it was perhaps in the commercial and trading domains that norms and regulatory mechanisms were formulated to facilitate coherence and uniformity in the precepts and practices of international trade. With the growth in trade and the increasing recognition of the emerging norms and regulations, a sense of universality of trading practices began to gain ground, gradually expanding to seafaring and maritime trade, where some of the most noticeable developments occurred. A significant part of this was the emergence and consolidation of the homogeneity of legal rules, habits, techniques and traditions.[11] The period was also noted for its preoccupation with the conception of the just war doctrine. The rise of prominent theologians such as St Augustine and St Thomas Aquinas provoked debate on the tenets and rationale of just war, helping frame the guideposts on how and when war was justified. Some of the mechanisms and principles that emerged from theological formulations were further engaged in the sixteenth and seventeenth centuries.

The sixteenth century is regarded as the receptacle of modern international law. The period saw the rise of France, Spain and England as the dominant powers in shaping the composition and trajectory of international norms through treaties and diplomatic exchanges.[12] But the century's specific significance to international law was that it coincided with the Golden Age of Spanish legal philosophy, from which key figures

---

[10] However the significance attached to the sequences of international norms-creation in earlier civilisations has been only cautiously received. Malcolm Shaw has, for instance, suggested that the dominant approach of ancient civilisations was limited by culture and geography, concluding that there was hardly a conception of an international community of states operating within a defined framework. What has been in existence, Shaw suggests, is a set of ideas relating to the sanctity of treaties which still remains an important component of social interaction. See Shaw, *International Law*, p. 16.

[11] Nussbaum, *A Concise History*, p. 31.   [12] *Ibid.*, p. 52.

such as Francisco Vitoria, Francisco Suarez and Balthasar Ayala emerged. The erudition of Francisco Vitoria helped to enunciate and clarify precepts of international law. Vitoria's early preoccupation was to reshape ideas about Spanish conquest of territories deemed to have lacked the right to remain self-governing. Using the South American Indians as a reference to his thesis, Vitoria argued strongly that the Indian peoples ought to be treated as nations with the right to define their own interests. This meant that war could only be waged against them on the basis of the existence of a just cause. Vitoria's assertion was constructed on the premise that the law of nations emanated from the law of nature whose jurisdiction extended to people of non-European origin. Yet this did not constitute the recognition or elevation of the Indian nations to equal standing and status as those of the European Christian states.[13] This was to be fossilised later in the encounters between international law and the Third World for much of the duration of colonial rule.

But it was Hugo Grotius who perhaps towered above the rest in the documentary history of the period. Often described as the 'father' of international law, Grotius developed remarkable scholarship in history, theology and law.[14] In one of his major works, *De Jure Belli ac Pacis*, Grotius outlined an elaborate exposition of his conception of private law. In Volume III he examined key features of customs and practices of war, calling for viable alternatives. Grotius proposed *temperamenta* in the conduct of warfare, laying the foundations for the subsequent development of the law of war. As Steve Forde puts it, Grotius' work represents 'not just a catalogue of the provisions of natural law and the law of nations on a wide variety of subjects; it is an ambitious attempt to forge a theoretical system that can account for these two types of law and define their relationship'.[15] This allowed Grotius to propose an alternative which he believed was crucial because the existing 'philosophies of war and peace were both too excessive and too absolute in the extent and limits they sought to place upon war'.[16] It is perhaps one of his most notable legacies, for as Kingsbury and Roberts note, 'what is clear is that the issues Grotius addressed, the concept and language he used, even the

---

[13] *Ibid.*   [14] *Ibid.*, p. 102.

[15] S. Forde, 'Hugo Grotius on Ethics and War', *American Political Science Review*, 92:3 (1998), 639–48 at 639.

[16] K. Nabulsi, *Traditions of War: Occupation, Resistance and the Law* (Oxford University Press, 1999), p. 54.

propositions he advanced, have become part of the common currency of international debate about war in general, and about particular wars'.[17]

The intellectual strength of Grotius and Vitoria stimulated scholarship in the seventeenth and eighteenth centuries, culminating in the emergence of some important norms and methods of international law. But the period was also characterised by a devastating European conflict, the Thirty Years War, from which a treaty emerged – the Peace of Westphalia – which fundamentally defined the notion of the sovereignty of the nation state. The restoration of peace through the treaty lasted for a century and became the main 'framework of European political organisation'.[18] By the beginning of the nineteenth century, the ideas and frameworks espoused by scholars in the previous centuries had been refined and moulded so much so that they had a profound impact on the outlook of international law. Some of this was later to condition the encounters between the discipline and non-European societies. Two interrelated factors were evident. First, the period witnessed the emergence and consolidation of a legal order which reflected the balance of European power following the end of the Napoleonic wars. Second, the exertion of power by the new political order culminated in the consolidation of a dimension of international law that was overwhelmingly Eurocentric, excluding, in effect, non-European nations. European empires expanded, nations were conquered and the values of the conquerors forced upon the conquered. Implicit in this was the increasing universalisation of international law to societies generally considered backward and uncivilised.[19]

But the role of international law in this 'civilising' mission was far from peripheral. In fact, as Anthony Anghie has persuasively argued, international law was complicit in European imperial expansionism and the vast exploitation that came with it.[20] With the dawn of the twentieth century, the development of international law entered a phase of contrasting paradoxes: one of turbulence and pessimism, and the other of hope and promise. Both periods were, ironically, shaped in the image

---

[17] B. Kingsbury and A. Roberts, 'Grotian Thoughts in International Relations' in H. Bull, B. Kingsbury and A. Roberts (eds.), *Hugo Grotius and International Relations* (Oxford: Clarendon Press, 1990), p. 26.

[18] Nussbaum, *A Concise History*, p. 90.

[19] See Cassese, *International Law*; M. Koskenniemi, *The Gentle Civilizer of Nations: The Rise and Fall of International Law 1870–1960* (Cambridge University Press, 2002).

[20] A. Anghie, *Imperialism, Sovereignty and the Making of International Law* (Cambridge University Press, 2004), p. 8.

of two World Wars. The First World War, spanning the period 1914–18, disrupted the narrative of Eurocentric triumphalism associated with the development of international law, not least because the presumed suprem-acy and dominance of European values, invincibility of their nations and dynamism of associated institutions were exposed by the horrors of the war and the failure to prevent them. New power-players such as the United States and the Soviet Union emerged, and, coupled with the gradual decline in colonial expansion, the Eurocentric strands of inter-national law dwindled. Within a short period, the edifice upon which international law was predominantly framed 'weakened and the univer-sally accepted assumptions of progress were increasingly doubted'.[21]

Following the end of the war, efforts to restore order were channelled towards the 1919 Treaty of Versailles, the outcome of which was the creation of the League of Nations. At its birth, the League embodied the most profound political innovations in the development of international law, as it constituted 'a juristic person of international law, capable of having international as well as private rights and duties of its own'.[22] Two key innovative devices of the League were rooted in its conception of the Mandate System and institutional international law. The Mandate System basically allowed territories previously held by the defeated powers to be handed to the Allies. Its significance was that the colonial dimension of international law was being extended through this novel approach, albeit in a less violent and more considered way. Article 22 of the League Covenant formulates the Mandate System as a sacred trust of civilisation:

> To those colonies and territories which as a consequence of the late war have ceased to be under the sovereignty of the States which formerly governed them and which are inhabited by peoples not yet able to stand themselves under the strenuous conditions of the modern world, there should be applied the principle that the well-being and development of such peoples form a sacred trust of civilization and that securities for the performance of this trust should be embodied in this Covenant.[23]

Institutional international law was the first serious attempt at creating international institutions with broad powers and jurisdictions. Under the League, a Permanent Court of International Justice (PCIJ) was established in 1921 and tasked with the function of settling international disputes as well as providing advisory opinions on disputes or questions

---

[21] Shaw, *International Law*, p. 30.   [22] Nussbaum, *A Concise History*, p. 249.
[23] League of Nations Covenant, Article XXII, paras. 1–2.

referred to it by member states.[24] The PCIJ was succeeded by the International Court of Justice (ICJ) in 1946. The idea of the League as a premier entity to manage and uphold international peace was, however, seriously tested in the 1930s by a series of invasions and state aggression, first by Japan's invasion of China, and following that by Italy's attack on Ethiopia and Germany's invasions of a number of states.

By 1940, with the emergence of the Second World War, the League had completely collapsed. Whilst the war represented the failure and ambitious attributes of the League of Nations, it also ushered in an era that sought to recalibrate the frames and dynamics of international politics through a new international legal order. In 1945 the United Nations was founded, primarily to maintain international peace and security. Naturally, as an offshoot of the war, the Preamble of the UN displays imprints of both the previous failing of institutional international law and the determination to minimise the prospects of its reoccurrence. Fundamentally, it undertakes to 'save succeeding generations from the scourge of war'. Over the decades, some of its legal instruments and institutional focus have sought to formulate, crystallise and, in many ways, universalise a regime of rights, norms and obligations which have significantly altered the shape of law, attitudes of states and entitlements of individuals and communities.

It is imperative to note, however, that the narrative of the development of international law has been increasingly contested on the basis that the dominant narration is Eurocentric and therefore oblivious to corresponding values shaped by societies elsewhere. In past decades some Third World scholars, such as R. P. Anand, T. O. Elias, Mohammed Bedjaoui and F. C. Okeye, have engaged in a series of excavations to challenge the dominant narrative of the development of international law as well as illustrate the role played by non-European societies in the norms-creation dimension of international law. These scholars explored the relationship between colonialism and international law, and embarked on articulating a framework capable of reflecting the needs of the Third World.[25] Their formulations sought to illustrate levels to

---

[24] *Ibid.*, Article XIV.

[25] R. P. Anand, 'Role of the "New" Asian-African Countries in the Present International Legal Order', *American Journal of International Law*, 56 (1962), 383–406; T. O. Elias, *Africa and the Development of International Law* (Leiden: A. W. Sijthoff; Kluwer Academic Publishers, 1972); Bedjaoui, 'General Introduction' in Bedjaoui, *International Law*; F. C. Okeye, *International Law and the New African States* (London: Sweet & Maxwell, 1972).

which Africa was immersed with practices and concepts that undergird international law as well as articulate a recreation of a typology of international law that could speak with and to the people of Third World nations.[26] Elias appeared convinced that:

> African communities and States have for centuries had contacts with countries of Europe and Asia and thereby shared with these a certain measure of common experiences in international living. These would entail the observance of certain practices in the field of diplomacy, the rules and practices of warfare, treaty-making, and patterns of international behaviour and of international morality.[27]

Whilst the focus of these scholars has been to reclaim Africa's contribution to international law, recent scholarship has taken a different route, one that aims to show the colonial origin of the discipline rather than glorify Africa's association with it. One such work is Anthony Anghie's *Imperialism, Sovereignty and the Making of International Law*.[28] In this study, Anghie offers a perspective that differs significantly from both the Eurocentric synopsis surveyed above and the reclamation exercise embarked on by earlier Third World scholars. The thrust of Anghie's study is that international law was central to the construction of the colonial machinery and the vast expanse of exploitation it engineered.[29] Put another way, colonialism was an operative decimal in the constitution of international law as the discipline's core doctrines 'were forged out of the attempt to create a legal system that could account for relations between the European and non-European worlds in the colonial confrontation'.[30]

The uneven encounters have, according to Anghie, continued to repeat themselves in many images and at varying habitats of the Third World. What this also means is that the actual scope of the effects is difficult to quantify, partly because 'the principles of international law, like rules in general, inevitably have disparate and unpredictable effects on differently situated people'.[31] Such a defining entity relates to the intersection between the civilising mission of international law and the doctrine of sovereignty. For Anghie,

> [s]overeignty was improvised out of the colonial encounter, and adopted unique forms which differed from and destabilized given notions of

---

[26] Bedjaoui, 'General Introduction' in Bedjaoui, *International Law*.
[27] Elias, *Africa and International Law*, p. 43.
[28] Anghie, *Imperialism, Sovereignty*.   [29] *Ibid.*, p. 2.   [30] *Ibid.*, p. 3.   [31] *Ibid.*, p. 35.

European sovereignty. As a consequence, Third World sovereignty is distinctive, and rendered uniquely vulnerable and dependent by international law.[32]

However, attempts to highlight some of these increasingly vociferous Third World perspectives have sometimes been muddled by a somewhat teleological reading of Third World struggles. For instance, in attempting to underscore the extent to which the underlying concepts of international law remain intact, Malcolm Shaw suggests that Third World states 'have eagerly embraced the ideas of sovereignty and equality of states and the principles of non-aggression and non-intervention, in their search for security within the bounds of a commonly accepted legal framework'.[33] Shaw is in effect echoing Wolfgang Friedmann, who, writing in the 1960s, asserted that 'whatever the differences may have been in the past, the facts of modern state organisation and internal life have completely overshadowed any traditional differences of outlook and philosophy'.[34] Of course these perspectives are overwhelmingly couched in state-centric terms and have the tendency to underwrite, if not mischaracterise, Third World struggles and the episodes upon which they are entrapped.

Purpose and focus of international law

Early formulations of international law were developed and articulated by a number of individual scholars, whose views and interpretations of key concepts shaped the subsequent scholarship on the discipline. Over the past century or so, the purpose of international law has been presented in many forms often with a certain focus or line of emphasis. For example Christian Tomuschat suggests that international law 'has a general function to fulfil, namely to safeguard international peace, security and justice in relations between States'.[35] The rationale and focus of this formulation strike at the hinterland of international law. But as Tomuschat further intimates, international law is also about promoting 'human rights as well as the rule of law domestically inside States for the benefit of beings'.[36] For Shaw, the object of international

---

[32] *Ibid.*, p. 6.   [33] Shaw, *International Law*, p. 39.
[34] Wolfgang Friedmann, 'The Position of Underdeveloped Countries and the Universality of International Law', *Columbia Society of International Law Bulletin*, 2 (1963), 5–12 at 6.
[35] C. Tomuschat, 'International Law: Ensuring the Survival of Mankind on the Eve of a New Century', *Recueil des Cours*, 23 (1999), 1–281 at 23.
[36] *Ibid.*

law is one that is both universal and general, focusing on the relations between states in all its habitats, and with additional functions of regulating international institutions.[37] The international regulatory regime Shaw alludes to does not attempt to create a framework of international morality. This is because although the two 'meet at certain points, the former discipline is a legal one both as regards its content and its form', whilst the concept of 'international morality is a branch of ethics'.[38]

Yet to entirely absolve international morality from the ethos and practice of international law is to undervalue some of the penetrating influences of international law methods and capabilities of norm-creation. Of course some of these are cumbersome, obscure and sometimes divisive. But they appear to straddle such a vast expanse of modern political challenges as to constitute a significant part of the preoccupations of international legal instruments and institutions. However, these are neither new nor accidental. In the eighteenth century, Immanuel Kant, one of the most erudite legal philosophers of his time, conceived an international law that is receptive to, and reflective of, certain normative strands. What it did was that it allowed Kant to formulate a theory of international law, and from this, ascribe it with a sense of purpose generally acknowledged as advanced and well ahead of his time. The departure point for Kant is to reconstitute the traditional focus of international law by moving away from the dual paradigm of the separation of the domestic and the international. The attribute of this duality has been that whilst the domestic realm strives to promote justice, the international sphere seeks order and compliance.[39]

For Kant this dichotomy seems both inadequate and improper, as its overwhelmingly statist orientation trumps some important variables in the domestic system. Thus Kant's alternative proposition is a conception of international law that offers a more organically integrated interface with the domestic jurisdictional system. The essence of this formulation is that the ability and moral legitimacy of states to conduct interstate relations is dependent on the extent to which their domestic order formulates and reinforces platforms for the attainment of individual freedom and autonomy. In his *Perpetual Peace*, Kant outlines the purpose of international law and its interaction with peace, arguing that peace as a social condition can only be achieved if the domestic order of

---

[37] Shaw, *International Law*, p. 2.   [38] *Ibid.*
[39] F. R. Teson, *A Philosophy of International Law* (Boulder, Colo.: Westview Press, 1998), p. 1.

nation states is free. The typology of international law Kant formulates is foregrounded in a kind of 'alliance of separate free nations, united by their moral commitment to individual freedom, by their allegiance to the international rule of law, and by the mutual advantages derived from peaceful intercourse'.[40] According to Kant, the respect for individual freedom and autonomy and the realisation of international peace are mutually dependent, and so must constitute the foundational ethos of international law.

Although Kant's formulation of international law is one of many theorisations, it is an innovative one nonetheless. This is because his rendition stems not only from the projection of the emergence of global international institutions, but also from being the first to seriously establish the intersections between international peace and individual freedom on the one hand, and between arbitrary government and externally directed aggression on the other.[41] In attempting to 'seek out and establish the supreme principle of morality' Kant is in effect challenging the assumption that 'human nature is not capable of good'.[42] Attempts have been made to explore the intersections between Kant's conception of international law and its role in securing freedom with provisions of the United Nations Charter. The comparisons seem to emanate from Kant's proposition of a global institution capable of advocating for a semblance of international legal order. Interpretations have varied though. Pauline Kleingeld suggests that what Kant seems to be proposing is actually a non-coercive league of states lacking a sense of legislative hierarchy 'as the only possible road to the ultimate ideal, a state of states'.[43]

The purpose of international law expanded in subsequent centuries, and by the dawn of the nineteenth century the discipline had gone through fundamental changes and acquired attributes that were shaped by and specific to the era. The different, and sometimes, differing interpretations and renditions of what the fundamental purpose of international law ought to be have persuaded Martti Koskenniemi to conclude that 'to enquire about the objectives of international law is to study the political preferences of international actors – what it is they

---

[40] *Ibid.*, p. 2.   [41] *Ibid.*, p. 2.

[42] I. Kant, *To Perpetual Peace: A Philosophical Sketch*, trans. T. Humphrey (Indianapolis: Hackett Publishing Company, 2003), 8:373.

[43] P. Kleingeld, 'Kant's Theory of Peace' in P. Guyer (ed.), *The Cambridge Companion to Kant and Modern Philosophy* (Cambridge University Press, 2006), p. 483.

wish to attain by international law'.[44] It is perhaps this interplay of 'political preference' that has shaped the development and ethos of international law. However, the most profound transformations in respect of the purpose and focus of international law occurred with the adoption of the UN Charter in 1945. The significance of this epoch was as much the outcome of the events that preceded it as it was the order that was constructed in its wake. Key principles central to the function and outlook of international law are set out in the Charter. Article 2 provides for the right to self-determination, peaceful settlement of disputes and the prohibition of the threat or use of force. Whilst this bore imprints of the horrors of the Second World War, the principles embody the focus of 'an international treaty of overriding importance [which] set forth the fundamental standards governing State action' and by so doing 'established the main goals of international institutions'.[45]

But the premise and promises of the emerging order had to negotiate complex and unforeseen circumstances in subsequent years. Two factors were responsible. First, although the formulated principles represented the fears of a bruised world, they appeared in a skeletal structure requiring a more elaborate and fleshed-out ordering. This, it was hoped, would encapsulate some of the values and perspectives that could form part of the international norms-creation agenda. Second, further challenges were brought to the fore with the emergence of new states. The expansion of international society with the progression of decolonisation meant that there emerged a disjuncture between what the more established states wanted and the aspirations of the new states. This is because for the most part, 'the language of argument employed by the new states seems to lack immediate relevance to the preoccupations of the world organization as conceived by the founders'.[46] The new states were entrapped in desperate situations having only recently emerged from colonial rule, needing, in effect, a sense of urgency to meet national ambitions and expectations. They were therefore 'keen to inject their own basic demands into international law so as to make it more consonant with current international realities'.[47]

---

[44] M. Koskenniemi, 'What is International Law For?' in Evans (ed.), *International Law*, p. 58.
[45] Cassese, *International Law*, p. 47.
[46] A. A. Mazrui, *Towards a Pax Africana: A Study of Ideology and Ambition* (London: Weidenfeld Goldbacks, 1967), p. 129.
[47] Cassese, *International Law*, p. 47.

The agitation for inclusion and an elaborate set of principles culminated in the 1970 UN Declaration on Friendly Relations.[48] The declaration elaborated on key concepts and unlike the UN Charter, which applied to member states, was directed at all states. The principles espoused have shaped the focus of international law and the preoccupations of international society. The principles were: equality of sovereignty of states; the right to self-determination; the prohibition of the use or threat of force; the prioritisation of peaceful settlement of disputes; the prohibition of intervention into the domestic affairs of other states; and the obligation to cooperate with others. The principles have fundamentally determined the direction of international law as well as the elements that frame its interfaces with states.

But given that transformational changes come by faster than the ability of law to adjust or respond to them, there is a presumption that an understanding of the purpose of international law cannot solely be anchored on the margins of these principles. This is so because the attempt to tackle conceptual questions about the purpose of international law has resulted in what Samantha Besson and John Tasioulas describe as the 'outpouring of theories about the nature and value of law, many of them developed in considerable detail and with remarkable ingenuity, often as a result of sustained dialectical exchange among their various proponents'.[49] Whilst the dialectical exchanges revolve around many strands, the enquiry as to the purpose of international law has remained virtually constant.

In sum, the above synopsis on the development of international law illustrates the extent to which the discipline has evolved through centuries of formulation, clarification and reaffirmation. The framework that has thus emerged conjures a sense of hope and promise on the one hand, and dilemmas and challenges on the other. The promises generate a particular kind of optimism driven by the realisation that 'the ambit of the authority claimed by international law has grown exponentially in recent years, with the proliferation of international legal institutions and norms entailing that many more aspects of life on our planet are now governed by international law than ever before in human

---

[48] Declaration on Principles of International Law concerning Friendly Relations and Cooperation among States in accordance with the Charter of the United Nations, General Assembly Resolution 2625 (XXV), 24 October 1970.

[49] S. Besson and J. Tasioulas, 'Introduction' in S. Besson and J. Tasioulas (eds.), *The Philosophy of International Law* (Oxford University Press, 2010), p. 1.

history'.[50] This may in some ways accentuate the capacity and value of law in serving or meeting demands of society.

Yet in the midst of this expansionism, challenges and catastrophic faultlines have opened up 'with the emergence of the intensification of various problems with a strong global dimension', a collective problem so deep as to almost overshadow the patina of progressive promises as well as 'outrun the problem-solving capacity of any individual state or group of states to deal with [it] adequately, and [which] seems to necessitate the development of appropriate international legal frameworks'.[51] Perhaps one area where these limitations have had profound implications is the realm of peacebuilding. In what follows, an attempt is made to disaggregate these implications.

International law and approaches to peacebuilding

In decades gone, attempts to arrest the scourge of conflicts had varied in scope and methods. Before the emergence of the new international legal order in 1945, international law approaches to conflicts were pursued through the classical approach, which was perhaps as old as the state.[52] Its primary instrument in tackling conflicts had been the utilisation of formal organs of the state. The process involved the application of mediation as the means through which negotiated resolution to conflicts was achieved. This was done by identifying leading parties to a conflict and encouraging them to negotiate a cease-fire agreement.[53] As the approach was largely concerned with the cessation of hostilities, the means to this end was less preoccupied with the underlying causes of conflicts. One reason was that the domestic jurisdiction of states fell outside the competence of third party mediators by virtue of the principle of sovereignty. Sovereignty was construed as the possession by a state of unlimited access to its territory and authority over its subjects. James Mayall describes this construction as 'an authority, supreme by virtue of its power,

---

[50] *Ibid.*, p. 4.   [51] *Ibid.*, p. 4.

[52] J. W. Cooley, 'A Classical Approach to Mediation Part II: The Socratic Method and Conflict Reframing in Mediation', *University of Dayton Law Review*, 19:2 (1993–94), 589–632 at 589.

[53] See T. Paffenholz, 'Western Approaches to Negotiation and Mediation: An Overview' in R. Reychler and T. Paffenholz (eds.), *Peace-building: A Field Guide* (Boulder, Colo.: Lynne Rienner, 2001), p. 77.

uncluttered by any mythological explanations of its mandate and beyond which there could be no appeal'.[54]

The relation with sovereignty implies that the evolution of the classical international law approach cannot be suffused outside the outlay of the Westphalian security paradigm. This approach's construction of the regulation of violence and conflict was framed around the state as the sole actor in facilitating internal and external security. The irony is that in dispensing this responsibility the state was expected to use modes of violence both against threats from entities emerging from within and outside its domestic space. In this sense, 'war functioned as an indispensable decimal in the construction of nationhood ... and [in] legitimising the state as supreme protector'.[55] Besides presenting a simplified rendition of the notion of peace, the classical international law approach had other faultlines. The supremacy of the state was predicated on the assumption that the maintenance of domestic order was a function the state was more than capable of discharging as it epitomised an efficient agency for the promotion of individual freedom. Jean Jacques Rousseau in particular saw the state as an embodiment of a social contract which the 'subjects do not need guarantees against ... because it is impossible to assume that the organism will want to damage its members'.[56] The state was in this sense regarded as the 'indispensable condition of value'.[57]

The Westphalian paradigm has had considerable influence in current perceptions and formulations of security. As Eboe Hutchful notes, it 'fundamentally shaped the theory and practice of [modern] statecraft and security'.[58] This was most evident at the dawn of the nineteenth century when the framework became increasingly institutionalised in modern international law. In the post-1945 legal order, however, the nature of this security paradigm has mutated into what could be labelled as neo-liberal international law approaches, which have acquired

---

[54] J. Mayall, 'International Society and International Theory' in M. Donelan (ed.), *The Reason of States: A Study in International Political Theory* (London: George Allen & Unwin, 1978), pp. 130–1.

[55] E. Hutchful, 'From Military Security to Human Security' in J. Akokpari, A. Ndinga-Muvumba and T. Murithi (eds.), *The African Union and its Institutions* (Johannesburg: Fanele Publishers, 2008), p. 67.

[56] J. Rousseau, *The Social Contract* (London, 1762, trans. edn Penguin, 1968), p. 23.

[57] R. E. Osgood and R. W. Tucker, *Force, Order and Justice* (Baltimore: Johns Hopkins University Press, 1967), p. 41.

[58] Hutchful, 'From Military Security', p. 68.

prominence in the aftermath of the Cold War. Yet what the approaches entail is fiercely contested.[59] To some, neo-liberal international law and its approaches refer to conflict resolution processes seeking to engage in mediation with the view to ending direct violence. For others, it essentially entails a variety of segments that include acknowledging past harm and 'remedying the necessity of allaying the fear of the victims'.[60] Neo-liberal international law approaches often imply a modification of liberal values to advance normatively induced conflict resolution approaches. The approaches encompass mechanisms for transforming conflicts by advocating for norms that could diffuse some of the causal factors of violence and conflicts.

Changing dynamics in the configuration of international society have made neo-liberal international law the dominant template for peacebuilding, especially in the Third World. As a result, the models of peacebuilding tend to provide a certain intellectual and practical framework around which proponents can justify and promote a particular version of peace.[61] Central to the visions and social construction of hegemonic neo-liberal internationalism is the objective of enhancing human freedom through empowerment of individual rights and spaces of autonomy. Freedom is considered crucial as it is believed to provide the guarantees necessary for a peaceful society. To this end, the neo-liberal international law emphasis on 'human freedom, the potential of agency over structure, the power of reason, and faith in the reconcilability of interests', John MacMillan asserts, 'equips it to be a distinctly pacifistic political philosophy'.[62] John M. Owen equally buttresses this perceived utility of neo-liberal international law. He notes that as an approach to conflicts, these sets of values are 'believed reasonable, predictable and trustworthy, because they are governed by their citizens' true interests, which harmonise with all individuals' true interests around the world'.[63]

---

[59] See J. Donnelly, 'In Defense of the Universal Declaration Model' in G. Lyons and J. Mayall (eds.), *International Human Rights in the 21st Century: Protecting the Rights of Groups* (London: Rowman & Littlefield Publishers, 2003), p. 26.

[60] J. Ho-Won, *Understanding Conflict and Conflict Analysis* (New York: SAGE Publishers, 2008), p. 40.

[61] R. Mac Ginty, *No War, No Peace: The Rejuvenation of Stalled Peace Processes and Peace Accords* (London: Palgrave Macmillan, 2006), p. 37.

[62] J. MacMillan, *On Liberal Peace: Democracy, War and the International Order* (New York: Tauris Academic Studies, 1998), p. 13.

[63] J. M. Owen, 'How Liberalism Produces Democratic Peace' in M. E. Brown, J. Lynn and S. E. Miller (eds.), *Debating the Democratic Peace* (Cambridge, Mass: MIT Press, 1996), p. 117.

Neo-liberal international law approaches have evolved over time and are constantly changing in an attempt, perhaps, to adapt to transform-ations in the social and political realm. Like classical approaches, their evolution could be partly associated with European Enlightenment visions as well as American constitutionalists.[64] The frames through which the approaches were conceptualised stood between libertarian values, moral philosophy and cosmopolitan visions. John Stuart Mill underscored the value of liberty and its potential in eroding fear and enhancing cohesion.[65] Similarly, Immanuel Kant was emphatic that the security and freedom of citizens cannot be guaranteed in social conditions predisposed to armed conflicts.[66] The relevance of the intersection between these European Enlightenment and post-Enlightenment visions and the contingent over-lay of neo-liberalism lies, perhaps, in the emphasis that core freedoms are essential to the progress of society and diffusion of social discord.

In recent decades, these transformations have broadened to incor-porate transitional justice, post-conflict reconciliation and a genre of value-laden conflict management systems.[67] The outgrowth also includes international standards of governance and donor-approved poverty-reduction measures.[68] There has also been a growing presence of devel-opment perspectives in these approaches. As Robert Muggah notes, this is mostly promoted by multilateral donors with a focus on the transition stage from war to peace, generally 'subsumed under the mantle of recon-struction and development'.[69] The expanding nature of these approaches and the ethos upon which they are framed have also meant that the social construction of peace through neo-liberal templates has been embraced so much so that these templates have almost become hom-ogenised by virtue of their dominance. Whilst the contributing factors for this are many, the role of international law has been particularly conspicuous. Three periods of development are apparent.

---

[64] L. Kriesberg, 'The Evolution of Conflict Resolution' in J. Bercovitch, V. Kreneyuk and I. W. Zartman (eds.), *The Sage Handbook of Conflict Resolution* (London: SAGE Publica-tions, 2009), p. 17.

[65] J. S. Mill, *On Liberty* (London: Longmans, 1869).

[66] I. Kant, *Perpetual Peace: A Philosophical Essay* (London: Vernor and Hood, 1795; Bibliolife Reproduction Series).

[67] Kriesberg, 'The Evolution', p. 15.

[68] M. Duffield, *Global Governance and the New Wars* (London: Zed Books, 2001), p. 8.

[69] R. Muggah, 'No Magic Bullet: A Critical Perspective on Disarmament, Demobilisation and Reintegration (DDR) and Weapons Reduction in Post-conflict Contexts', *The Round Table: The Commonwealth Journal of International Affairs*, 94:379 (2005), 239–52 at 242.

First, the period after 1918 saw major efforts in the institutionalisation of international legal norms following the war years. The First World War orchestrated destruction on a large scale and shattered assumed illusions of international solidarity.[70] Failings in international structures and statist diplomacy in averting the horrors of war were clear. This culminated in a battle of ideas of which Woodrow Wilson, the United States President at the time, represented the liberal response.[71] In a set of proposals presented in his January 1918 'Fourteen Points Speech', and thereafter at the Versailles peace talks, Wilson formulated what he considered to be an accountable world order that ascribed to the values of democracy, freedom and equality.[72] His notions of peace also meant recharacterising liberal approaches to acquire purchase inside states' borders so as to include 'justice to all peoples and nationalities, and their right to live on equal terms of liberty and safety with one another'.[73] Adjoining this was the imperative for the removal, 'so far as possible, of all economic barriers and the establishment of an equality of trade conditions among all the nations consenting to the peace and associating themselves for its maintenance'.[74] The League of Nations emerged from this but collapsed shortly after.

The second phase in neo-liberal internationalism followed the end of the Second World War. The atrocities of that conflict had exposed the falsity of international legal capabilities and ambitions. In 1941, the Atlantic Charter had been instituted as the governing framework for Anglo-American cooperation in prosecuting the war. The Charter proclaimed the 'right of all peoples to choose the form of government under which they will live' as well as providing for 'access, on equal terms, to the trade and to the raw materials of the world which are needed for their economic prosperity'.[75] This was more than mere rhetoric. It set the frame of reference for the new world order and the adoption of liberal values as its operating guide. The UN was founded in 1945

---

[70] Kriesberg, 'The Evolution', p. 17.

[71] E. J. Dillon, *The Inside Story of the Peace Conference* (New York: Harper & Brothers, 1920), p. 90.

[72] Address by President Woodrow Wilson to Sixty-Fifth Congress, 1st Session, Senate Document No. 5, 2 April 1917, http://historymatters.gmu.edu/d/4943/ (last visited November 2010).

[73] Speech delivered by Woodrow Wilson to a Joint Session of Congress, 8 January 1918.

[74] *Ibid.*

[75] See text of the Atlantic Charter, available at www.socialsecurity.gov/history/acharter2.html (last visited November 2010).

on the back of this international liberal agenda. Its Charter, whilst appearing to speak with a universal language and to a global audience, still displays imprints of hegemonic liberalism.[76] Central to its institutions and governing instruments are the virtues of economic liberalism where, according to Upendra Baxi, markets are presumed to have the qualities to confront suffering by way of offering a pathway to individual emancipation.[77]

The third phase followed the end of the Cold War. During this period, hegemonic neo-liberal international law approaches acquired renewed vigour. There are two reasons behind this. First, the end of the Cold War provided space for the extension of neo-liberal values to territories and regional institutions whose principal actors and policy engagement had been aligned to the former Soviet Union. Second, the period also witnessed the proliferation of civil societies and non-governmental organisations that were mostly funded by Western governments and agencies. Their operations and the philosophy that underpins them are largely constituted within neo-liberal internationalism. Neo-liberal approaches embrace the idea of democracy as a transitional process and prescriptive mechanism for the advancement of peace in societies displaying potentials of conflict and violence. Democracy, it is assumed, provides the appropriate environment for the consolidation of a human rights culture capable of empowering individual worth and freedoms.[78]

With the influence of international economic institutions such as the World Bank and International Monetary Fund, an economic dimension to liberal internationalism emerged and expanded through market values and the presumed imperative of integrating Third World nations into the global economic order.[79] The internationalisation of liberal approaches appears to suggest that initial Eurocentric essentials and

---

[76] See C. J. Nolan, 'Road to the Charter: America, Liberty and the Founding of the United Nations', Global Society, 3:1 (1989), 24–37.

[77] See U. Baxi, The Future of Human Rights (Delhi: Oxford University Press, 2006); M. Mandelbaum, The Ideas that Conquered the World: Peace, Democracy, and Free Markets in the Twenty-first Century (New York: Public Affairs Press, 2004).

[78] See generally M. E. Brown, S. M. Lynne-Jones and S. E. Miller, Debating the Democratic Peace (Cambridge, Mass: MIT Press, 1996); J. Donnelly, 'In Defense of the Universal Declaration Model' in Lyons and Mayall (eds.), International Human Rights.

[79] The appropriation of spaces of engagement in approaches to conflict and peace by IFIs and other transnational institutions is clearly evident in their programmes as well as their in-house publications. See World Bank, Building Social Capital Through Peacemaking Circles (Washington, DC: The World Bank, 2004); Oxfam International, Towards Global Equity: Strategic Plan 2001–2004 (London: Oxfam International, 2004).

processes that characterise classical approaches have been replaced by a set of values that often tendentiously acquire a universal language and form. Their imposition on societies caught up in warfare has been increasingly accentuated through largely unaccountable civil society groups and NGOs. These agencies have acted as mediums of peace-building through a process that Amitav Acharya calls norms localisation. The notion of localisation, according to Acharya, 'involves the active construction of foreign ideas by local actors, which results in the former developing significant congruence with local beliefs and practices'.[80]

The utility of neo-liberal international law as a conceptual and methodological approach to confronting violence and internal conflicts has had particular endorsement amongst liberal scholars, filtering into the normative inclination of transnational institutions. Mark Duffield has characterised neo-liberal international peacebuilding as a political project that is manifestly inclusive. The aim, he argues, 'is to transform the dysfunctional and war-affected societies that it encounters on its borders into cooperative, representative and, especially, stable entities'.[81] According to Duffield, because neo-liberal approaches are ameliorative and encompassing in their transformational measures, they also embody 'reconstructing social networks, strengthening civil and representative institutions, promoting the rule of law, and security sector reform in the context of a functioning market economy'.[82] Jack Donnelly agrees, arguing, in effect, that liberalism and its neo-liberal incarnation are premised on the commitment to liberty and individual autonomy, essential factors making possible self-governance and the availability of choices.[83] What Donnelly seems to be suggesting is that the constitutive existence of these values promotes a kind of cohesion that diminishes possibilities of social discord or even armed conflict.

But no one, perhaps, appears to go further than Francis Fukuyama in glorifying the absolute dominance of neo-liberal peacebuilding, to the extent of equating its intellectual triumph and universality to the end of history. In his *The End of History and the Last Man*, Fukuyama argues that neo-liberal values and the democratic culture they espouse may signal the end-road of humanity's socio-cultural travails.[84] This final

---

[80] A. Acharya, 'How Ideas Spread: Whose Norms Matter? Norms Localisation and Institutional Change in Asian Regionalism', *International Organisation*, 58 (2004), 239–75 at 245.

[81] Duffield, *Global Governance*, p. 11.   [82] *Ibid.*

[83] Donnelly, 'In Defense' in Lyons and Mayall (eds.), *International Human Rights*, p. 26.

[84] F. Fukuyama, *The End of History and the Last Man* (New York: Free Press, 1992).

triumph, according to Fukuyama, will provide a uniform template for the advent of government and a form of political process that will have no alternative. He had concluded in the foundational essay of the book that 'what we may be witnessing is not just the end of the Cold War, or the passing of a particular period of post-war history, but the end of history as such: that is, the end of mankind's ideological evolution and the universalisation of western liberal democracy as the final form of government'.[85] Writing subsequently in the London-based *Guardian* newspaper, Fukuyama restates the core of his book with two crucial emphases. First, that 'the desire to live in a modern society and to be free of tyranny is universal, or nearly so'. But this desire, he argues, does not necessarily translate into an actual ability to do so. For 'long before you have a liberal democracy, you have to have a functioning state'.[86] Second, that transnational governance would emerge as a universal rule that would transcend sovereignty and traditional spaces of power.[87]

Fukuyama's prophecy on transnational governance becoming the new hegemon is not to suggest that the state as a juridical entity has become weaker or has lost its political pedigree. But like Duffield, he is implying that the transformational powers of hegemonic neo-liberal internationalism have fundamentally altered the nature and authority of the traditional sovereignty power base. Michael Hardt and Antonio Negri have taken a similar view, albeit with a neo-Marxist persuasion. They argue that sovereignty has not actually eroded in the sense formulated by the emerging scholarship. What is happening, in effect, is the emergence of a global form of sovereignty.[88] According to Hardt and Negri this diffuse, decentred and deterritorising apparatus called 'empire' progressively incorporates the entire global realm with 'its open expanding frontiers ... [and] manages hybrid identities, flexible hierarchies, and plural exchanges through modulating networks of command'.[89] This possibility has been brought about by methods of governance and assumptions of universalism through which modern transnational institutions and Western governments could assert influence and authority.

---

[85] F. Fukuyama, 'The End of History', *The National Interest*, Summer 1989, 1–12 at 4.
[86] F. Fukuyama, 'The History at the End of History', 3 April 2007, available at www.guardian.co.uk/commentisfree/2007/apr/03/thehistoryattheendofhist (last visited December 2010).
[87] *Ibid.*
[88] M. Hardt, and A. Negri, *Empire* (Cambridge, Mass: Harvard University Press, 2000), p. xii.
[89] *Ibid.*, pp. xii–xiii.

Faultlines of neo-liberal international law approaches

Martti Koskenniemi, that perceptive voice of current international law scholarship, asserts in his influential *From Apology to Utopia* that 'law is unable to fulfil any functions unless it has a degree of autonomy from particular state behaviour, will and interest'.[90] Implicit in the fulfilment of such functions is the capability to provide determinate outcomes to normative problems.[91] The continuous dependence of law on political and social forces implies that the degree of autonomy it requires in order to achieve functionalism is greatly constrained. The limitation also quite often affects the extent to which approaches to conflict conceived through international law are enforced. There are several important aspects to this. First, neo-liberal international law approaches to conflict are overwhelmingly burdened by the patterns and pathologies of state sovereignty. Sovereignty occupies centre stage as the apparatus for the organisation of social life and 'western experience of space and time'.[92] It has the capacity and tendency to be expansive in outreach and authoritative in both theory and practice. As Camilleri and Falk explain,

> it is a way of speaking about the world, a way of acting in the world. It is central to the language of politics but also to the politics of language. It is part of the more general discourse of power whose function is not only to describe political and economic arrangements but to explain and justify them as if they belong to the natural order of things.[93]

For the modern nation state, the notion of sovereignty provides the legal frame for legitimate authority, whilst also constructing the basis for its existence and boundaries of engagement. This allows the state to be bound only by matters to which it has granted consent. The focus and sometimes reliance on the consent and authority of the state creates conditions of disproportionate interaction with international law. By virtue of the primacy of the state, the efficacy of international law is greatly dependent on the willingness and the extent to which the state wishes to cooperate. The implication is that approaches to conflicts framed through international law are also affected. For instance, neo-liberal approaches that rely on conflict resolution are limited in what

---

[90] M. Koskenniemi, *From Apology to Utopia: The Structure of International Legal Argument* (Helsinki: Finnish Lawyers Publishing Company, 1989), p. 5.

[91] *Ibid.*

[92] J. Camilleri and J. Falk, *The End of Sovereignty? The Politics of a Shrinking and Fragmenting World* (Aldershot: Edward Elgar, 1992), p. 11.

[93] *Ibid.*

they can achieve. In the context of postcolonial internal conflicts, the consent and cooperation of the state is vitally important for any settlement to occur either through mediation or conciliation. Where these have made some rare headway, they are almost exclusively focused on resolution rather than advancing proactive approaches such as deepening engagement with social institutions and promoting integration.[94]

What this points to is that constraints imposed through the structures of international law in the pursuit of transformative peacebuilding are hardly accidental. They are for the most part configured to be compatible with the exercise of state sovereignty.[95] And of course in its attempts to adhere to a simulacrum of international legality the state is merely framing such an engagement to its own will and interest. After all, as Koskenniemi reminds us, 'the virtues of sovereignty remain as palpable as its vices'.[96] Thus, whilst the exercise of sovereignty may appear irreconcilable with a centralised hierarchy of international law, 'it is not at all inconsistent with a decentralised, and hence weak and ineffective, international legal order'.[97] From this frame, both sovereignty and the assumed supremacy of the nation state are at work. Sovereignty conjures duality of functions that transcend its traditional normative remits. Its unequal engagement and constrictive relationship with international law makes possible the elevation of the state to levels that are at times difficult to contain or subject to effective scrutiny. As an entity that has 'compulsory political association with continuous organisation', the state ascribes itself with the function of serving as the primary focal point through which social life is organised.[98] It cannot achieve this with competing variables, institutional or organic, social or political in outlook.

This primacy has been, since the evolution of the modern state, a jealously guarded prerogative. And so, for what it is worth, international law and its approaches to conflicts have been confined to the backwater of subservience. The impact is by no means minor. It defines both the scope of, and relationship between, international law and its engagement

---

[94] J. P. Lederach, *Building Sustainable Peace: Sustainable Reconciliation in Divided Societies* (Washington, DC: United States Institute of Peace Press, 1997), p. 16.

[95] K. W. B. Middleton, 'Sovereignty in Theory and Practice' in W. J. Stankiewicz (ed.), *The Defense of Sovereignty* (New York: Oxford University Press, 1969), p. 153.

[96] Koskenniemi, *From Apology to Utopia* (Cambridge University Press, 2005 reprint), p. xiii.

[97] H. Morgenthau, *Politics Among Nations* (New York: Alfred Knopf, 1978), p. 300.

[98] M. Weber, *The Theory of Social and Economic Organisation* (New York: Oxford University Press, 1947), p. 154.

with postcolonial internal conflicts. Neo-liberal international law approaches rely on the state's goodwill to acquire any degree of purchase. Although their development was partly influenced by the authoritative tendencies of state behaviour, the optimism that pervaded their theorisation has been largely transient. In the main, these approaches perceive internal conflicts as an inchoate result of the crisis of governance.[99] Thus, prescriptions put forward are often framed within a context that navigates between internalising ameliorative measures whilst simultaneously configured to conform to the prerogative spaces of the state. For example, despite the moral and practical relevance of instituting good governance and upholding the virtues of social inclusion as means of tackling the underlying causes of conflicts, the role of the state is both pivotal and vigorously sought.

Second, the anatomy of neo-liberal approaches appears to be preoccupied with the cessation of hostilities once an armed conflict erupts. Part of this is pursued through statist diplomacy, whilst others prescribe social inclusion and transparency. With close scrutiny, however, these approaches tend to conceptualise peace in the form of the attainment of cease-fire agreements or absence of violence. Yet essentials of peace are more nuanced than this realist paradigm projects. This is so because peacebuilding is a process and a social condition whose attainment encompasses the reflection of deeper structural and normative imperatives. Emmanuel Hansen has suggested that peace be perceived not only in the context of minimising conflict, but also 'in the positive sense of creating material conditions which provide for the mass of the people a certain minimum condition of security, economic welfare, political efficacy and psychic wellbeing'.[100] The notion of negative and positive peace has been generally associated with the Norwegian sociologist and peace scholar Johan Galtung. According to Galtung, negative peace is preoccupied with the provision of structures that seek to contain direct physical violence.[101] This version of peace is not so much concerned with confronting the underlying causes of violence, but only its

---

[99] See S. Stedman, 'Conflict and Conflict Resolution in Africa' in F. M. Deng and I. W. Zartman (eds.), *Conflict Resolution in Africa* (Washington, DC: The Brookings Institution, 1991), p. 387.

[100] E. Hansen (ed.), *Africa: Perspectives on Peace and Development* (London: Zed Books, 1987), p. 4.

[101] See J. Galtung, 'Violence, Peace and Peace Research', *Journal of Peace Research*, 6 (1969), 167–91 at 169.

immediate manifestations. In contrast, positive peace seeks to tackle causes of conflicts by promoting justice, cooperation and social integration.

Third, there is also an interconnected dimension to international law's attitude to the challenges and problematic of peacebuilding. Quite often, once any of its approaches succeeds in facilitating the cessation of hostilities, however brief, the assumption that the state is the primary provider of security takes immediate effect. But structural violence as theorised by Galtung could still persist with even far-reaching ramifications. Its possibilities are accentuated by the assumed supremacy of sovereign authority. V. S. Peterson notes that in view of the evident fragility of the weak postcolonial state where 'direct violence is the ultimate arbiter of conflict(s), peace can only be *negative peace* as violence can only be regulated but not transcended'.[102] This construction of peace, however, continues to be an operating denominator in contemporary neo-liberal approaches.

Fourth, even if a concession is made, *gratia argumentandi*, that the attainment of peace is the fundamental purpose of international law, the perception of neo-liberal international peacebuilding that has filtered through the evolution of international law appears historically conceptualised from the context of maintenance of order. The meaning of order in the language of international law, howsoever articulated, has very limited undertakings. It simply implies a measure of predictability so as to assist a given social setting in the advancement of its futures.[103] Maintaining order through the existing instruments and structures of neo-liberal international law approaches would, in this sense, almost inevitably require the consolidation of the traditional functions of the state. The implication is that the emphasis on order relates more to the international sphere than the domestic. As Quincy Wright equally admitted, this dimension of international law is essentially intended to regulate (interstate warfare) as well as stabilise balance of power. Thus this construction of peace has little to offer to the dilemmas underlying postcolonial internal conflicts.

The suggestion here is that all these approaches conceived within the frame of international law and the state institutional apparatus have a

---

[102] V. S. Peterson, 'Security and Sovereign States: What is at Stake in Taking Feminism Seriously?' in V. S. Peterson (ed.), *Gendered States: Feminist (Re)Visions of International Relations Theory* (Boulder, Colo.: Lynne Rienner Publishers, 1992), p. 48.

[103] See Q. Wright, *The Role of International Law in the Elimination of War* (Manchester University Press, 1961), p. 6.

certain particularity that makes them fundamentally removed from the types of conflicts they are often confronted by. And for the most part, the tendency of these approaches is to disentangle conflicts outside their social context.[104] They often thrive on the belief that the state exercises its sovereign virtues responsibly, as the adherents of democracy and the fundamentals underpinning free market values only operate in a strong state system. In Third World or postcolonial African states, the utility or even prospects of realising these values is not axiomatic. And even where attempts are made through the diffuse networks alluded to by Hardt and Negri, these processes produce a set of complexities that exacerbate social tensions and fragile political conditions. Thus they end up neither achieving nor tackling the underlying root causes of conflicts.

In light of these inadequacies, there is a strong basis for alternative thinking that considers and engages propositions from Third World approaches to international law and their relevance to the need for conceptual recasting of approaches to violence and conflicts. This is particularly compelling given that, for the most part, postcolonial African statehood has been largely characterised by the eruption of wars and conflicts, most of which have been, since the end of the Cold War, consigned to the internal boundaries of states. And for the most part too, the encounters between international law and postcolonial African statehood have provided little respite by way of offering viable approaches to confronting these complex sets of conflicts. It is perhaps due to this bifurcation between international law and Africa that postcolonial peacebuilding has become both a challenge and an imperative worthy of vigorous pursuit.

Third World Approaches to International Law

The philosophy of international law espouses a set of values ascribed with universal attributes, most of which have been consolidated historically through non-consensual methods. This has also filtered into international law's conception and approaches to peacebuilding. But the dominance and claims to universalism by international law and its peacebuilding dispositions have not gone uncontested. In the past decades, its Eurocentric

---

[104] P. Richards, 'New War: An Ethnographic Approach' in P. Richards (ed.), *No Peace, No War: An Anthropology of Contemporary Armed Conflicts* (Oxford: James Currey, 2005), p. 18.

mediums of interactions have come under scrutiny from a school of critical legal discourse labelled Third World Approaches to International Law (TWAIL). Its meaning and methodologies are diverse and still evolving. But simply put, TWAIL is an intellectual, ideological and political movement seeking to counter some of the domineering conceptual foundations and material assumptions underlining international law and its encounters with the Third World. The approach essentially highlights what it perceives as 'tyrannical' tendencies of international law. Its focus is to promote just and equitable encounters between international law and peoples of the Third World.[105]

TWAIL's driving force hinges on a historical and cultural empiricism that exposes the Eurocentric narrative of contemporary international law and its influence on the institutionalised mechanisms of interaction with some of the challenges of the Third World. Thus TWAIL functions as a 'redemptive force' seeking to recapture authentic representations of past and present lived realities of the Third World. Its strong appeal lies perhaps in the underlying narrative that international law's engagement with Third World societies be viewed in a historical and colonial context rather than simply validated by contemporary experiences.[106] The relevance of TWAIL relates both to its methodological and historical critique of international law and for the provision of a platform for the reorientation of contemporary international law.

The Third World and the quest for 'relevance'

There is a fair amount of consensus that Third World Approaches to International Law is not a recent phenomenon.[107] It has a long history inspired by, and interwoven with, decolonisation movements from Latin America, Asia and Africa.[108] The focus of the ideology in challenging

---

[105] P. D. Fidler, 'Revolt Against or From Within the West? TWAIL, the Developing World, and the Future Direction of International Law', *Chinese Journal of International Law*, (2003), 29–76 at 29.

[106] See A. Anghie, 'Time Present and Time Past: Globalisation, International Financial Institutions, and the Third World', *N.Y.U.J Int'l L. & Pol.*, 32 (2000), 243–90 at 245–6; O. C. Okafor, 'Newness, Imperialism, and International Legal Reform in Our Time: A TWAIL Perspective', *Osgoode Hall Law Journal*, 43:1 (2005), 172–91 at 176.

[107] See M. W. Mutua, 'What is TWAIL?', *A.S.I.L. Proceedings*, 32 (2000), 31–9; Anghie, *Imperialism, Sovereignty*.

[108] J. Gathii, 'Rejoinder: Twailing International Law', *Mich. L. Rev.*, 98:6 (2000), 2066–71 at 2066.

presumptions and capabilities of international law as an instrument of international social order and a means to which interstate behaviour is organised is foregrounded in a certain tradition of critical international thinking.[109] This has been formulated through a number of approaches such as New Approaches to International Law (NAIL), Critical Legal Studies (CLS), Critical Race Approaches to International Law and Marxist Approaches to International Law. Their combined effects have impacted, and to some degree influenced, the evolution of TWAIL. But it is perhaps decolonisation as a struggle and site of resistance that framed the historical, political and socio-legal context upon which TWAIL and Third World themes are organised and articulated.

Decolonisation provided a platform from which agencies of colonial subjugation and dominance were challenged by nationalist leaders from the Third World. The role of colonial international law was critical to the conditions of the colonised. This is because in its encounters with them international law created patterns of behaviour and routines that prolonged the oppression of Third World peoples.[110] Colonial international legal regimes deployed state sovereignty as the denominator upon which countries could participate in international society. This excluded non-European societies. Its implication was that treaties and forcible occupation could be used to impose and acquire sovereignty over non-European peoples.[111] Anti-colonial struggles – comprising indigenous activists, trade unions and armed liberation movements – set out to dislodge this imperial architecture. In doing so, they were in effect attempting to arrest the coercive culture of the institutional colonial machinery, in which international law was complicit.

The convergence between TWAIL and decolonisation is found in the idea of the Third World. The emergence of the Third World, it is said, has not only been one of the most distinctive features of post-war international relations, but has also reshaped contemporary international

---

[109] For perspectives on points of convergence see M. Mutua, 'Critical Race Theory and International law: The View of an Insider-Outsider', *Vill. L. Rev.*, 45 (2000), 841–53.

[110] See Anghie, *Imperialism, Sovereignty*; A. Anghie, B. S. Chimni, K. Mickelson and O. C. Okafor (eds.), *The Third World and International Order: Law, Politics and Globalisation* (Leiden: Martinus Nijhoff Publishers, 2003); R. Falk, B. Rajagopal and J. Stevens (eds.), *International Law and the Third World: Reshaping Justice* (London: Routledge-Cavendish, 2008).

[111] R. P. Anand, *International Law and the Developing Countries: Confrontation or Cooperation?* (Dordrecht: Martinus Nijhoff Publishers, 1987), p. 28.

law and discourse.[112] As a broad label the Third World is a mosaic of complex communities whose anatomy is foregrounded in a geographic and historic concept relating to southern states that obtained political independence from imperial powers.[113] Although the states attributed to the label tend to be from the global south, emphasis on who fits the description is placed on a sense of historical *victimhood* and continuing marginalisation arising either from colonial subjugation or contemporary global dominance. Julius Nyerere, the former Tanzanian President, captures eloquently both this sense of victimhood and mode of dominance:

> [The] Third World consists of the victims and the powerless in the international economy . . . Together we constitute a majority of the world population, possess the largest part of certain important raw materials, but we have no control and hardly any influence over the manner in which the nations of the world arrange their economic affairs.[114]

The Third World as an organised ideological tool of resistance can be traced from the Bandung conference, which, by providing a platform for the renewal of solidarity, was perceived to have 'symbolised the moment of arrival for the Third World'.[115] Newly independent states from Asia and the bulk of the colonies from Africa used the label to engender Third World solidarity through anti-colonial rhetoric. Thus Bandung became the touchstone of collective narratives, initiatives and patterns of beliefs that embodied 'Third Worldism'.[116] The Third World as a concept continues to acquire varying interpretations. Jim Norwine and Alfonso Gonzalez note that the Third World 'actually is at once intellectual, metaphysical and *experiential*; thus, it is much more than merely a helpful but fundamentally trivial – or even non-existent – idea'. As a result the Third World 'is a mental region – an image . . . but a tremendously profound and vital image'.[117]

---

[112] T. Wang, 'The Third World and International Law' in R. Macdonald and D. M. Johnston (eds.), *The Structure and Process of International Law: Essays in Legal Philosophy Doctrine and Theory* (Dordrecht: Martinus Nijhoff Publishers, 1986), p. 956.

[113] *Ibid.*

[114] J. Nyerere, 'South-South Option' in A. Gauhar (ed.), *The Third World Strategy: Economic and Political Cohesion in the South* (Westport: Praeger Publishers, 1983), p. 10.

[115] M. T. Berger, 'After the Third World? History, Destiny and the Fate of Third Worldism', *Third World Quarterly*, 25:1 (2004), 9–39 at 10.

[116] *Ibid.*

[117] J. Norwine and A. Gonzalez, *The Third World: States of Mind and Being* (Boston, Mass: Unwin Hyman, 1988), p. 2.

The significance of that image translates into a purpose, one that makes the Third World a representation of a 'historically constituted, alternative and oppositional stance within the international system', so that 'its very contingency, involving an insistence on history and continuity, may in fact be one of its strengths'.[118] Recent reflections on the term perceive it as 'a contingent and shifting space of engagement and interaction of differences that are irreconcilable sometimes, and overlapping and reinforcing in others'.[119] The end of the Cold War triggered debate as to the existence, sense of worth and geographical visibility of the Third World.[120] Those adamant on the term's lack of conceptual utility have pointed to what they consider as its growing redundancy as an effective methodological and analytic tool.[121] They contend that the Third World has no practical essences, for its utilities are merely chronicles of contingencies. Guy Arnold has, for instance, suggested that the term was a creation of the Cold War, and once a new world order emerged with the end of the Cold War, 'there was no place for a Third World in this new dispensation'. The reason, he explains, owes to the fact that rules governing relations between north and south fundamentally changed, making the label 'an anachronism of history'.[122]

But these perspectives have been contested. B. S. Chimni rejects any suggestions of Third World redundancy. He argues that the growing north–south divide not only provides sufficient grounds for the category of the Third World, but that 'its continuing usefulness lies in pointing to certain structural constraints that the world economy imposes on one set of countries as opposed to others'.[123] This finds resonance elsewhere. For instance Balakrishnan Rajagopal appears convinced that the category Third World continues to command relevance even after the Cold War because of two fundamental reasons. First, the category exposes the

---

[118] K. Mickelson, 'Rhetoric and Rage: Third World Voices in International Legal Discourse', *Wis. Int'l L. J.*, 16 (1997–8), 353–420 at 360.

[119] See Albany Law School, 'The Third World and International Law Conference: TWAIL III', www.albanylaw.edu/twail (last visited June 2010).

[120] See M. T. Berger, 'The End of the Third World?', *Third World Quarterly*, 15:2 (1994), 257–75; G. Arnold, *The End of the Third World* (New York: St Martin's Press, 1993).

[121] See D. Otto, 'Subalternity and International Law: The Problems of Global Community and the Incommensurability of Difference', *Soc. & Legal Stud.*, 5 (1996), 337–64 at 353; J. Ravenhill, 'The North-South Balance of Power', *International Affairs*, 66:4 (1990), 731–48.

[122] See Arnold, *The End of the Third World*, pp. 1–3.

[123] B. S. Chimni, 'Third World Approaches to International Law: A Manifesto', *International Community Law Review*, 8 (2006), 3–27 at 5.

hierarchical ordering of the international community at state and trans-state levels.[124] Second, it serves to 'locate the historic-cultural roots of this hierarchical ordering in the historical experience of colonialism and imperialism'.[125] And to the extent that other terminologies such as 'developing world' and 'postcolonial societies' 'do not capture these sensibilities fully', Rajagopal concludes, the Third World, then, 'remains relevant particularly as a polemical or counter-hegemonic term that is designed to rupture received patterns of thinking'.[126]

What Rajagopal's interpretation points to is the imperative of the Third World as an accessible platform for alternative thinking. Upendra Baxi considers this instrumental to ongoing Third World struggles to the extent that it 'offers the best possible readings of the critique of the European Enlightenment and of the universalising form of capitalism'.[127] As regards its contingent relevance, Baxi goes on to say that 'Third Worldism offers histories of mentalities of self-determination and self-governance, based on the insistence of the recognition of radical cultural and civilizational plurality and diversity'. Also important according to Baxi is that 'as an ideological formation, of world historic pertinence, Third Worldism actively survives the obituaries at the demise of the Third World as a distinct geopolitical entity', and so it 'spawns many a genre of postcolonial, and even postmodernist, thought practices; more critically, it renews people's struggles within the spaces of the postcolonial and postmodern'.[128] It was perhaps this understanding of the essence and image of the Third World and the quest for the consolidation of its utilitarian dimensions that facilitated the emergence of TWAIL as an intellectual, ideological and methodological technique.

Evolution and estuaries of TWAIL

Third World Approaches to International Law is largely a progeny of the 'uneven encounters' between international law and the Third World. The scope, impact and implications of the encounters culminated in modes of injustices and misrepresentation that inspired a group of Third World

---

[124] B. Rajagopal, 'Locating the Third World in Cultural Geography', *Third World Legal Studies*, (1998–99), 1–20 at 3.
[125] *Ibid.*   [126] *Ibid.*
[127] U. Baxi, 'What May the "Third World" Expect from International Law?' in Falk, Rajagopal and Stevens (eds.), *Reshaping Justice*, p. 10.
[128] *Ibid.*

international lawyers.[129] Their mission was to highlight the binaries of disempowerment that characterise international law by 're-read[ing] international law in a third world mode' in an attempt to chronicle 'the shared experience of third-world peoples into international legal discourse'.[130] These early attempts, labelled as TWAIL (I), emerged against the backdrop of decolonisation struggles of the 1950s and 1960s. The prevailing view at the time was that political independence could usher in an era of tremendous domestic and international progress with potential benefits to Third World peoples. But these hopes were overshadowed by obstacles that were not easily visible to Third World struggles.[131]

In the years following decolonisation, efforts were channelled to international institution-building with the creation of the United Nations Conference on Trade and Development (UNCTAD) in 1964. It was viewed as a permanent intergovernmental body with the mission to help 'maximise trade, investment and development opportunities of developing countries and assist them in their effort to integrate into the world economy on an equitable basis'.[132] Third World initiatives pursued through UNCTAD culminated in the proposition for the New International Economic Order (NIEO).[133] It is these endeavours in imagining an international institutional architecture sensitive to, and reflective of, Third World challenges that perhaps paved the way for Mohammed Bedjaoui's influential work, *Towards a New International Economic Order*.[134]

Bedjaoui's work straddles two propositional platforms. The first is what he calls the 'international order of poverty', and the second the 'poverty of the international order'. According to Bedjaoui, the two are symbiotic to the extent that the existence of either one may have considerable impact on the conditions of the Third World and its quest

---

[129] These scholars include Mohammed Bedjaoui, R. P. Anand, Upendra Baxi, C. G. Weeramantry, Taslim Oliwale Elias, Georges Abi-Saab, and Keba M'bye.

[130] O. C. Okafor, 'The Third World, International Law, and the "Post-9/11 Era": An Introduction', *Osgoode Hall Law Journal*, 43:1 (2005), 1–5 at 1.

[131] See Mickelson, 'Rhetoric and Rage'.

[132] See UNCTAD, www.unctad.org/Templates/StartPage.asp?intItemID=2068 (last visited March 2010).

[133] *Declaration on the Establishment of a New International Economic Order*, UN Doc. A/RES/3201(S-VI) (1 May 1974). For a mainstream counter-critique to the NIEO see R. Rothstein, 'Limits and Possibilities of Weak Theory: Interpreting North-South', *J. of Int'l Affairs*, 44 (1990), 159.

[134] M. Bedjaoui, *Towards a New International Economic Order* (New York: UNESCO, 1979).

for international justice. He devotes considerable space to the indictment of the existing international order and the constantly growing disparities between the north and the Third World.[135] The scale of the disparities emerging from the backdrop of liberal trade policies, Bedjaoui notes, amounts to a 'new form of slavery of modern times'.[136] Drawing on a theme that has become well received amongst contemporary TWAIL scholars, Bedjaoui tackles the colonial and historical factor in the subjugation of non-European peoples. He notes that 'classical international law . . . recognised and enforced a *right of dominion* for the benefit of the *civilised nations*', which was seen as a 'colonial and imperial right, institutionalised at the 1885 Berlin Conference on the Congo'.[137]

The themes that anchor Bedjaoui's work correlate to some extent with the scholarship of T. O. Elias. But unlike Bedjaoui, Elias focuses on the specific encounters between international law and the Third World, seeking, in effect, to construct a past and future Africa that maintains reciprocal outlets of dialogue with international law. Elias grounds his critique in the *trenches* of international law's engagement with African societies, an express intent in recapturing a place in international legal history for Africa. A prominent part of Elias' work relates to Africa's participation in the formation of international law outlined in his *Africa and the Development of International Law*.[138] The work challenges the view that both international law and its universal mission are a product of European culture and ambitions. Foregrounding a counter-argument leads Elias to indulge in some historical romanticism, attempted through an excavation of the social structures of medieval African kingdoms to demonstrate African participation in the areas of commerce, history and international law.

Contemporary TWAIL's visions have been generally shaped by a group of leading scholars active in the domain: Anthony Anghie, Balakrishnan Rajagopal, B. S. Chimni, Makau wa Mutua, Obiora Chinedu Okafor, James Gathii and Karin Mickelson. Their individual, collaborative and combined works have added refreshing perspectives in highlighting international law's encounters with the Third World and the disruption that often follows. In a short, yet influential brief, Makau Mutua formulates a three-part interrelated TWAIL vision seeking to critique past and continuing modes of dominance and disempowering essentials of international law.[139] The first, he suggests, 'is to understand, deconstruct, and

---

[135] *Ibid.*, p. 26.   [136] *Ibid.*, p. 35.   [137] *Ibid.*, p. 49.
[138] Elias, *Africa and International Law*.   [139] Mutua, 'What is TWAIL?', 31.

unpack the issues of international law as a medium for the creation and perpetuation of a racialised hierarchy of international norms and institutions' that thrive on subordination.[140] The second, Mutua explains, is to 'construct and present an alternative normative legal edifice for international governance'. The third is to attempt 'through scholarship, policy, and politics to eradicate the conditions of underdevelopment in the Third World'.[141]

These objectives do not, however, limit either TWAIL's ontology or the nature of its methodological critique. Its 'broad dialectic of opposition' is deliberately constructed to acquire the tendencies to respond to the manifold challenges faced by Third World peoples and institutions. In this context, Mutua insists that TWAIL must be construed in ways that transcend the boundaries of a mere site for resistance. It is, he claims, an intellectual and political movement that is not axiomatically bound by geography.[142] The rationale for TWAIL's nuances could also be understood from international law's heritage of dominance that Mutua considers as a predatory system, one that consolidates the plunder and subordination of the Third World.[143] This also filters through international institutions such as the UN. And even with the rhetoric of sovereign equality that sustains international society, and the 'fictions of neutrality and universality' upon which it is framed, current international law institutions are complicit in making possible the dominance of northern and European states to the extent of determining the contours of international peace and stability.[144]

Yet, Mutua's critique of international law is not solely limited to the discipline's structural outlay. It also filters to the human rights movement and discourse. His query in this domain lies in the presentation of human rights as an instrument of salvation by 'mainstream' scholarship. The assumption of salvation in the ontology of human rights is perceived by TWAIL scholars as integral to the civilising and universalising mission of European value systems during and after the colonial period.[145] For Mutua, the 'human rights corpus, though well-meaning, is fundamentally Eurocentric, and suffers from several basic and interdependent flaws'.[146] The suspicion is rooted in the presumption of the

---

[140] *Ibid.*   [141] *Ibid.*   [142] *Ibid.*, p. 38.   [143] *Ibid.*, p. 36.

[144] M. W. Mutua, 'Savages, Victims and Saviours: The Metaphor of Human Rights', *Harv. Int'l L. J.*, 42:1 (2001), 201–45 at 206.

[145] See Anghie, 'Time Present and Time Past', at 249–50.

[146] Mutua, 'Savages, Victims and Saviours', at 204.

universal applicability of human rights values because of what is viewed as their cultural neutrality. The latter had generated tension between proponents of the universal and cultural relativists. Mutua dismisses prevailing assumptions and imprimaturs conditioning both the normative hierarchy and contemporary discourse of human rights, indicating that what in essence exist are a metaphor of 'savages-victims-saviours'.[147] He argues that the transformatory credentials of human rights remain 'ultimately a set of culturally based norms and practices that inhere in liberal thought and philosophy' and as a result the anatomy of the movement that propagates it 'falls within the historical continuum of the Eurocentric colonial project, in which actors are cast into superior and subordinate positions'.[148]

Like Mutua, Balakrishnan Rajagopal's study on the nature of resistance in the world of social movements provides valuable insights into the sometimes parochial outlook of Third World critique and periodisation.[149] The critique stems from the premise of prevailing legal scholarship that international law is constitutive of sovereign states whose social interaction is enforced by international officialdom and institutions. He challenges this assumption partly on the grounds that it does not account for or recognise non-state actors and social movements as legitimate embodiments of social change. He argues that contrary to mainstream perspectives, Third World peoples play a central role in the renewal of international institutions.[150]

In a subsequent co-edited volume, Rajagopal resuscitates the question of legitimacy of the narrative and structure of the contemporary international order by intensifying the exposition of TWAIL's interrogation of the encounters between the Third World and international law.[151] In the volume's introduction, the editors reiterate TWAIL's undercurrent that 'the Westphalian foundations of international law seem oddly inadequate in explaining the nature of power, legitimacy, effectiveness or even resistance in international relations'.[152] The implication is that 'the production of more international law cannot automatically be assumed to be in the interest of the South, or produce a legal system

---

[147] *Ibid.*   [148] *Ibid.*

[149] See B. Rajagopal, *International Law from Below: Development, Social Movements and Third World Resistance* (Cambridge University Press, 2003).

[150] B. Rajagopal, 'From Resistance to Renewal: Third World, Social Movements and the Expansion of International Institutions', *American International Law Journal*, 41:2 (2000) , 529–78 at 542.

[151] See Falk, Rajagopal and Stevens (eds.), *Reshaping Justice.*   [152] *Ibid.*, p. 2.

that is minimally just'.[153] The volume's overarching themes resonate with much of the scholarship that animates TWAIL's methodological techniques: given that Third World encounters with international law are historically contingent, there is a need for a conceptual recasting so as to envision the construction of alternative modes of international justice.[154] In the context of peacebuilding, this quest for recasting is imperative, if not inevitable.

Utility of TWAIL to peacebuilding

There is consensus in TWAIL scholarship that the dominant structures of international law continue to have widespread effects on the institutional and social conditions of Third World peoples. Consensus also exists that the construction of those conditions was central to the anatomy of colonialism and the imposition of international law as a civilising mission. In this light, reliance on the overtures of contemporary international legal norms to appreciate such struggles without deeper interrogation may amount to validating the variegated legacies of dominance and coercion. And because of its history, international law lacks the legitimacy to appropriate grounds of neutrality and 'to the extent it purports to do so, it remains indifferent both to human suffering and to its own historical complicity with injustice'.[155] As regards peacebuilding, TWAIL's postmodernist critique offers avenues of reference through which peace could be conceived and approaches to it formulated.

TWAIL's ideological strands offer a framework through which an engagement of the assumptions that undergird international law might be conceived. There is consensus in TWAIL scholarship that the avenues of law-making and the very essence of law itself need rethinking. For that to happen, though, international law must be examined so as to understand manifestations of the present and their implications for Third World futures.[156] This is a necessary condition in the quest to make contemporary international law reflective of the sensibilities of Third World struggles, because 'law can renew its youth only by breaking with its own past ... for the idea of the law is an eternal Becoming; but that

---

[153] *Ibid.*, p. 3.   [154] See generally Falk, Rajagopal and Stevens (eds.), *Reshaping Justice.*
[155] Mickelson, 'Rhetoric and Rage', at 353.
[156] See B. S. Chimni, 'The Past, Present and Future of International Law: A Critical Third World Approach', *Melbourne Journal of International Law*, 8:2 (2007), 499–515.

which has Become must yield to the new Becoming'.[157] The point here is that the disempowering tendencies of international law cannot be attenuated with what C. W. Jenks calls the 'intellectual baggage of yesterday'.[158] Christopher Weeramantry, a former judge of the International Court of Justice, has similarly warned that unless these past and present problems are engaged, future international law will lack the capacity to fulfil expectations and will thereby be unable to actualise its ascribed universal mission.[159]

The interrogation of the origin of the normative disposition of international law leads to TWAIL's second utility as a postmodern critique. The crisis of legitimacy of international law hinges on its largely 'monocultural' constructs and the indigenisation of vestiges of Western normative values. The outgrowth of this institutionalised mindset disenfranchised and made invisible, traditional institutions and social values of Third World societies. What this points to is that most of the early developments of international legal norms and processes have been largely inconsiderate to the social settings and foundations of the Third World. TWAIL's critique of this historical dynamic provides a valuable platform from which to explore the potential of peacebuilding approaches embedded in endogenous institutions and instruments that attempt to reclaim spaces of legitimacy and sense of ownership. TWAIL's resistance to calls to render the category Third World as 'an artefact of thought that closes the doors of perception' is partly rooted on grounds of memory, to celebrate the category's re-inscription of 'its peoples as inaugural actors on a world historic scene'.[160]

The third utility of TWAIL is the possibility of serving as an outlet for alternative propositions to peacebuilding. There is potential in this outlet because issues of legitimacy and agency that TWAIL advocates for in respect of Third World peoples are, in effect, a call for reclamation of the voices and destinies that have either been silenced or marginalised in the encounters with neo-liberal international law institutions. TWAIL's quest for the reorientation of the institutional and normative structures

---

[157] Anand, *International Law and the Developing Countries*, citing V. Jhering, *The Struggle for Law*, trans. Lalor (Berlin: Breitkopf, 1879).

[158] C. W. Jenks, *Law in the World Community* (London: Stevens Publishers, 1967), pp. 1–2.

[159] C. G. Weeramantry, 'International Law and the Developing World: A Millennial Analysis – Keynote Address', *Harvard International Law Journal*, 41:2 (2000), 277–86 at 278.

[160] Baxi, 'What May the "Third World" Expect?' in Falk, Rajagopal and Stevens (eds.), *Reshaping Justice*, p. 15.

of international law, given the history that propels them, provides a contextual framework through which it is possible to gauge the extent to which the peacebuilding disposition embedded in the Constitutive Act of the African Union represents a departure from international law approaches. Doing so provides the springboard from which the book interrogates both the applicability and capacity of international law in confronting the complexity of postcolonial internal conflicts.

Conclusion

The focus of this chapter has been to outline the analytic framework that provides the basis and context for the broader and specific themes explored in this book. The overview of the development of international law establishes the discipline's points of reference as a way of situating the inadequacies that characterise its peacebuilding approaches. The assessment of neo-liberal approaches illustrates the extent to which their historical chronicles have been influenced by both the formation of the state system and Eurocentric philosophical persuasions that have, in the aftermath of the Cold War, ascribed a sense of universalism in form and language. The convergence of these elements ensured that even when conceptualised within some of the more proactive inclinations of international law, the limitations of these approaches manifest themselves considerably.

The historical overview also offers a medium through which a post-modern critique of the identity and identification of international law has been anchored. The analytical framework offers an articulation of international law through Third World Approaches to International Law. The objective is to interrogate international law with the view to provoking a re-imagination of approaches to conflicts so as to make them sensitive to postcolonial peace. This opens up a pathway for the possibilities of potential alternatives capable of engaging constituencies largely invisible to the past and current outlay of international law. The inadequacies of international law peacebuilding approaches pertain to the normative inability and structural inhibitions that characterise them. This therefore necessitates a conceptual recasting.

The need for a recasting is consolidated by the platform offered by TWAIL in relation to the perceived doubts on the legitimacy and relevance of international law and its approaches to conflicts. The imperative of incorporating Third World perspectives in international law approaches to peacebuilding is particularly poignant. This is because the conventional international law influences and approaches to peacebuilding have been so dominant that alternatives framed around Third World points of view have often been perceived as either incongruent or inapplicable. It is to the basis of this framework that the syntheses of the analyses and arguments in this book are anchored.

3

Violence and conflicts in Africa

By not averting . . . colossal human tragedies, African leaders have failed the peoples of Africa; the international community has failed them; the United Nations has failed them. We have failed them by not adequately addressing the causes of conflict; by not doing enough to ensure peace; and by our repeated inability to create the conditions for sustainable development.

Kofi Annan, UN Secretary General[1]

Introduction

Africa often conjures a telling of sorrow and contrasting ironies. The telling suggests that most of its geographic and social spaces have been riddled with upheavals such as economic crises, political turbulence, impoverishment and armed conflicts. Their causal factors also appear many and varied. Some could be located in the fissures of the immediate aftermath of decolonisation struggles, whilst considerably more emerged from the strains that accompanied the exercise of postcolonial nation-building. Their combined effects had, and continue to have, devastating impact on peoples and institutions, exacerbating the risk of conflicts, fragmentation and disruption in the social spaces and political processes. As a result, a huge part of Africa's expectations in the decades after independence was replaced by what Olusegun Obasanjo, the former Nigerian President, characterises as the culture of rising frustrations.[2] He asserts that this came with the backdrop of Africa's unenviable position of being 'the theatre for more endemic deadly conflicts than

---

[1] UN Secretary General, *The Causes of Conflict and the Promotion of Durable Peace and Sustainable Development in Africa* (New York: United Nations Department of Public Information, 1998).

[2] See O. Obasanjo, 'Preface' in F. M. Deng and I. W. Zartman (eds.), *Conflict Resolution in Africa* (Washington, DC: Brookings Institute, 1991), p. xiv.

any other region of the world', concluding that 'there is no sub-region in Africa that is immune from conflicts and large-scale violence'.[3]

Empirical evidence on conflicts in Africa overwhelmingly validates Obasanjo's pessimistic view. For most of Africa's postcoloniality, conflicts and violence have occupied a significant part of its recent history. What this has done, in addition to the human and material devastations, is to impose strains and limitations on the endogenous normative and institutional frames through which social relations are often negotiated. Quite often too, where social structures have been disrupted and distorted, the ability of formal state institutions to acquire a semblance of functionalism is greatly affected, gradually leading to crises, state inversion or conflicts as has been the case in many countries. But why is Africa so prone to conflicts? And what might be the underlying reasons for the constant oscillation of violence and conflicts and their transcending teleologies? The bases of these questions are worth synthesising.

But a word or two needs saying about the focus of this chapter. Given that there is considerable literature on conflicts in Africa from a variety of multidisciplinary perspectives, the scope and nature of conflicts explored here are neither exhaustive nor representative in totality. Rather, the overriding objective is to provide a snapshot of the prevalence and pervasiveness of conflicts, and their constant oscillation.

Overview of conflicts in Africa

To many observers of Africa, a continent with an enormous potential, the constant oscillation from violence and conflicts, disasters and conditions of impoverishment is perhaps one of the more painful of its many paradoxes. Although some degree of caution ought to be exercised in any excursus on African conflicts so as to avoid consolidating the very generalisations and stereotypes that have defined some academic representations of the discourse, it is still plausible to suggest that with the exception of a handful of countries, virtually every state and every region in postcolonial Africa has experienced, at some stage and to some degree, a sequence of violence and armed conflicts. In many such instances, the scale and depths of conflicts have been so intense as to consume the political, economic and social energies of people and institutions. There

---

[3] *Ibid.*

are numerous examples to illustrate this. Mozambique and Angola, two countries that have recently enjoyed relative peace and stability, were for most of their post-independence history desolated by decades of violence originating from political and ideological power struggles, and colonial and Cold War intervening factors.[4] During decades of disorder an entire generation grew up around conflicts and the fear of an uncertain future. What made the civil wars in both countries critical was that they were the longest-running proxy wars in Africa.[5] Unlike most other countries, whose fragility increased with the end of the Cold War, Mozambique and Angola were only then able to pursue transformative peacebuilding initiatives.

The Democratic Republic of Congo (DRC), formerly Zaire, also had an uneasy postcolonial transition. Upon gaining independence in 1960, rival political groupings and secession attempts in the province of Katanga polarised the country, plunging it into a bloody civil war that threatened the very survival of that state. It was only partly defused by a United Nations-led multilateral intervention force.[6] Three decades later, the fall of the regime triggered a civil war that nudged the country to near collapse.[7] Steered by multitudinous actors, Congo's internal conflict has gone through several life cycles, each generating devastating consequences on lives and property.[8]

Even countries that managed to secure a fairly orderly post-independence transitional statehood were strangled by sequences of violence, institutional collapse and unsettling military coups. The breakdown of order and erosion of basic civil liberties under intolerant military dictatorships sowed seeds of discord in Nigeria, Central African Republic, Ghana

---

[4] See A. Adedeji (ed.), *Comprehending and Mastering African Conflicts: The Search for Sustainable Peace and Good Governance* (London: Zed Books, 1999).

[5] D. Francis, *Uniting Africa – Building Regional Peace and Security Systems* (Aldershot: Ashgate Publishing, 2006), p. 74.

[6] See D. Gondola, *The History of Congo* (London: Greenwood Press, 2002).

[7] See generally R. G. Edgerton, *The Troubled Heart of Africa: A History of the Congo* (New York: Palgrave Macmillan, 2002); L. Zeilig, *The Congo: Plunder and Resistance* (New York: Zed Books, 2007); T. Turner, *The Congo Wars: Conflict, Myth and Reality* (New York: Zed Books, 2007).

[8] For insightful commentary on the range of actors in Congo's civil war see J. Clark, *The African Stakes in the Congo War* (New York: Palgrave Macmillan, 2002); International Crisis Group, *Congo at War: A Briefing of the Internal and External Players in the Central African Conflict* (Africa Report No. 2, 17 November 1998); C. Kabemba, 'Whither the DRC? Causes of the Conflict in the DRC, and the Way Forward', *Policy Issues and Actors*, 11:6 (1999).

and Guinea-Bissau.[9] The impasse degenerated into social fragmentation and insecurity, occasioning disruptions in human relations and governance structures.

Elsewhere, post-independence nation-building ushered in disparities in vision between competing political elites, the result of which led to politically instigated conflicts over coveted resources amongst dominant and minority social groups.[10] In these unsettling and often fragile situations, tension grew with the inability of state institutions to cope with expectations that accompanied obligations of statehood and the burden and responsibilities of governing and governance. Civil wars in Uganda, Liberia, Sierra Leone, Ivory Coast and Burundi soon ignited in the 1980s, lasting through much of the 1990s. Whilst some of the reasons for those conflicts might be construed as reflective of the specific settings of the respective countries and the legacies bequeathed to them, there were common denominators in the form of excesses of power and rights abuses, widespread discontent about living conditions, militarisation of politics and subsequent emergence of insurgent groups.[11]

Similarly, the Horn of Africa – comprising Eritrea, Djibouti, Ethiopia and Somalia – has been almost continuously entrapped in conflicts.[12] With colonialism came additional artificial layers of complications that collided with indigenous forces creating volatile social conditions. This state of uncertainty continued with the process of postcolonial statecraft when 'colonial dispositions were rectified in the interests of indigenous statehood'.[13] As regards the Somali segment of the Horn's ongoing crisis, the overriding causes partly originated from the obsession of Somali nationalists to unify all Somali-speaking people scattered across international boundaries in Ethiopia, Kenya and Djibouti. Whilst this ambitious nation-building exercise generated excitement, a sense of belonging and national pride at the domestic level, the impact outside Somalia was

---

[9] For a historical overview of post-independence African crises see M. Meredith, *The State of Africa: A History of Fifty Years Since Independence* (London: The Free Press, 2005).

[10] S. Brown, *The Causes and Prevention of War* (Basingstoke: Macmillan Press, 1994), p. 31.

[11] See generally T. M. Ali and R. O. Mathews (eds.), *Civil Wars in Africa: Roots and Resolutions* (Montreal: Queens University Press, 1999). See also W. Reno, *Warlord Politics and African States* (London: Lynne Rienner Publishers, 1999); C. Clapham (ed.), *African Guerrillas* (London: James Currey, 1998).

[12] M. Chege, 'Conflict in the Horn of Africa' in E. Hansen (ed.), *Africa: Perspectives on Peace and Development* (London: Zed Books, 1987), pp. 88–9.

[13] C. Clapham, 'The Horn of Africa: A Conflict Zone' in O. Furley (ed.), *Conflict in Africa* (London: Tauris Academic Studies, 1995), p. 73.

far more sombre and at times deeply unsettling. That fixation with unification, cherished and pursued by Somali post-independence leaders, was to culminate in the Ethiopian–Somali conflict of 1977–78, and was in part responsible for tension during and after the collapse of the Somali state in 1991.[14]

Other forceful determinants have also been at play in the Horn's recent resurgence of violence, of which Somalia has borne the brunt of the human cost. The lack of functioning state institutions since 1991 implies that formal structures traditionally relied on for economic growth and fiscal discipline have long ceased to exist. Trade and commercial relations have therefore largely being conducted within regulatory structures of clan and cross-clan interactions. What is equally intriguing is that the void in formal state institutions has not led to the complete erosion of commercial entrepreneurship. What has in fact emerged is a fairly chaotic, yet marginally functional private sector that has survived state collapse and the anarchy that followed. In the wake of this chaos, the provision of public goods is scarcely attainable; most of the post-independence infrastructure is either dysfunctional or has vanished in the shadows of war and plunder.[15] The absence of visible presence of governance structures and the continuous inability of international law and institutions to guide Somalia to a home-grown progressive path have produced a sequence of tragedies. The most recent, of course, relates to the devastating 2011–12 famine which has disrupted and claimed the lives of millions of Somalis betrayed by war, law and the world.

Old wars, though, are still raging on in Africa. Until the Naivasha Peace Agreements that paved the way for the independence referendum held in South Sudan in January 2011, the first (1955–72) and second (1983–2005) sequences of conflicts made Sudan's civil wars, in cumulative terms, Africa's longest-running internal conflict having effectively begun in 1955. It would be churlish, however, to assume that the recently acquired independence of South Sudan will dowse the flames of conflict. Tensions and conflict have already flared between the North and South over ownership of the Abeyei territory and distribution of oil resources,

---

[14] See I. M. Lewis, *A Modern History of Somalia: Nation and State in the Horn of Africa* (London: James Currey, 2002).

[15] See A. A. Mohamoud, *State Collapse and Post-Conflict Development in Africa* (Indiana: Purdue University Press, 2006); M. H. Brons, *Society, Security, Sovereignty and the State in Somalia: From Statelessness to Statelessness?* (Utrecht: International Books, 2001).

implying that Sudan remains volatile and its future uncertain. In fact the extent and further risk of Sudan's social fragmentation and its potential for continual implosion had long led Peter Woodward to label it as seemingly intractable, a kind of 'war without end'.[16] In its many imageries and transformations, the Sudanese civil war continues to challenge adequacies of international structures, viability of regional mechanisms and capacity of domestic institutions in advancing appropriate conflict transformation and peacebuilding initiatives. In between the sequence of wars, military interventions in Sudan's political life instituted patterns and mindsets that were often antithetical to the process of reconciliation and social healing.[17]

In the civil war's most recent incarnation in the form of the Darfur conflict, hundreds of thousands of civilians have been killed, a vast amount of infrastructure destroyed and a generation of minority social groups exposed and left vulnerable to the *Janjaweed* rebels.[18] Darfur is, indeed, particularly unsettling on two fronts. First it shows how old conflicts and tensions that remain unresolved can mutate and acquire new characteristics with even bigger sets of challenges. Second, in the process of mutation, the frontiers of causes of the conflict have expanded in ways exacerbated by specific interests of new actors. The external characters of the two competing interests – China and Russia – often converge at the UN Security Council as veto-wielding powers willing and wilful in stalling the very limited peace initiatives in Darfur.

Perhaps none of these episodes have shocked the world and exposed the inadequacies of international law approaches to conflicts more than the 1994 genocide in Rwanda. For most of the 1980s, Rwanda's internal politics was driven by state policies that had the tendency to create circumstances of segregated coexistence amongst the country's dominant ethnic groups, the Tutsis and Hutus.[19] In the early 1990s, marginalisation of the Tutsis led to sequences of violence, and a civil war erupted

---

[16] P. Woodward, 'Sudan: War Without End' in Furley (ed.), *Conflict in Africa*, p. 93.

[17] G. N. Anderson, *Sudan in Crisis: The Failure of Democracy* (University Press of Florida, 1999); P. K. Bechtold, *Politics in the Sudan: Parliamentary and Military Rule in an Emerging African Nation* (California: Praeger Press, 1976).

[18] See the *Report of the International Commission of Inquiry on Darfur to the United Nations Secretary-General*, 2004, www.un.org/News/dh/sudan/com_inq_darfur.pdf (last visited November 2010).

[19] For an account of these policies, from colonial to postcolonial, see J. D. Eller, *From Culture to Ethnicity to Conflict* (Ann Arbor: The University of Michigan Press, 2002).

thereafter degenerating into terror and insecurity. Worse was to come. In 1994 the aeroplane carrying the President of Rwanda (and Burundi) was shot down. Prominent Hutu personalities blamed Tutsi militants for the assassination and instigated a campaign of terror that incited large groups of Hutus to hunt down and kill any Tutsi in sight. In the space of several weeks, over 800,000 Tutsi and their sympathisers were killed.[20] Like conflicts in Darfur, Angola, Mozambique and Somalia, the Rwandan genocide could neither be contained nor prevented by existing international law mechanisms or regional mediation processes. In fact there is a perception that had it not been for 'its extent [close to a million killed] and timing [post-Cold War period], the Rwandan crisis would have been dismissed as another example of Africa's perennial ethnic conflicts'.[21]

Whilst the immediate causes of the genocide were predominantly internally driven, there were external factors that triggered a chain of events crucial in the narrative of the conflict and the atrocities that came from it. The role of Tutsi exiles in Uganda was important in this regard. In 1988 a group of these exiles founded the Rwandan Patriotic Front (RPF) as a political and military movement. One of its aims was to attempt to repatriate Tutsi refugees in Uganda as well as overthrow the Hutu-led Government in Rwanda. The RPF leadership utilised its contacts and experience, having served and fought with Yoweri Museveni, to successfully seize power through the National Resistance Movement. On 1 October 1990 the RPF launched its first attack, on the Rwandan border post of Kagitumba, killing one person and destroying the outpost.[22] The response from the Rwandan Government and its affiliated media outlets was to label Tutsis inside the country as collaborators. The distrust and animosity that followed laid the foundation for some of the vicious reprisals that occurred in the 1994 genocide.

---

[20] P. Gourevitch, *We Wish to Inform You that Tomorrow We will be Killed with Our Families: Stories from Rwanda* (New York: Picador, 1999).

[21] A. Alao and F. Olonisakin, 'Post Cold War Africa: Ethnicity, Ethnic Conflict and Security' in A. Oyebade and A. Alao (eds.), *Africa After the Cold War* (Asmara, Eritrea: Africa World Press, 1998), p. 117.

[22] G. Prunier, *The Rwanda Crisis: History of a Genocide* (London: Hurst and Company, 1995), p. 93; See also A. J. Kuperman, *The Limits of Humanitarian Intervention* (Washington, DC: The Brookings Institution, 2001); M. Mamdani, *When Victims Become Killers: Colonialism, Nativism, and the Genocide in Rwanda* (Princeton University Press, 2001).

The prevalence and intensity of violence and conflicts in Africa appear to have both increased and receded in the post-Cold War period. For some regions, the end of the Cold War exposed states' dependence levels on the United States and the former Soviet Union. In the Horn of Africa, for instance, both Ethiopia and Somalia had been at the centre stage of superpower rivalry due to their strategic locations.[23] The end of the Cold War was the final straw in the collapse of the Somali state, whilst Ethiopia could not prosecute its war with Eritrea in the absence of massive injections of external military aid.[24] For Mozambique and Angola, the post-Cold War period opened up a window of opportunity, ushering in a new era of peacebuilding. But in states whose dependence on the two superpowers stretched across all sectors of their political economies, internal disintegration followed inability of formal state institutions to fulfil the most basic of functions. This turning point in the dynamics of the state system exposed traditional suppositions on the ability of the state to exert effective control over its domestic jurisdiction. Many doubted the ability of some of the Cold War-dependent states to fend for themselves.

Since the end of the Cold War, violence and conflicts in Africa have remained largely internal in character, accounting for substantial warfare casualties. According to the 2002 UNDP Human Development Report, an estimated 3.6 million people had been killed in internal conflicts since the 1990s as opposed to an estimated 220,000 deaths in interstate wars.[25] The Report laments that particularly tragic is the fact that it is civilians, and not soldiers, who are increasingly the victims of Africa's conflicts, accounting for over 90 per cent of the casualties.[26] More often than not, given their vulnerability and difficulties in mobility during conflicts, children and women account for half of the civilian casualties.[27] The manner of internal conflicts is further complicated by high rates of conscription of children as combatants, 'a remarkable phenomenon that has caused surprise and concern'.[28] A disconcerting pattern across these episodes is that increasingly, the totality of their character results in destruction of civilian life and minority groups, challenging the very

---

[23] See Lewis, *A Modern History of Somalia*.

[24] J. Lefebvre, 'Post-Cold War Clouds on the Horn of Africa: The Eritrea-Sudan Crisis', *Middle East Policy*, 4 (1995), 34.

[25] United Nations Development Programme Human Development Report, *Deepening Democracy in a Fragmented World* (Oxford University Press, 2002), p. 16.

[26] *Ibid.*   [27] *Ibid.*

[28] O. Furley, 'Child Soldiers in Africa' in Furley (ed.), *Conflict in Africa*, p. 28.

ethos of post-war international legal structures and instruments.[29] But given their seemingly intractable nature, what are the predominant causes and characteristics of postcolonial conflicts? And how might these pose challenges to contemporary international legal structures and instruments?

Causes of internal conflicts in Africa

Africa is vast, diverse and an inherently complex continent. It comprises a mosaic of communities with individual histories, different geopolitical circumstances, contrasting economic strengths and varying patterns of internal and international interactions.[30] It is partly this intricate postcolonial social order that makes the underlying causes of internal conflicts in Africa equally diverse and varied in nature and significance. Yet it is also true that there are incredible similarities in the backdrop of the diversity that provide a common thread of lived experiences and sometimes overlapping sociological and anthropological constructs. The commonalities also extend to the very sources of internal conflicts, which come in the form of historical legacies, ethnic factors, bad governance and a host of intervening internal and external precipitants.[31] Most conflicts have elements of these factors.

Historical legacies and burden of inheritance

Despite the elapse of space and time the colonial inheritance continues to burden Africa. Although the Berlin Conference of 1884–85, which consolidated Empire's expansion to Africa, took place over a century ago, transformational changes on the continent not only constructed the immediate context for African political and social orders, but continue to impose constraints and shape futures.[32] The cultural historian and

---

[29] The Preamble to the United Nations Charter employs the essence of the collective (we the people) to announce that the principal aim of the new organisation and the legal order it represents is to 'save succeeding generations from the scourge of war'. See Preamble to Charter of the United Nations, available at www.un-documents.net/ch-ppp. htm (last visited November 2010).

[30] Report of the Secretary General, *The Causes of Conflict*, p. 3. See also M. Mwanasali, 'From the Organisation of African Unity to the African Union' in M. Baregu and C. Lansberg (eds.), *From Cape to Congo: Southern Africa's Evolving Security Challenges* (Boulder, Colo.: Lynne Rienner, 2003), p. 206.

[31] UN Secretary General Report, *The Causes of Conflict*, p. 3.

[32] D. L. Gordon, 'African Politics' in A. A. Gordon and D. L. Gordon (eds.), *Understanding Contemporary Africa* (London: Lynne Rienner Publishers, 2001), p. 40.

novelist V. S. Naipaul agrees. He locates the depths and defining attributes of colonial legacies in the claim that although 'the empires of our time were short lived . . . they have altered the world forever' and that 'their passing away is their least significant feature'.[33] The alterations Naipaul alludes to are being manifested through the state and formal institutions associated with it. Thus this 'messy afterlife of colonialism', as Shashi Tharoor labels it, could in many ways be attributed to 'yesterday's colonial attempts at order'.[34] Perhaps nowhere is this more evident than in the nature and continuing trials and tribulations of the post-colonial African state. As a progeny of colonial legacies, it continues to retain structures of the colonial machinery.

Territorial boundaries demarcated by colonial authorities have remained virtually unchanged, as have the institutions and structures of government. The state is the entity through which these legacies are consolidated. Its influence as a political phenomenon has been tremendous, to the extent that it is viewed as an indispensable political unit without which modern society can hardly exist.[35] But this notion of statehood, and the parameters upon which it is defined and negotiated, are a novelty in modern African political history. The effect on post-colonial statehood is that it induces a sense of incoherent ambiguities that impose an adverse strain on its social fabric, creating tension and unequal subsidiaries.

Indeed, it is the artificiality of the African state and the manner in which it was constructed by colonial order that is frequently identified as a contributory source of internal conflicts. Part of the reason hinges on the premise that the postcolonial African state is an amalgamation of traditions, routines and mentalities of the colonial state.[36] That is to say, it is by and large a by-product of colonial tinkering where boundaries came first and nations subsequently emerged from them.[37] Such an arbitrary colonial partition implied that complex and variable sets of diverse ethnic and cultural elements had to 'negotiate' an interaction on often uneven, and subsequently devastating, platforms.[38] A. E. Moodie claims that this was not the 'visible expression of the age-long efforts of

---

[33] V. S. Naipaul, *The Mimic Men* (London: Vintage Books, 1985), p. 32.
[34] S. Tharoor, 'The Messy Afterlife of Colonialism', *Global Governance*, 8:1 (2002), 1–5 at 5.
[35] Mohamoud, *State Collapse*, p. 15.
[36] C. Young, 'The End of the Post-Colonial State? Reflections on Changing African Political Dynamics', *African Affairs*, 103 (2004), 23–49 at 23.
[37] C. Clapham, 'Rethinking African States', *African Security Review*, 10:3 (2001), 1–12 at 2.
[38] *Ibid.*, at 6.

peoples to achieve political adjustment between themselves and the physical conditions in which they live'.[39] Rather, it was a form of construction whose fragility could hardly sustain internal coherence, often leading to weak and dysfunctional state apparatuses.[40] The unease that has long characterised relations between Somalia and its neighbours, for instance, has been partly fanned by the former's rejection of colonial borders, opting instead to unify the Somali-speaking people scattered across Kenya, Ethiopia and Djibouti.

The susceptibility of Africa to the vicissitudes of conflict also lies in the very nature of the historically conditioned weakness of the postcolonial African state.[41] It is this weakness that has subjected it to constant struggles with social forces within its boundaries. The combined impact of such struggles has often had profound effects on the existence as well as the symbolic and political relevance of the state.[42] The traditional role of the state is to, primarily, exercise effective control and provide governance structures in a defined territorial space. Max Weber expands the construction of this role to encapsulate 'claim to the monopoly of the legitimate use of physical force in the enforcement of its order ... over all action taking place in the area of its jurisdiction'.[43] Weber's formulation lays particular emphasis on the empirical attributes of statehood. Taken literally, it is difficult to situate this in the context of Africa given that the reality of a large part of African statehood has hardly 'been objictified in the sense that it has in Western Europe'.[44]

---

[39] A. E. Moodie, 'Fragmented Europe' in W. E. Gordon and A. E. Moodie (eds.), *The Changing World: Studies in Political Geography*, cited in J. C. Anene, *The International Boundaries of Nigeria 1885–1960: The Framework of an Emergent African Nation* (Ibadan: Ibadan History Series, 1970), p. 3.

[40] Whilst dysfunctional state structures and collapse are often caused by numerous factors, there is a credible link between state disintegration and the legacy of colonialism. For further exposition on this see generally O. C. Okafor, *Re-defining Legitimate Statehood: International Law and State Fragmentation* (Dordrecht: Martinus Nijhoff Publishers, 1999).

[41] See J. W. Harbeson and D. Rothchild (eds.), *The African State System in Flux* (Boulder, Colo.: Westview Press, 2000).

[42] See D. Rothchild and E. J. Keller (eds.), *Africa in the New International Order: Rethinking State Sovereignty and Regional Security* (Boulder, Colo.: Lynne Rienner, 1996).

[43] M. Weber, *The Theory of Social and Economic Organisation*, trans. A. Henderson and T. Parson (London: Free Press, 1964), pp. 154–6.

[44] R. Lemarchand, 'The State and Society in Africa: Ethnic Stratification and Restratification in Historical and Comparative Perspective' in D. Rothchild and V. A. Olorunsola (eds.), *State Versus Ethnic Claims: African Policy Dilemmas* (Boulder, Colo.: Westview Press, 1983), p. 44.

The existence, then, of the postcolonial African state has not been entirely dependent on the strength of its empirical attributes. For the most part, it has been unable to extend its jurisdiction beyond urban spaces and the narrow confines of legitimacy. Its survival has been largely due to emphasis on juridical statehood by the post-war international dispensation.[45] And of course, in its attempt to regain or consolidate authority, the state comes under challenge from 'parallel' entities such as ethnic or indigenous social groups and institutions. The ensuing tension has caused civil wars in Liberia, Somalia, Sierra Leone and Ivory Coast. There is also a broader implication additional to the fragility of the African postcolonial state. The disjuncture in the empirical attribute exposes the falsity inherent in the state and its inability to nurture frameworks capable of organising social relations arising from colonial constructed order. As Ali Mazrui notes, 'the African state is sometimes excessively authoritarian to disguise the fact that it is inadequately authoritative'.[46]

Ethnic claims as sources of conflicts

The impact and influence of ethnicity in shaping relations and the unmaking of communities has remained a well-pursued argument and a point of disagreement amongst scholars. Perhaps this may be due to the nature of the ethnicity argument on one hand, and its associated terminological confusion and inadequacy of knowledge on the other.[47] George DeVos defines the phenomenon of ethnicity as a group's 'subjective symbolic or emblematic use of any aspect of culture, in order to differentiate themselves from other groups'.[48] For Anthony Smith, ethnicity invokes 'a myth of common ancestry, shared memories and

---

[45] See R. H. Jackson and C. G. Rosberg, 'Why Africa's Weak States Persist: The Empirical and the Juridical in Statehood', *World Politics*, 35:1 (1982), 1–24; R. H. Jackson and C. G. Rosenberg, *Personal Rule in Black Africa: Prince, Autocrat, Prophet, Tyrant* (Berkeley: University of California Press, 1982); R. H. Jackson and C. G. Rosenberg, 'Sovereignty and Underdevelopment: Juridical Statehood in the African Crisis', *The Journal of Modern African Studies*, 24:1 (1986), 1–31.

[46] A. Mazrui, 'Political Engineering in Africa', *International Social Science Journal*, 35:96 (1983), 279–95 at 293.

[47] J. D. Eller, *From Culture to Ethnicity to Conflict: An Anthropological Perspective on International Ethnic Conflict* (Ann Arbor: University of Michigan Press, 1999), p. 7.

[48] G. DeVos, 'Ethnic Pluralism: Conflict and Accommodation' in G. DeVos and L. Romanucci-Ross (eds.), *Ethnic Identity: Cultural Continuities and Change* (University of Chicago Press, 1975), p. 16.

cultural elements, a link with an historic territory or homeland and a measure of solidarity'.[49] A constant in these formulations is the recurrence of the notion of identity and sense of belonging, two factors that are central to shaping relations and determining balance between the state as an organic political institution and national groups as competing social variables.

Thus, control over what appears to be a delicate balance has not been particularly easy in postcolonial Africa given that ethnic affiliation is for the most part 'self-defined in the sense that members of a group rather than outsiders draw its boundaries'.[50] Conceived this way, membership of an ethnic group serves as a source of security whose overriding object is to 'make use of certain cultural traits from their past to ensure perpetual cohesion'.[51] Once individuals see ethnic affiliations as paramount to their survival, loyalty to that group trumps an individual's otherwise rational encounters with those outside of that group, and the 'other' is almost perceived as an unnecessary burden rather than an essential entity for social coexistence. This inward-looking perception of the 'other' widens divisions in a heterogeneous society.[52] Ethnicity as a source of conflict is anchored on a number of factors. First, it has been argued that the arbitrary colonial partition has ensured that the current postcolonial African state has not been built on strong nationalist foundations and is therefore susceptible to competing political, sociological and anthropological factors.[53] Makau Mutua considers this factor as critical to postcolonial crises, arguing that it created a situation where 'states or entities with a history of tension and war between them were lumped into the same state'. And 'in other cases', Mutua notes, 'the new frontiers split ethnic and linguistic groups from their political societies

[49] A. Smith, 'The Ethnic Source of Nationalism', *Survival*, 35:1 (1993), 48–62 at 49.

[50] H. Bienen, 'The State and Ethnicity: Integrative Formulas in Africa' in Rothchild and Olorunsola (eds.), *State Versus Ethnic Claims*, p. 100.

[51] E. Rosen, *Creating Ethnicity: The Process of Ethnogenesis* (London: SAGE Publishers, 1989), p. 12.

[52] The potential task of a divided society to heal its ethnic differences can be daunting. As Donald Horowitz explains, a divided society often 'propels ethnic conflict to the centre of politics and social relations', which eventually strains 'the bonds that sustain civility and is often seen as the root of violence'. See D. Horowitz, *Ethnic Groups in Conflict* (Berkeley: University of California Press, 1985), p. 12.

[53] Of all the postcolonial African states, only Eritrea has had its borders 'redrawn' to reflect a homogenous ethnic composition embodying commonly shared cultural values and national identity. M. W. Mutua, 'Why Redraw the Map of Africa: A Moral and Legal Inquiry', *Michigan Journal of International Law*, 16 (1994–95), 1136.

and located them in different states'.[54] For Mahmood Mamdani, the colonial element of ethnic construction must be seen in the context that more than any other subject of Empire, the African was containerised not as an autonomous native, but solely as a tribesperson.[55] Jean-François Bayart goes even further, asserting, in effect, that the precipitation and articulation of ethnic identities become incomprehensible when dissociated from colonial rule.[56] What this seems to point to is that so deeply entrenched is the ethnicity factor that past ethnic solidarities may invade the present, giving rise to problems of political organisation and fanning tensions and instabilities.

Second, ethnicity has also been used as a way of giving effect to claims of self-determination. Whilst the fixation with the exercise of this right has been a hallmark of the post-war legal order, it has also been a recipe for conflicts with complexities that have challenged the normative construct of both municipal and international law. Conflicts arising from this are often exacerbated by a feeling of alienation on the part of ethnic groups that occupy a certain territory. The injustice they endure emboldens their desire to seek political autonomy or complete self-rule in some cases. The ongoing violence in the Delta region of Nigeria is a case in point. This is in part a result of the legacies bequeathed to the post-colonial state as well as the inability of post-independence nation-building to construct states along a genuine basis of nationalism.

The complicity of colonial legislation and policy in this imbroglio cannot be underrepresented. Fundamental to British colonial policy was the enforcement of a mission to 'civilise' Africans as cohering communities and not individual constituents of communities.[57] The indirect rule system pioneered by Lord Lugard as the engine for colonial administrative machinery was laden with references to, and composites of, the tribe as the defining unit of organisation. Policy instruments were specifically formulated to reflect this mindset, as the 1930 *Native Administration Memorandum on Native Courts* of Tangayika illustrates. The instrument noted that tribes were entities with 'common language, a single social system, and an established

---

[54] *Ibid.*

[55] M. Mamdani, *Citizen and Subject: Contemporary Africa and the Legacy of Late Colonialism* (Princeton University Press, 1996), p. 22.

[56] J. F. Bayart, *The State in Africa: The Politics of the Belly* (London: Longman Group, 1993), p. 51.

[57] Mamdani, *Citizen and Subject*, p. 22.

customary law'.[58] Of course this reinforced the perception and image of a tribalised Africa, and 'where there did not exist a clearly demarcated tribe with a distinct central authority', Mamdani explains, 'then one had to be created in the interest of [colonially crafted] order'.[59]

The ethnicity proposition as cause of conflicts has been increasingly challenged. In a study edited by Adebayo Adedeji, an argument is made for the need to move away from ethnic-oriented approaches to the understanding of African conflicts to empirical, proactive, policy-oriented research and strategic studies.[60] Adedeji asserts that 'it is quite simplistic to regard conflict, civil strife and political turmoil as merely postcolonial teething problems of independent states and to resort to stereotypic and facile analysis of dumping everything at the door of ethnicism and tribalism'.[61] The point is that in order to understand the complex dynamics of conflicts drawn from ethnic identities, it is imperative to look beyond the degree of violence, simply because conflicts emanating within ethnic communities do not erupt spontaneously.[62] Seen this way, 'ethnicity is not the ultimate, irreducible source of violent conflict'.[63] Mamdani also agrees, indicating that an internal conflict cannot exhaustively define or account for the ethnic phenomenon given that 'references to tribalism accent more the interethnic than the intraethnic, the conflict between the tribes and not that within a tribe'. His point though is 'not to deny the existence of the former, but to claim that the nature of conflict between ethnic groups in the larger polity is difficult to grasp unless we relate it to the conflict within a tribe'. For 'without the connection', Mamdani concludes, 'we will be left with no more than a tautology: different tribes fight because they are different'.[64]

Others, like David Francis, reason that 'because ethnicity is socially constructed, it is not a static concept', therefore 'constantly mutating and . . . reconstructed over time'.[65] For Francis, ethnicity is not so much the

---

[58] *Native Administration Memorandum on Native Courts*, Tangayika, 1930, cited in Mamdani, *ibid.*, p. 79.

[59] Mamdani, *ibid.*, p. 79.

[60] Adedeji (ed.), *Comprehending and Mastering African Conflicts*, p. 7.   [61] *Ibid.*

[62] S. Wolff, *Ethnic Conflict: A Global Perspective* (New York: Oxford University Press, 2006), p. 3.

[63] B. Rogers and D. D. Laitin, 'Ethnic and Nationalist Violence', *Annual Review of Sociology*, 24 (1998), 423–52 at 425.

[64] Mamdani, *Citizen and Subject*, pp. 184–5.

[65] D. Francis, *Uniting Africa – Building Regional Peace and Security Systems* (Aldershot: Ashgate, 2006), p. 77.

problem, as often claimed, but rather it is the 'politicisation, exploitation and manipulation of ethnicism' that consolidate prejudice and lay the foundation for discord.[66] In their bid to acquire power and control over state resources, Francis explains, postcolonial political elites have resorted to colonial tactics of demonstrating 'remarkable recklessness and a total lack of restraint in manipulating ethnicity by peddling stereotypes and prejudices against opposing groups'.[67] The argument finds support elsewhere. Donald Rothchild has, for instance, underlined the danger of mobilising ethnic solidarity for purposes of garrisoning against dominance or fulfilment of class political interest. Rothchild argues that in situations where there exists a looming fear by ruling state elites and their constituents of the 'consequences of a fundamental re-ordering of regime procedures or where political minorities remain deeply anxious over their subordination or their cultural or physical survival', the ethnic factor may not only be an operative decimal, but conflicts arising from it are likely to be intense and highly destructive.[68]

Perhaps what these perspectives illustrate, in a sense, is that ethnicity-induced conflicts are context dependent, as they arise from what Donald Horowitz describes as the main evaluative significance accorded by the groups in acknowledging their perceived differences and then played out in public rituals of affirmation and contradiction.[69] In other words, a conflict that is described as ethnically motivated is often a progeny of some bigger mitigating element that transpires into what Hizkias Assefa calls 'a self-fulfilling prophecy engulfing [an] entire ethnic group'.[70] The Carnegie Commission on Preventing Deadly Conflict has warned against the usage of expressions such as 'tribal' and 'ethnic' as they do not offer a holistic understanding of the dynamics of violence.[71] The Commission notes that to label a conflict as overwhelmingly ethnic could result in misguided policy choices by fostering a certain perception that differences emanating from ethnic, cultural or religious identities inevitably lead to violence and conflict and that such differences must therefore be suppressed.[72]

---

[66] Ibid., pp. 77–8.   [67] Ibid., p. 78.

[68] D. Rothchild, 'An Interactive Model for State-Ethnic Relations' in Deng and Zartman (eds.), Conflict Resolution in Africa, p. 190.

[69] Horowitz, Ethnic Groups in Conflict, p. 227.

[70] H. Assefa, 'Crucible of Civilisation and Conflicts: Ethiopia' in P. Anyang' Nyong'o (ed.), Arms and Daggers in the Heart of Africa (Nairobi: African Academy of Sciences, 1993), p. 23.

[71] Carnegie Commission, Carnegie Commission on Preventing Deadly Conflict (New York: Carnegie Corporation, 1997), p. 29.

[72] Ibid.

Efforts to buttress this proposition often point to the fact that if ethnicity on its own is capable of initiating violence, then conflicts in what are largely homogenous societies such as Somalia and Rwanda would make little sense. In Rwanda, the ethnographic profile of Hutus and Tutsis shows patterns of similarities: same language, same territory and cultural trends and mindsets. From this perspective the existence of common ethnicity, then, does not appear to automatically translate into unity and harmonisation of aspirations. There is also a perception that these homogenous societies are perhaps the exceptions rather than the norm. And that even in the cases of Rwanda and Somalia, ethnic-related distinctions, however minor, have been used to fan violence, suggesting perhaps, that the incidence of conflicts in these states is not so much dependent on the existence of a common ethnic identity as such, but more crucially, the substantive character of this 'identity in terms of the shared attitudes towards issues of political authority and control that embodies it'.[73]

Yet even when huge segments of the literature on ethnicity and conflicts lead to one-dimensional conclusions and assumptions, it is difficult to totalise their validity. This is because, irrespective of their differences, it is highly unlikely that a Tutsi, say, would willingly and without remorse kill a Hutu in the absence of a compelling and provoking intervening agent, factor or element. As Jean-François Bayart notes, manifestations of ethnicity often involve some kind of social dimensions and so far as the contemporary state is concerned, an ethnicity-induced conflict erupts largely as an agent of accumulation and extraction of wealth, political power and survival.[74] Other possible agents could be attributed to fears of security, safety and uncertainty, dispute over resources and interplay of politics occasioning in marginalisation, exclusion and dominance. The point here is that where conflicts have an ethnic dimension, they would almost certainly have been triggered by other agents or factors. They do not erupt in moments of spontaneity.

Bad governance, politics of exclusion and beyond

There is growing consensus that bad governance and the politics of exclusion are major factors in Africa's postcolonial crises. With a few exceptions, Africa's internal conflicts considerably relate to underlying

---

[73] Clapham, 'Rethinking African States', 2.   [74] Bayart, The State in Africa, p. 55.

paucity in the nature and structures of good governance.[75] There is hardly an exhaustive catalogue of what constitutes good governance or its most essential components. Governance generally includes the network of institutions and relationships from which people articulate their views, choices and preferences, through accountable and transparent mechanisms and processes.[76] What it simply means is the prevalence of conditions conducive for the advancement of the rule of law, human security and the utilisation of institutional resources in the interest of the collective good. Its antonym, bad governance, encompasses everything that good governance is inclined to eradicate. Bad governance is usually the culmination of end products of historically constituted practices of exclusion, which are antithetical to the attainment of peace, social justice and progressive democratic order.[77]

Adebayo Adedeji has attempted to establish links between the erosion of democratic values and the proliferation of conflicts in Africa.[78] Adedeji contends that the presence of freedom through the deepening of democracy is a prerequisite for the advancement of social justice, progress and development.[79] He further argues that conditions of internal strife and conflicts are generally reactions to the pervasive lack of democracy, erosion of human rights, suppression of people's sovereignty, absence of accountability frameworks and culture, and above all, prevalence of bad governance.[80] In societies afflicted with violence, Adedeji notes, 'justice which encompasses equity and fair play as the ethical basis of national politics is [often] conspicuous for its absence', concluding that 'such an absence is reason enough for political instability and violence, conflicts and wars'.[81] The relationship between freedom, democratic governance and economic progress has been elaborately explored by Amartya Sen, who illustrates that economic and political freedoms have a mutually reinforcing existence whose benefits could significantly promote social justice and mitigate grievances associated with injustice.[82]

---

[75] T. Awori, 'Foreword' in Adedeji (ed.), *Comprehending and Mastering African Conflicts*, p. xiii.

[76] K. Jenkins and W. Plowden, *Governance and Nationbuilding: The Failure of International Intervention* (Cheltenham: Edward Elgar, 2006), p. 8.

[77] T. E. Paupp, *Achieving Inclusionary Governance: Advancing Peace and Development in First and Third World Nations* (New York: Transnational Publishers, 2000), p. 288.

[78] See Adedeji (ed.), *Comprehending and Mastering African Conflicts*.

[79] *Ibid.*, p. 7.　　[80] *Ibid.*　　[81] *Ibid.*

[82] A. Sen, *Development as Freedom* (Oxford University Press, 1999).

Bad governance does not occur in a vacuum. It is often a culmination of factors, faultlines or even failures in the social, institutional and political management and architecture of a state. The politics of exclusion is one such factor. By exclusion is meant a process where access to decision-making, resources and opportunities are appropriated by or restricted to a chosen class or group. An exclusionary political system creates conditions where a favoured class or group often wields considerable power and influence that facilitate means to dominate and define the direction of policy and the category of its beneficiaries. In these conditions, the excluded group or class feels unrepresented and perceives political institutions and constitutional arrangements as contemptible and lacking in legitimacy.

The link between exclusion and violence is well documented. Terence Edward Paupp is of the view that any prospects of avoiding armed conflicts in a country would depend 'upon the type and fairness of its political system'.[83] A society that has adequacy of representation strengthened by social and political inclusion could greatly mitigate dangers of social instability and political violence.[84] What this means is that social and political violence tend to take effect more strongly in exclusionary political systems than in inclusionary ones.[85] This is because an ethos of inclusion leads to practical power-sharing arrangements in ethnically divided societies.[86] The strand finds favour amongst governance advocates treating its promise as a fait accompli.[87]

Patterns of exclusion have been at the centre of a number of internal conflicts, from Angola to Zimbabwe, and DRC to Ivory Coast. The exclusion of groups from equal access to political and economic benefits, and services, for instance, contributed to the second Sudanese civil war that has claimed the lives of thousands of people over the past decades. In the DRC, exclusion of a large number of ethnic and social groups led to violence and a civil war that continues to rage. The effects of politics of exclusion show, quite clearly, that what has also been in short supply in Africa, especially in relation to its nation-building initiatives, are leaders with the qualities to unify, 'bind wounds, hold everything and everyone together, mobilise and motivate their people, pursue a policy of

---

[83] Paupp, *Achieving Inclusionary Governance*, p. 314.   [84] *Ibid.*   [85] *Ibid.*

[86] *Ibid.*

[87] See *Kenya at the Crossroads: Demands for Constitutional Reforms Intensify* (New York: Robert F. Kennedy Center for Human Rights, 1997).

inclusion rather than exclusion and [who] are seen by one and all to be of the highest integrity and beyond suspicion'.[88]

Beyond bad governance and the politics of exclusion, there are other historically conditioned factors that play a part in the oscillation of violence and conflicts in Africa. Although the causes of African conflicts are a combination of different factors as shown above, they cannot, as Obiora Chinedu Okafor aptly observes, 'be neatly divorced from the enduring crisis of internal legitimacy that the postcolonial African state has always experienced'.[89] The crisis of legitimacy and the chaos of internal social and political dynamics have created a centre-point of friction that makes many African state structures edge ever closer to fragmentation and reconfiguration.[90] Bertrand Badie and Pierre Birnbaum have similarly pointed to these fissures of legitimacy, asserting that postcolonial societies approach state construction by a kind of mimicry of forced acceptance of exterior models emanating from the West and artificially grafted on socio-political structures which probably demanded different organisational models.[91] They conclude, therefore, that the state in Africa remains 'a purely imported product, a pale imitation of the diametrically opposite European political and social systems, a foreign body, which is moreover overweight, inefficient and a source of violence'.[92]

Postcolonial Africa's enduring difficulties in mediating its crisis of statehood are to some degree due to the desire to underwrite the symbolic role of socio-cultural cleavages as operative links with the past and spaces of loyalty for the present. The continued reoccurrence of this struggle may well point to the shallow grounding of political spaces and the loose interstices between formal political institutions and indigenous social structures. Remnants of precolonial cleavages and their traditional social affiliations are often perceived by structures and representations of the contemporary African state 'as the embodiment of the historical and cultural consciousness of the people and the bedrock of ethnicity, as a threat to its hegemony

---

[88] See A. Adedeji, 'The Nigerian Political Economy in the Next Millennium: What Prospects?' Second Quarterly Club Lecture, Yoruba Tennis Club, Lagos, June 1997, p. 11, cited in S. Odunuga, 'Achieving Good Governance in Post-Conflict Situations: The Dialectic between Conflict and Good Governance' in A. Adedeji (ed.), *Comprehending and Mastering African Conflicts*, p. 41.

[89] Okafor, *Re-defining Legitimate Statehood*, p. 38.   [90] *Ibid.*

[91] B. Badie and P. Birnbaum, *The Sociology of the State* (The University of Chicago Press, 1983), p. 178.

[92] *Ibid.*, p. 181.

and secular values'.[93] This is aggravated when the state further poses as the 'crucible of modernity and the sole symbol of international sovereignty'.[94] Society on the other hand struggles in a desperate attempt 'to escape the clutches of the state'.[95] In the ensuing struggle, instruments of coercion are utilised as a way of imposing 'order' in circumstances that do not have platforms to support it. The result has, occasionally, been the emergence of military and one-party dictatorships and the inevitable eruption of violence and conflicts. Such unsettling contestations breed tension and instability, widening the state–society disconnect and margins of exclusion. But these conditions also exist simultaneously with the parallel system of a personalised state. This is a system that operates with a paternalistic mode of governance where the personality of an individual overshadows the state and the primacy of its sovereign functions.[96] Decolonisation struggles mostly succeeded due to the resilience of colonial subjects. But the charisma of leadership was vital and helped sustain the agenda of self-rule and the means to bring it to reality. This phenomenon of personalisation has filtered down through the whole postcolonial era.

Unlike its positive effects in anti-colonial struggles, personalisation of the African state exacerbates dysfunctional institutions and may well rupture the fragile ethnic patchwork that binds African nationhood. Personalisation of the state has resulted in a number of negative outcomes. First, the overgrowth in the influence and authority of a leader defines the relationship between society and the state. Where this has eroded faith in state institutions, the fate of a nation falls in the hands of individuals who, in many instances, lack constitutional legitimacy and public recognition. Second, personalised rule is an expensive phenomenon that employs patronage as a means of maintaining hegemony.[97] In postcolonial Africa, ruling elites' obsession with political patronage often comes with what Dwayne Woods calls the 'burden of cooptation'.[98]

---

[93] E. Hutchful, 'The Fall and Rise of the State in Ghana' in A. Samatar and A. I. Samatar (eds.), *The African State: Reconsiderations* (Portsmouth: Heinemann, 2002), p. 105.

[94] *Ibid.*

[95] J. Herbst, 'War and the State in Africa', *International Security*, 14:4 (1990), 117–39 at 127.

[96] See generally Jackson and Rosenberg, *Personal Rule in Black Africa*.

[97] See J. A. Ayoade, 'States Without Citizens: An Emerging African Phenomenon' in D. Rothchild and N. Chazan (eds.), *The Precarious Balance: State and Society in Africa* (Boulder, Colo.: Westview Press, 1988).

[98] D. Woods, 'Côte d'Ivoire: The Crisis of Distributive Politics' in L. A. Villalon and P. A. Huxtable (eds.), *The African State at a Critical Juncture: Between Disintegration and Reconfiguration* (Boulder, Colo.: Lynne Rienner, 1998), p. 213.

Patronage almost certainly leads to untenable expansion and centralisation of the state. Elizabeth Colson adds nuance to this by explaining that African postcolonial expansion and centralisation is not inspired by the desire to deliver public goods effectively, but rather is a means of informalising the formal state.[99] Unable to reach out to society and establish points of mediation with law and supervisory institutions and processes of legitimate governance, the state eventually 'turns in on itself'.[100]

Rights violations and the yearning for freedom

The quest for freedom and dignity of the individual are natural aspirations found in values, belief systems and cultural traditions across civilisations. In the post-war international legal order, the dominance of neo-liberal concepts and ideology have culminated in the consolidation of the premises and promises of rights and values, so much so that there emerges an intellectual and ideological mindset that proselytises what has been described as 'uncompromising autonomy of the individual, rights-bearing, physically discrete, monied, market-driven, materially inviolate human subject'.[101] Justification for this line of thought is often framed around the belief that a society that enshrines and enforces rights and freedoms for its people is almost always a society at ease with itself and in peace with like-minded others beyond its boundaries. Such a social and political ordering provides and makes possible alternative platforms through which views, aspirations, grievances and national energies could be channelled. Where the normative and institutional framework is visible and well established, not only is 'certainty' in the social spaces 'guaranteed', but that a reasonable amount of predictability exists.

Human rights constitute an important part of this post-war agenda. In the context of Africa, the idea of human rights acquires poignancy on two fronts. The first is that Africa occupies an experimental and paradoxical site for the global human rights movement. Experiment comes into the fray to the extent that Africa is often the natural choice for civil

---

[99] E. Colson, 'Competence and Incompetence in the Context of Independence', *Current Anthropology*, 8 (1967), 92–111 at 93.

[100] C. Boone, *Merchant Capital and the Roots of State Power in Senegal 1930–1985* (Cambridge University Press, 1992), p. 13.

[101] J. L. Comaroff and J. Comaroff, 'Introduction' in J. L. Comaroff and J. Comaroff (eds.), *Civil Society and the Political Imagination in Africa: Critical Perspectives* (Chicago University Press, 1999), p. 3.

society groups and, increasingly too, international financial institutions, to pilot-project programmes, policies, campaigns and initiatives on human rights violations. Paradoxically, the increasing focus on Africa also produces methods of norms localisation that activate prejudices that are at one level antithetical to the narrative of inclusion, and on the other, the means through which human rights acquire purchase.[102] Where rights are violated, agitation for a remedy or their restoration may lead to tension and violence. The reverse is also true in that where violence exists, human rights almost certainly become one of its casualties. The symbiosis is even stronger than often acknowledged.

Over the decades, there have been attempts by international institutions to reflect these linkages in their legal and policy instruments, forming part of the integrated approaches to conflicts. In a report to the UN General Assembly, the UN High Commissioner for Human Rights emphasises the importance of a human rights approach to conflict prevention, noting that 'it will be important in the future to have as early notice as possible of situations in which various elements of the United Nations human rights program could play a role in preventing the outbreak of serious violations of human rights'.[103] The UN Charter provides for sets of principles that seek to promote peace and security through the respect for the sanctity of human life. This is also echoed in Article 23(1) of the African Charter on Human and Peoples' Rights as well as Article 3(d)–(h) of the Constitutive Act of the African Union.

Quite often too, prescriptions for peacebuilding and prevention of conflicts are framed around democratic governance. John Tesha has reiterated the symbiosis of these prescriptions by noting that democracy and human rights are indispensable to the procurement of peace in Africa given that 'conflicts may lead to human rights violations and human rights violations may also lead to conflict'.[104] Recent empirical evidence from North Africa in the shape of the so-called 'Arab spring' of 2010–11 validates this. The three countries mostly affected – Tunisia, Egypt and Libya – shared a common political culture of oppression and

---

[102] See M. Mutua, 'Savages, Victims and Saviors: The Metaphor of Human Rights', *Harvard International Law Journal*, 36:3 (2001), 201–45.

[103] UN High Commissioner for Human Rights, *First Report to the UN General Assembly*, A/49/36, cited in R. Murray, 'Preventing Conflicts in Africa: The Need for a Wider Perspective', *Journal of African Law*, 45:1 (2001), 13–24 at 14.

[104] J. Tesha, 'Addressing the Challenges of Peace and Security in Africa', Conflict Management Centre, OAU Secretariat, Addis Ababa, Ethiopia Occasional Paper Series No. 1/1999, at 22.

rights abuses, though with varying degrees of impunity. For the most part of the life cycles of the regimes of Ben Ali in Tunisia, Mubarak in Egypt and Ghaddaffi in Libya, violations of human rights and denial of freedoms had been so entrenched that violence or revolt of some sort, and at some stage, was more than probable. It was inevitable. Although Egypt and Tunisia effected regime change without an armed conflict, the Libyan uprising resulted in warfare.

There has also been a trend of violence erupting in the aftermath of disputed or inconclusive elections, where incumbents have resisted consti-tutional requirements to hand over power even when results adequately suggest defeat. This was the case in Kenya's 2008 elections when the incumbent, Mwai Kibaki, and the main opposition leader, Raila Odinga, both claimed victory resulting in violence. A similar situation also occurred in Zimbabwe in 2008 leading to social disorder, and in Côte d'Ivoire in 2010, again culminating in violence and bloody reprisals. Until certainty, fairness and transparency exist in electoral processes and outcomes in Africa, it is likely that this trend will continue well into the future as people become increasingly intolerant of electoral malpractices, especially in an era when technology and social media are making tre-mendous leaps in the way information is shared, stored and accessed.

The causes of violence and conflicts in Africa are diverse, but also closely interrelated. The causal factors occur in the context of an imposed state system, whose representations, inabilities, activities and modes of operation are often mediums of contestation and sources of tension. It is also the very diversity of the causes that makes the depths and pattern of these conflicts vary. These changing dynamics require analyses that are capable of encapsulating the contradiction inherent in contemporary Africa and the challenges posed to international legal structures and instruments. Violence and internal conflicts are complex and it is sometimes difficult to determine their true character. But given that they occur within postcolonial statehood, there are commonalities that can be identified. Although it is dangerous to totalise such a nature, it is still possible to identify some common traits.

Attributes of internal conflicts in Africa

The UN Charter and the Geneva Conventions of 1949 provide, respect-ively, legal frameworks that regulate conflicts on the one hand, and humanise warfare on the other. With the exception of Common Article 3 of the Geneva Conventions and Protocol II of the 1977 Geneva supplements, most of the post-war warfare regulatory regime was primarily concerned with the prevention or management of interstate conflicts. This state-centric focus, though a conditioned product of the Westphalian influences on international law, was not reflective of the emerging trends in warfare, especially those relating to post-independence Africa. In fact, soon after the formulation of the UN Charter and the ratification of the Geneva Conventions, anti-colonial armed movements were increasingly challenging post-war international approaches to conflicts, ultimately rendering them anachronistic. The inability of international structures and instruments to effectively confront internal conflicts is encrusted in layers of historical, normative and institutional outlays. There are a number of aspects to internal conflicts that ought to be set out.

The first is that internal conflicts have acquired certain defining attributes that make them fall outside traditional warfare classification or categorisation. In other words, their dynamics have evolved so much beyond the sphere of the ordinary that they cannot simply be perceived as conventional wars or conflicts. This is partly because postcolonial internal conflicts tend to acquire a certain element of indeterminacy and novelty. This arises when the actual actors and factors propelling them lack an identifiable profile, as they are characterised by what Volker Boege calls 'an entanglement of a host of actors, issues and motives'.[105] Actors in this context are sourced from unstable and dynamic constituents ranging from minority social groups to peasants to professionals, and to more vulnerable actors such as children and women. Each group is in turn motivated by a certain consensual or enforced commonality of interest or social bond either territorial, ethnic or in a collective desire to bring about change. Perhaps the only certainty in this intricate relationship is that as dynamics change so does the role of individual or collective membership.

The distinctive incarnation of the actors and motives of postcolonial internal conflicts imply that certain assumptions that underpin conventional state-centric approaches to conflicts are exposed, challenged and disrupted. For instance, under the conventional categorisation of conflicts, there is scope and adherence to international principles such as sovereignty, territorial integrity and distinctions between combatants and civilians. And it is through this ethos that international approaches

---

[105] V. Boege, 'Traditional Approaches to Conflict Transformation – Potentials and Limits', Berghof Research Center for Constructive Conflict Management (2006), at 2, available at www.berghof-handbook.net/documents/publications/boege_handbook.pdf.

to violence are conceptualised and implemented. The diversity of causes and socially constructed nature of postcolonial African conflicts blur the assumed and outlined ambits of the boundaries between state, society and subjects. Where conflicts take firm root, the scope and nature of participation have an extensive range, often including lineage structures, ethno-linguistic groups, social group affiliations and religious entities, who not only redefine the contours of the conventional sociological outlook on conflicts but also introduce their own agendas into the overall setting.[106] The significance attached to these social entities lies, perhaps, in their tendency to organise people into certain groupings that are often sources for political and emotional loyalties, making internal conflicts enduring, complicated and often devastating.

The nature of these agendas is also different to the extent that they cannot be entirely framed in neo-liberal constructions such as political power or economic ambitions.[107] Rather, they are driven by a mixture of the dictates of modernity and the demands of social traits such as lineage obligations and security. Often also, these agendas are neither easily discernible nor are they readily reconcilable within the framework and mindset of contemporary international governing instruments and regulatory regimes. Once a conflict erupts and begins to be entrenched, the complex web of social actors and its vicissitude also acquire characteristics that are often particular in outlook. For instance, a leader in a given social group who traditionally serves as the fulcrum of reference and social cohesion in a locality assumes, by virtue of the particular qualities of a conflict, the functions of an organising entity. The role of lineage structure in the organisation of social life and distribution of political power may sometimes be optimised to advance individual agendas, thereby playing a major role in shaping people's lives and providing them with identities.[108]

The second attribute relates to the contradictory pattern of postcolonial internal conflicts. On the one hand, internal conflicts erupt from weak or fragile states, and on the other their challenge on the legitimacy of postcolonial statehood paradoxically results in state fragility and collapse. As Volker Boege explains, 'all too often the [postcolonial] state is weak because it has no legitimacy in the eyes of the people', meaning those 'on the ground do not perceive themselves as citizens of the state'.[109] It is a factor that makes the state an entity to be 'perceived as

---

[106] *Ibid.*, at 3.   [107] *Ibid.*   [108] Reno, *Warlord Politics and African States*, p. 19.
[109] Boege, 'Traditional Approaches to Conflict Transformation', at 12.

an alien external force' resulting in the ascription of loyalty to traditional groups and social institutions.[110] Once that character of the state as the central organ through which social life is organised dissipates, or is even appropriated by dynamic non-state social forces, the state then loses its essence as a primary focal actor which serves as the traditional organising framework of reference.[111] These irregularities are reflected in the very nature of the composition and combustive characteristics of armed groups populating internal conflicts in Africa. Often, the groups do not conform to orthodox templates of categorisation. This is also compounded by the fact that the conflicts sometimes represent 'political projects which no longer seek or even need to establish territorial, bureaucratic or consent-based political authority in the traditional sense'.[112]

Third, social resistance to postcolonial state excesses has diminished the capacity of the state to regulate and enforce law and order. Society and state become disentangled as people dissociate themselves from the state or its formalised representative organs. The state in the eyes of the people transforms from a necessary variable that should protect and promote notions of order and justice to a symbol of evil that becomes an agent of criminality.[113] Weak state structures are themselves breeding grounds for the emergence and functioning of parallel social entities that operate in contrast with, and opposition to, the Westphalian model of the formal state. Tensions arising from these complex variables have degenerated into violence and prolonged internal armed conflicts. In the ensuing struggles between the adherents of the formal state and those social entities seeking to contest it, a disorder is created that resembles what William Reno calls the 'shadow state'.[114] Shadow states comprise a mix of warlords, ethnic networks and primordial lineage and tend to operate parallel structures which contest the legitimate existence of the formal state, whilst often remaining invisible to the regulatory regimes of international law.[115] Shadow states have increasingly succeeded in defining the totality of existence of people along localised boundaries and

---

[110] *Ibid.*   [111] *Ibid.*

[112] C. Tshitereke, 'On the Origins of War in Africa', *Africa Security Review*, 12:2 (2003), 32–40.

[113] See J. F. Bayart, S. Ellis and B. Hibou, *The Criminalization of the State in Africa* (London: James Currey, 1999).

[114] See Reno, *Warlord Politics and African States.*

[115] C. Newbury, 'States at War: Confronting Conflict in Africa', *African Studies Review*, 45:1 (2002), 1–20 at 8.

militia-constructed instruments of violence.[116] Christopher Clapham has warned that any prolongation of breeding spaces of shadow states could potentially lead to warlords creating 'their own ethnicities by consolidating different groups within a common military system'.[117]

Fourth, there is also an attempt to interpret internal conflicts in Africa as the personification of a form of retreat from modernity and advance to postmodernity.[118] The reference to modernity as agent of resistance could relate to those continuing representations of the legacy of the colonial state, the Westphalian model of statehood and sovereignty, as well as a recalibration of these images in the form of globalisation. A central aspect of the postcolonial assault on modernity relates in part to the latter's social embodiments and structure of thought, which are self-consciously Western.[119] This includes the incoherently ambiguous character of the postcolonial state and its continuing battles to entrench legacies of Westphalia. In so doing, a chaotic encounter emerges where 'the new clashes with the old, tradition battles with modernity, the indigenous engages the alien, and nemesis catches up with colonial structures'.[120]

Advances to postmodernity by contrast could be understood as the 'disenchantment with the philosophical structures and grand narratives of modernity'.[121] It is a process that is often disjointed and involves attempts to reclaim authority or relevance of certain indigenous pre-colonial identities that were effaced by the construction of the colonial state and the emergence of its postcolonial predecessor. These inter-faces are sources of conflict which also convey a certain character of postcolonial internal conflicts that sets them apart from conventional warfare. The implications are particularly poignant and may have the potential of mapping a kind of African postmodern statecraft. In Somaliland, for instance, the collapse of the Somali Republic resulted in the reconstitution of the state through unique conflict transformation and peacebuilding initiatives that propelled traditional institutions to the forefront of institution-building. What has emerged is a hybrid state

---

[116] O. Ndoli, *Ethnic Conflicts in Africa* (Dakar: CODESRIA Book Series, 1998).

[117] Clapham, 'Rethinking African States', at 7.

[118] A. A. Mazrui, 'Conflict as a Retreat from Modernity: A Comparative Overview' in Furley (ed.), *Conflict in Africa*, p. 19.

[119] H. Schepel, 'Legal Pluralism in the European Union' in P. Fitzpatrick and H. Bergeron (eds.), *Europe's Other: European Law Between Modernity and Postmodernity* (Aldershot: Ashgate, 1998), p. 70.

[120] Mazrui, 'Conflict as a Retreat from Modernity', p. 23.

[121] Schepel, 'Legal Pluralism', p. 69.

system that has incorporated distinctive derivatives from primordial kinship. It could be argued that these are alien to the philosophical construct from which international law is sourced and the structures that set out to universalise it.

Ramifications of conflicts in Africa

The constant oscillation from one conflict to another has had devastating impacts on the people, economies, prospects and fragile security architecture of a significant portion of Africa. Progress in whatever way conceived, whether through human rights or development-based approaches, has been threatened and impeded by the recurrence of armed violence and social upheaval. There are a number of tangents to this. The first is that conflicts are almost certainly an assault on the sanctity of human life and dignity. Human life is a treasured ideal and entity, and its protection is fundamental to the advancement of the human project. It is in part the ethos behind this that inspired the formulation of the post-war international legal order. The intensity and ubiquity of internal conflicts attack the very essence upon which this ethos is founded. Beyond this, disruption of the ethical paradigm impacts enormously on the physical and material conditions of Africa. Besides the immediate negative impact on growth, labour and human wellbeing, conflicts deprive Africa of talent, opportunities and stability, all of which are essential determinants in securing futures framed around the realisation of collective prosperity and fulfilment of individual aspirations.

Second, conflicts have a certain expensive dimension. For many African states where formal institutional structures and the delivery of public goods are generally inadequate, the redirection of resources to finance conflicts imposes strain on what is already a pretty desperate resource pool. Often too, there is an irrational inclination to increase military expenditures beyond available means. Mass spending on military hardware implies that resources for the improvement of social life such as education, health and infrastructure are diverted for purposes of prosecuting warfare. In its first Human Development Report in 1990, the UNDP expressed concern over what it labelled as 'the military-social imbalance' where defence expenditures in most African states were threefold higher than those on health.[122] Analyses on this,

---

[122] United Nations Development Programme, *Human Development Report* (Oxford University Press, 1990), pp. 162–163.

though, are few and far between. Francis Stewart and Valpy Fitzgerald have pointed out that although conflicts remain 'one of the main causes of human suffering and economic underdevelopment', it is difficult to fathom why 'economic analysis of developing countries at war is relatively rare'.[123]

There are other significant ramifications of conflicts in Africa. Contemporary international society projects itself as a system driven by sovereign equality. Some of the African states afflicted by conflicts do not perceive themselves in the same rosy platitudes represented by international structures and instruments. And of course this perception of indifference has left a poisonous legacy that continues to undermine confidence and trust between developing and developed countries.[124] In the past it had led to apprehension amongst weaker states, given that some of Africa's political landscape is susceptible to external interventions. Also, conflicts have restricted Africa's proactive contributions to the shaping of an international policy sensitive to Third World concerns. The recurrence of violence and conflicts confines many countries in Africa in a state of 'receivership', where their right, and perhaps obligation, to participate fully in the conduct and affairs of international society is dismissed with indifference or even ridiculed. The effect has been disenfranchisement of peoples' voices and erosion of sovereign interests and powers.

Indeed, Africa's post-independence travails have been a narrative of two halves. On the one hand, independence brought excitement, expectations and hope for a progressive future, one that would be characterised by justice and freedom, pride and ambition, constitutionalism and responsible governance. On the other hand, however, what emerged in many African states has been a telling of violence and conflicts, social frustrations and impoverishment. The conditions have been all-consuming, and in other instances both defining and totalising. In the few states where progress was made to arrest the scourge of conflicts, the initiatives succeeded in some, but failed in most others as there appeared to have been the existence of operating dynamics which when converged with other defining factors have the potential to reignite conflicts. This has been the trend in many parts of Africa.

---

[123] F. Stewart and V. Fitzgerald, *War and Underdevelopment*, vol. I: *The Economic and Social Consequences of Conflict* (New York: Oxford University Press, 2001), p. 1.

[124] Report of the UN Secretary General, *The Causes of Conflict and the Promotion of Durable Peace and Sustainable Development in Africa*, 16 April 1998, UN Report A/57/172.

Alternative perspectives on internal conflicts

The impact of conflicts in Africa has led to the need for searching enquiries on ways to overcome tragedies and underdevelopment. One recent trend has been to initiate distinctive thinking in policy and research so as to provoke recuperation of the narrative of internal conflicts. Its importance lies in the fact that the description and identification of a problem affect its orientation. As Boaventura de Sousa Santos observes,

> the way the crisis is identified conditions the direction of the epistemo-
> logical turn ... Knowledge, particularly critical knowledge, moves
> between ontology (the reading of crisis) and epistemology (the crisis of
> reading), and in the end it is not up to it to decide which of the two
> statuses will prevail and for how long.[125]

Alternative perspectives on internal conflicts revolve around two funda-mental factors. The first pertains to the 'non-emancipated' postcolonial state, and the second is the notion of re-traditionalisation of society and crisis of governance.

The 'non-emancipated' postcolonial state

The African postcolonial state has perhaps been subjected to more scrutiny in recent times than any equivalent in other geographic appel-lations. The scrutiny has also been enriched by increasingly expanding perspectives from interdisciplinary approaches. But from whatever per-spective it is viewed, there is near consensus that the postcolonial African state exhibits characteristics of the colonial state, having being funda-mentally affected by Empire's methods of domination and the residual effects of colonial policies.[126] The mode upon which the colonial state was crafted implies that its successor – the postcolonial state – is a progeny of unedifying inheritance consolidated by an unevenly sketched international legal order. This has provided the state with little room for reinventing, having lacked the capacity and appropriate settings, resulting in constant challenges to its authority and legitimacy. Its crisis, though, straddles vast spaces in the social and political spheres,

---

[125] B. Sousa Santos, *Towards a New Common Sense: Law, Science and Politics in the Paradigmatic Transition* (New York: Routledge, 1995), p. 7.
[126] J. B. Barron, 'African Boundary Conflict: An Empirical Study', *African Studies Review*, 22:3 (1979), 1–14 at 1.

ultimately raising doubts over its relevance as a functional variable in light of 'shrinkage in the competence, credibility and probity' of the state.[127]

It is not surprising, therefore, that the proliferation of conflicts has not only posed challenges to the postcolonial state, but also that they constitute distinctive elements of its current critical juncture.[128] In many ways too, this disjuncture represents a paradox that culminates in what Rene Lemarchand calls a 'kind of conceptual borderline area where the encounter of traditional and modern institutions generates its own perverse effects'.[129] Corollary to the many contingent effects, institutional disintegration and crisis of identity present problems and challenges to the state as a model of social and political organisation as well as to the international system whose operational functionalism cannot be distilled from the dis(order) at the municipal level. As a result, the reliance on the postcolonial state as an entity for peacebuilding and primary point of reference for interfaces with international law appears to be untenable. There are two elements to this.

First, by virtue of the fluid circumstances of its birth, the postcolonial African state was from the onset convicted as an alien apparatus with an inclination for oppression and tyranny.[130] In its quest to dispose of its acquired misfortune, the state has resorted to colonial modes of dominion through coercion, occasionally tempted by 'populist ideologies of doubtful logical integrity'.[131] For TWAIL, the outlay of international law and the general inadequacies of the postcolonial state cannot be understood outside the context of the lived histories of Third World peoples, simply because the process that framed the formation and evolution of the postcolonial state conditioned the internalisation of conflicts and authoritarianism.[132] Whilst the role of colonialism in this episode has been fairly explored, the complicity of international law in postcolonial

---

[127] C. Young, 'Zaire: Is There a State?', *Canadian Journal of African Studies*, 18:1 (1984), 80–2 at 80.

[128] J. B. Forrest, 'State Inversion and Nonstate Politics' in Villalon and Huxtable (eds.), *The African State at a Critical Juncture*, p. 45.

[129] R. Lemarchand, 'The State, the Parallel Economy, and the Changing Structure of Patronage Systems' in Rothchild and Chazan (eds.), *The Precarious Balance*, p. 149.

[130] Ayoade, 'States Without Citizens' in Rothchild and Chazan (eds.), *The Precarious Balance*, p. 115.

[131] *Ibid.*, p. 116.

[132] See A. Anghie and B. S. Chimni, 'Third World Approaches to International Law and Individual Responsibility in Internal Conflicts', *Chinese Journal of International Law*, (2003), 78–103 at 78.

African crises is perhaps only seriously engaged by TWAIL scholarship. The causes of internal conflicts in Africa must therefore be aligned to, and understood from, the prism of the encounters between international law and the Third World, and the role of colonialism in providing the incubator from which an uneven relation was violently forged. In this sense, the inadequacy of the postcolonial state is, in effect, an indictment of the structures of the contemporary international legal order, of which international law serves as the main engine-room.

Second, the narrative on internal conflicts disproportionately dilates on the economic and political causes without critically interrogating the social dimension of the continued effects of hegemonic aspects of international law. The distillation of alternative thoughts on this issue points to Upendra Baxi's characterisation of some of the social conditions in the Third World as constituting 'geographies of injustice' partly created by the commissions and omissions of international legal structures and instruments. Besides depriving people of the ability 'to be and remain human', the impact of the fissures of international law produces tragedies and victims who are then categorised as needing salvation through the same mechanisms that shaped the plight of these people in the first place. The injustices are various and varying in outlook, yet constitute sufficient capacity to trigger tensions and contestations that may result in violence and conflicts. Often though, those entangled in anti-hegemonic revolts and violence emanating from these episodes are seen in different lights. The traditional reaction has been one that shifts from the characterisation of their plight as either misfortunate or injustice. Judith Shklar has drawn attention to the nuances that separate these, suggesting that 'the difference between misfortune and injustice frequently involves our willingness and our capacity to act or not to act on behalf of the victims, to blame or to absolve, to help, mitigate, and compensate, or to just turn away'.[133]

The inadequate assessment of these episodes is, of course, lamentable considering that their continuing effects in Africa expose the falsity of the triumphalism that accompanies the post-war international legal order, whose faultlines in the arena of peacebuilding are indicative of the 'baleful statistic that half of Africa's wars have reignited within a decade of ending'.[134] Transformations are therefore needed so as to

---

[133] J. Shklar, *The Faces of Injustice* (New Haven and London: Yale University Press, 1990), p. 2.
[134] O. Furley and R. May, 'Introduction' in O. Furley and R. May (eds.), *Ending Africa's Wars: Progressing to Peace* (Aldershot: Ashgate, 2006), p. 5.

confront these episodes as part of approaches to internal conflicts in Africa. To initiate this, the prescription from TWAIL seems to be that there must exist the conceptual and normative frame that not only attempts to reconnect the postcolonial state and society, but also seeks a transformation of the borders, contents and boundaries of international law in ways that seriously reflect the needs and particularities of Third World peoples.[135] But as Anthony Anghie has reminded us, 'international law remains oblivious to its imperial structures even when continuing to reproduce them, which is why the traditional law regards imperialism as a thing of the past'.[136] The response to this is, of course, the quest for the reclamation of voices and legitimacy, which 'suggests the importance of speaking to, and with, the suffering others'.[137] This is imperative, for as Judith Shklar illuminates once again:

> Whatever decisions we do make will, however, be unjust unless we take the victim's view into account and give her voice its full weight. Anything less is not only unfair, it is also politically dangerous.[138]

Re-traditionalisation of society

To the extent that the postcolonial African state is largely a product of colonial tinkering, there are bound to be attempts to induce contestation of an order perceived as alien. The contestations have triggered transformations which represent a remarkable resurgence in the patterns of resistance, reinvention and renewal of traditional social institutions in Africa. The characterisation of this phenomenon has shifted through many imageries, with some calling it a resistance to the tragedies of modernity whilst others perceive it as an advent of 're-traditionalisation' of African society. Whatever the tag, the evolving process impinges on the foundational frame underpinning classical notions of sovereignty and the legitimacy of the postcolonial African state. Patrick Chabal and Jean-Pascal Daloz have argued that what has been unfolding 'confounds expectations of modernization' as there seems to be a noticeable

---

[135] See also Anghie and Chimni, 'Third World Approaches', at 101.

[136] A. Anghie, *Imperialism, Sovereignty and the Making of International Law* (Cambridge University Press, 2005), p. 312.

[137] U. Baxi, 'Epilogue: Whom May We Speak For, With, and After? Re-Silencing Human Rights' in G. Bhambra and R. Shilliam (eds.), *Silencing Human Rights: Critical Engagements with a Contested Project* (London: Palgrave Macmillan, 2009), p. 259.

[138] Shklar, *The Faces of Injustice*, p. 126.

resurgence of the traditional.[139] They emphasise, however, that there are dimensions to this which straddle the visibly modern and the ostensibly traditional, and that the failure to adequately understand this contradiction is 'the result of an analytical convention which tends to assume a paradigmatic dichotomy between the realms of the modern and the traditional'.[140]

Similarly, Boaventura de Sousa Santos has attempted to highlight the heterogeneous nature of the postcolonial African state and the intense hybridisation growing within it. An important dimension of his formulation is the expansion of the ambit and influence of traditional elements, which distil 'the modern equation between the unity of the state, on one hand, and the unity of its legal and administrative operation, on the other hand'.[141] The hybridisation has been made possible by the weakness of the state's bureaucratic apparatuses, which when combined with external factors generates devastating consequences such as fragile formal institutions and internal conflicts. Related to this is the global factor, which has constrained the centrality and dominance of the state in the backdrop of the emergence of suprastate political processes.[142] What is however intriguing, Santos explains, is the emergence also of infrastate actors determined to challenge the centrality of the postcolonial state.

But unlike others who perceive the resurgence of the traditional dimension as a retreat from modernity, Santos suggests that the 'recovery of the traditional in Africa, far from it being a non-modern alternative to Western modernity, is the expression of a claim to an alternative modernity'.[143] Irrespective of how this is viewed, the significance of the resurgence must not be underrepresented, not least because traditional entities conjure perhaps the 'paradigmatic example of what cannot be globalised in Africa'. And of course what 'cannot be globalised is of no interest to neoliberal globalization and, as such, can be easily stigmatized as an African particularity'.[144] But what ultimately 'becomes the object of stigmatization', Santos concludes, 'may be reappropriated by the subaltern social groups as something positive and specific, as a source of resistance against excluding global (Western) modernity'.[145]

---

[139] P. Chabal and J. P. Daloz, *Africa Works: Disorder as Political Instrument* (Oxford: James Currey, 1999), p. 45.

[140] *Ibid.*, p. 46.

[141] B. Sousa Santos, 'The Heterogeneous State and Legal Pluralism in Mozambique', *Law and Society Review*, 40:1 (2006), 39–76 at 39.

[142] *Ibid.*, at 43–4.   [143] *Ibid.*, at 61.   [144] *Ibid.*, at 60.   [145] *Ibid.*, at 60–1.

Whilst the frame of analyses on the resurgence of the traditional often varies, the constant appears to be the indolence, indifference and acquiescence of the legacy of the colonial dimensions of international law and their continued manifestation in the Third World. In postcolonial Africa the manifestations gestate in a host of entities, such as transnational institutions, state and non-state actors and, increasingly, through globalisation. Their impact has generated consequences of which violence, conflicts and famine have been the more visible. It is in this context that Anghie and Chimni assert that unless the challenges of conflicts in Africa are understood beyond particular embryonic circumstances, solutions can be at best artificial. This is because internal conflicts in Africa, especially those viewed through ethnic lenses, are 'not simply the latest expression of primordial forces', but their outlooks are 'all inextricably linked both with colonialism and with the very modern forces of globalisation that inevitably involve North-South economic relations'.[146]

Conclusion

Much of the recent history of Africa has been one of paradoxes. At independence, euphoria, hope and optimistic ambitions took hold in the minds of people and political leadership in Africa. The expectations hinged on the possibilities of self-rule and the assumption that the state has the capacity, will and legitimacy to realise its national and international obligations. But it was not long before euphoria turned into disappointment and optimism transformed into gloom as political disorder and conflicts slowly engulfed many countries from virtually all regions in Africa. With a defective international legal order, the presence of a disruptive Cold War politics and a host of compelling social transformations in Africa, internal conflicts appropriated patterns that made them enduring and devastating. But ever since the end of the Cold War, conflicts in Africa have constantly mutated, challenging and testing the structures and instruments of international law. Their effects continue to be felt across the continent.

As illustrated in this chapter, the causes of violence and conflicts in Africa are many and varied; so also are the theoretical analyses underpinning them. The relevance of the analyses has, however, been shaped by some of the historical factors that underline postcolonial Africa. The

---

[146] Anghie and Chimni, 'Third World Approaches', at 96.

historical episodes that conditioned its construction imply that the state is locked in an almost constant battle with 'parallel' entities contesting its legitimacy, abilities and relevance. The rhetoric of nationalism and nation-building that followed independence painted images of the need for social emancipation. But the emancipation could not be extended to the state, the failure of which was to provide the foundation for future crises. There was also a lack of constitutive elements to enforce a progressive transformation of the coercive culture of colonial structures. As Franz Fanon points out, 'an authentic national liberation exists only to the precise degree to which the individual has irreversibly begun his own liberation'.[147] Historians have often seen this as the reference point for the continuing disconnect between the state and the people.

The influence and impact of international law in formulating uneven interfaces with both the social conditions of the Third World and its formal institutions cannot be overemphasised. The growth of transnational bodies, non-state actors and a vast expanse of other entities has dwindled the centrality of the state and its traditional monopoly over power and resources. The impact and influence of the external dynamics of internal conflicts cannot be ignored. The pervasiveness of the conflicts has also led to searching enquiries towards confronting them. But the prescribed solutions and approaches have been in the main conditioned by the inherent limitations of international legal structures and instruments. Thus their inability to provide viable frameworks consolidates the search and quest for alternative approaches to conflict and peace-building, particularly in the context of Africa.

---

[147] F. Fanon, *Toward the African Liberation* (New York: Grove Press, 1967), p. 103.

4

International law responses to conflicts

Armed conflict either reveals lacunae in the law or demonstrates how law designed for yesterday's wars falls short when applied to contemporary conflict. When that happens, international law reacts by allowing provisions to fall into desuetude, embracing new interpretations of existing prescriptions, or generating new norms through practice or codification.

Schmitt and Pejic[1]

Introduction

Documented legal history of warfare suggests that violence and conflicts have in some shape or form almost always afflicted communities and societies across civilisations. The disorder, disruption and challenges to life that often accompanied conflicts meant that different societies had in varying degrees developed tremendous capacities to resolve them. Anthropological studies have shown that although conflict in some form was prevalent in most societies, it was often highly ritualised and in some instances almost bloodless.[2] The initiatives often involved a consolidation of peacebuilding frameworks, processes or rituals formulated through social practices, moral philosophy and a continuum of religious norms. The frameworks emanated from what could be viewed as the conscious desire by communities to tackle the scourge of conflict. As Douglas Fry notes, although people across cultures have displayed the capacity to create mayhem, they have also shown remarkable abilities to deal with conflicts.[3]

---

[1] M. Schmitt and J. Pejic (eds.), *International Law and Armed Conflict: Exploring the Faultlines: Essays in Honour of Yoram Dinstein* (Dordrecht: Martinus Nijhoff Publishers, 2007).

[2] M. Howard, 'Constraints on Warfare' in M. Howard, J. Andreopoulos and M. R. Shulman (eds.), *The Laws of War: Constraints on Warfare in the Western World* (New Haven: Yale University Press, 1994), p. 2.

[3] D. Fry, *Beyond War: The Human Potential for Peace* (Oxford University Press, 2007), p. 2.

This capacity and preoccupation with the quest for peace have been constant in human civilisation.

Modern institutional responses to conflicts have evolved over many decades. In the aftermath of World War II the condemnation of violence and prohibition of armed conflicts between states were enshrined in the UN Charter, with certain exceptions. Although part of the rationale that underlies the limitations of war emerged from the League of Nations, the nature in which it has been framed owes much to the horrors and disorder of World War II. However, this post-war internationalist dispensation has had a particularly desperate and intense relation to negotiation with Africa's postcolonial order. The nature and attributes of these conflicts have prompted theoretical reflections as well as regional or internationally sanctioned mechanisms towards more robust regulatory regimes. For the most part, the techniques and focus of the approaches, howsoever articulated, often fall short in fashioning an integrated conception capable of confronting the particularities and typology of internal conflicts that have emerged from Africa.

This chapter focuses on the encounters between international law and internal conflicts. It engages the institutional and normative responses that have been deployed in confronting conflicts as well as Africa's institutional legal frameworks that existed prior to the creation of the African Union. The aim is as much to contextualise the theoretical and analytic approach of the book as it is an affirmation of the contention that internal conflicts in Africa have largely remained invisible to international law's regulatory frameworks. The task here is to highlight responses to conflicts framed through international law's institutional architecture and normative ordering, and their relevance and adequacy towards confronting internal conflicts in Africa.

International law, the United Nations and internal conflicts

International legal frameworks have had a symbiotic relationship with armed conflicts for many centuries. This coexistence has thrived on the presumption that for law to effectively serve a social need it must acquire normative relevance and pragmatic spaces. Following the reconstitution of the international legal order in 1945 the function of international law in relation to conflicts acquired a particularly urgent focus. Its traditional role was amended to focus on the maintenance of order and promotion of justice. The operative rationale underpinning this enforced recalibration was rooted in the premise that for the conceptual shift to gain purchase international law needed to procure positive responses to the maintenance of peace by regulating warfare.[4] In the post-1945 era that quest has in part been moderated through the *jus ad bellum* regime embedded in the UN Charter. The regime essentially prohibits the threat or use of force in the conduct of interstate relations, with exceptions only relating to individual and collective self-defence, maintenance of order by regional organisations and Security Council enforcement action.

But this regime did not, *stricto sensu*, resolve a fundamental in the encounters between international law and postcolonial internal conflicts. The significance of this unresolved dynamic is profound, especially given that internal conflicts continue to pose numerous problems to international legal structures and instruments. The challenge is often manifestly acute in recurrent situations where conflicts increasingly expose the inability of law to govern them. To assess the extent of this challenge there is a need to examine the *jus ad bellum* regime that has developed and the relevance of its reflection in the UN Charter, as well as its limited applicability to internal conflicts.

The just war theory: a brief appraisal

Modern international law attitudes to conflicts have antecedents in medieval European cultures and their efforts to regulate and restrain armed violence. This legacy takes root from moral and historical presumptions against violent conduct and aggressive behaviour. However, with the changing nature of legal and political orders, and the emergence of new structures in European societies, the strong moral position on violence began to diminish with the propagation of the just war theory. The focus of early just war doctrine sought to provide a framework that would establish the basis upon which the waging of war could be justified. Its underlying philosophy was to reconcile *might* and *right*, making war a just response and an 'ultimate means for restoring a right that had been violated'.[5] An ancillary of this conception was that any such war was carried out by a specific belligerent for certain defined reasons. What this meant was that rights and

---

[4] Q. Wright, *The Role of International Law in the Elimination of War* (Manchester University Press, 1961), pp. 7–8.

[5] R. Kolb, 'Origin of the Twin Terms *Jus ad Bellum* and *Jus in Bello*', *IRRC*, 320 (1997), 553–62 at 553.

obligations of belligerents differed and depended on the causes triggering the war and their material justness.[6]

Dominant scholarship on the just war theory traces its formulation
in Western legal and social traditions. Part of this is firmly rooted in early
Christian theological conceptions.[7] A key player in this was the institution
of the *collegium fetiale*, a congregation of priests who administered the
jus fetiale, a task that involved the consideration of whether there was
sufficient ground for Rome to wage war with an adversary.[8] The *fetiale*
embodied a legal entity that was in many ways striking. No matter how
compelling circumstances for war appeared, prior approval from the
collegium was an ultimate procedural necessity, material requirement
and legal prerequisite. War conducted in the absence of an approval was
unlawful and deemed an assault on the dignity of the *collegium*. Some
of the functional and operative elements of the *fetiale* did creep into the
early part of the foundation of modern international law, a factor that
probably underscores the binding synthesis in the evolutionary history
of the discipline. The doctrine of *bellum justum* did not disappear with
the emergence of the *jus fetiale*.[9] Rather, the Christian credentials of the
Roman state shaped attitudes on the nature and condition of warfare.[10]

At the forefront of the Christian conception of war was St Augustine,
who conceived a kind of *bellum justum* theorised on Christian notions of
love.[11] In Augustine's view, the Christian obligation of love towards one's
neighbour also extended to the battlefield, where military action ought
to be rational, considerate and proportional. Traces of Augustine's
bellum justum could be found in the philosophies of subsequent theologians, most notably St Thomas Aquinas. Aquinas' influence in the just
war conception was immense and his formulation continues to resurface
in modern legal instruments.[12] Being the first to set out the conditions
for just war, Aquinas' formulation transcends its ascribed historical and

---

[6] P. Haggenmacher, *Grotius et la Doctrine de la Guerre Juste* (Paris: Calmann-Lévy, 1983), p. 250.

[7] J. T. Johnson, 'Historical Tradition and Moral Judgment: The Case of Just War Tradition',
The Journal of Religion, (1984), 299–317 at 301.

[8] I. Shearer, 'A Revival of the Just War Theory?' in Schmitt and Pejic (eds.), *International
Law and Armed Conflict*, p. 3.

[9] See J. von Elbe, 'The Evolution of the Concept of Just War in International Law', *AJIL*, 33
(1939), 665–88 at 667.

[10] See Y. Dinstein, *War, Aggression and Self-Defence* (Cambridge University Press, 2005), p. 64.

[11] See P. Ramsey, *War and the Christian Conscience* (Durham, NC: Duke University Press, 1961).

[12] According to Aquinas, there are three requirements for just war: (i) war had to be waged
by legitimate authority; (ii) there had to be a 'just cause'; and (iii) that just cause had to
be complemented with right intentions. See Shearer, 'A Revival', p. 5.

theological symbolism, especially as the approach was varyingly adopted by subsequent theorists. Although some of the normative variations were conditioned by certain features of an individual era, others were clearly borne out of the over-zealous punditry of some scholars. For Ivan Shearer, the variations represented compromises because what has eventually emerged is in 'a sense a perversion of the doctrine, since almost anything could – and did – form grounds for offence and thus for a just response in war'.[13]

Aquinas' just war conception has been reflected in the development of international legal theory and partly incorporated in modern legal instruments seeking to confront conflicts. Most notable perhaps is its recent reincarnation, constituting the cornerstone of the Responsibility to Protect doctrine. However, by the end of the nineteenth century the just war theory had experienced a substantive decline.[14] The period saw a shift from *jus ad bellum* to peacebuilding initiatives, and subsequently the propagation of the concept of *jus in bello*, which sought to humanise warfare. Besides reshaping discourses on legal approaches to violence, the transition paved the way for the rise of modern international institutions.[15] The creation of the League of Nations in 1919 was one such outcome. Its significance was that, for the first time, the unilateral approach that characterised responses to armed conflict through the just war theory was now substituted for the concept of collective security, a principle to be codified in the UN Charter.[16] The emergence of the principle signalled an enforced negotiated shift in the legal and philosophical synthesis between morality, warfare and modern law.

Jus ad bellum, *international law and the UN Charter*

Conceived from the ashes of war, the UN's primary task is the maintenance of international peace and security.[17] It provides a recognised,

---

[13] Shearer, *ibid.*

[14] See generally L. Freedman (ed.), *War* (Oxford University Press, 1994); R. Holmes, *On War and Morality* (Princeton University Press, 1989).

[15] A. Nussbaum, *A Concise History of the Law of Nations* (New York: Macmillan, 1954), pp. 10–11.

[16] See Shearer, 'A Revival'.

[17] The general purpose of the United Nations is enshrined in Article 1(1) of the UN Charter: 'To maintain international peace and security, and to that end: to take effective collective measures for the prevention and removal of threats to the peace, and for the suppression of acts of aggression or other breaches of the peace'. See United Nations Charter, adopted on 26 June 1945, 9 Int. Leg. 327, 332.

though imperfect, framework that seeks to regulate threats to global peace and security. The UN's mandate was founded on the premise to 'save succeeding generations from the scourge of war' and help 'establish conditions under which justice and respect for the obligations arising from treaties and other sources of international law could be maintained'.[18] The maintenance of peace and security acquired renewed importance largely because the friction between the use of force and the supremacy of law had been magnified by World War II.[19] And so from the onset, it had become clear that unless serious restraints were put on violence and conflicts, the world would be heading for catastrophe.[20]

The current *jus ad bellum* regime revolves around Article 2(4) of the UN Charter. The provision proclaims that '[a]ll Members shall refrain in their international relations from the threat or use of force against the territorial integrity or political independence of any state, or in any other manner inconsistent with the Purposes of the United Nations'. The two exceptions are contained in Article 51 and Chapter VII of the Charter. Article 51 makes allowance for the right of individual or collective self-defence in the event of an armed attack. Self-defence in this case is a stop-gap, a transitional measure to avail a state the right to defend its territorial integrity until such time when the Security Council can take action. The opening under self-defence is limited as it can only be invoked in situations of an armed attack.[21] The second exception is Chapter VII, a provision for the use of force to counter threats to, and breaches of, international peace and security as well as acts of aggression. Article 42 empowers the Security Council to impose military action in the fulfilment of its mandate to maintain peace and international security. Over the years, the provision on self-defence under Article 51 has attracted expansive interpretations, some of which have sought to include not only occurrence of armed attack, but also when such attacks are imminent.

Like most treaty law of the post-war era, Article 2(4) is not without flaws. Its language has inspired debate as to its scope and margin of ambiguity, which to some extent dictate applicability of *jus ad bellum* in the context of contemporary internal conflicts. There are two aspects to this. The first is that the provision is selective in its use of 'force' rather

---

[18] Preamble of the United Nations Charter, *ibid.*
[19] A. Cassese, *International Law* (Oxford University Press, 2005), p. 320.   [20] *Ibid.*
[21] W. Scholtz, 'The Changing Rules of *Jus ad Bellum*: Conflicts in Kosovo, Iraq and Afghanistan', *Potchefstroom Electronic Law Journal*, 2 (2004), 1–37 at 3.

than 'war'. The aim, it is believed, was to encapsulate as many of the modes of violence as possible. It follows, then, that the prohibition extends to war as well as other forcible measures that are short of war. The scope of the term 'force' to which Article 2(4) applies still remains a subject of enquiry.[22] The established position is that the provision transcends recourse to force regardless of whether a particular situation acquires basic constitutive elements of war.[23] In other words, Article 2(4) does not require an illegal threat to be supplemented with an order or demand, as a threat of force inconsistent with the Charter simply passes the test of an unlawful act, an interpretation much favoured by the International Court of Justice.[24]

The second aspect is that the Charter's reference to 'against the territorial integrity and political independence of any State' also raises issues of ambiguity, part of which has triggered an interpretation that places overstretched qualifications on the use of force under Article 2(4). It has been argued that the unilateral use of force within the borders of a state is not a violation of 'territorial integrity' and 'political independence' so long as a part of that territory is not permanently lost.[25] A similar line of argument was advanced by the United Kingdom in the *Corfu Channel* case.[26] But as Ian Brownlie, the veteran international lawyer, explains, this argument is not entirely persuasive because the 'phrasing was introduced precisely to provide some form of guarantee to small States and was not, *a priori*, intended to have a restricted effect'.[27]

---

[22] Does, for example, Article 2(4) extend to situations of economic pressure? Or is such a pressure only under the purview of Article 2(4) if it is accompanied by the use or the threat of force? On this see R. D. Kearney and R. E. Dalton, 'The Treaty on Treaties', *AJIL*, 64 (1970), 495.

[23] A. Randelzhofer, 'Article 2(4)' in B. Simma (ed.), *The Charter of the United Nations: A Commentary* (Oxford University Press, 2002), pp. 117–18 .

[24] In its Advisory Opinion on the Legality of the Threat or Use of Nuclear Weapons, the International Court of Justice reasoned that 'the notions of "threat" and "use" of force under Article 2, paragraph 4, of the Charter stand together in the sense that if the use of force itself in a given case is illegal – for whatever reason – the threat to use such force will likewise be illegal'. See Advisory Opinion on the Legality of the Threat or Use of Nuclear Weapons [1996] ICJ Rep. 226, 246.

[25] A. D'Amato, *International Law: Process and Prospect* (New York: Transnational Publishers, 1987), pp. 58–9. See also A. D'Amato, 'The Invasion of Panama was a Lawful Response to Tyranny', *AJIL*, 84 (1990), 516–24 at 520.

[26] ICJ Reports (1949), at 4.

[27] I. Brownlie, *Principles of Public International Law*, 7th edn (Oxford University Press, 2008), p. 733.

The interpretations perhaps suggest that the operative reflex of Article 2(4) as the baseline for the current *jus ad bellum* regime is inadvertently sheltering its own ghost. Tom Farer has described the selective and varying interpretations as a manifestation of choice between a textual orientation of a classical view and an approach leaning towards legal realism.[28] As Farer notes, the classical view departs from the presumption that parties to a treaty 'had an original intention which can be discovered primarily through textual analysis and which, in the absence of some foreseen change in circumstances, must be respected until the agreement has expired according to its terms or be replaced by mutual consent'.[29] The legal realist approach, Farer explains, perceives 'implicit and explicit agreements, formal texts, and state behaviour as being in a condition of effervescent interaction, unceasingly creating, modifying and replacing norms'.[30]

The Charter's *jus ad bellum* regime has attracted diverging views. The traditional position in international legal scholarship is that the current *jus ad bellum* regime has retained certain 'mentalities' of the just war theory. The claim is based on the premise that the UN Charter constructs what appears to be a *restrictionist* framework that leans towards the maintenance of international peace by tightening up the recourse to force. Yet the burden of ambiguity and imperfection that pervades the Charter creates a tension between the *desiderata* of perpetual peace and perfect justice.[31] The tension partly revolves around the notion of state sovereignty which was the centre of attention when the Charter came into force in 1945.[32] This perhaps explains the equation of sovereignty as a restraining determinative element in the scope and applicability of *jus ad bellum*. For instance, Article 2(7) of the Charter states that 'nothing contained in the present Charter shall authorise the United Nations to intervene in matters which are essentially within the domestic jurisdiction of any state'. The impact of the tension is especially felt in situations of internal conflicts, where the impulse of Article 2(4) does not follow the same scope as its regulation of international conflicts.

---

[28] T. Farer, 'An Inquiry into the Legitimacy of Humanitarian Intervention' in L. Damrosch and D. Scheffer (eds.), *Law and Force in the New International Order* (Boulder, Colo.: Westview, 1991), p. 185.

[29] *Ibid.*   [30] *Ibid.*

[31] See T. Franck, *Recourse to Force: State Action Against Threats and Armed Attacks: The Hersch Lauterpacht Memorial Lectures* (Cambridge University Press, 2002), p. 14.

[32] See J. Charney, 'NATO's Kosovo Intervention – Anticipatory Humanitarian Intervention in Kosovo', *AJIL*, 93 (1999), 834.

Jus ad bellum *and internal conflicts*

The UN Charter epitomises the focus, organising frame and ethos of the post-war international legal order. The Charter's promises provide a semblance of a collective will to negotiate a sense of coexistence and common security concerns. Despite its flaws, the collective security architecture provides, to a certain degree, a fairly acceptable and generally cohesive regulation for the recourse to armed conflicts. Its scope of application has also generated relative consensus in the manner of enforcement and legitimacy. But this perceived cohesion in the *jus ad bellum* regime pertains largely to international conflicts. The same is not true of conflicts that are of an internal nature. The rendition and attitudes of international legal frameworks to internal conflicts are still overwhelmingly shaped by the legacy of the Treaty of Westphalia. The legacy's progeny includes the presumption that the maintenance of order in a country falls within the domain of the jurisdiction of states. Also aligned to this is the view that the business of international law has always been to regulate the conduct of interstate relations in international affairs.[33] Therefore, encroachment into the domestic jurisdiction of a state is prohibited, especially where it impacts on matters in which 'each State is permitted, by the principle of State sovereignty to decide freely' its domestic affairs such as the 'choice of political, economic, social and cultural system'.[34]

The question, though, of whether the scope of *jus ad bellum* extends to internal conflicts had occupied international lawyers for many decades. Quincy Wright wrestled with it for much of the 1950s.[35] Like those who engaged the question much later, Wright's articulations were neither conclusive nor suggestive of a desirable theorisation, partly because the historically instructive inclination of the idea and institution of sovereignty had always conditioned an international law weak in its ordering and subordinate to the principles designed at Westphalia. Both Lauterpacht and Oppenheim added their perspectives. Writing in 1963, Lauterpacht noted that 'the Law of Nations does not treat civil war

---

[33] See H. Kelsen, *The Law of the United Nations: A Critical Analysis of its Fundamental Problems* (New York: Frederick A. Praeger, 1964).

[34] Case Concerning Military and Paramilitary Activities in and Around Nicaragua, *Nicaragua v. United States of America (Merits)* 1986 ICJ Rep. 14, at 107–8.

[35] See Q. Wright, *The Role of International Law in the Elimination of War* (Manchester University Press, 1961).

as illegal'.[36] In a project on civil war commissioned by the American Society of International Law in 1970, John Norton Moore echoed the prevailing view at the time on the applicability of *jus ad bellum* to internal conflicts:

> The normative standards for differentiating permissible from impermissible resort to force have, like the other principal strands in the international law of conflict management, largely evolved in response to conventional warfare across national boundaries. Thus for the most part, they provide only minimal guidance, if any, to normative judgements concerning conflicts purely within national boundaries.[37]

Moore's perspectives have been ascribed to and consolidated by many scholars. Michael Akehurst's *Modern Introduction to International Law* is emphatic in this regard. He argues that 'there is no rule in international law against civil wars. Article 2(4) of the United Nations Charter prohibits the use or threat of force in international relations only.'[38] Akehurst thus concludes that 'it is possible that each side will regard the other side as traitors from the point of view of municipal law, but neither the insurgents nor the established authorities are guilty of any breach of international law'.[39] Akehurst's reference to the absence of a breach of international law in relation to internal conflicts pertains to the question of legality and jurisdiction with the 'absoluteness' of state sovereignty clearly in mind.

Yoram Dinstein, another international lawyer with considerable pedigree, claims similarly that the current *jus ad bellum* regime only abolishes the use of force in international relations of states, and internal conflicts 'are out of the reach of the Charter's provision'.[40] In the early editions of his now increasingly authoritative text, Malcolm Shaw proclaimed that nation states are traditionally free to act without restraint within their borders. Shaw explained that 'international law is based on the concept of the state. The state in its turn lies upon the foundation of sovereignty, which expresses internally the supremacy of governmental institutions and externally the supremacy of the State as a legal person'.[41] In this

---

[36] L. Oppenheim and H. Lauterpacht (eds.), *International Law* (London: Longmans, 1963), p. 248.

[37] J. N. Moore (ed.), *Law and Civil War in the Modern World* (Baltimore: Johns Hopkins University Press, 1974), p. xiii.

[38] A. Akehurst, *Modern Introduction to International Law*, 6th edn (London: Routledge, 1992), p. 281.

[39] *Ibid.*, pp. 281–2.   [40] Dinstein, *War*, p. 85.

[41] M. Shaw, *International Law*, 3rd edn (Cambridge University Press, 1991), pp. 276–7.

sense, the inviolability of territorial sovereignty of a state is a foundational principle of international law.[42] It has shaped theories on modern statecraft and defined the privileges and conduct of statehood.

Despite vast transformations in the focus and mindset of international law scholarship, recent engagement on the applicability of the *jus ad bellum* regime to internal conflicts shows no radical departure from traditional thinking. If anything the discourses seem to embrace the reluctance embedded in the line of thought. For instance, in a collection of critical essays in honour of Yoram Dinstein published in 2007, Marco Sassoli emphasises that 'no international *ius ad bellum* exists concerning non-international armed conflicts, since such conflicts are neither justified nor prohibited by international law'.[43] He explains that the only category of conflicts 'that has been considered as having a justification in international law – national liberation wars in which a people exercises its right to self-determination – has been moved into the category of international armed conflicts'.[44] Sassoli posits, however, that given the monopoly on violence conferred on state organs by the Westphalian conception of the nation state and its legacy, there is an automatic presumption that a *jus ad bellum* regime for internal conflicts does exist in domestic legislation.[45]

But Sassoli's remark on the exception is not shared by Heather Wilson.[46] Wilson contends that although there has been a trend to extend *jus ad bellum* to national liberation movements, the use of force in these conflicts 'remained a matter of self-help beyond the purview of international law'.[47] According to Wilson, the very nature of the use of force was a privilege exclusive to governments, and that elements opposed to an establishment, for whatever cause, could not exercise this

---

[42] It must be added though that the absoluteness of this principle has not always prevailed. In the aftermath of the French Revolution, self-determination had emerged as a moderating concept almost negotiating the plight of subjugated subjects and the excesses of state authority. For more on this, see generally A. Buchanan, *Justice, Legitimacy and Self-Determination: Moral Foundations for International Law* (Oxford University Press, 2007); A. Cassese, *Self-Determination of Peoples: A Legal Reappraisal* (Cambridge University Press, 1999).

[43] M. Sassoli, '*Ius ad Bellum* and *Ius in Bello* – The Separation between the Legality of the Use of Force and Humanitarian Rules to be Respected in Warfare: Crucial or Outdated' in Schmitt and Pejic (eds.), *International Law and Armed Conflict*, p. 254.

[44] *Ibid.*, pp. 254–5.   [45] *Ibid.*, p. 225.

[46] H. Wilson, *International Law and the Use of Force by National Liberation Movements* (Oxford: Clarendon Press, 1988), p. 136.

[47] *Ibid.*, p. 28.

right as it was 'neither condoned nor condemned by customary inter-national law'.[48] Wilson goes on to say that 'for the most part, traditional international law is silent on the use of force within the borders of States'. And 'given that by the nineteenth century, international law was a body of rules governing relationships between States, violence within a State was considered beyond the bounds of international legal regulation'.[49] The point of agreement amongst international lawyers is that the regulatory framework of *jus ad bellum* is considerably limited in internal conflicts. François Bugnion situates this in the context of the recognition that every state has the right to resort to force so as to preserve its territorial integrity and crush a rebellion if need be.[50] The law, Bugnion reasons, 'remains rudimentary and responds in only a very limited manner to such conflicts for protection generated by internecine strife'.[51]

There appears to be a relative consensus in the traditional perception of the scope of *jus ad bellum* that internal conflicts are neither justified nor outlawed by international law. What is not so clear is the legal foundation upon which these assumptions are based. As Kirsti Samuels observes, lack of detail from the discourse in the old and contemporary literature shows that the issue is often approached more as a moral judgement, shaped by a particular traditional historical narrative, than as solid insightful legal analyses.[52] Even in rare cases where there is an attempt at legal theorisation, this is often confined in the conventional view. Thus, only a few scholars have attempted to theorise an approach that departs from this position. Ruth Wedgwood, for instance, has undertaken a study to enquire whether a parallel principle to the *jus ad bellum* regime applicable to international affairs could be equally applicable to internal conflicts, 'given that intervention in civil war precipitates internal conflicts'.[53] Wedgwood asserts that 'with civil wars now fought by means that are as massively destructive as international conflicts ... threats to international peace and security ... are now read

---

[48] *Ibid.*   [49] *Ibid.*, p. 22.

[50] F. Bugnion, '*Jus ad Bellum, Jus in Bello* and Non-International Armed Conflicts', *Yearbook of International Humanitarian Law*, 6 (2003), 168–98 at 168.

[51] *Ibid.*

[52] K. Samuels, '*Jus ad Bellum* and Civil Conflicts: A Case Study of the International Community's Approach to Violence in the Conflict in Sierra Leone', *Journal of Conflict and Security Law*, 8:2 (2003), 315–38 at 315.

[53] See R. Wedgwood, 'Limiting the Use of Force in Civil Disputes' in D. Wippman (ed.), *International Law and Ethnic Conflict* (Ithaca: Cornell University Press, 1998), p. 245.

to include civil wars ... and that textbook scruple is mustered only to the extent of preferring that the Charter be amended to conform to new practice'.[54]

However, to take the conventional view as all-encompassing would of course run the risk of undermining some of the inroads made by international law in confronting internal violence. In fact, as Ian Brownlie notes, the concept of reserved domain or domestic jurisdiction is 'rapidly becoming relative given that a state cannot plead provisions of its own law or deficiencies in that law in answer to a claim against it for an alleged breach of its obligations under international law'.[55] And although international society remains organised in nation states and is sovereign in name, the contemporary legal order is far more complex than the narrative suggests.[56] Certain levels of violence could induce the arrogation of legal rights and duties by non-state actors as well as attract a regime of prohibitions.[57] Increasingly, the corpus of human rights law functions as a medium of dialogue between the traditional shortfalls of the current international legal architecture and the elusive character of internal violence.

Although this chorus is yet to result in the extension of *jus ad bellum* to internal violence, the human rights movement has nonetheless galvanised initiatives and concern about the effects of these armed conflicts.[58] Conduct and behaviour deemed inconsistent with certain normative values is prohibited and could well give rise to some level of sanction. Human rights law propounds a philosophy of collective morality that confronts impunity irrespective of the imbalance of the international legal order and the inadequacies inherent in normative instruments. The approach's rationale has filtered, in a measured way, through the jurisprudence of some of the international criminal tribunals and UN Security Council resolutions. These reinventions and normative

---

[54] *Ibid.*

[55] I. Brownlie, *Principles of Public International Law* (Oxford University Press, 1998), p. 293.

[56] D. Kennedy, *Of War and Law* (Princeton University Press, 2006), p. 14.

[57] See R. A. Falk, 'Janus Tormented: The International Law of Internal War' in J. N. Rosenau (ed.), *Internal Aspects of Civil Strife* (Princeton University Press, 1964), p. 197. See also J. Baloro, 'International Humanitarian Law and Situations of Internal Armed Conflicts in Africa', *African Journal of International and Comparative Law*, 4 (1992), 449; R. Myren, 'Applying International Laws of War to Non-International Armed Conflicts: Past Attempts, Future Strategies', *Netherlands International Law Review*, 37 (1990), 347.

[58] *Second Interim Report of the Committee on the Enforcement of Human Rights Law*, in International Law Association, *Report of the Sixty-third Conference*, 1988, at 40.

proclamations lack the capacity to substitute the limited applicability of *jus ad bellum* in internal violence. What then is the alternative? What has been the response through international norms and instruments to re-engage these faultlines? And how have structures of international law been *forced* to attempt a modicum of reorientation so as to be sensitive to dilemmas posed by internal conflicts? Answers to some of these questions have been attempted through the doctrine of intervention and the Responsibility to Protect.

Intervention and Responsibility to Protect in internal conflicts

With the limited applicability of *jus ad bellum* to internal conflicts, attention has increasingly turned to the doctrines of intervention and Responsibility to Protect as means of confronting conflicts and halting their excesses. The resurgence of these doctrines has been shaped by the very debate that interrogates what international law really ought to be, given the state of social conditions in societies afflicted with internal violence.[59] The correlation between intervention and the applicability of *jus ad bellum* in internal conflicts hinges on two dialectical and mutually reinforcing strands. The first is that the moral foundation upon which the doctrine of intervention is premised suggests an avocation to protect people and preserve justice and order. Its operative moral denominator follows the stream that the suffering of people, no matter how distant, ought to be an affront on the conscience of humanity.

The second strand reinforces the traditional international law scholarship arguing that what happens in the domestic affairs of a state is beyond the purview of international instruments and external intervention. From this view, a government's legitimacy also depends on the extent to which it is able to defend its borders and exert authority in its territorial spaces without external intervention. However, where an internally directed aggression is at play, the varying interpretations converge to tolerate a principled basis through which a *jus ad bellum* regime could be formulated. This opening has helped facilitate the elevation of the notion of Responsibility to Protect as a variation of the traditional conception of *jus ad bellum* in internal conflicts.

The recurrence of internal conflicts and their historical disjuncture with international law have had the effect of inadvertently providing

---

[59] O. Ramsbotham and T. Woodhouse, *Humanitarian Intervention in Contemporary Conflict: A Reconceptualisation* (Cambridge: Polity Press, 1996), p. 65.

space for the UN to shape, modify and revitalise discourses on intervention, largely conceptualised within the prism of its philosophical
progenitor – 'the responsibility to protect mandate'. The UN's two
previous Secretary Generals, Boutros Boutros-Gali and Kofi Annan, have
been instrumental in this regard. The former had, in his 1992 *Agenda
for Peace*, suggested that 'respect for ... [the state's] fundamental sovereignty and integrity are crucial' for the maintenance of international
peace and security, but also recognised that 'the time of absolute and
exclusive sovereignty ... has passed; its theory was never matched by
reality'.[60] Boutros-Gali subsequently called on the international community to formulate 'a balance between good internal governance and the
requirements of an ever-more interdependent world'.[61]

Boutros-Gali's immediate successor, Kofi Annan, challenged the international community to develop a common ground that would underpin a
concerted response to systematic abuses and serious violations of international law in domestic conflicts.[62] Annan's challenge was preceded by
two defining events – Rwanda and Kosovo. In 1994 mass killings and
genocide broke out in Rwanda. The episode could not be contained
as state sovereignty stood in the way of any prospect of intervention from
the international community, even though a UN mission was already
stationed in Kigali, the Rwandan capital. The use of sovereignty to forestall
any form of preventive action led Kofi Annan to quip, in what is his most
quoted line in the debate on intervention:

> If humanitarian intervention is, indeed, an assault on sovereignty, how
> should we respond to a Rwanda, to a Srebrenica – to gross and systematic
> violations of human rights that affect every precept of our common
> humanity?[63]

Kosovo involved, on the other hand, a contentious intervention that
triggered questions as to its legitimacy in a sovereign state. The intervention by the North Atlantic Treaty Organisation (NATO), without
explicit UN Security Council authorisation, was deemed by many to
have amounted to an assault on the international legal order. Allegations

---

[60] *Ibid.*, p. 38.
[61] B. Boutros-Gali, *Agenda for Peace* (New York: United Nations, 1992), p. 9.
[62] K. Annan, 'Two Concepts of Sovereignty', *The Economist*, 18 September 1999.
[63] *Ibid.* For an account of the genocide and the nature of weaponry used, see L. Melvern,
Conspiracy to Murder: The Rwandan Genocide (New York: Verso, 2004); and for a
historical context, see M. Mamdani, *When Victims Become Killers: Colonialism, Nativism,
and the Genocide in Rwanda* (Princeton University Press, 2002).

of carnage committed by the NATO bombings raised the issue of proportionality and brought to the fore doubts over the suitability of violent countermeasures as a way of confronting impunity.[64] In the aftermath of Kosovo, the intensity surrounding intervention heightened. This culminated in another plea from Kofi Annan to the UN General Assembly in 2000.[65] The call persuaded the Canadian Government to initiate the International Commission on Intervention and State Sovereignty (ICISS), whose task was to wrestle with some of the critical questions relating to the discourse on intervention.[66]

The Responsibility to Protect principle seeks a moderate engagement of the dilemmas of intervention and a reorientation of its merits. It departs from a traditional sovereignty platform that recognises states as the primary entities to protect the rights and welfare of their citizens. The protection mandate includes a responsible duty to take precautionary measures to mitigate the risk of exposing people to the scourge of violence, disease and impoverishment. The emphasis on responsible state obligations recharacterises the concept of sovereignty from that of a relative absolute control to sovereignty as responsibility. The principle leans on the assertion that given the increasing fusion of global norms and polities, sovereignty is overwhelmingly conditional and therefore can no longer be a shield against international scrutiny.[67] What this means is that when a state lacks the capacity or is unwilling to protect its population or is perhaps the very source of impunity, the Responsibility to Protect then shifts to the international community. According to the ICISS Report, once responsibility is deemed to have been transferred, the international community can avail itself of options that include military countermeasures to avert or arrest impunity in the violating state.

---

[64] For opinions protesting the illegality of NATO's bombings, see I. Brownlie and J. C. Apperley, 'Kosovo Crisis Inquiry: Memorandum on the International Law Aspects', *International and Comparative Law Quarterly*, 49 (2000), 878; J. Lobel, 'Benign Hegemony? Kosovo and Article 2(4) of the UN Charter', *Chi. J. Int'l. L.*, 1 (2000), 19.

[65] K. Annan, *We the Peoples: The Role of the United Nations in the 21st Century*, The Secretary General's Millennium Report to the General Assembly of the United Nations, 3 April 2000, www.un.org/millennium/sg/report/full.htm (last visited April 2010).

[66] The Commission was co-chaired by Gareth Evans and Mohamed Sahnoun and comprised the following ten members: Gisele Cote-Harper, Lee Hamilton, Michael Ignatieff, Vladimir Lukin, Klaus Naumann, Cyril Ramaphosa, Fidel Ramos, Cornelio Sommaruga, Edwardo Stein and Ramesh Thakur. See www.iciss.ca/members-en.asp (last visited July 2010).

[67] See L. Gene and M. Mastanduno, *Beyond Westphalia? State Sovereignty and International Intervention* (Baltimore: Johns Hopkins University Press, 1995).

The imperative of transfer of responsibility implies that consent at this stage becomes irrelevant. The ICISS locates the foundation of the Responsibility to Protect in Article 24 of the UN Charter[68] as well as international legal instruments, notably human rights covenants and treaties framing the corpus of international humanitarian law.[69]

The discourse framing contemporary international law's scholarship on intervention, though far from achieving consensus, is perhaps more nuanced than the ethical perspectives reviewed above. In the legal realm the debate straddles what has been classified as restrictionist and counter-restrictionist interpretations of the UN Charter's *jus ad bellum* regime.[70] Many have questioned any definitive prospects of reconciling the concept of the Responsibility to Protect through intervention within the framework of the Charter. Opponents of intervention rely on the prohibition of the use of armed violence against the territory of a sovereign state. The argument continues that not even the use of collective self-defence pursuant to Article 51 of the Charter could in any way justify unauthorised intervention regardless of its purpose. And so for what it's worth, 'neither human rights, democracy or self-determination are acceptable legal grounds for waging war, nor for that matter, are traditional just war causes or righting wrongs'.[71] This position had been earlier articulated in the 1986 ICJ Nicaragua judgment where the court held that the 'use of force could not be the appropriate method to monitor or ensure ... respect for human rights'.[72]

---

[68] Article 24 mandates the Security Council to be the primary agent for the responsibility of international security.

[69] ICISS, p. xi. Whilst accepting that military intervention could be used as a tool to curb impunity, the ICISS emphasise that it is nonetheless 'an exceptional and extraordinary measure'. For it to be warranted, the Commission notes, there must be imminent or irreparable harm to human life. To better avert human suffering the Report embraces certain key elements of prevention, reaction and rebuilding and its functional dynamics encapsulate the popular mantra of good governance and 'reinforce the link between security and development'. See K. Powell, 'The African Union's Emerging Peace and Security Regime: Opportunities and Challenges for Delivering on the Responsibility to Protect', ISS Monograph Series, 119 (2005), at 4.

[70] The disagreements could be classified under four headings: (i) interpretation of the Charter; (ii) interpretations of UN General Assembly Resolutions as well as judgments of the International Court of Justice; (iii) interpretation of customary international law; and (iv) assessment of possible consequences. See Ramsbotham and Woodhouse, *Humanitarian Intervention*, p. 61.

[71] O. Schachter, *International Law in Theory and Practice* (Dordrecht: Martinus Nijhoff, 1991), p. 128.

[72] ICJ Reports (1986), para. 268.

In a deliberation on NATO's attacks on the former Yugoslavia, Bruno Simma and Antonio Cassese confront the legal parameters of intervention. Cassese's view takes its cue from the position that intervention without Security Council authorisation is not acceptable within the framework of the UN Charter. He asserts that the framework upon which the international community operates is underpinned by an overarching system that symbolises peace, human rights and self-determination.[73] Where conflict emerges between these values, Cassese argues, peace must be allowed to prevail. He further notes that 'under the UN Charter system, as complemented by the international standards which emerged in the last 50 years, respect for human rights and self-determination of peoples, however important and crucial it may be, is never allowed to put peace in jeopardy'.[74] This kind of perspective echoes moderation where the strictures of legal requirements are weighed against the dictates of moral and human compassion.[75]

Conversely, Simma adopts a restrictionist approach, construing countermeasures in response to gross violations as irreconcilable with the spirit and character of the UN Charter. He argues that a teleological and historical interpretation of Article 2(4) suggest that 'the prohibition enacted therein was, and is, intended to be of a comprehensive nature'.[76] The prohibition in Article 2(4), Simma submits, is part of *jus cogens* and thus 'cannot be contracted out of at the regional level'.[77] The only exception in Simma's formulation relates to the occurrence of genocide, where the use of countermeasures by states becomes an obligation. This restrictive reading naturally extends to Article 51, which allows the use of self-defence to justify violent countermeasures. According to Simma, it is only available if crises transcend borders 'and lead to armed attacks'.[78] But Simma's distinction between what constitutes an internal matter (not warranting intervention) and a cross-border problem (possibly

---

[73] A. Cassese, '*Ex iniuria ius oritur*: Are We Moving towards International Legitimation of Forcible Humanitarian Countermeasures in the World Community?', *EJIL*, 10 (1999), 23–30 at 24.

[74] *Ibid.*, at 25.

[75] Richard Lillich adopts a similar balancing act when he says that 'to require a state to sit back and watch the slaughter of innocent people in order to avoid blanket prohibitions against the use of force is to stress blackletter [law] at the expense of far more fundamental values'. See R. Lillich, 'Forcible Self-help by States to Protect Human Rights', *Iowa Law Review*, 53 (1967), 325–51 at 344.

[76] B. Simma, 'NATO, the UN and the Use of Force: Legal Aspects', *EJIL*, 10 (1999), 1–22 at 2.

[77] *Ibid.*, at 3.   [78] *Ibid.*, at 5.

giving effect to Article 51) could give rise to complex and ambiguous sets of circumstances with varying degrees of threshold.

The different perspectives demonstrate the ambiguities inherent in the contemporary *jus ad bellum* regime and the extent to which they have shaped international law's treatment of internal conflicts. And in the context of intervention, whether it is the moderation in the interpretation of the UN Charter suggested by Cassese or a restrictionist approach advocated by Simma, doubts and questions remain as to the viability and utility of these approaches to the nature and complexities of postcolonial internal conflicts. In a broader sense also, the ambiguities and shifting premises upon which they are framed expose the normative limitations of institutional approaches to conflicts through the *jus ad bellum* regime and the difficulties that may arise in reconciling them with the challenges of peacebuilding in postcolonial societies.

Limitations of the contemporary *jus ad bellum* regime

International legal instruments humanise and shape the nature of armed conflicts by using institutional frameworks to impose normative limits on the manner and conduct of warfare. In this sense, as David Kennedy explains, international law is perceived 'as a broadly humanist and civilising force, standing back from war, judging it as just or unjust, while offering itself as a code of conduct to limit violence on the battlefield'.[79] But the proactive inclination also exposes the extent of its historical and normative limitations. In the process, international law approaches to conflict are forced into what could perhaps be described as a state of compulsive-obsessive disorder. Only that as regards the regulation of postcolonial internal conflicts, international law's perceived obsession as a civilising force promises so much, yet delivers so little. This state of ambivalence further projects the anachronistic nature of modern international law, implying that today's armed conflict 'reveals lacunae in the law or demonstrates how law designed for yesterday's wars falls short when applied to contemporary conflict'.[80] When this happens international law and its institutional instruments react 'by allowing provisions to fall into desuetude, embracing new interpretations of existing prescriptions'.[81] The limitations of *jus ad bellum* have a certain correlation with the architecture of the international legal order.

---

[79] Kennedy, *Of War and Law*, p. 6.
[80] Schmitt and Pejic (eds.), *International Law and Armed Conflict*.   [81] *Ibid.*

The approaches to conflicts through the prism of law had been for many centuries modelled on the distinction between the state of *war* and that of *peace*. In a consideration by the Judicial Committee of the House of Lords (UK), this traditional distinction was reiterated when the Law Lords noted that 'the law recognises a state of peace and a state of war, but that it knows nothing of an intermediate state which is neither one thing nor the other'.[82] War and peace were therefore seen as distinct legal frameworks determining the dialectical application of international law.[83] This attitude shaped the views of most international law scholars at the turn of the nineteenth century. Lassa Oppenheim's classic treatise *Oppenheim's International Law* embraced the binary and frames of this dichotomy. But as Carsten Stahn notes, 'war and peace are no longer perceived as strict organising frameworks for the categorisation of rules of international law'.[84] The shift was precipitated by attempts in the twentieth century to advocate for a legal order with an inclination to outlaw war.[85] Emphasis on international peace resulted in the reduction of interstate conflicts making the peace-war dichotomy increasingly untenable and irrelevant to postcolonial realities.

Proclamations against war have had little impact in the mitigation of the normative flaws inherent in international law and its institutional responses to conflicts. Even with the removal of the classical distinction, contemporary international law still retains some of the mentality, materiality and perhaps particularity of the old order. It is still organised in a type of dualist framework of *jus ad bellum* and *jus in bello*. The two bodies have mostly been kept distinct 'in order to postulate the principle that all conflicts shall be fought humanely, irrespective of the cause of armed violence'.[86] In this sense, the framework reflects the nineteenth-century traditional dichotomy between war and peace.[87] *Jus ad bellum* is perceived to denote conditions triggering the transition from peace to war, whilst *jus in bello* is concerned with the imposition of limits on

---

[82] Lord Macnaghten, *Jason v. Driefontein Consolidated Mines Ltd* [1902] AC 484.

[83] See S. C. Neff, *War and the Law of Nations: A General History* (Cambridge University Press, 2005), pp. 177–95.

[84] C. Stahn, '*Jus ad bellum, jus in bello . . . jus pos bellum*? Rethinking the Conception of the Law of Armed Force', *EJIL*, 17:5 (2006), 921–43 at 922.

[85] The Kellogg-Briand Pact under the aegis of the League of Nations and the UN Charter both made moves in prohibiting aggressive warfare in international affairs. See Q. Wright, 'The Outlawry of War and the Law of War', *AJIL*, 47 (1953), 365–76 at 365.

[86] Stahn, '*Jus ad bellum*', 925.   [87] *Ibid.*, 926.

proscribed conduct in warfare.[88] But as Kennedy explains, war and peace 'are far more continuous with one another than our rhetorical habits of distinction ... would suggest'.[89]

The flaws show that the idolisation of international law as an instrument of emancipation and, as 'always something of a cultural myth, has been demythologised'.[90] The intricate nature of internal conflicts illustrates how the contextual relevance of a particular body of law determines the applicability of another body. Yet the constitutive subsets of the *jus ad bellum* conception thrive on a set of presumptions, based on the capacity and ability of the nation state to serve as an agent of legality and norms enforcement. It follows that the nation state is perceived to have the capabilities to appreciate and adhere to the frameworks governing warfare and its prohibition. The challenge posed by the quest for peace in postcolonial states, particularly in Africa, does not follow this normatively regimented stream. In fact, if anything, the African postcolonial state is an incoherent, ambiguous concept whose artificiality carries certain antinomies.

Given that the dualist framework is almost exclusively focused on situations or conditions of armed conflicts, it has little relevance to societies in a period of transition from conflicts or at the 'critical transformative period of movement toward armed confrontation'.[91] This is a situation that features in many postcolonial societies, perhaps suggesting why the quest for transformative approaches to peacebuilding ought to be viewed as a continuous process. Western European legal approaches have historically been unable to reflect this, influencing international law's approach. A case in point is an 1830 English tribunal ruling where the court refused to recognise the existence of a transformative period in the principality of India, denying the contention 'that the country was unsettled, or in a state of passage'.[92] It noted that 'such a state is unknown in our laws' and that a 'country must either be in a state of war or state of peace'.[93] Although this is not authority in contemporary international law, it nonetheless shows the approach's

---

[88] See G. Best, *War and Law Since* 1945 (Oxford University Press, 1994).

[89] Kennedy, *Of War and Law*, p. 3.

[90] T. M. Franck, 'Who Killed Article 2(4)? Changing Norms Governing the Use of Force by States', *AJIL*, 64 (1970), 809–37 at 836.

[91] J. P. Lederach, *Building Peace: Sustainable Reconciliation in Divided Societies* (Washington, DC: United States Institute of Peace, 1997), p. 73.

[92] *Elphinstone* v. *Bedreechund* [1830] 1 Knapp 316; (1830) 12 Tindle Reprint 340.

[93] *Ibid.*

long-rooted historical perceptions. The implication is that the transformative periods of postcolonial states are almost certainly outside the radar of the *jus ad bellum* framework. Postcolonial states are increasingly trapped in an analogous transition where the absence of violence 'may mask a profound sense of latent conflict that may be awaiting an opportunity to come to the surface'.[94] Yet the institutional international law response through the *jus ad bellum* framework seems to 'present a simplified account of the sequencing and categorisation of human conduct throughout armed hostilities'.[95]

Faultlines in institutional international law responses also lie in the anatomy of *jus ad bellum*. There are two notable dimensions to this. The notion of *jus ad bellum* is predicated on the limitations in the human capacity to inflict violence. From this perspective, it has relative peace-building dispensation to the extent that it prolongs the conditions of 'peace' by narrowing the circumstances for the recourse to force. The doctrine flourishes on the basis that only when certain conditions – of often much higher threshold – are met can the use of force be permitted. Peace therefore becomes a 'subdued' condition to the extent that the recourse to force is restrained, requiring the permission of a competent authority. On the other hand, the doctrine is conceptually limited as it falls short of sustaining the full concept of *progressive peace*. By progressive peace is meant the existence of a social order that transcends the mere absence of violence. The effect is tension in the doctrine's sets of principles and structures, leading to a struggle between the sustenance of the traditional role of law and the need to tackle the social challenges confronting it.

It may well be that the conditions for determining when violence or conflict is justified imply that *jus ad bellum* neither anticipates nor strives to create sustainable or permanent conditions for 'zero wars' or 'zero prospects for wars'. The framework only provides moral guidelines for waging war that are neither unrestricted nor too restrictive. This weak orientation permeates through the UN Charter. Antonio Cassese notes that what this faultline in *jus ad bellum* shows is the fact that the Charter has 'left a huge host of potentially dangerous strains to be dealt with at the discretion of individual states, should political dissension

---

[94] W. J. Foltz, 'The Organisation of African Unity and the Resolution of Africa's Conflicts' in F. M. Deng and I. W. Zartman, *Conflict Resolution in Africa* (Washington, DC: Brookings Institute, 1991), p. 369.

[95] Stahn, '*Jus ad bellum*', at 926.

and demands for change intensify to the point of armed conflict'.[96] International lawyers are almost unanimous that the Charter's historical imperatives are frozen by the adoption of *negative peace* as opposed to *positive peace*. Negative peace equates to the desire to enforce order through the absence of war. Positive peace, on the other hand, requires the promotion of justice for the purposes of confronting the underlying causes of conflict. Thus the Charter and its *jus ad bellum* regime are almost totally oriented towards negative peace.

Indeed, the role and contribution of international law through the UN in confronting conflicts and promoting international peace and security has been, and remains, valuable. Through its *jus ad bellum* regime, the UN represents a crucial though imperfect *universal* endeavour in what its Preamble describes as the determination to save 'succeeding generations from the scourge of war'. It has in many respects achieved a modicum of success in its mission. But its *jus ad bellum* approach to internal conflicts remains critical. Besides the historical Western European cultural heritage upon which its norms are largely sourced, the legal framework is neither clear nor capable of confronting the changing nature of violence and internal conflicts in postcolonial societies. As William Schabas observes, the increasing intrusion of law in warfare regulation does not mean that conflict is becoming any easier to resolve.[97] If recent experiences are anything to go by, as the body of law becomes more elaborate and constraining, it becomes increasingly contentious. The ambiguity of the applicability of *jus ad bellum* suggests that the presumed sophistication of institutional international law and its rendition of internal conflicts are overstated.

Embodiment of regional international law in Africa

Despite the seeming inability of international law to deal with violence and internal conflicts, approaches adopted in postcolonial Africa were still arranged around the dominant structures and approaches of international law instruments. The Organisation of African Unity (OAU) was the embodiment of this approach. As an institution that emerged in the post-1945 international order, its structures and philosophy also

---

[96] Cassese, *International Law*, p. 325.

[97] W. Schabas, 'International Law and Response to Conflict' in C. Crocker, F. Hampson and P. Aall (eds.), *Turbulent Peace: The Challenges of Managing International Conflict* (Washington, DC: United States Institute of Peace, 2001), p. 603.

replicated to a considerable degree the ethos of international law. It was therefore far from being just a mere example. Given its relationship with the historical determinants of international law, it is imperative to establish the extent to which the OAU's burden of inheritance influenced the organisation's approach to internal conflicts and the correlation this had with the inadequacies in confronting internal conflicts. This will illustrate how the convergence between the foundational principles of international law and the OAU offered little hope in the quest for alternative peacebuilding approaches in Africa. It will also provide a sketch of the factors that stirred the compelling need for normative and institutional recasting of the OAU and the legal order under which it operated.

Background and principles of the OAU

Post-war anti-colonial struggles in Africa had impacts beyond accelerating independence campaigns. The movements enabled the birth of new states claiming a place in international society. Independence brought a sense of identity, optimism and the desire for greater cooperation amongst the new states. Largely influenced by Pan-African ideals of the time – emancipation, Africa for Africans and the values of unity and solidarity – a common narrative developed that saw promise in an African project of institution-building. The need for unity and cooperation was also shaped by internal disorder, rivalry between elites and political uncertainty engulfing the new states. Along with the euphoria of decolonisation, political turbulence was slowly unravelling in Africa. Yet amidst the tension that arose from these waves of social upheavals, there was still some unity of purpose amongst African political elites. This served as a common denominator that unity and cooperation were crucial in the attainment of prosperity and security.[98] Part of it was influenced by Pan-African ideals and conceptions, which not only provided the template for African nationalism to evolve as an organised site for resistance against exploitation and dominance, but also helped in framing the ideological basis for the proposition of an African institutional legal order.[99]

---

[98] P. M. Munya, 'The Organisation of African Unity and its Role in Regional Conflicts Resolution and Dispute Settlement: A Critical Evaluation', B. C. Third World L. J., 19 (1999), 537–91 at 541.

[99] T. Murithi, The African Union: Pan-Africanism, Peacebuilding and Development (Aldershot: Ashgate, 2005), pp. 23–33. See also C. O. Amate, Inside the OAU: Pan-Africanism in Practice (New York: St Martin's Press, 1986).

Yet the realisation of a continental organisation was fraught with obstacles that initially hampered prospects for a unified Africa.[100] Lack of consensus as to the direction and essence of the anticipated continental institution culminated in competing regional and ideological groupings. By early 1960, the ideological divide had given birth to four major groupings: the Brazzaville Group, Casablanca Group, Monrovia Group and Pan-African Freedom Movement of Eastern, Central and Southern Africa.[101] The manifest ideological divide brought in individual oppositional perspectives and initially forestalled ambitions for the hitherto romanticised continental institution-building. However, after a series of meetings and consultations, a number of proposals seeking to determine the mandate and shape of the proposed organisation were presented to Councils of Ministers from independent African states, from which a consensus was reached that mediated between the main proposals, ultimately paving the way for a moderate organisation.

The OAU was finally inaugurated in Addis Ababa, Ethiopia on 25 May 1963. The creation of the OAU represented the social and political aspirations of postcolonial Africa. Its Preamble outlined this vision by reiterating the inalienable right to self-determination, equality, justice

---

[100] R. Murray, *Human Rights in Africa: From the OAU to the African Union* (Cambridge University Press, 2004), pp. 2–3.

[101] The Brazzaville Group comprised mostly French-speaking countries and represented what was then viewed as 'moderate voices'. It included Chad, Senegal, Gabon, Central African Republic, Ivory Coast, Republic of Congo, Madagascar, Cameroun and Dahomey (Benin). The group was noted for its conservative approach to the question of African unity and integration. Although it acknowledged the imperative of a united Africa, its members preferred a gradual process of cooperation and consolidation. The Casablanca Group was the most radical and comprised Ghana, Guinea Conakry, Algeria, Egypt, Libya, Mali and Morocco. The group's perspectives on the African unity project were in sharp contrast to those of the others. It advocated for an immediate creation of a united continental government capable of challenging neo-colonialism and its pathologies of dominance. The Monrovia Group had Nigeria, Liberia, Somalia, Togo, Ethiopia, Sierra Leone and Tunisia amongst its key members. Its line of thinking was that although unity and integration were crucial in shaping Africa's place and future in the world, the approach needed to be gradual, steady and reassuring to those states that expressed fear of losing their sovereign status. The Pan-African Freedom Movement of Eastern, Central and Southern Africa was not particularly prominent in the debates and disagreements that anchored the times, partly because some of the members were locked in brutal anti-colonial liberation struggles. For informed perspectives on this see generally Murray, *Human Rights in Africa*, and R. Cox, *Pan-Africanism in Practice: An Eastern African Study 1958–1964* (Oxford University Press, 1968).

and dignity.[102] It went on to underscore the essentials of cooperation and the need for solidarity in a larger unity transcending ethnic and national differences. Fundamentally, the Charter buttressed the continent's desire to safeguard its sovereignty and territorial integrity, and fight neo-colonialism. To realise this, the Preamble reaffirmed Africa's faith in the UN as an institution that 'provide[s] a solid foundation for peaceful and positive co-operation'.[103]

The purposes of the OAU were set out in Article 2 of its Charter. These included the promotion of unity and solidarity,[104] cooperation for the realisation of better conditions of life for Africa,[105] to defend Africa's sovereignty, territorial integrity and independence,[106] eradicate colonialism and promote international cooperation with due regard to the UN Charter and the UDHR.[107] In pursuance of these purposes, Article 3 of the Charter outlined a number of principles that were to govern OAU membership. These were sovereign equality and non-interference in the internal affairs of states,[108] respect for sovereignty and territorial integrity,[109] peaceful settlement of disputes by negotiation, mediation, conciliation or arbitration,[110] condemnation of political assassination as well as dedication to the emancipation of Africa and an affirmation of a policy of non-alignment.[111] It is worth noting, though, that these principles clearly reflected the history, structure and intersection of the prevailing international order and precepts of international law.

The incorporation of non-intervention, sovereign equality and territorial integrity in the Charter of the OAU attracted various and varying interpretations. Taslim Elias situates it in the context of the complementarity of sovereign equality with non-interference in the domestic affairs of sovereign states. He argues that 'the desire to be left alone, to be allowed to choose its particular political, economic, and social systems ... is a legitimate one ... and the freedoms thus claimed are

---

[102] Preamble of the Charter of the former Organisation of African Unity, available at www.africa-union.org/root/au/Documents/Treaties/text/OAU_Charter_1963.pdf (last visited August 2010).
[103] Ibid.   [104] Article 2(1)(a), Charter of the OAU.   [105] Ibid., Article 2(1)(b).
[106] Article 2(1)(c).   [107] Article 2(1)(d) and (e).   [108] Article 3(1) and (2).
[109] Article 3(3).   [110] Article 3(4).
[111] Articles 3, 5–7. It is to be noted that the inclusion of the condemnation of political assassination as a principle governing the OAU was most probably triggered by the assassination of Silvanus Olympio, the first Togolese post-independence leader. The assassination occurred in 1963, a few months before the adoption of the final OAU Charter.

inevitable attributes of the sovereignty of every state'.[112] On territorial integrity, Elias notes that its purpose is to help protect the inviolability of the territory of a state from external interference or encroachment, and by so doing enhances continuity and the exercise of prerogative rights.[113] Although the reference to sovereign equality echoes Article 2 of the UN Charter, Elias proclaims that its incorporation was 'to allay the fears of the smaller [states] in the context of the new spirit of unity and solidarity'.[114]

James Mayall locates the rationale for the incorporation of these principles from the perspective of the psychology of fear, as the radical Pan-Africanism propounded by Kwame Nkrumah of Ghana sought to create a continental union government. This vision, Mayall explains, 'was greeted with extreme nervousness by most of his neighbours', whose 'response was to insist on entrenching the principles of State sovereignty, territorial integrity and non-interference in domestic affairs as the basis of the OAU Charter'.[115] Mayall then concludes that 'the new orthodoxy, which effectively stripped pan-Africanism of its subversive appeal, stemmed not from a rejection of the artificial State thesis but from a generally fearful acceptance of it'.[116] Tim Murithi construes these encapsulations in the context of the cliché that 'politics is the art of the possible', proclaiming that the OAU was based on the lowest common denominator and not a representation of the highest aspirations of African visionaries.[117]

Plausible as these perspectives are, it appears that both Elias and Mayall – and to some extent Murithi – theorise the OAU's adoption of some of the defining international law principles rather incorrectly. Their perspectives are almost oblivious of the legacy of Africa's encounter with imperialism and international law. There is little doubt that sovereignty was seen by new states as denoting equality, and that Nkrumah's union government proposal scarcely found favour. But these were peripheral factors in the scheme of things. The political differences were more in relation to the approaches to the question of African unity than an interrogation of Westphalian normative precepts and structures

---

[112] T. O. Elias, *Africa and the Development of International Law* (Leiden: A. W. Sijthoff, 1972), p. 127.
[113] *Ibid.*   [114] *Ibid.*, p. 126.
[115] J. Mayall, 'The Hopes and Fears of Independence: Africa and the World 1960–1990' in D. Rimmer (ed.), *Africa 30 Years On* (London: James Currey, 1991), p. 25.
[116] *Ibid.*   [117] Murithi, *The African Union*, p. 27.

governing international society. As Felix Okoye explains, the ideological differences were manifested in the political considerations for the achievement of unity. Consequently, the Casablanca Group began 'projecting international political institutions, whereas the Monrovia [Group] followed essentially a functional approach to unity, expecting it to develop gradually from collaboration on economic and social matters'.[118]

It is imperative to note also, that the idea of the OAU as a premier continental institution was itself a progeny of Pan-Africanism, whose main objective has been the propagation of a certain ideology that galvanises a sense of African unity.[119] It was the manner in which unity was to be conceptualised, negotiated and achieved that gave rise to political compromises and ideological differences. Beyond this, however, the broader reason for the OAU's conformity with the strictures of international society lies elsewhere. At the dawn of independence, the African state had already undergone centuries of externally induced conceptual and physical orientation through colonially scripted patterns and mindsets. This discarded, almost beyond recognition, some of the constitutive anatomy of precolonial African polities. In fact, the reconfiguration was so deep that it is almost impossible to disentangle postcolonial Africa from the patterns and residues of imperialism. For the new postcolonial African state, the burden of inheritance conditioned by encounters with international law played some part in limiting prospects for reinvention. Over a long period, most of the African colonial states had not experienced a culture outside of that framework.

This burden of cooptation made it possible for the concepts of sovereignty, territorial integrity, equality of states and non-interference to shape the international legal order operating at the time of the founding of the OAU. The organisation, and indeed its membership, could not realistically arrogate exception to the structure of the prevailing international order, nor was the OAU capable of reinventing inherited notions of statehood. The international rules and institutions – the systems under which the OAU operated – were already in place at the dawn of postcolonial statehood.[120] From this perspective, the

---

[118] F. C. Okoye, *International Law and the New Africa States* (London: Sweet & Maxwell, 1972), p. 124.

[119] R. Emerson, 'Pan-Africanism', *International Organisation*, 16:2 (1962), 275–90 at 282.

[120] D. Francis, *Uniting Africa – Building Regional Peace and Security Systems* (Aldershot: Ashgate, 2006), p. 49.

international order functioned as 'post-imperial ordering devices'.[121] It is this legacy, and the events and order it conditioned, that perhaps explain why the objectives and principles outlined in the Charter of the OAU corresponded to similar provisions in the UN Charter. For instance, paragraph 1 of Article 2 of the UN Charter proclaims the adherence to sovereign equality of member states, whilst Article 2(4) prohibits the violation of territorial integrity and political independence of states. Similarly, Article 2(7) of the UN Charter provides for non-interference in the domestic affairs of states. The peaceful settlement of disputes through mediation, conciliation and arbitration is the subject of Article 33.

It follows, therefore, that the inclusion of these principles in the OAU's Charter was a natural entry point into international society. It is this burden of inheritance that fictionalises the assumed autonomy of the African postcolonial state, subjecting it to what could be called conditions of choiceless conformity. Its implications transcended the OAU's normative conformity with international legality. Of course this is not to suggest that international law is entirely responsible for the creation, configuration and subsequent failings of the OAU. There were considerable political, social, economic and personal inputs from African leaders who conceived and empowered the OAU. However, the point made here is that despite the exercise of agency by African leaders, their efforts and those of the OAU were, in some respect, limited by international law as the operating frame of reference in international society. This was particularly evident in the context of approaches to conflict and peace-building in Africa. To put this in proper context, it is imperative to examine, briefly, the nature of the OAU's approaches to conflicts and the extent to which they were shaped by structures of international order.

The OAU and internal conflicts

The principal organs for the accomplishment of the purposes of the OAU were provided for under Article 7 of the Charter. They were the Assembly of Heads of State and Government, Council of Ministers, General Secretariat and Commission of Mediation, Conciliation and Arbitration. The Assembly was composed of heads of state and government and their appointed representatives. Its main function was to

---

[121] P. Lyons, 'New States and International Order' in A. James (ed.), *The Bases of International Order: Essays in Honour of C. A. W. Manning*, cited in Francis, *ibid.*

provide leadership in the formulation of the political and ideological direction of the organisation. Its other functions included the adoption of declarations and resolutions, and the approval of the appointment of Secretary General. The Council of Ministers comprised ministers from member states and functioned as the policy formulation forum of the OAU. Headed by the Secretary General, the Secretariat was the principal administrative body mandated to oversee the implementation of decisions from the organs of the OAU. It was based in Addis Ababa, Ethiopia.

The initial attempts by the OAU to confront violence and conflicts were embedded in the Commission of Mediation, Conciliation and Arbitration. The Commission's mandate, functions and composition were outlined in a separate protocol which came into effect soon after the creation of the OAU.[122] The Protocol was divided into six main parts. Part I dealt with issues of establishment and organisation, whilst composition, qualification and tenure of members of the Commission were provided for under Parts II and III. Perhaps the most important section of the Protocol was Part II, which enumerated the General Provisions dealing with the settlement of disputes. The mandate of the Commission was restricted to disputes between member states, although non-members could refer disputes between themselves and member states to the Commission.[123]

Given the confinement of the Commission's work to disputes amongst member states, the means and methods of dispute settlement had a largely non-confrontational character, rooted in classical statist diplomacy. Like most of the Charter's provisions, the emphasis on mediation, conciliation and arbitration reflected values rooted in modern international law. The provisions outlining the processes assumed that conflicts in Africa could be categorised into layers that progress in a predictable, orderly fashion. The Commission's operation also depended on the willingness and consent of disputants. No wonder, then, that the Commission was never constituted and so not a single dispute could ever be referred to it.[124] It is worthy of note that the provisions and approaches to conflicts under the Commission were primarily aimed at

---

[122] Protocol Establishing the Commission of Mediation, Conciliation and Arbitration, reprinted in L. B. Sohn (ed.), *Basic Documents of African Regional Organisations* (New York: Ocean Publications, 1971).

[123] See Article XI of the Protocol.

[124] T. Maluwa, *International Law in Postcolonial Africa* (Leiden: Kluwer Law International, 1999), p. 245.

echoing the prohibition of the use of force personified by the post-1945 international legal order. Whilst the Commission's overriding objective was to help in the peaceful settlement of disputes amongst member states, its almost verbatim rendition of the UN Charter's approach to conflicts meant that neither the Commission nor the OAU Charter could incorporate alternative approaches to confronting conflicts beyond the existing conventional ones.

In the absence of the operation of the Commission, the many conflicts that afflicted most parts of Africa continued with little or no meaningful attempts by the OAU to confront them. Where attempts were made, these involved the munificence of ad hoc committees and diplomatic endeavours fronted by some political leaders. This alternative was mostly favoured by African states that ignored the Commission on the basis, perhaps, that 'less formal procedures are more attuned to the fluidity and rapidity of African conflicts, which tend to defy overly legalistic and time consuming formal solutions'.[125] The perceived flexibility and accessibility of informal mechanisms could, sometimes, provide effective means of confronting conflicts that were not suitable for formalised processes of arbitration.[126] The process had been attempted in two notable internal conflicts – the Congo crisis of the 1960s and the Biafra civil war of 1967–70. In the case of the Congo, the cessation of Belgian colonial rule in 1960 led to a wave of squabbles amongst Congo's political elites. As the differences widened, the mineral-rich Katanga province attempted secession.[127] In the ensuing mêlée, the incumbent Prime Minister, Patrice Lumumba, was assassinated.[128] The new government found support from the UN but was shunned by many OAU members.

Faced by an impending crisis, the OAU enlisted the services of the then Kenyan President, Jomo Kenyatta, to initiate mediation between the warring parties.[129] However, neither the OAU hierarchy nor the diplomacy that ensued could make any impact in defusing the conflict. In Nigeria's Biafra, similar encounters and results characterised the OAU's attempted engagement. The Biafra civil war of 1967 erupted

---

[125] Munya, 'The Organisation of African Unity and its Role', at 552.
[126] See J. A. Meyer, 'Collective Self-Defense and Regional Security: Necessary Exception to a Globalist Doctrine', *Boston University International Law Journal*, 11:2 (1993), 391–434.
[127] See Munya, 'The Organisation of African Unity and its Role', at 570.
[128] P. Schuler, *Who Killed the Congo?* (New York: Devin-Adair, 1962), pp. 243–7.
[129] Munya, 'The Organisation of African Unity and its Role', at 571.

as a result of numerous factors such as political competition amongst social groups, perceived insecurity of the Igbo, the politicisation of the military as well as the growing economic importance of oil. Some of these factors contributed to the Nigerian military coup in 1966, followed by the civil war a year later when Odumegwu Ojukwu made a unilateral declaration of independence for the state of Biafra.[130] When Federal Government forces moved to nullify the attempted secession the conflict escalated into a bloody civil war. In this instance, diplomatic initiatives were pursued only to the extent that they benefitted the Federal Government of Nigeria. In the early 1980s a civil war erupted in Chad, which triggered the involvement of the OAU. Unlike in earlier internal conflicts, the OAU despatched a peacekeeping mission. But like the record of the organisation in other peacebuilding initiatives, the Chadian mission failed and the OAU withdrew.

What the OAU ad hoc committees and diplomatic peace efforts showed was that their effectiveness tended to have little impact on internal conflicts. Despite these attempts the ad hoc committees were far from ideal – many African leaders had established groups of friends and sympathisers amongst their peers, and some of the close relations meant that where conflicts erupted, ad hoc committees were more inclined towards preserving and protecting incumbents than working for swift and effective settlement through neutrality and fair play. Moreover, the ad hoc committees by their very nature lacked coherence and clear direction in achieving durable peace. They were largely constituted at the discretion and will of the Assembly and were often more reactive than proactive and preventive.[131]

By the early 1990s, it was becoming increasingly obvious that the OAU's normative and institutional settings were insufficient to confront violence and conflicts in Africa. At least for a while, that realism provoked debate on the need to reconceptualise and reinterpret some of the principles that anchored the OAU Charter. As these principles were averse to advancing transformative approaches to conflicts, the organisation's then Secretary General, Salim Ahmed Salim, spoke of the need to 'maintain a balance between national sovereignty and international

---

[130] Ibid., at 573.
[131] G. Naldi, 'Future Trends in Human Rights in Africa: The Increased Role of the OAU' in M. Evans and R. Murray (eds.), The African Charter on Human and Peoples' Rights: The System in Practice, 1986–2000 (Cambridge University Press, 2002), p. 98.

responsibility'.[132] Salim questioned the relevance of some of the principles underpinning the OAU Charter, noting in particular that 'the doctrine of non-intervention precludes the possibility of accountability on the part of states'.[133] The Secretary General's pronouncements, however persuasive, could not induce the OAU into the kind of changes that were required at the time. A significant development, however, was the creation of the Mechanism for Conflict Prevention, Management and Resolution (MCPMR) following a decision by the Assembly in June 1993.[134] The OAU declaration introduced the MCPMR as an organ that was needed so as to 'bring to the processes of dealing with conflicts in . . . the continent a new institutional dynamism, enabling speedy action to prevent or manage and ultimately resolve conflicts when and where they occur'.[135] A year later, the Rwandan genocide occurred, and by that time the OAU had lost its relevance. In 2001, the OAU and its Charter were disbanded and a new organisation, the African Union, was created. The MCPMR was subsequently drafted into the Peace and Security Council of the African Union.

Limitations and failures of the OAU

The OAU came under increasing criticism in the 1980s for its inability to proffer transformative changes that were desperately needed in post-independence Africa. But it was the organisation's institutional and normative weaknesses in confronting armed conflicts that attracted most condemnation.[136] The sense of apathy and ineptitude caused vast human misery in many parts of Africa.[137] The failing prospects of the organisation led many to conclude that if positive steps were not taken

---

[132] Statement by Salim Ahmed Salim, Secretary General of the OAU, in O. Obasanjo and F. G. N. Mosha (eds.), *Africa: Rise to Challenge* (Abeokuta: Africa Leadership Forum, 1993), p. 343.

[133] *Ibid.*, p. 346.

[134] Assembly of the Heads of State and Government, Twenty-ninth Ordinary Session, Cairo, Egypt, 28–30 June 1993, AHG/Decl.3 (XXIX).

[135] *Ibid.*, para. 13.

[136] See G. E. Achuku, 'Peaceful Settlement of Disputes: Unsolved Problem for the OAU', *Africa Today*, 24:4 (1977); Munya, 'The Organisation of African Unity and its Role'; R. K. Ramphul, 'The Role of International and Regional Organisations in the Peaceful Settlement of Internal Disputes (With Special Emphasis on the Organisation of African Unity)', *Ga. J. Int'l & Comp. L.*, 13 (1983), 371–84.

[137] Foltz, 'The OAU and Resolution of Africa's Conflicts' in Deng and Zartman (eds.), *Conflict Resolution in Africa*, p. 347.

to renew and revamp its conflict management frameworks, it was 'hard to see an effective future for the OAU'.[138] This was because the deficiencies of the OAU were embedded in the very nature of the organisation and its emergence at a poignant epoch of the international legal order. The Cold War was at its peak and global geopolitics ever so fragile. Compounding this was the interplay of the burden of inheritance that confronted new African states at the onset of independence. The deficiencies of the OAU could be classified into structural inadequacies and normative failings.

Structural inadequacies of the OAU

Structurally, the OAU Charter delineated functions that made it difficult for swift action to be taken to confront internal conflicts. The organisation's traditional response to social turbulence was often defined and dependent on decision-making processes of its key institutions. For instance, meetings at the level of Council of Ministers and Heads of Government required a quorum of two-thirds, which also applied to all decisions in summits.[139] Bureaucratic formalism was deeply enshrined, which amounted to what William Foltz calls a demonstration of 'a protective preference for inaction and delay over decisive movement'.[140] Likewise, the original focus of the OAU also played a role in its limitations. The OAU was fundamentally a political organisation which sought to accelerate decolonisation struggles as well as salvage what little was left of the African unity project. In this sense, it was merely a platform to provide solidarity and a sense of identity amongst states, and was not, therefore, set out to establish functional institutional machinery that could proactively generate norms and enforce policies.

Moreover, the absence of enforcement and capacity in the life of the organisation made it more of a loose association of sovereign states designed to promote essential international relations without offending the tenet of sovereign equality.[141] It was perhaps in conjunction with this outlook of the OAU that William Zartman proclaimed that 'there is no OAU; there are only members, and their interests come first'.[142] Lacking

---

[138] *African Confidential*, 30 (1989), 11 August, at 4.
[139] See Article XXVII on the interpretation of the OAU Charter.
[140] Foltz, 'The OAU and Resolution of Africa's Conflicts', p. 350.
[141] Munya, 'The Organisation of African Unity and its Role', at 583.
[142] I. W. Zartman, 'The OAU in the African State System' in Y. El-Ayouty and I. W. Zartman (eds.), *The OAU After Twenty Years* (New York: Praeger, 1984), p. 41.

an elaboration of norms of behaviour, the OAU thus became a 'complex pattern of ordered interactions among states'.[143] But this flawed conceptualisation of international relations was typical of post-war regional organisations and the OAU might just have been another victim of the hierarchies created by elements of the international order.[144] As Ellen Frey-Wouters writes:

> The limited character of existing regional organisations shapes their response to internal conflict. The decision making process of the Organisation of African Unity ... is of an intergovernmental character. There is no supranational regional centre of power above member states; the regional system is limited to direct interaction between the power centres of the member units. The regional secretariats are merely administrative organs, exercising no executive power and entrusted with little scope for independent initiative.[145]

The conformity to order resulted in an institutional structure that was conservative, unable and unwilling to cultivate a proactive normative blueprint relevant to Africa.

Normative inadequacies of the OAU

Perhaps the most definitive factor for the limitations of the OAU, leading eventually to its collapse, was the very nature of the normative architecture underpinning its Charter. The organisation was structured along four fundamental principles: *sovereignty*; *non-interference*; *territorial integrity*; and *African solutions to African problems*. The strict reverence to these principles implied that conditions of violence, conflicts and rights abuses in Africa were mostly unattended to by the OAU. The failure to empanel the Commission provided under the Charter for conflict resolution was, for instance, an offshoot of the non-interference principle. Even if, under the Charter, member states had a basis to submit disputes for the purposes of peaceful settlement, the jurisdiction of the Commission was, in theory, optional rather than compulsory. Critically, the Commission's mandate was confined to interstate conflicts only. The exclusion of internal conflicts was a major flaw, especially

---

[143] Foltz, 'The OAU and Resolution of Africa's Conflicts', p. 350.

[144] E. Frey-Wouters, 'The Relevance of Regional Arrangements to Internal Conflicts in the Developing World' in J. N. Moore (ed.), *Law and Civil War in the Modern World* (Baltimore: Johns Hopkins University Press, 1974), p. 460.

[145] *Ibid.*

given that a substantial number of conflicts in most of Africa's post-independence have been in the form of civil war. This narrow conception not only suggests that there was little enthusiasm for the Commission's proactive involvement in internal conflicts, but also that the sanctity of sovereignty and the principle of non-interference were more than just mere guiding principles. They were at the centre of the OAU's existence. Sam Ibok, the OAU's former Director of Political Affairs, writes:

> A strong view pervaded the OAU that conflicts within States fell within the exclusive competence of the States concerned. Arising from that basic assertion, was the equally strong view that it was not the business of the OAU, to pronounce itself on those conflicts and that the organisation certainly had no mandate to involve itself in the resolution of problems of that nature.[146]

And by the time the MCPMR was established the organisation had become increasingly alienated. Catherine Hoskyns explains that the balancing act embedded in the OAU Charter transformed it into 'a curious hotchpotch of principles and purposes, which combined rather conservative statements designed to protect the status quo in inter-African relations with radical commitments towards the outside world'.[147] It was the OAU's dogmatic resolve to fulfil this delicate equation with a cumbersome institutional structure that made its impact in confronting Africa's postcolonial peace and human security dilemmas minimal and largely subdued.[148] Confronting internal armed conflicts was subordinate to the broader goal of maintaining harmony amongst states.[149] As a result, the OAU demonstrated profound hesitation in intervening in internal violence, and even 'when it did intervene', Obiora Chinedu Okafor asserts, 'it ha[d] almost always been on the side of the established order'.[150]

In the Biafra civil war of 1967, for instance, the crisis was deemed by the OAU as an internal conflict that fell outside the purview of its Charter, and so the organisation's involvement was only to place the 'services of the Assembly at the disposal of the Federal Government of

---

[146] S. Ibok, 'Conflict Prevention, Management and Resolution in Africa' (2000), http://unpan1.un.org/intradoc/groups/public/documents/CAFRAD/UNPAN011836.pdf (last visited June 2010).

[147] C. Hoskyns, 'The Organisation of African Unity and Eastern Africa', cited in W. Tordoff, *Government and Politics in Africa* (Bloomington: Indiana University Press, 1984), p. 277.

[148] *Ibid.*   [149] Foltz, 'The OAU and Resolution of Africa's Conflicts', p. 354.

[150] O. C. Okafor, *Redefining Legitimate Statehood: International Law and State Fragmentation in Africa* (The Hague: Martinus Nijhoff Publishers, 1999), p. 138.

Nigeria'.[151] A similar position was adopted following the 1972 genocide in Burundi. Other internal crises that led to atrocities remained unattended to for far too long. Ugandan President Yoweri Museveni made reference to this at his maiden OAU summit in 1986:

> Over a period of 20 years three quarters of a million Ugandans perished at the hands of governments that should have protected their lives ... Ugandans felt a deep sense of betrayal that most of Africa kept silent ... the reason for not condemning such massive crimes had supposedly been a desire not to interfere in the internal affairs of a Member State, in accordance with the Charter of the OAU and the UN.[152]

But these 'perverse principles with negative effects'[153] are largely progenies of the international legal system that emerged in the post-war period. The result has been that international organisations that emerged were, by default and design, loose associations of states intended to promote a sense of harmony. The implication in the context of postcolonial Africa is that, at its birth, the OAU was constrained by the existence of an order operating in a political dispensation that could neither challenge nor shed its burden of inheritance. From this perspective, the functional normative limitations made the OAU an Oedipal child of international law, whose sins and weaknesses as regards approaches to internal conflicts were, in effect, also those of international law. For instance, one of international law's key principles, non-intervention, not only shaped the mandate and operational structure of the OAU's Commission of Mediation, Conciliation and Arbitration, but also reduced it to levels of negative capability. The inability of the OAU to fashion transformative approaches to internal conflicts was, by extension, the failure of institutional international law.

Beyond this, principles of sovereign equality and non-interference shielded and bolstered the mantra African solutions to African problems. The mantra had been premised on what Berhanykun Andemicael labels 'try OAU first' before resorting to the UN Security Council.[154]

---

[151] J. J. Stremlau, *The International Politics of the Nigeria Civil War 1967–1970* (Princeton University Press, 1977), p. 4.

[152] President Yoweri Museveni of Uganda, Maiden Speech to the Ordinary Session of Heads of State and Government of the OAU, 22nd Ordinary Session, Addis Ababa, Ethiopia, July 1986.

[153] E. Kodjo, 'Et Demain L'Afrique', cited by Foltz, 'The OAU and Resolution of Africa's Conflicts', at 352.

[154] B. Andemicael, *The OAU and the UN: Relations Between the Organisation of African Unity and the United Nations* (New York: Africana, 1976).

Article 52(2) of the UN Charter allows regional organisations to take measures in settling regional disputes through peaceful means before forwarding such matters to the Security Council. The prioritisation of the OAU as an organisation of first instance in settling disputes had been an effective strategy of keeping most internal conflicts outside the bounds of international legal instruments. Even if internal conflicts could not be settled by the OAU, interference from outside the continent was greeted with apprehension.[155] The absence of external scrutiny allowed problems to escalate as the OAU hung on to its African solution mantra, which ironically found harmony with international law's non-interference principle. Not even the crises in Biafra in 1966, and in Eritrea and Sudan for much of the 1980s and early 1990s, could make any impact on the need to reconsider norms underlying the OAU.

By the early 1990s, the impact of the normative and institutional inadequacies was so acute that the need for reformation dominated the 1991 OAU Summit, with the adoption of the Draft Treaty on Economic Integration as a decisive outcome.[156] But the nature of Africa's problems required a comprehensive overhaul of its institutions. The move towards institutional reformation coincided with the end of the Cold War. The optimism ushered in by the period was couched in a spectrum of a shift in superpower political and economic contention. The reconstitution of the balances of global political rivalry between the United States and the former Soviet Union devalued Africa's strategic importance and, to some extent, contributed to the continent's increasing marginalisation. The effect of this shift on Africa was not insignificant. In July 1990, the OAU admitted in a declaration that the end of the Cold War would fundamentally transform the geopolitical landscape of the world and that Africa needed to revive and strengthen its indigenous institutions so as to engage emerging global challenges.[157] It led the continent to accelerate reforms, and by 2001 the OAU was dissolved and the African Union created.

---

[155] Foltz, 'The OAU and Resolution of Africa's Conflicts', p. 355.

[156] Treaty Establishing the African Economic Community, adopted 3 June 1991, available at www.africa-union.org/root/au/Documents/Treaties/Text/AEC_Treaty_1991.pdf (last visited August 2010).

[157] See OAU, *The Political and Socio-economic Situation in Africa and the Fundamental Changes Taking Place in the World*, AHG/Dec.1 (XXVI), 1990.

Conclusion

The extent to which international law approaches to conflicts embedded in the UN Charter and the Responsibility to Protect are applicable to conflicts of an internal nature remains limited. This is particularly evident in the context of internal conflicts in Africa. The reasons may point to the fact that the normative principles and institutional structure underpinning the current framework are shaped and inspired by a particular mindset that has struggled to initiate avenues of engagement with the underlying causes of internal conflicts. And so for the most part the approaches remain absorbed in the particularities of a dysfunctional architecture through the *jus ad bellum* regime. The limitations in the *jus ad bellum* in relation to internal conflicts lend strength to the view that internal conflicts have been traditionally neither justified nor outlawed by international law. The UN Charter is not, *expressis verbis*, helpful on this front. Its lack of clarity arising from the incoherent balancing act of sovereign authority and international legality has fashioned a near consensus that international law's encounters with internal conflicts are limited by virtue of the traditional monopoly of state domestic jurisdiction; it is the frame upon which the doctrine of non-interference hinges.

In a broader sense too, the nature of international law approaches bear faultlines that make them increasingly unsuitable in confronting internal conflicts. Faced with this legacy, the OAU, as Africa's premier continental organisation, could neither acquire the platform to depart from the international legal order, nor offer a parallel challenge to approaches to conflicts. Even where in rare instances it attempted to tackle internal conflicts, international legal principles stood in the way of the organisation. Thus the normative and institutional structures embodied by the OAU neither added to nor improved the already conceptually inadequate international law responses to conflicts. As a loose political organisation, the OAU sought to cater for the needs of its members within the ambits of a defined international legal order.[158] The OAU Charter simply 'codified' the general attitude of international law to internal conflicts. In particular, its incorporation of the principles of non-interference and territorial integrity facilitated the continuation of the limited applicability of *jus ad bellum* in internal conflicts. In this sense, the shortcomings of the OAU in confronting internal conflicts in Africa reflected the broader inadequacies of international law.

---

[158] Tordoff, *Government and Politics in Africa*, p. 261.

5

The genesis of the African Union

There are occasions when African nationalists are evidently guilty of a misapplication of old evaluative concepts to new situations. But the student of political events must allow for the possibility of a re-interpretation of old concepts to cope with new challenges.

Ali A. Mazrui[1]

Introduction

In July 2002, a congregation of African heads of state and government presided over the official launch of the African Union in the South African city of Durban. The new organisation replaced the OAU, which had steered Africa's political and ideological matters since its inception in 1963. The launch was characterised by rapturous affirmations of the potential attributes of the new organisation and the satisfaction that Africa had taken significant leaps towards mapping a progressive future capable of shaping identities, protecting interests and granting agency to its people. This sense of optimism was in part predicated on a popular belief that the institutional and normative settings upon which Africa was organised were being disentangled to provide a break from a troubled past and usher in an era that promised a different future. The launch was therefore seen as symbolic to the extent that it signalled an end, at least in theory, to the old institutional order embodied by the OAU.

Yet the sequences of events that triggered the launch – completing the transition from the OAU to the African Union – were far from straightforward. In fact, the need for institutional reformation had to endure a lukewarm reception for many decades, due in part to the effects of the

---

[1] A. A. Mazrui, *Towards a Pax Africana: A Study of Ideology and Ambition* (London: Weidenfeld Goldbacks, 1967), p. 19.

Cold War and the structural rigours of the international legal order. In this sense, transformations in the configuration of international society presented an opportunity for a process of international engagement and normative reorientation. For Africa, this culminated in the inception of a new continental architecture embodied by the African Union. The normative values of the African Union and its institutional objectives are guided by a Constitutive Act, Protocol Relating to the Establishment of the Peace and Security Council and a number of important framework instruments. These instruments and the conceptions and institutions they represent are predicated on certain principles that attempt to calibrate the focus, emphasis and approaches to the challenges facing Africa, especially as regards peace and security.

The search for peace through normative principles constitutes a significant component of the Constitutive Act's peace and security architecture. And so the purpose and focus of this chapter is to account for the chain of events and wider historical outlays that ultimately informed the genesis and normative framework of the Constitutive Act of the African Union. There are three key aspects of this genesis. The first is the rubric of Pan-Africanism and its role and continued relevance in the process of African institution-building. The second relates to the Cold War and how its aftermath provided an opening for Africa to appropriate space and ownership in the conception and formulation of norms relating to institution-building and approaches to peace. And the third is the role of key African personalities and their battle for ideas in the final stages of the transition from the OAU to the African Union. These account for the combined internal and external factors and their signification in the norms formulation processes that ultimately inspired the creation of the African Union.

Normative origins of the African Union

Africa has long had encounters with ideas, concepts and institutions. Due to their depths, intensity and varying strands, the encounters have been internally and externally driven. Internally, norms had been conceived from a process of cross-cultural dialogue by various empires and kingdoms at different times occasioning in demographic transformations, trading links and educational exchanges.[2] Externally formulated

---

[2] See B. Davidson, *Africa in History: Themes and Outlines* (London: Touchstone Books, 1995).

norms emanated from three main outlets. The first was slavery and European colonialism. This outlet of encounters exposed Africa to a cultural frame and mindset from which emerged a social and political order that was alien to the continent and its people. The second encounter came through trade and religious missionary expansionism. Trade and commerce provided avenues for interaction between African communities and those of other societies and civilisations, whilst Islam and Christianity introduced norms and belief systems that continue to shape lives and political and social orders. The third took the shape of counter-hegemonic anti-imperial ideologies, and was preoccupied with the emancipation and the reassertion of the dignity of the African. Although most of the encounters have had a violent and devastating impact on Africa, one such interface has presented a much more subtle and defining outlook. This is Pan-Africanism, and its subsidiary norms formulation processes.

Pan-African ideals and visions

There is perhaps scarcely a phenomenon that has become so suffused with the visions, instruments and institutions of Africa than the rubric of Pan-Africanism. Emerging from and imaging through varying habitats, Pan-Africanism has remained a defining component of Africa's resistance, reinvention and renewal initiatives. But what the concept means exactly has occupied scholars for many decades. The search for a definition of Pan-Africanism has been difficult and varied. And although it is, as Colin Legum suggests, 'possible to talk about the way Pan-Africanism expresses itself, it is not so easy to give a concise definition'.[3] This is because the concept has been used by 'its protagonists and antagonists as if it were a declaration of political principles'.[4] Equally problematic is what Jabez Ayodele Langley perceives as the lack of a 'single intellectual pedigree' of Pan-Africanism, making it 'difficult to define comprehensively for the simple reason that it has assumed different meanings and orientations at various stages in its evolution'.[5]

Definitions have been attempted nevertheless. Ofuatey-Kodjoe has, for instance, defined Pan-Africanism as the 'acceptance of oneness of all people of African descent and the commitment to the betterment of

---

[3] C. Legum, *Pan-Africanism: A Short Political Guide* (London: Pall Mall Press, 1961), p. 14.
[4] *Ibid.*
[5] J. A. Langley, *Pan-Africanism and Nationalism in West Africa 1900–1945* (Oxford: Clarendon Press, 1973), p. 7.

all people of African descent'.[6] For Robert Chrisman, at the heart of Pan-African vision is the 'basic premise that ... the people of African descent throughout the globe constitute a common cultural and political community'.[7] Pan-Africanism has also been interpreted as 'essentially a movement of ideas and emotions; at times it achieves a synthesis: at times it remains at the level of antithesis'.[8] The term's Latin origin is not entirely helpful in conceiving a definition. 'Pan' in Latin means 'all', and so 'Pan-African' simply translates as 'all African'. To this end, Walter Rodney suggests that 'any pan-concept is an exercise in self-definition by the people, in the establishment of a broader re-definition of themselves than that which has so far been permitted by those in power'. And so, 'invariably, however, this exercise is undertaken by a specific social group or class which speaks on behalf of the population as a whole'.[9] Legum has identified key elements of Pan-Africanism through sets of guiding principles, which range from emotions, solidarity, pride and ownership to sense of belonging.

What the varying interpretative strands of Pan-African values perhaps suggest is the cohering theme of the resolve for greater solidarity, unity and cohesion. Pan-Africanism has a long history which developed through what George Shepperson calls 'a complicated Atlantic triangle of influences'.[10] Its documentary expression can be traced from the proceedings of the 1893 Congress on Africa held in Chicago.[11] It was at this conference that the term began to gather purchase as a principle and ideological instrument. Initial formulations construed Pan-Africanism as an idea to advance unity, emancipation and empowerment of the black race.[12] The idea was received enthusiastically, providing inspiration and contributing to the creation of the African Association in London in 1897.[13] In years to follow, the ideals

---

[6] W. Ofuatey-Kodjoe, *Pan-Africanism: New Direction in Strategy* (Lanham: University Press of America, 1986), p. 388.

[7] R. Chrisman, 'Aspects of Pan-Africanism', *Black Scholar*, 4:10 (1973), 2–5 at 2.

[8] Legum, *Pan-Africanism*, p. 14.

[9] W. Rodney, 'Towards the Sixth Pan-African Congress: Aspects of the International Class Struggle in Africa, the Caribbean, and America' in M. K. Asante and A. S. Abarry (eds.), *African Intellectual Heritage: A Book of Sources* (Philadelphia: Temple University Press, 1996), p. 729. See also W. Rodney, *Walter Rodney Speaks: The Making of an African Intellectual* (Trenton: Africa World Press, 1990).

[10] G. Shepperson, 'Notes on Negro American Influences on the Emergence of African Nationalism', *Journal of African History*, 1:2 (1960), 299–331 at 299.

[11] F. P. Noble, *The Chicago Congress on Africa* (Washington, DC: Library of Congress, 1894), pp. 280–1.

[12] *Ibid.*, p. 286.

[13] P. O. Esedebe, *Pan-Africanism: The Idea and the Movement 1776–1963* (Washington, DC: Howard University Press, 1982), p. 46.

espoused at the Chicago Congress framed broader consensus for the need to institutionalise some of the norms shaping up at the time. But in most of its early formulation Pan-Africanism largely remained an 'informal organisation of memories'.[14]

The momentum generated by the agitations of previous gatherings led to the first Pan-African Conference held in London in 1900 under the chairmanship of Alexander Walters.[15] The conference was a significant advance on the precepts, identification and direction of the hitherto nascent outlook of Pan-Africanism. Subsequent conferences were held in Paris in 1919, London in 1923 and New York in 1927.[16] It was not, however, until the Manchester Conference of 1945 that the movement's emancipatory rhetoric was fused with African nationalism. This was a poignant epoch that helped locate Pan-Africanism within the struggles and challenges facing Africa. In fact, so important was the Manchester Conference that Kwame Nkrumah was to later claim that the 1945 conference 'provided the outlet for African nationalism and brought the awakening of African political consciousness', transforming it into 'a mass movement of Africa for the Africans'.[17] Pan-Africanism had, by the 1950s, become deeply aligned to, and morphed into, the political philosophies of indigenous nationalist movements, and subsequently acquired a powerful ideological platform whose residual persuasions and normative inclination continue to be fossilised in African institution-building initiatives.[18]

Pan-Africanism is not, however, a homogeneous concept. It has meant different things at different times and for different purposes. The diversity in meaning and purpose therefore implies that Pan-Africanism 'is not a movement that should be boxed and frozen into epochs and categories'.[19] In its early political imagery the concept evoked elements of counter-hegemonic resistance against forces of exploitation and imperial dominance.[20] This was a strand popularised during anti-imperial struggles and featured nationalism and principles of self-determination. Its ideological premise was and largely remained focused on protecting

---

[14] Langley, *Pan-Africanism and Nationalism*, p. 18.
[15] A. Walters, *My Life and Work* (New York: Fleming H. Revel Company, 1917), p. 253.
[16] W. E. B. Du Bois, *The World and Africa* (New York: International Publishers, 1979), p. 240.
[17] K. Nkrumah, *The Autobiography of Kwame Nkrumah* (Edinburgh University Press, 1957).
[18] T. Murithi, *The African Union, Pan-Africanism, Peacebuilding and Development* (Aldershot: Ashgate, 2005).
[19] Langley, *Pan-Africanism and Nationalism*, p. viii.
[20] Walters, *My Life and Work*, p. 253.

what is viewed as truly 'belonging' to Africa. As a sociological discourse, Pan-Africanism is an interactive process that 'embraces the language, narratives, communicative action and frames of reference which serve to construct actors' understandings of their interests, identities, norms, values'.[21]

There have been attempts to appropriate the Pan-African language of 'unity in diversity' as a tool for mobilisation and conscience-building amongst the peoples of Africa and the African diaspora.[22] This dimension of Pan-Africanism seeks to reclaim lost identities as well as provide spaces for memory and empowerment. The rationale is to deploy the rallying qualities of Pan-Africanism as an antidote to the marginalisation and alienation of Africa and its people with the hope that closer integration and empowerment would consolidate shared visions and neutralise indifference. The underlying wisdom is that the 'power of the individual country or society is amplified exponentially when it is combined with the forces of other [historically related] countries and societies'.[23] It was in the context of the essence of collective strength that upon gaining independence for Ghana, Kwame Nkrumah declared that independence for his country was meaningless until aligned to the total liberation of the African continent. For Nkrumah, like most of his contemporaries, Pan-Africanism offered a medium through which the lived experiences of Africans could be documented and deployed as a prism for the formulation of emancipatory futures.

But the most profound impact of Pan-Africanism as a norm-engendering ideology lies, perhaps, in its ability to help transform and optimise African institutions. This is evident in the periodic transformations of Pan-Africanism which often appear to personify particular projects of African institution-building. The early evolution and orientations of Pan-Africanism in Africa were primarily preoccupied with anti-colonial struggles resulting in the incorporation of the language of decolonisation movements and ideologies into its rhetoric. For example, the Mau Mau rebellion in Kenya and the anti-colonial nationalist movement in Algeria both sourced inspiration from, and had close association with, the Pan-African movement.[24] In recent times, this transformation has seen a

[21] D. Francis, *Uniting Africa – Building Regional Peace and Security Systems* (Aldershot: Ashgate, 2006), p. 14.

[22] See Murithi, *The African Union.*   [23] *Ibid.,* p. 26.

[24] See J. B. Adekson, 'The Algerian and Mau Mau Revolts: A Comparative Study in Revolutionary Warfare', *Comparative Strategy*, 3:1 (1981), 69–92.

noticeable attempt to shift from the movement's anti-colonial reactionary rhetoric to a more proactive engagement with issues of social justice, governance, human security and peacebuilding.[25] According to Tim Murithi, this shift represents patterns of 'organised Pan-Africanism' which symbolise a 'pragmatic transition which seeks to regenerate African solidarity and unity to confront [amongst others] the adverse consequences of economic and predatory globalisation'.[26] It is these elements that had been the stimulants behind the creation of the OAU and the subsequent formation of the African Union.

Pan-Africanism during the Cold War

The paradigmatic transition of the Pan-African movement and its consolidation in Africa largely took place in the aftermath of the Manchester Conference of 1945. New opportunities and networks of engagements had emerged whose purpose was to galvanise an adequate articulation of the plight and rights of colonial subjects. This was a defining period in international politics as it was the beginning of the Cold War and the emergence of the new international legal order. But this epoch also had considerable impact on the rise of liberation movements and the increasing agitation for independence. The gradual success of liberation struggles reset the conception of Pan-Africanism in Africa. New priorities of independent Africa triggered an enforced recasting of the focus and vision of Pan-Africanism, ultimately leading to a loose separation of the ideology from its originating roots in the Caribbean and the United States.[27] What emerged subsequently was a version of Pan-Africanism increasingly moderated through formalised initiatives that transformed it 'from a movement of peoples to a movement of governments'.[28]

The intellectual and geographic 'separation' of Pan-Africanism from its founding roots subjected the movement to the influences and specific agendas of actors whose circumstances were different from those of the ideology's initial custodians. In the process, Pan-Africanism went through sequences of incarnations conditioned by the politics of the Cold War. Two progenies of the Cold War in Africa impacted on

---

[25] P. G. Adogamhe, 'Pan-Africanism Revisited: Vision and Reality of African Unity and Development', *African Review of Integration*, 2:2 (2008), 1–34 at 27.

[26] Murithi, *The African Union*, p. 23.   [27] Mazrui, *Towards a Pax Africana*, p. 3.

[28] S. M. Makinda and F. W. Okumu, *The African Union: Challenges of Globalisation, Security and Governance* (New York: Routledge, 2008), p. 19.

Pan-Africanism. The first was the set of ideological groupings that emerged in independent Africa. With the normative recasting and nudging of the Pan-African focus onto Africa-specific ambitions, calls for unity and closer integration through formalised institutions and initiatives gained ground. Although common denominators existed on the significance of these grand ambitions, the means and methods of achieving them created divisions and differences in views and approaches. The divisions converged in two main camps: one advocating for a political union, and the other, whilst acknowledging the importance of such a move, proffering a gradual approach. The positions represented particular interpretations of Pan-Africanism which, to some extent, reflected the influences of the competing superpower ideological strands of the Cold War.

The second impact of the Cold War was the ascription of the doctrine of non-alignment. The doctrine was both an affirmation of an aspect of Pan-Africanism and a departure from it. Non-alignment was a principle largely associated with countries that wanted to express their sense of freedom by arrogating the 'right to be and remain to be' during the Cold War's deeply internationally tribalised politics and political behaviour. For non-aligned countries, the propagation of neutrality was a pathway to making freedom a default setting in the governance and methods of politics. With this it was possible to assert difference without being indifferent. This was an operating decimal in the movement, as the 1961 Belgrade Declaration of the Non-Aligned Conference emphasised: 'all peoples and nations have to solve the problems of their own political, economic, social and cultural systems in accordance with their own conditions, needs and potentialities'.[29]

The interfaces between Pan-Africanism and non-alignment illustrate subtle convergences and divergences, which are in part located in the propositional frames of the two concepts. The underlying focus of Pan-Africanism in all its defining epochs over the decades has been to make people of African descent more visible, and in the aftermath of the 1945 Manchester Conference, shifted towards asserting the importance of Africa and the dignity of its people in international politics and political agreements. This was of specific significance to African nationalists because, as Kwame Nkrumah was to lament, 'for far too long Africa has spoken through the voices of others'. And so the notion of

---

[29] Proceedings of the Belgrade Conference of Heads of State or Government of Non-Aligned Countries, 1–6 September 1961, p. 255.

African personality was conceived so that Africa could make 'its proper impact and will let the world know it through the voices of Africa's own sons [and daughters]'.[30] Implicit in this is an ambition to move towards political integration as a means to accentuating Africa's standing in the world. Thus the premise and promise that Africa ought to chart its own course has been and remains central to the narrative of Pan-Africanism.

Non-alignment, on the other hand, was largely a diplomatic ethic that sought to provide individual member countries with the freedom and the tools to rise above the lure of ideological blocs associated with the politics of Cold War bipolar rivalry. One of the key resolutions of the Belgrade Declaration noted that 'the non-aligned countries represented at this Conference do not wish to form a new bloc and cannot be a bloc'.[31] As Ali Mazrui notes, whilst the ultimate undertaking of Pan-Africanism has been the desire for a more powerful Africa in world politics, the ultimate objective of non-alignment was to reconcile Africa's vulnerability with a degree of diplomatic freedom.[32] The desire for power may complement the ambition for freedom to the extent that as the progenies of Pan-Africanism and non-alignment, these elements are 'different aspects of the same ethical orientation'.[33]

There was divergence in the interfaces between Pan-Africanism and non-alignment. Continental unity as an ultimate ambition of Pan-Africanism has meant that the failure of achieving it would subject the continent into a 'bloc of like-minded African states'.[34] What this points to is that the disparities in the orientation of Pan-Africanism and non-alignment suggest that the two were not wholly complementary in a manner it was generally assumed they were. Of course, the divisive politics of the Cold War encouraged this divergence to the extent that the orientation of non-alignment and Pan-Africanism assumed defensive interfaces as means of resistance to bipolar rivalry and the disunity and marginalisation it was capable of creating. And so where Pan-African ideals approached this with unity as power, proponents of non-alignment proposed *freedom* and *individuality* in the conduct and politics of interstate relations. Taken together, though, Pan-Africanism and non-alignment

---

[30] K. Nkrumah, *I Speak of Freedom: A Statement of African Ideology* (London: Heinemann, 1961), p. 125.
[31] Proceedings of the Belgrade Conference, p. 256.
[32] Mazrui, *Towards a Pax Africana*, p. 165.   [33] *Ibid.*, p. 167.   [34] *Ibid.*, p. 175.

provided independent Africa with the spaces to project an affirmation of relevance in international society. Mazrui puts it succinctly:

> The desire for power and the desire for freedom together amount to an African quest for significance. It is a desire to assert what in a more straightforward idiom would be the proposition that 'Africa matters in the world'. Pending the formation of a continental or sub-continental African federation nothing has contributed more to the feeling that 'Africa matters in the world' than the part which African states have been able to play in the cold war and as a result of the cold war.[35]

But the interaction between Pan-Africanism and non-alignment 'introduced' Africa to an alliance with a collective of countries of the eastern and central European bloc whose traditional political constituency was moderated through communist and socialist dogmas. The Cold War provided the platform through which this was facilitated. The interaction raised questions as to the compatibility of Pan-Africanism with communist precepts and practices. The close ties between communist states and a fair number of African political leaders was a development frowned upon by prominent Pan-Africanists in America and the Caribbean. In fact George Padmore, who had previously expressed sympathy with communism, did attempt to tilt the pendulum towards a more prioritised Pan-African movement. Writing in the 1950s, Padmore wrestled with this issue and ultimately concluded that in the 'struggle for national freedom, human dignity and social redemption, Pan-Africanism offers an ideological alternative to communism'.[36] His optimism was welded to the belief that Pan-Africanism is less tribal as it operates well above the narrow confines of class, race and religion.[37] The Soviets, of course, disagreed with Padmore's attempt at drawing nuances and subjectivised battlegrounds. This view reflected the growing divide in the direction of Pan-Africanism during the Cold War. From this perspective, the Cold War further consolidated the intellectual and geographic separation of Pan-Africanism from its original American and Caribbean roots.

In sum, Pan-Africanism, as Horace Campbell notes, embodies the search for dignity, one that has gone through numerous iterations in the recent and distant past.[38] In other ways also, Pan-Africanism has

---

[35] *Ibid.*, p. 165.

[36] G. Padmore, *Pan-Africanism or Communism? The Coming Struggle for Africa* (London: Dobson, 1956), p. 379.

[37] *Ibid.*

[38] H. G. Campbell, 'Walter Rodney and Pan-Africanism Today', paper presented at the Africana Studies Research Centre, Cornell University, Ithaca, New York. Africa

been a constant phenomenon in Africa's norms formulation and institution-building processes. It has remained a point of reference for the promotion of unity and the advancement of integration initiatives. During the Cold War, Pan-Africanism acquired a certain mutation that sought to assert Africa's relevance in world politics and, in the process, drew lines of interfaces with the non-aligned movement. Pan-African ideology has acquired renewed relevance in Africa's search for an endogenous order capable of advancing the course of the continent and its people. In the process, the ideology has been reinterpreted and recalibrated to make it relevant, functional and focused on Africa's quest for a progressive future.

Cold War impact and its aftermath

The proposition that the Cold War had significant political, economic and social impact on Africa is now generally accepted. The nature of this impact ranged from the specific to the broad. On the political front, a large part of Africa became entangled in the dynamics of bipolar rivalry and competing interests. The struggles of the erstwhile major powers for influence on the continent and the corresponding clamour for alignment on the part of African countries resulted in an ideological divide in Africa. The divide generated distrust, reducing a substantial part of Africa to the influence and dictates of external powers. This was such a prominent feature of the Cold War that the choice of a particular country's political leaders – a natural prerogative of citizens – was being determined by, and aligned to, the competing national interests of Cold War protagonists. Those leaders who resisted were violently overthrown, mostly through externally orchestrated military coups. Consequently, one of the primary casualties was Africa's claim to sovereign governance.

The bipolar configuration of Cold War politics impacted the economic and social spheres considerably. Political alignment created a sense of a 'pastoral' clientele that thrived on economic dependence. What this meant was that African countries sought to benefit from the economic and military might of the particular power they were aligned to. Whilst national economies became disproportionately dependent on the largesse of the aligned external powers, the capacity of those countries to forge a future independent of Cold War politics became

Colloquium Series, 28 September 2005, available at www.library.cornell.edu/africana/lecture/campbell.pdf (last visited June 2011).

increasingly doubtful. The inhabitants of Cold War client states did not fare any better either. Their expectations of national statehood and the freedom it was meant to embody were betrayed by alignment with the geopolitical interests of external powers. The inability to manifest sovereign autonomy impinged on the capacity of individuals to freely fulfil their aspirations outside the milieu of Cold War clientele politics, the reason being that Cold War alignment generally limited the scope of cross-cultural dialogue to countries that had common ideological strands. What existed outside of their territories became, for the most part, an element of painful curiosity.

Perhaps the most defining impact of the Cold War on Africa, as was discussed in Chapter 3, pertains to the recurrence of violence and conflicts. Cold War ideological orientations accentuated social and political divides, which almost always ended up fomenting social discord. This ideological warfare disrupted already fragile post-independence transitions in much of African postcoloniality. One major result was the emergence of proxy wars which had devastating effects on lives, property and national economies. Resources that could potentially have made vital contributions to critical sectors were diverted to fund exorbitantly expensive wars. Initially attempts were made, through the nonalignment movement, to contain the ills, hindrances and excesses of the Cold War in Africa. But their effects on conflicts were limited, in part because the OAU as a progeny of the prevailing international order neither had the normative instruments nor the institutional capacity to confront the scourge of conflicts.

The end of the Cold War was a welcome respite for Africa, for with it there emerged an opportunity to shed some of the hitherto defining ideological effects of the process. Gone were the bipolar rivalry and the pastoral clientele relationship that it manifested in Africa. However, the aftermath also exposed the scale of dependence of many African states on the United States and the former Soviet Union. Deprived of crucial external support, many of the bipolar client states had to face new challenges whose scope tested their capacity to sustain themselves. Many struggled and gradually faced institutional disintegration, civil war and, in some instances, prolonged disintegration as exemplified by the case of Somalia. The new challenges further exposed the weaknesses of the OAU and galvanised some initiatives aimed at transforming Africa's normative and institutional settings.

The first serious attempt to address this came at the 1990 OAU Heads of State and Government summit. The summit was poignant on two levels. First, it came on the fringes of the immediate aftermath of the Cold War. The period was unsettling considering the dilemmas faced by many countries that had excessively relied on the largesse and political support of the two superpowers. For most of Africa's political leadership present at the summit, the uncertainty that loomed required concerted responses lest their countries and the continent's institutions be condemned to an even more disempowering appendage of international society. Second, some of the variegated vestiges of the aftermath of the Cold War had begun to aggravate layers of tragedies in some countries in the form of internal conflicts, food shortages and weak state institutions. All these, of course, were happening with the backdrop of an increasingly alienated OAU. Once again, the vulnerability of Africa was laid bare.

The response from the summit was a series of initiatives, some rhetorical, others pragmatic. The Declaration of the Assembly of Heads of State and Government, whilst acknowledging the problems and challenges faced by Africa, reaffirmed the leaders' 'commitment to revive the ideals of Pan-Africanism' so as to maintain unity and solidarity as well as 'face the challenges of the decades of the 1990s and beyond'.[39] The Declaration concluded that the objectives set out by the summit 'will be constrained so long as an atmosphere of lasting peace and stability does not prevail in Africa'.[40] Thus although the end of the Cold War ushered in uncertainty and unsettling episodes, it nonetheless provided the rallying ground for the preliminary formulation of the processes that subsequently led to the transition from the OAU to the African Union.

Fears of globalisation and marginalisation

Globalisation has become both cherished and feared. Straddling many civilisations and invoking varying perceptions, globalisation is an increasingly powerful phenomenon which, according to Robert Keohane, 'means the shrinkage of distance on a worldwide scale through the emergence and thickening of networks of connections'.[41] Andrew Hurrell and Ngaire Woods have also underscored the importance of globalisation in the

---

[39] *Declaration of the Assembly of Heads of State and Government of the Organisation of African Unity on the Political and Socio-economic Situation in Africa and the Fundamental Changes Taking Place in the World*, 11 July 1990, Twenty-sixth session of AHSG.

[40] *Ibid.*, para.11.

[41] R. O. Keohane, 'Governance in a Partially Globalized World', *American Political Science Review*, 95:1 (2001), 1–13 at 1.

rhetoric of contemporary international relations, describing its elements as a 'process of increasing interdependence and global enmeshment which occurs as money, people, images, values, and ideas flow ever more swiftly and smoothly across national boundaries'.[42] Despite the optimistic ambitions and realm of possibilities in which it is often depicted, globalisation's growing entrenchment continues to raise a number of concerns and fears.

The entrenchment unfolds through what Joe Oloka-Onyango calls a 'complex set of developments often operating in contradictory, oppositional or even conflictual manner'.[43] The fears and uncertainty this generates often shape responses and initiatives aimed at containing its excesses. In the context of Africa, the fears of globalisation are exacerbated by the continent's past encounters and historical susceptibility to concepts and phenomena that take universalism as a departure point. Part of the fears initially hinged on the perception that globalisation can disrupt frames of identity, exacerbate margins of socio-economic differences, introduce security risks and undermine good governance in Africa.[44] Other elements of the fears have been drawn from the divisive character of globalisation and its overhyped prescriptive qualities. In his farewell address to the UN General Assembly as Secretary General in 2006, Kofi Annan emphasised that 'globalization is not a tide that lifts all boats' and that 'even among those who the statistics tell us are benefiting many are deeply insecure, and strongly resent the apparent complacency of those more fortunate than themselves'.[45]

The scepticisms suggest that whilst it is good to embrace the positive affirmations of globalisation, it is imperative also to put in place mechanisms to contain its excesses. In Africa, the urge for containment has been largely conceived and pursued through continental institutional structures made possible by the end of the Cold War. Central to this approach is the determination to confront the recurrence of violence and

---

[42] A. Hurrell and N. Woods, 'Globalization and Inequality', *Millennium*, 25:3 (1995), 447–70 at 447.

[43] J. Oloka-Onyango, 'Globalisation in the Context of Increased Incidents of Racism, Racial Discrimination and Xenophobia', Working Paper of the United Nations Sub-Commission on the Promotion and Protection of Human Rights, 22 June 1999 (E/CN4/Sub2/1999/8), para. 2.

[44] Makinda and Okumu, *The African Union*, p. 2.

[45] K. Annan, 'Ten Years After: A Farewell Statement to the UN General Assembly', 19 September 2006, at www.un.org/News/ossg/sg/stories/statments_search_full.asp?statID=4 (last visited June 2011).

armed conflicts, underdevelopment and marginalisation. Tiyanjana Maluwa is adamant that integral to the political context within which the transformations from the OAU to the African Union should be understood is the reality of the threats and challenges of globalisation and Africa's response to them.[46] Thus the African Union, Maluwa explains, is 'predicated on the premise that the construction of a large integrated regional bloc is the only efficient response to the challenge of globalisation'.[47] Pusch Commey also suggests that 'globalisation and the need for a fundamental change of the iniquitous international economic system' have been responsible for the overhaul of the OAU and the creation of the African Union.[48]

A major fear of globalisation is the concern that its vestiges may result in the marginalisation of Africa. One of the many features of globalisation is the ability to penetrate boundaries and thereby gather the world into a global village. The process also makes it possible for competition and inter-cultural dialogue. But given the gaps in the so-called 'digital divide' and the existence of weak production and service industries in Africa, the continent is largely unable to compete on the same levels and terms with other continents. In this respect the need for change and reformation of institutional structures was galvanised by fears of marginalisation. Opinions vary, though, as to the elements most vulnerable to marginalisation. The overwhelming perception is that it is the African state that is most affected. Philip Ndegwa has suggested that marginalisation is not a 'natural and harmless gradual reduction of contacts between African economies and the rest of the world', but that 'what the process actually involves is the deepening of the poverty of an already very poor people, widespread unemployment, political instability and other economic and social hardships'.[49]

Nevertheless, the fears of globalisation, coupled with the effects and aftermath of the Cold War as well as Africa's weak endogenous institutions, made the need for institutional and normative reformation all the more palpable. But the need for containing global power and dominance is not a new argument. Kwame Nkrumah had repeatedly warned

---

[46] T. Maluwa, 'The Constitutive Act of the African Union and Institution Building in Postcolonial Africa', *Leiden Journal of International Law*, 16 (2003), 157–72 at 162.

[47] *Ibid.*

[48] P. Commey, 'African Union – What Next?', *New African*, 1:410 (September 2002), 12–17.

[49] P. Ndegwa, 'Africa and the World: Africa on its Own' in O. Obasanjo and F. G. N. Mosha (eds.), *Africa: Rise to Challenge* (Otta: Africa Leadership Forum, 1992), p. 13.

in the 1960s that Africa's strength and future relevance reside in its ability to withstand manipulative externalities. To mitigate these he suggested that Africa needed a united and integrated front if it wanted to 'become one of the greatest forces for good in the world'.[50] It is perhaps the interfaces between those early rhetorical snapshots on the need for a united and integrated Africa in tackling external forces and marginalisation that have made the Pan-African dimension of post-Cold War transformations in Africa all the more profound. The end of the Cold War heightened fears and accentuated the need for reform, especially with the backdrop of the increasing irrelevance of the OAU. As C. A. Parker and D. Rukare observe, the time for genuine reformation could not have been more appropriate, and 'by the time of its thirtieth anniversary, most analysts of the OAU concluded that the organisation could not meet future demands without serious reforms and reorganisation'.[51]

Transition from the OAU to the African Union

At the beginning of the 1990s the OAU had become so disconnected from the realities and challenges of post-Cold War Africa that it was generally acknowledged, and even echoed, by some of Africa's most ardent apologists that the institution needed a major or complete overhaul. Although it is hard to determine the specific defining epoch that triggered the need for normative and institutional transformation, it is plausible to suggest that the inability of the OAU to confront violence and conflicts, especially in the 1990s, and the broader challenges of an increasingly globalised world, were the major factors. Pan-Africanism provided the rallying baton and battle-cry for the acceleration of reforms. The urge for transformation was therefore more inevitable than accidental. But in the run-up to the transition process from the OAU to the African Union, other factors were also at play that helped provide the essential narrative and political synergy to translate ambitions into practical outcomes. This was manifested through a battle for ideas fronted by leading personalities from three major countries.

---

[50] Nkrumah, *The Autobiography*, p. 9.
[51] C. A. Parker and D. Rukare, 'The New African Union and its Constitutive Act', *American Journal of International Law*, 96:2 (2002), 367–9 at 367.

Battle for ideas in the quest for continental reform[52]

The final prelude to the transition from the OAU to the African Union was characterised by disagreement and accommodation of competing political, ideological and individual strategic interests.[53] This mainly revolved around personalities and countries who intended to arrogate dominant roles in Africa's post-Cold War reformation agenda. The competing interests were at times tense, reminiscent perhaps, of the tempestuous ideological groupings that preceded the founding of the OAU in the early 1960s. The competing dynamics were spearheaded by the political leaderships of Nigeria, Libya and South Africa, accentuated by their desire to shape the ethos and trajectory of continental institution-building. The initiatives were framed around specific domestic circumstances of the three countries and the ambitious personalities of their leaders at the time. But why were the initiatives for reform led by these three countries?

Thomas Kwasi Tieku has identified key factors that propelled Nigeria, Libya and South Africa to the forefront of Africa's institutional reform. In the case of Nigeria, the process began in the late 1990s when the country emerged from military interregnum, steering it onto a pathway to bolster its democratic credentials in a bid to recapture lost glory in Africa's geopolitics. Coinciding with general disaffection with the OAU, the country's leadership saw an opening through which Nigerian foreign policy influence could be exerted to shape the direction of continental institutional reform. Like Nigeria, South Africa had also emerged from a difficult period – apartheid and the international isolationism it embodied. South Africa's readmission to international diplomacy provided it with a platform to formulate a foreign policy framework that could promote stability and democratic culture across Africa.[54] For Libya, its poor international image following prolonged isolation generated considerable political desperation in the context of widespread disenchantment with its domestic constituents. International transformations in the aftermath of the Cold War brought an opportunity for Ghaddaffi to attempt an exercise in image-building.[55]

---

[52] The perspectives, and to some extent organisation, of this section have significantly benefitted from Thomas Kwasi Tieku, who was perhaps the first scholar to seriously excavate some of the deeper underlying factors that triggered the transformation from the OAU to the Africa Union. See T. Kwasi Tieku, 'Explaining the Clash and Accommodation of Interests of Major Actors in the Creation of the African Union', *African Affairs*, (2004), 249–67.

[53] *Ibid.*, at 253.   [54] *Ibid.*, at 253–5.   [55] *Ibid.*, at 261.

The specific circumstances of the three countries and the desire of their respective political leaderships to influence Africa's future found an appropriate interface in a dysfunctional OAU and a continent very much in need of an organised narrative in a period of rising frustration. Subsequent attempts to claim ownership over the transformation from the OAU to the African Union became straddled with competing viewpoints which converged in the personalities of Thabo Mbeki, Olusegun Obasanjo and Muammar Ghaddaffi, who made different propositions as to how and what a new African organisation should constitute. Whilst their ambition for Africa was similar, the approaches to achieving it were as diverse as their respective personalities. And so to understand the founding of the African Union's purpose and design, it is imperative to put in context the broader interests and visions that the three main actors tried to reflect. These appeared in the shape of the quest for African Renaissance, normative formulation through the African Leadership Forum and a resurgence of 'radical' Pan-Africanism.

Thabo Mbeki's African Renaissance

The fall of apartheid in 1990 unshackled South Africa from a certain isolation directed towards it, particularly from African states. The new order availed the country the opportunity to be involved in tackling wider challenges facing Africa. In the pursuit of this goal the new governing African National Congress (ANC) set out to formulate a vision of an Africa that was receptive to the values of good governance, human rights and liberal internationalism.[56] A perception emerged that for South Africa to progress it must calibrate its policy objectives and visions to speak to and with Africa. It appears that at some stage the ANC was so devoted to this line of thinking that there is a genetic link between its post-apartheid visions and the narrative of the African Union.[57] But the acquired responsibilities of the new South Africa appeared to impose a layer of burden and challenges on the country's political leadership.

The ANC had been enmeshed in decades of anti-apartheid struggles that moulded its policies, political rhetoric and support base from an overwhelmingly ideological standpoint which had the potential of being inconsistent with South Africa's post-apartheid international engagement. The second challenge was that after decades of isolation within

---

[56] *Ibid.*, at 253.   [57] *Ibid.*

Africa, South Africa was eager to play a part in international diplomacy, especially in the processes of Africa's normative formulation and institutional reformation. The presence of a revered figure in Nelson Mandela made South Africa's eagerness all the more palpable.[58] But these factors also meant that the ANC had to abandon its populist and socialist ideas and the radical ideological rhetoric upon which they were framed, and advance towards liberal internationalism.[59] The first major opportunity for Mandela to unveil his country's vision arose at the 1994 OAU summit in Tunisia, where he spoke of a South Africa that 'would use its abilities and potentials to help advance the common struggle to secure Africa's rightful place within the world'.[60] Mandela pursued this line of policy, and where the opportunity arose he was determined to make clear his views on important issues affecting Africa's progress, even at the risk of antagonising some of his peers. It was Mandela's uncompromising stance on the improvement of the social plight and human rights situation in Africa that culminated in a fierce confrontation with General Sani Abacha, the late Nigerian military dictator.[61] This outreach approach was a rare departure from the OAU's culture of non-interference, which Mandela was not only challenging, but perhaps also hoping to highlight by drawing attention to the absurdities that characterise the continental legal architecture, and by so doing, help provoke efforts aimed at promoting a more people-centred normative order.

Thabo Mbeki, the successor to the South African presidency, had been an understudy to Mandela for many years and showed some determination to pursue an agenda of reform. Mbeki's Africa policy was framed around the belief that for South Africa to prosper it must align its interests to, and seek, social integration as well as political and economic stability in Africa.[62] He gradually reshaped and expanded the concept of 'African Renaissance', which he had earlier popularised as Deputy President.[63] Mbeki's vision was essentially an aspiration for a kind of

---

[58] *Ibid.*, at 253–4.   [59] *Ibid.*, at 253.

[60] N. Mandela, 'Statement of the President of the Republic of South Africa at the OAU Heads of State and Government Summit', Tunisia, 1994, www.search.gov.za/info/ previewDocument.jsp (last visited April 2010).

[61] C. Lansberg, 'Promoting Democracy: The Mandela-Mbeki Doctrine', *Journal of Democracy*, 11:3 (2000), 107–21 at 110.

[62] *Ibid.*, at 109–10.

[63] T. Mbeki, 'The African Renaissance', 13 August 1998, www.anc.org.za/ancdocs/history/ mbeki/1998/tm0813.htm (last visited April 2010).

change that could overhaul some of Africa's dysfunctional institutional settings. In its literal meaning, 'Renaissance' implies a revival or renewal of interest in an idea, object or order.[64] This is often sought where an existing system lacks the capacity to produce progressive outcomes. In a speech to the United Nations University before assuming the South African presidency, Mbeki idealised for Africa 'a system of government in which the people are empowered to determine their destiny and to resolve any disputes among themselves by peaceful political means'.[65] He emphasised that Africa's problems cannot be tackled solely by its weak institutional structures, and that an approach that combines institutional and normative reform was needed to accelerate integration and interdependence. He continued:

> We are trying to convey the message that African underdevelopment must be a matter of concern to everybody else in the world, that the victory of the African Renaissance addresses not only the improvement of the conditions of life of the peoples of Africa but also the extension of the frontiers of human dignity to all humanity. Accordingly, we believe that it is important that the international community should agree that Africa constitutes the principal development challenge in the world.[66]

It was the beginning of his African Renaissance project, some of which subsequently filtered through to the normative framework of the African Union. The renewal implied a redirection of focus sufficient to advance a collectively defined agenda for the purpose of initiating social change and integration as means towards achieving conditions of peace, development, social justice and responsible governance. At the 1998 Africa Renaissance Conference, Mbeki elaborated on the tenets of renewal as an undertaking for 'making foreign to Africa the disempowerment of the masses' and accordingly wanting 'to see an African continent in which people participate in systems of governance ... and put behind us the notions of democracy and human rights as particularly Western concepts'.[67] The shift in rhetoric not only symbolised an elevation of a particular kind of consciousness, but also suggested a renewed political advocacy for an integrated Africa that would accelerate development

---

[64] *Concise Oxford English Dictionary* (Oxford University Press, 2006), p. 1217.

[65] T. Mbeki, 'The African Renaissance, South Africa and the World', speech at the United Nations University, 9 April 1998, www.unu.edu/unupress/mbeki.html (last visited April 2010).

[66] *Ibid.*

[67] 'Statement by Deputy President Mbeki at the African Renaissance Conference, Johannesburg, 28 September 1998', www.anc.org.za.andocs/history/mbeki/1998tm0928.htm (last visited April 2010).

and confront violence and conflicts. It was within this framework that Mbeki's renaissance vision represented a sense of African political consciousness which shaped some of the values of the Constitutive Act of the African Union.

It is worth noting, however, that Mbeki's renaissance conception had been informed by a combination of intervening historical factors and contemporary socio-political expediencies. From a normative perspective, Mbeki's renaissance was an amalgamation of these influences and reflections of the internal reorientation of the ANC. 'Renaissance' also had certain African features that suggested a consolidation of Pan-Africanism and a reconstitution of its functional ideals in a post-Cold War context. The crucial difference here is in the modifications Mbeki injected into Pan-Africanism through renaissance, with the view to reflecting the contingent problems and needs of Africa and its particular response to global economic and political forces. For Mbeki, the object of renaissance was to recharacterise Pan-Africanism to enable a rebirth of Africa.[68] This embodied a vision of a dynamic, stable and integrated Africa. It was these elements that persuaded him to push for the overhaul of the OAU. At the 1999 Algiers OAU Summit, Mbeki generated a political consensus on the need for institutional reformation so as to facilitate integration, cultivation of democratic culture and principles of rule of law.[69]

The ALF and the quest for normative formulation

In addition to Mbeki's attempt to push for continental reform, Nigeria's Olusegun Obasanjo also played a pivotal role in the transition from the OAU to the African Union. Like Mbeki, Obasanjo's vision for Africa was shaped by precepts of modernised Pan-Africanism and the propagation of sets of values for a progressive Africa. In 1988, Obasanjo created the Nigeria-based African Leadership Forum (ALF), whose aim is to enhance the quality of leadership and responsible governance in Africa.[70] The ALF operates as an independent think tank, and its role in

---

[68] T. Mbeki, 'Statement at the 35th Ordinary Session of the OAU Assembly of Heads of State and Government', Algiers, 13 July 1999, www.thepresidency.gov.za/president/sp/1999/tm0713.html (last visited April 2010).

[69] Assembly of Heads of State and Government, Thirty-fifth Ordinary Session of the OAU, 12–14 July 1999, AHG/Dec.1 (XXXV).

[70] Africa Leadership Forum, 'Vision and Mission', www.africaleadership.org/Missionobjectives.htm (last visited April 2010).

shaping the ethos of the African Union is often undervalued. Through Obasanjo's guidance and initiatives, the ALF formed partnerships with civil society groups and multilateral donor agencies such as the United Nations Economic Commission for Africa (ECA), Organisation for Cooperation and Security in Europe (OCSE) and the OAU. A series of workshops were subsequently organised with the objectives of generating norms to 'initiate a process capable of operationalizing emerging para- digms, concepts and new attitudes as a means of increasing the capacity of the continent to deal with its own problems'.[71]

In May 1991, the Kampala Forum was convened as a constituent of a deliberative process in the search for Africa's appropriate response to issues relating to security, stability, integration, democratic governance and human rights.[72] The forum culminated in the adoption of a pro- posal for a Conference on Security, Stability, Development and Cooper- ation in Africa (CSSDCA).[73] Known also as the Kampala Document, the CSSDCA represents an important framework that embodies a collective ambition for responsive governance, peace, security and development through cooperation and integration. Obasanjo's election as Nigerian President in 1999 provided the political platform that was to later help in the transformation of the CSSDCA into a major reference point for policy formulation in Africa.

Obasanjo's political offering to the CSSDCA was an impassioned appeal to the 1999 OAU Algiers Summit, where he urged his colleagues to adopt the Kampala Document as the guiding framework for Africa's pathway to an integrated normative order.[74] But the more subtle significance of the summit related to the emergence of a part- nership between Mbeki and Obasanjo, one that was perhaps borne out of the desire of the former to promote his African Renaissance against the latter's ALF normative principles. Despite variances in

---

[71] Africa Leadership Forum, 'Origins of the Conference on Security, Stability, Development and Cooperation in Africa', www.africaleadership.org/CSSDCA.htm (last visited April 2010).

[72] The forum was attended by heads of government, academics, civil society groups, trade unionists and senior officials from donor agencies. For informed commentary on the scope and dynamics of the Kampala Forum, see F. M. Deng and I. W. Zartman (eds.), *A Strategic Vision for Africa: The Kampala Movement* (Washington, DC: The Brookings Institution Press, 2002).

[73] O. Obasanjo and F. G. N. Mosha (eds.), *Africa Rise to the Challenge: Conference Report on the Kampala Forum* (Abeokuta/New York: Africa Leadership Forum, 1992).

[74] See Tieku, 'Explaining the Clash and Accommodation of Interests', at 259–60.

individual interests and competing philosophical strands, their visions were reconcilable in so far as their overriding objective was to initiate reform. Noticeable too, were the flickers of similarities and relative consensus that existed on the need to overhaul the OAU and pursue an internalisation agenda of responsive governance, rule of law, security, development and integration initiatives in Africa.

The need for the actualisation of the ethos underpinning the agenda for reform compelled Mbeki and Obasanjo to appreciate the extent to which 'they needed each other to provide the leadership and the sustained political will to drive the reform process'.[75] In a sense, what the enforced *entente cordiale* did was to help create a mutual point of convergence that facilitated the CSSDCA initiative to function as a framework for reform. The tacit support for Obasanjo's 'strategic vision for Africa' provided him the impetus with which to build on. On 28 August 1999, Obasanjo co-chaired a consultative meeting in Abuja, Nigeria. Its primary focus was to mobilise further support and initiate the groundwork for the full integration of the CSSDCA into the OAU structure.[76] Official recognition was finally accorded to the CSSDCA at the 1999 OAU Summit held in Sirte, Libya. The Sirte Summit adopted a resolution requesting the OAU Secretariat to convene a Ministerial Conference that would study the CSSDCA initiative. The conference was held in Abuja in May 2000.

Ever since its cooptation and subsequent formalisation into the OAU processes, the CSSDCA has remained an invaluable policy reference and norms formulation outlet. Its significance and the period from which the process emerged have also meant that the CSSDCA has had a profound influence not only on the transition from OAU to African Union, but also on the shaping of the institutional architecture and normative order that emerged thereafter. Fundamentally, the CSSDCA provided the much-needed compass for policy definition for African institutions and agencies at a time of unsettling uncertainty in international society.[77] In fact the foundational principles embedded in the Constitutive Act and other African Union institutional instruments owe a great deal to the values espoused in the CSSDCA. This was clearly acknowledged by the African Heads of State and Government at the official launch of the African Union.

[75] Francis, *Uniting Africa*, p. 28.   [76] See ALF, 'Vision and Mission'.   [77] *Ibid.*

The CSSDCA process has added an urgent and vital dynamism and vigour to the activities of the OAU/AU Secretariat. It has provided a forum for the progressive development and advancement of common values and a structure that consolidates the constructive implementation of the agendas of the Political and Community Affairs Department by relating activities in the sphere of security, stability, development and cooperation more closely to each other and interfacing their initiatives.[78]

The ALF's quest for normative formulation accounts for, and constitutes, an important part of the genesis and narrative of the African Union. Obasanjo's role has been – in both his personal capacity as a statesman and through his leadership of the ALF – crucial in keeping up the momentum necessary for the creation of what he has described as a 'comprehensive and a systematic regional framework with the adequate mechanisms to effectively address and simultaneously solve ... interrelated [African] problems'.[79] With the support and collaboration of a number of agencies, and the political partnership with Mbeki, Obasanjo's task was to ensure that a bargaining point was opened for the 'diffusion' and accommodation of competing strands and interests. Yet the Mbeki–Obasanjo partnership was not, on its own, sufficient to bring about the reforms the duo set out to achieve. For that to happen, they needed the exuberance, forceful charm and idiosyncrasy of an unlikely ally, Colonel Muammar Ghaddaffi.

Pan-Africanism and the Ghaddaffi factor

With its history and flexible orientations, the capacity of Pan-Africanism to adapt to changing circumstances as well as initiate transformational reforms is profound, as evident in the various stages of its evolution. But Ghaddaffi's entry into the sequel of the African Union's narrative was an improbable prospect, not least because his reputation, controversial personality and divisive politics seemed irreconcilable with the kind of reforms Mbeki and Obasanjo had occupied themselves with. Yet his role in the transition to the African Union is not by any means peripheral. Ghaddaffi's expressed desire to be involved in Africa's institutional

---

[78] Assembly of Heads of State and Government, Thirty-eighth Ordinary Session of the Organisation of African Unity, *Decision on the Conference on Security, Stability, Development and Cooperation*, AHG/Dec.175 (XXXVIII).

[79] O. Obasanjo, 'Opening Statement at the Brainstorming Meeting on Conference on Security, Stability, Development and Co-operation in Africa', Addis Ababa, 17–18 November 1990.

transformations was demonstrated by his eagerness to convene an extra-ordinary summit at his home town of Sirte, Libya, in September 1999. The aim of the summit was 'to discuss ways and means of making the OAU effective so as to keep pace with the political and economic developments taking place in the world and the preparation required of Africa within the context of globalisation so as to preserve its social, economic and political potentials'.[80]

But of course Ghaddaffi's opportune involvement also exposed his own vision for Africa. This was particularly important given that for most of the 1990s Libya was ostracised in the wake of allegations of human rights abuses and terrorist activities. The end of the Cold War brought an opportunity for Ghaddaffi to begin a rehabilitation exercise that would include attempts at rebranding Libya and himself.[81] The Sirte Summit provided him with a platform to launch his 'comeback' and add his voice to the quest for continental reform.[82] But unlike Mbeki and Obasanjo, whose Pan-African visions were distilled with integrated normative values, Ghaddaffi's vision was suffused with residues of radical Pan-Africanism, evident in the proposals he presented to the summit.

The perception of many African leaders was that although there was sympathy for Ghaddaffi's proposals, the magnitude of reform needed for Africa at what was a particularly critical time transcended the emancipatory rhetoric upon which his proposals were couched. Thus the lack of consensus on the proposals from Mbeki, Obasanjo and Ghaddaffi culminated in compromise between those who wanted a revolutionary approach and those who opted for a gradualist approach.[83] The Sirte Summit chose to pursue a moderate approach to continental reform, aligning strongly with Obasanjo's CSSDCA process, whilst also endorsing Mbeki's renaissance conception, especially its affirmation of the need to cultivate good governance and values predicated on the rule of law. At the July 2000 OAU Summit in Lomé, Togo, a Constitutive Act forming the basis for the African Union structures was adopted. Ghaddaffi's radical rendition of Pan-Africanism had reached a dead-end. But this

---

[80] Assembly of Heads of State and Government, Thirty-fifth Ordinary Session of the OAU, 12–14 July 1999, AHG/Dec.140 (XXXV).

[81] Tieku, 'Explaining the Clash and Accommodation of Interests', at 261.

[82] A. Huliaras, 'Qadhafi's Comeback: Libya and Sub-Saharan Africa in the 1990s', *African Affairs*, 100:398 (2001), 5–25 at 17.

[83] B. Kioko, 'The Right of Intervention under the African Union's Constitutive Act: From Non-interference to Non-intervention', *International Review of the Red Cross*, 85:852 (2003), 807–25 at 811.

was by no means a defeat for Pan-Africanism. Rather, it was a restatement of the wisdom underpinning the concept's long history – that it is neither static nor homogeneous, and thus has the remarkable quality and capacity of adopting and adapting to changing political, social and economic circumstances. Africa's endogenous institution-building foreshadows the patterns and depths of the institutionalisation of Pan-Africanism. The normative formulation agenda of the African Union is in many ways part of a sequence of the transformative dimensions of Pan-Africanism.

Although his proposal hardly won favour amongst African leaders, Ghaddaffi's inputs must not be totally discounted. His personal resolve combined with a fiery Pan-African rhetoric accelerated the pace for the overhaul of the OAU. Equally important was his persistence in arguing, at least at the Sirte Summit, that the political energies of the competing powers must be synchronised to make the necessary reforms possible. This, in effect, rallied African leaders to appreciate the significance of a collectively defined agenda, as demonstrated in the Sirte Declaration. Tiyanjana Maluwa provides a good summation of the significance of the declaration:

> The Sirte Declaration represents a significant step in the march towards the renewal, consolidation and repositioning of the OAU. It was born out of the perceived need to strengthen the continental organisation and to rekindle the aspirations of the African people for further unity, solidarity and cohesion in a larger community transcending linguistic, ideological, ethnic and national differences. In adopting the declaration, African leaders apparently recognised that the continent would be stronger and the collective voices of the African nations more effective, if all African were involved in the establishment of a community of peoples.[84]

The final transition and transformation of the OAU was completed with the adoption of the Constitutive Act of the African Union in 2001 and the launch of the African Union in July 2002. By a twist of irony, the energetic Ghaddaffi, who had so passionately envisioned an Africa driven by the wishes of its people, was to himself deny the voices of disenchantment in his own Libya, culminating in his violent overthrow through a peoples' uprising in 2011. He died soon after his capture in circumstances yet to be fully established.

---

[84] T. Maluwa, 'Re-imagining African Unity: Some Preliminary Reflections on the Constitutive Act of the African Union', *African Yearbook of International Law*, (2002), 3–38 at 21.

Conclusion

The genesis of, and the process leading to, the reformation of Africa's institutional and normative framework has been the product of a long history, one that has meandered through Africa's fears, crises and vulnerabilities. The urge to mitigate them has also meant that there is often a sense of desperation and expectation in the continent's endogenous institutions and their potential to confront challenges of often great magnitude. One constant in this quest for answers, however, has been the resurgence of Pan-Africanism as an ideological variable and a reference point for social consciousness, political synergy and continental institutional reformation. And like the founding of the OAU, Pan-Africanism has been central to the creation of the African Union. Its transformative orientation makes it possible for kinds of adoption and adaptations that may cope with changing circumstances. Yet other external intervening factors had to come into play, especially in the aftermath of the Cold War. Transformations in international society presented an opportunity for the recasting of Africa's institutional and normative ordering.

But above all, however, the transition from the OAU to the African Union must also be understood in the broader context of the pervasiveness of postcolonial African conflicts. Over the past decades, the intensity and effects of armed conflicts have posed numerous challenges to Africa's leadership and political institutions. The scale of these conflicts and the many actors that characterised them had almost always overwhelmed the capacity of indigenous institutions to deal with them. Yet despite the OAU providing an interactive political platform for African leaders to engage and reflect, its normative and structural inadequacies could no longer serve as dependable denominators in tackling Africa's postcolonial disorder. Under its watch Africa witnessed a proliferation of problems ranging from violent conflicts, human rights abuses and state institutional failure to deepening impoverishment. In the end, neither Africa's institutions, nor the instruments and structures of international law, could make much difference. But with the disbanding of the OAU, a new instrument – the Constitutive Act of the African Union – was installed as part of attempts to forge a way forward, especially in the context of peacebuilding.

6

Philosophy and structures of the African Union

> No more, never again. Africans cannot . . . watch the tragedies developing in the continent and say it is the UN's responsibility or somebody else's responsibility. We have moved from the concept of non-interference to non-indifference. We cannot as Africans remain indifferent to the tragedy of our people.
>
> Ambassador Said Djinnit[1]

Introduction

The philosophy of the Constitutive Act of the African Union and the structures it formulates hinge on a kind of narrative that taps into the promises of a united, integrated and peaceful Africa. The framework upon which this narrative is anchored takes cue from Africa's perceived and actual vulnerabilities and the imperative for a constant search for alternatives. The narrative's optimistic inclination and Pan-African orientations also imply that it cannot be understood outside the genesis and historical overture of the founding of the African Union. Since the July 2002 official launch in Durban, South Africa, aspects of the African Union's evolving instruments and institutions have together been heralded as a milestone in the evolution of the continent's security architecture and the beginning of a particular kind of African norms formulation agenda. This positive reception stems from the perceived potential of the Constitutive Act of the African Union in not only helping to actualise the aspirations of the people of Africa, but also in providing a window of opportunity through which approaches to violence and conflicts can be conceptualised.

---

[1] Ambassador Said Djinnit, former African Union Peace and Security Commissioner, cited in K. Powell, 'The African Union's Emerging Peace and Security Regime: Opportunities and Challenges for Delivering on the Responsibility to Protect', ISS Monograph Series, 119 (2005), at 1.

Although the inspirations for the paradigmatic shift embodied by the new normative and institutional architecture come from a number of dimensions, they nonetheless signify an admission that conventional modalities for confronting violence and conflicts have had little impact in large parts of Africa. The realisation came in the wake of an apparent institutional paralysis and normative faultlines of the former OAU and their prolonged and combined consequential effects on the political, economic and social conditions of Africa. From this perspective, the emerging African Union's framework is meant to be a conscious representation of a leap into the future and an attempted departure from the muses of past failings. Whilst this leap and what it attempts to achieve could be attributed to a conflation of factors, the perceived departure seeks to ascribe a sense of reorientation of Africa's institutions and norms-creation mechanisms. Although the significance of this shift straddles many areas, its resonance with the search for alternative approaches to the conflict and peace problematic in Africa is profound. In the context of peacebuilding, the reorientation may potentially constitute parameters of what could be termed an African-induced recharacterisation of approaches to internal conflicts.

The constituents of those parameters need, of course, to be determined, assessed and contextualised. So the focus in this chapter is to examine the capacity and depths of the African Union's institutional and normative order. The aim is to gauge not only the specific and broader relevance of this architecture, but also the extent to which it provides viable processes and mechanisms in confronting violence and internal conflicts in Africa. Emphases are placed on the normative principles that underlie the Constitutive Act's peace and security architecture, which attempts an alteration of the international law ethos that conditioned the African postcolonial institutional legal order under the OAU.

Philosophy of the Constitutive Act

Transformations in international society, a resurgence of Pan-Africanism and the convergence of interests and visions of competing actors in African politics provided the final drive for the reformation agenda of the OAU and the subsequent transition to the African Union. A key instrument that embodies this reform agenda is the Constitutive Act of the African Union. The Constitutive Act was adopted by the Assembly of Heads of State and Government of the OAU on 11 July 2000, in the

Togolese capital of Lomé.[2] The Constitutive Act entered into force on 26 May 2001 after the deposit of the required ratification of two-thirds of member states as stipulated by the instrument's Article 28. The African Union was officially launched in Durban, South Africa, in July 2002. Upon ratification of the Constitutive Act, a transition period was provided for to facilitate an orderly devolution. Article 33(1) provides that:

> This Act shall replace the Charter of the Organisation of African Unity. However the Charter shall remain operative for a transitional period of one year or such further period as may be determined by the Assembly, following the entry into force of the Act, for the purpose of enabling the OAU/AEC to undertake the necessary measures regarding the devolution of its assets and liabilities to the Union.[3]

The legal basis for the African Union architecture is provided for by both the UN Charter and the Constitutive Act. By virtue of its founding history as an institution predisposed to the maintenance of international peace and security, the UN Charter opens up the possibility for the creation of regional organisations for purposes generally compatible with those of the UN. The Charter's Article 52 provides that nothing 'precludes the existence of regional arrangements or agencies for dealing with such matters relating to the maintenance of international peace and security as are appropriate for regional action, provided that such arrangements or agencies and their activities are consistent with the Purposes and Principles of the United Nations'. The basis for creation is less detailed in the Constitutive Act. Its Article 2 states, only briefly, that 'the African Union is hereby established in accordance with the principles of this Act'. The Constitutive Act's principles are variously complementary of the UN Charter and thus the legal basis for creation of the African Union corresponds to the object and purposes of the Charter's Article 52.

But unlike the Charter of the defunct OAU, the Constitutive Act falls short of indicating whether the African Union is actually an international organisation bequeathed with the full benefits and privileges of international legal personality.[4] The legal personality of international

---

[2] The Constitutive Act of the African Union, OAU Doc.CAB/LEG23.15 (11 July 2000).

[3] See also OAU *Decision on the Implementation of the Sirte Summit*, Decision of the 37th Ordinary Session of the African Union Assembly of Heads of State and Government, Lusaka, Zambia, July 2001, AHG/Dec.1 (XXXVII), para. 7.

[4] The legal personality of international organisations was recognised by the International Court of Justice in *Reparations for Injuries Suffered in the Service of the United Nations*

organisations essentially relates to their capacity to possess rights and duties that may be enforceable at law. The concept was recognised by the International Court of Justice (ICJ) in the *Reparations for Injuries* case and subsequently reaffirmed in the *Expenses of the United Nations* case.[5] But the extent to which an organisation possesses international legal personality will hinge upon its constitutional arrangements, power and practices.[6] Gino Naldi and Konstantinos Magliveras have suggested that the loose expression of legal personality in the Constitutive Act could be attributed to the logical presumption that the African Union, as a natural successor to the OAU, was expected to inherit its legal personality.[7] In fact, Article 33 of the Constitutive Act – which manages the transitional phase of the new order – is reflective of, and makes considerations for, an organised succession that facilitates the devolution of the assets and liabilities of the OAU to the African Union. The devolution would naturally include privileges, obligations and legal entitlements.

Explicit articulation, though, is not conditional to determining legal personality. In the absence of such articulation, personality could be inferred from the purpose, character, authority and even behaviour of an organisation. This is the most common yardstick of determining personality and was adopted as a settled principle by the ICJ. In determining entitlement of legal personality by the UN, the ICJ emphasises that by entrusting functions to the United Nations with corresponding duties and responsibilities, its members 'have clothed it with the competence required to enable those functions to be effectively discharged'.[8] In another Advisory Opinion, the ICJ indicates that the rationale of the constituent legal instruments of international organisations 'is to create new subjects of law endowed with a certain autonomy, to which the parties entrust the task of realizing common goals'.[9] The responsibilities

---

(1949) ICJ 174. The principle was later reaffirmed in *Certain Expenses of the United Nations* (1962) ICJ Rep. 151. For discussion on the concept see generally J. E. Nijma, *The Concept of International Legal Personality: An Enquiry into the History and Theory of International Law* (The Hague: T. M. C. Asser Press, 2004).

[5] *Reparation for Injuries Suffered in the Service of the United Nations* (1949) ICJ 174; *Certain Expenses of the United Nations* (1962) ICJ Rep. 151.

[6] M. N. Shaw, *International Law* (Cambridge University Press, 2008), p. 260.

[7] G. Naldi and K. D. Magliveras, 'The African Union – A New Dawn for Africa?', *ICQ*, 51 (2002), 415–25 at 415.

[8] See *Reparation* case, at 318.

[9] ICJ Advisory Opinion on Legality of the Use by a State of Nuclear Weapons in Armed Conflict, at para. 19.

and functions of the African Union resonate with the criteria formulated by the ICJ, affirming, in effect, both the organisation's legal basis and its ascription of personality.

The essence of the African Union's legal personality is anchored in, and driven by, the Constitutive Act and its related instruments. As its governing instrument, the Constitutive Act espouses a sense of philosophy that provides the frame of reference for Africa's institutional continental order. In theory, the outreach of the ethos transcends the structural limitations of the defunct OAU and its normative orientation. The potential of the new dispensation is perhaps more profoundly embedded in its attempt, howsoever limited, to envision an integrated approach to violence and conflicts in Africa. As this is the thrust of the book, it is a dimension worth illuminating.

Objectives and principles of the African Union

The Preamble to the Constitutive Act provides a documentary expression of the resolve of African leaders to confront what they view as the multifaceted challenges facing Africa. These are partly situated in the context of the political, economic and social transformations around the world.[10] The Preamble also acknowledges the pervasive nature of the scourge of armed conflicts as a major impediment to the socio-economic development of Africa.[11] In this light, the Preamble goes on to underscore that African leaders are conscious 'of the need to promote peace, security and stability as a prerequisite for the implementation of [Africa's] development and integration agenda'.[12] To achieve this, the Preamble speaks of a determination 'to take all necessary measures to strengthen ... common institutions and provide them with the necessary powers and resources to discharge their respective mandates effectively'.[13]

The Constitutive Act enumerates fourteen objectives that serve as the operational pillars of the African Union. These include an undertaking to achieve greater unity and enhance solidarity in Africa;[14] accelerate political cooperation and socio-economic integration;[15] propagate peace, security and stability;[16] as well as promote and protect human rights, democratic values, good governance and the establishment of appropriate conditions that would enable Africa's participation in

---

[10] Constitutive Act, para. 5.   [11] *Ibid.*, para. 8.   [12] *Ibid.*   [13] *Ibid.*, para. 10.
[14] Article 3(a), Constitutive Act.   [15] Article 3(c), *ibid.*   [16] Article 3(f), *ibid.*

the global economy and related international affairs.[17] The objectives are organically aligned to sets of principles. Article 4 outlines sixteen principles of which four are inherited from Article II of the defunct OAU Charter. The four are sovereign equality of member states,[18] peaceful resolution of disputes amongst member states,[19] non-interference by any member into the internal affairs of another[20] and condemnation and rejection of impunity and political assassination.[21] Their cooptation into the Constitutive Act is testament perhaps to their continued relevance to Africa's socio-legal contexts and the need to institute balance between radical reform and conformity with international legality.

The foundations of those core principles are not, on their own, sufficient to usher in the kinds of transformational changes necessary in shedding the past patrimonies of the OAU. New principles have therefore been added to strengthen the African Union's normative architecture. These include participation of the African people in the activities of the Union,[22] prohibition of the use of force amongst members[23] and the right of the Union to intervene in a member state in respect of grave circumstances such as war crimes, crimes against humanity and genocide.[24] By the same token, member states have a right to request intervention from the Union to restore peace and stability.[25] Other principles of critical value include the promotion of gender equality and social justice,[26] condemnation and rejection of unconstitutional changes of government,[27] respect for the sanctity of human life[28] and creation of a common defence policy.[29]

The Constitutive Act was first amended in July 2003.[30] The amendment constituted the addition of a number of objectives that initially had gone unnoticed or been ignored. For instance, Article 2 of the Preamble has been amended to shed its patriarchal constructs so that the original phrasing of 'founding fathers' was replaced with the more gender-neutral 'founders'. Similarly, Article 3 of the objectives incorporated three new subparagraphs that advocate for the effective participation of women in

---

[17] Article 3(g), (h) and (i), *ibid.*   [18] Article 4(a), *ibid.*   [19] Article 4(e), *ibid.*
[20] Article 4(g), *ibid.*   [21] Article 4(o), *ibid.*   [22] Article 4(c), *ibid.*
[23] Article 4(f), *ibid.* There is a direct correlation between this provision and Article 2(4) of the UN Charter.
[24] Article 4(h), Constitutive Act.   [25] Article 4(j), *ibid.*   [26] Article 4(l), *ibid.*
[27] Article 4(p), *ibid.*   [28] Article 4(o), *ibid.*   [29] Article 4(d), *ibid.*
[30] Protocol on Amendments to the Constitutive Act of the African Union, adopted in Maputo, Mozambique, 11 July 2003, www.africa-union.org/root/au/Documents/Treaties/treaties.htm (last visited April 2010).

decision-making processes,[31] promotion of common policies on trade, defence and foreign relations[32] and the encouragement of the participation of the African diaspora in the advancement of the African Union.[33] Article 4 of the principles has also undergone a minor, yet potentially significant amendment. The provision on the right of the African Union to intervene in the internal affairs of member states has been expanded to cover not only war crimes, crimes against humanity and genocide, but also 'serious threat to legitimate order to restore peace and stability to a Member State'.[34]

The objectives of the African Union have a wider scope than those of the OAU.[35] There are a number of possible reasons for this. First, the OAU was created in the shadows of competing ideological persuasions. Compromises were made that ultimately scaled down the prospects for an institution capable of arrogating broad functions and objectives. Second, most of the OAU's existence coincided with a critical period shaped by the challenges of post-independence political struggles in Africa. The overriding concern at the time was to create a semblance of functionality and survival of newly independent states. Values such as human rights, good governance and social justice were hardly on the agenda of African leaders. The African Union, on the other hand, emerged at a critical juncture of Africa's quest for political renewal, accelerated by transformations in international society. Unlike with the OAU, the difficulties the African Union endured in the build-up to its creation were more a result of the desperate need for reformation than a contestation to it. It would have been a missed opportunity had the African Union's objectives merely replicated those of the OAU.

Like the objectives, the African Union's principles suggest a shift in the continent's ethos, focus and political ideology. Whilst the influence of Pan-African ideals appears strong, other ideals have an integrated normative predisposition considered paramount to Africa's participation in the global world and the containment of some of the effects of globalisation,

---

[31] To be inserted under Article 3(i).   [32] To constitute Article 3(p).

[33] To constitute Article 3(q).   [34] To be incorporated into Article 4(h).

[35] The OAU had only four main objectives, outlined in Article II of its Charter: '(a) to promote the unity and solidarity of the African States; (b) to co-ordinate and intensify their co-operation and efforts to achieve a better life for the peoples of Africa; (c) to defend their sovereignty, their territorial integrity and independence; (d) to eradicate all forms of colonialism from Africa; and (e) to promote international co-operation, having due regard to the Charter of the United Nations and the Universal Declaration of Human Rights'. (See Article II(1) of the OAU Charter, 479 UNTS 39.)

impoverishment and impunity.[36] A major concern associated with globalisation is the potential marginalisation of Africa and the impact it may have not only on the continent's endogenous institutions, but also on the vast expanse of a constituency of people who are vulnerable to, and excluded from, the manifest bearings of globalisation. The narrative which might plausibly lie behind the expanded objectives and principles is the affirmation of the belief that for Africa to develop it must overhaul its institutional structures and initiate a genuine normative transformation, one that is conscious of global changes and the needs of Africans.

Thus taken together, the principles and objectives espoused by the Constitutive Act aspire to create a kind of continental order that seeks to benefit from the essence of Pan-African ideals, harness normative values and accentuate integration and interdependence as important elements in the formulation of durable peace and progressive futures. This leans on, and departs from, a Pan-African strand that eulogises unity and the strength that comes with the harmonisation of interdependent attitudes and values. Beyond the benefits of integration is also the belief that the attainment of social justice, sustainable development, peace, stability and human security cannot be fulfilled on an individual basis, especially given that Africa is a mosaic of overlapping communities with shared history and concerns.[37] The understanding seems to be that such an achievement requires concerted efforts founded on political, social and economic integration.[38] All these, of course, are dependent on the existence of collective political will and robust institutions and structures.

Structures and institutions of the African Union

At the time of its adoption, the Constitutive Act initially established nine organs as supporting pillars for the African Union. Article 5 stipulates that the African Union shall comprise the Assembly of the Union, the Executive Council, the Pan-African Parliament, the Court of Justice, the Commission, the Permanent Representatives Committee, the Specialised Technical Committees, the Economic, Social and Cultural Council and the Financial Institutions. By virtue of Articles 5(2) and 9(d) which grant the Assembly the power to create any organ it deems necessary, the Peace and Security Council (PSC) was subsequently created through

---

[36] See S. M. Makinda and F. W. Okumu, *The African Union: Challenges of Globalisation, Security and Governance* (New York: Routledge, 2008), p. 34.
[37] Naldi and Magliveras, 'The African Union', at 416.   [38] *Ibid.*

a protocol adopted on 9 July 2002.[39] In a sense, the organs reflect the natural order of the structural outlay of contemporary international organisations. Individual tasks are assigned to the organs with the view to achieving the African Union's objectives through the set of principles espoused by the Constitutive Act. This needs to be delineated.

Like the OAU, the Assembly is the supreme organ of the African Union. It comprises heads of state and government or their delegated representatives. The Assembly meets twice a year, usually in January and July. Each meeting requires the satisfaction of two-thirds of the total membership of the African Union. The Assembly elects a chair for a year's duration, which is renewable where compelling circumstances exist. But this is rare, and aside from Olusegun Obasanjo's re-election as chair, has not reoccurred. In light of the problems of non-attendance at summit meetings in the past, the high threshold for a quorum could potentially be problematic. The Constitutive Act envisions, nonetheless, a strong institutional architecture that propagates certain values in advancing the collective aspiration of Africa. Adequate representation and effective participation in the affairs of the Union is anticipated to provide means of making the African Union acquire a meaningful presence in the lives of Africans.

The powers and functions of the Assembly are delineated in Article 9(1) and include the determination of the common policies of the Union, consideration of requests for membership, monitoring of implementation of policies and decisions as well as ensuring compliance. Article 7(1) provides that the Assembly shall take its decisions by consensus or failing which a two-thirds majority will suffice. However, the need for consensus does not extend to procedural matters, which only require a simple majority.[40] The idea of decision by consensus is steeped in African traditional governance processes 'as a manifestation of an immanent approach to social interaction'.[41] Its utility in contemporary decision-making serves as antidote to forestall the trivialisation of the right of the minority to have an effect on decision-making.[42] In the complex dynamics of contemporary international politics, decision by consensus could

---

[39] Protocol Relating to the Establishment of the Peace and Security Council of the African Union, adopted in Durban, South Africa, 9 July 2002, www.africa-union.org/root/au/Documents/Treaties/treaties.htm (last visited April 2010).

[40] Article 7(1), Constitutive Act.

[41] K. Wiredu, *Cultural Universals and Particulars: An African Perspective* (Bloomington: Indiana University Press, 1996), p. 163.

[42] *Ibid.*

be fraught with difficulties and could likely result in a 'type of inaction that may well impact on the organisation's operational competence'.[43] The Assembly also has the crucial function of directing the Executive Council on confronting conflicts, managing emergency situations and mapping and sustaining the restoration of peace. Article 9(2) grants the Assembly the discretion to delegate any of its functions to any organ of the Union.

The Executive Council constitutes another of the African Union's institutions. Article 10 provides that the Council shall comprise Ministers of Foreign Affairs or equivalent authorities designated by governments of member states. The Council is accountable to the Assembly and is required to meet at least twice a year for ordinary sessions. Its functions are similar to those of its equivalent in the defunct OAU.[44] According to Article 13, the Executive Council is charged with the coordination of policies in areas of common interest to member states and makes appropriate decisions thereto. The Council also has the mandate to monitor the implementation of policies formulated by the Assembly.[45] Although its areas of competence seem to be broad and reflective of some of the challenges confronting Africa, they do not sufficiently correspond to either the narrative inscribed in the Preamble or the values espoused in the Constitutive Act. The eleven areas of interest falling within the functional jurisdiction of the Executive Council do not include some of the causal factors that have been central to violence and conflicts in Africa. The excluded areas include the promotion and protection of human rights, respect for and sanctity of human life, consolidation of mutual coexistence and peacebuilding initiatives, promotion of interdependence and integration and institutionalisation of good governance and democratic culture. Considering that the Council is mandated to play a 'filtering' role for policy-making and implementation, the restriction of its competence makes little sense. What the exclusions could potentially do is marginalise the jurisdictional competence of the Council, consigning it to issues of a largely technical nature.[46]

---

[43] Naldi and Magliveras, 'The African Union', at 420.

[44] Articles XII–XIV of the OAU Charter provided for a Council of Ministers which performed advisory functions to the Assembly.

[45] Article 13(2), Constitutive Act.

[46] It ought to be noted that some of these excluded areas do fall under the functions of the Peace and Security Council. But the Commission could still have been involved in these very important issues.

The operational functionality of the Assembly and Executive Council or the African Union as a whole is dependent on the existence of a vibrant administrative support. To this end, Article 20 provides for the establishment of a Commission which shall constitute the Secretariat of the Union. For historical and practical reasons, Article 24 stipulates that the Commission shall be seated in the Ethiopian capital of Addis Ababa. Corinne Parker and Donald Rukare have suggested that the decision of where to locate the African Union's Commission seemed not to be an issue during the *travaux préparatoires* of the Constitutive Act, despite the city's diminished significance today compared to other cities such as Nairobi, Lagos and Dakar.[47] According to Article 20(2) the Commission shall be headed by a Chairperson, his or her deputies and Commissioners. They shall be assisted by support staff. As the organ responsible for the day-to-day management of the African Union, its functions have recently been delineated to include, amongst others: represent and defend the Union and its interests; elaborate draft common positions of the Union; prepare strategic plans and studies for the consideration of the Executive Council; elaborate, promote and coordinate the programmes and policies of the Union and harmonise them with those of the RECs; ensure the mainstreaming of gender in all programmes and activities of the Union.[48]

It should be noted that the powers and functions of the Chairperson were not initially outlined in the Constitutive Act. This was delegated for the Assembly to determine in due course. The benefit of such an arrangement was to open the door for the possibility of 'granting that official a broad array of duties as the Union unfolds'.[49] In July 2003, the Executive Council adopted a Report on the proposed structure, human resource and condition of service of the Commission.[50] The Report outlined a range of functions for the Chairperson which reflect the much expanded competence of the Union. The expanded functions and powers of the Chairperson are an attempt to correct the inadequacies that paralysed the Secretariat of the former OAU. The new functions

---

[47] C. Parker and D. Rukare, 'The New African Union and its Constitutive Act', *American Journal of International Law*, 96:2 (2002), 265–78 at 375.

[48] 'African Union in a Nutshell', www.africa-union.org (last visited June 2010).

[49] Parker and Rukare, 'The New African Union', at 375.

[50] *Report of the Third Ordinary Session of the Executive Council on the Proposed Structure, Human Resource Requirements and Condition of Service for the Staff of the Commission of the African Union and their Financial Implications*, Maputo, Mozambique, 4–8 July 2003, Doc.Ex/CL/39/III.

allow the Chairperson to play a more proactive role in the advancement of the Union's principles and objectives in conjunction with other organs. In addition, Article 7 of the Protocol Relating to the Establishment of the Peace and Security Council provides that the Chairperson is expected to be proactive in conflict transformation, peacebuilding initiatives and the implementation of the normative values of the Union.

The Constitutive Act provides for Specialised Technical Committees whose functions and composition are outlined in Articles 14–16. Their range of competence suggests an attempt towards making the African Union structurally stronger than its predecessor. Responsible to the Executive Council, and an improvement on the OAU's Specialised Commissions,[51] the seven Specialised Committees shall be a source of expert knowledge and technical assistance and may be expanded if the Assembly deems it necessary.[52] Their functions are to prepare projects and policies, supervise, follow up and evaluate the implementation of decisions taken by the Union's organs as well as coordinate and harmonise them. Furthermore, Articles 17–19 establish the Pan-African Parliament, Court of Justice (which has been merged with the African Court of Human Rights to become the African Court of Justice and Human Rights) and Financial Institutions. The Financial Institutions are provided for by Article 19 and comprise three institutions: the African Central Bank, the African Monetary Fund and the African Investment Bank. The Constitutive Act stipulates that the functions, composition and rules of operation of the Financial Institutions will be defined in a protocol relating thereto.

The creation of the Pan-African Parliament is indeed a new development. Its main functions are spelt out in Article 17 and relate largely to facilitating the full participation of the African people in the development and economic integration of the continent. The powers, functions

---

[51] The OAU only had three Specialised Commissions, whose functions fell short of those of the African Union Specialised Committees. The Commissions were established by Article XX of the OAU Charter and were as follows: Economic and Social Commission; Educational, Scientific, Cultural and Health Commission; and Defence Commission.

[52] The seven Committees established under Article 14 shall be composed of ministers or senior officials responsible for sectors falling within their respective areas of competence. The Committees are as follows: The Committee on Rural Economy and Agricultural Matters; The Committee on Monetary and Financial Affairs; The Committee on Trade, Customs and Immigration Matters; The Committee on Industry, Science and Technology, Energy, Natural Resources and Environment; The Committee on Transport, Communications and Tourism; The Committee on Health, Labour and Social Affairs; and The Committee on Education, Culture and Human Resources.

and composition of the Pan-African Parliament are outlined in the Protocol to the Treaty Establishing the African Economic Community relating to the Pan-African Parliament.[53] These include, among others: to examine, discuss and make recommendations on the implementation of the Union's policies; work towards the harmonisation and coordination of legislation of member states; promote solidarity and economic integration with regional groups; and other functions the Parliament may deem appropriate. Whilst indicating that the Pan-African Parliament shall be vested with legislative powers to be defined by the Assembly, Article 11 however stipulates that during its first term of existence (2003–08) it shall exercise advisory and consultative powers only. A review is expected to be conducted to determine, among others, whether its members will be elected by universal suffrage. Meanwhile, members of the Assembly are elected from the national legislatures of member countries.

In the context of peacebuilding, the institution whose functions are critical to tackling violence and conflicts in Africa is the Peace and Security Council (PSC). Created by a separate protocol, the PSC is an amalgamation of some of the conflict resolution and management structures that existed under the OAU, aspirational values of the treaty relating to the establishment of the African Economic Community (AEC) and the integrated normative principles underlying the Constitutive Act.[54] Article 2 of its Protocol states that the PSC is the standing decision-making organ for the prevention, management and resolution of conflicts, and therefore perceived as a collective security and early-warning arrangement to facilitate timely and efficient response to conflict and crisis situations in Africa.

The Protocol further stipulates that the PSC shall be supported by a Panel of the Wise, a Continental Early Warning System, an African Standby Force and a Special Fund for Peace. Article 11 of the PSC Protocol provides that the Panel of the Wise shall be selected by the Chairperson of the African Union Commission and be composed of five highly respected African personalities from various segments of society.

---

[53] The Protocol was adopted on 2 March 2001 and entered into force on 14 December 2003. Available at www.africa-union.org/root/au/Documents/Treaties/treaties.htm (last visited April 2010).

[54] The Protocol was adopted in July 2002 by the Assembly of the Heads of State and Government of the AU, meeting in Durban, South Africa. It entered into force on 26 December 2003. (Protocol Relating to the Establishment of the Peace and Security Council of the African Union, adopted in Durban, South Africa, 9 July 2002, www.africa-union.org/root/au/Documents/Treaties/treaties.htm (last visited April 2010).

In determining the members of the Panel, regard must be had to their outstanding contribution to the causes of peace, security and development. The Panel's main function is to advise the PSC and the African Union Commission on matters relating to the promotion and maintenance of peace, security and stability in Africa. The Continental Early Warning System was absent from the OAU conflict resolution structures. It is composed of an observation and monitoring centre (the Situation Room) and is responsible for data collection and analysis which shall be used to monitor developments and recommend the best course of action. The Standby Force is created to assist the PSC in its conflict transformation functions, such as peace support deployments and intervention missions pursuant to Article 4(h) and (j), and is anticipated to serve as a rapid deployment unit in situations of emergency.[55] In this sense, the Standby Force constitutes an important part of the emergency dimension of the Constitutive Act's peace and security architecture.

The collective objectives of the African Union's institutions are mainly to promote peace and security, closer integration and creation of conditions for sustainable development, and to anticipate and prevent conflicts.[56] In circumstances where conflicts occur, the PSC shall have the responsibility to resolve them through transformative approaches and in due regard to the principles espoused by the Constitutive Act. In order to strengthen and consolidate durable approaches to conflict, the Protocol mandates the PSC to broaden its outreach capabilities by promoting and encouraging democratic values, good governance, human rights and respect for the sanctity of human life and international humanitarian law. It also re-echoes the need for interdependence and socio-economic integration through an organic relationship between the PSC and regional mechanisms for conflict management and resolution. What this points to is the reaffirmation that regional mechanisms are important components of the overall security architecture and are required to keep the PSC fully informed of their activities. The incorporation of these values and institutions is part of an integrated framework and approach to conflicts.[57]

---

[55] The idea of an African force is not new. Before and after the creation of the OAU, Kwame Nkrumah had led an abortive campaign to mobilise opinion on the establishment of an African High Command to promote security and stability. The idea was considered overambitious at the time. See B. Franke, 'A Pan-African Army: The Evolution of an Idea and its Eventual Realisation in the African Standby Force', *Africa Security Review*, 15:4 (2006), 1–16 at 4.

[56] Article 3(a)–(b), Constitutive Act.   [57] Article 3(f), *ibid*.

Given its wide range of responsibilities, the effectiveness of the PSC is vitally important to the successful realisation of the Constitutive Act's peacebuilding framework. It has a range of powers and functions which represent a significant departure from the OAU conflict management structures. However, the structural set-up of the PSC could have gone beyond its existing configuration. For instance, there are concerns that the final *decision* to authorise intervention pursuant to Article 4 of the Constitutive Act should have fallen within the competence of the PSC rather than the Assembly. As the PSC can only *recommend* intervention or any other course of action to the Assembly, this may give rise to inaction that could have devastating consequences.[58] This was certainly the case with the OAU's Assembly, whose reluctance, and in many instances refusal, to intervene in internal conflicts was borne out of the fear that doing so would make states susceptible to intervention in their domestic affairs.[59] One comparative advantage the existing arrangement has is the possibility of reducing a potential standoff between two organs should the final decision be taken to intervene under the purview of the PSC.

Perspectives on the structure of the African Union

Although the African Union organs enunciate a relatively integrated approach and proactive involvement, opinions on their number and scope have ranged from optimism to concern to indifference. It has been submitted that the institutional framework has the potential for enhancing economic cooperation and social integration and inter-dependence.[60] Others have berated the resemblance of the African Union's institutional configuration to that of the European Union organs, stressing that the imitation is deceptive and would not necessarily usher in progress. Amadou Sesay is, for instance, reluctant to embrace the African Union's 'impressive array of new institutions and organs', indicating that they do not follow a logic that is aligned to the past and present expediencies of Africa.[61] Sesay is adamant that 'the institutions and organs represent at one level, impersonations of organisations in other parts of the world that bear no direct relevance

---

[58] Parker and Rukare, 'The New African Union', at 373.
[59] *Ibid.*   [60] Naldi and Magliveras, 'The African Union', at 425.
[61] A. Sesay, 'The African Union: Forward March or About Face-Turn?', *Clauke Ake Memorial Papers No. 3*, (2008), at 21 (Nordic African Institute, Uppsala).

to the African continent's historical, socio-economic, political and cultural development'.[62] He goes on to say that the African Union 'seems to have committed what can be described as "political mimicry" by reflecting in Africa institutions that are set up in other parts of the world, especially from the EU'.[63]

Sesay's suggested parallels are misplaced for two reasons. First, the disparities in the historical and philosophical origins of the two institutions make the comparisons illogical. The African Union is a progeny of nineteenth-century struggles against racism, colonialism, slavery, oppression and exploitation of Africa and peoples of African descent. Pan-Africanism has been, and continues to be, a struggle for the advancement of African social spaces and institutions through unity, integration and development. It is a vision that played an active part in shaping the configuration of the African Union. In contrast, the European Union is an 'establishment' institution that evolved from the European Coal and Steel Community. Its overriding vision has been the consolidation of European power and stability through economic integration. Second, the idea of an African Union has a strong genetic link with early Pan-African ideology. It is the substance underlying this link that inspired anti-colonial struggles and post-independence institutions such as the OAU.

So when contextualised within the Pan-African narrative, the African Union and its instruments largely reflect Kwame Nkrumah's visions of a supranational continental government advocated for by him in the 1940s, 50s and 60s. Not only do the African Union's institutions resonate with Nkrumah's visions – however far-fetched they appeared at the time – but instruments such as the African Standby Force and the Common Defence Policy typically represent Pan-African ambitions. From this perspective, the creation of the African Union is largely symbolic of, and consistent with, the long travails of the institutionalisation of Pan-African ideals and visions. And of course in all its many philosophical incarnations, one constant in Pan-Africanism has been the desire to advance continental unity through a robust supranational body. These Pan-African visions surely predate the EU, and so the suggested ostensible 'mimicry' is more coincidental than intentional. Thus the idea of the African Union is hardly a simulacrum of the EU.

---

[62] *Ibid.*   [63] *Ibid.*

There are also suggestions that given scarcity of resources has been emblematic of African institutions, it is illogical to 'load' the Constitutive Act with an ambitious expanse of organs, as in the future this could not only lead to cumbersome operation of the Union, but also present a financial burden.[64] The concerns are legitimate, and the impending fear they allude to has in certain respects, relatively speaking, constrained some of the current engagements of the African Union. Nonetheless, the interaction between the organs and their overlapping functions follow a rational balancing act that initiates a more elaborate and institutionally mediated decision-making structure. This is because as a representation of a major normative shift, with expectations of addressing social integration, economic, political and human security challenges, it is hard to conceive of a continental organisation with such a broad scope of responsibilities operated by a limited ordering of organs and institutions. In view of Africa's challenges and the urgent need to address them, these institutions could play a positive role in following up decisions and facilitating their implementation. It is a crucial factor, given that the ineptitude symptomatic of the OAU was partly due to the organisation lacking both the will and means to uphold its decisions.[65]

Of course, this is not to suggest that their existence would have served as the definitive solution to the enormous challenges facing Africa. It would be churlish to do so. There is already a history – both documented and through the lived experiences of people as shown by their suffering and struggles – of the neglect, incompetence and failings of Africa's endogenous institutions. There are also, rightly so, considerable doubts and pessimism about the possibilities of agency in the continent's institutions. Yet this should not dampen the need for, and pursuit of, the conception of an ensemble of institutions that could open a window of opportunity towards rectifying what have been sequences of challenges and great injustices to Africa and its people. For the African Union to accentuate the ethos of its Constitutive Act there is a need to empower its organs with human, financial and material resources. In the context of peacebuilding, the Constitutive Act presents an opening through which approaches to conflicts could be conceptualised by virtue of its normative shift.

---

[64] Naldi and Magliveras, 'The African Union', at 419.

[65] J. Cilliers and K. Sturman, 'Challenges Facing the AU's Peace and Security Council', *African Security Review*, 13:1 (2004), 97–104 at 97.

The Constitutive Act's normative shift and
peacebuilding approaches

The post-1945 international legal order obligated the OAU to be structured upon the principles of sovereignty, non-interference and territorial integrity. Sovereignty provided the frame of reference for the OAU's strict reverence for the doctrine of non-interference. Serious violations of human rights and international humanitarian law were committed with little or no response from the OAU. Compounding this was the fact that international law's approaches to internal conflicts have been shaped, influenced and constrained by state-centric conceptions of peacebuilding rendering them fundamentally limited in what they can do to confront the complexities of conflicts in Africa. For real change to occur, therefore, a recasting of the institutional norms, particularly those relating to peacebuilding, became both necessary and imperative. In the Constitutive Act, there appears to emerge an opportunity for the formulation of an integrated approach to conflicts in Africa.

The approaches embedded in the Constitutive Act conjure a typology of conflict transformation. Transformative approaches to conflicts are not entirely new. Some have been advanced in the past decade as conceptual responses to the inadequacies of liberal peacebuilding approaches. Joseph Folger and Robert Baruch Bush have, for instance, propounded transformative mediation as an alternative to what they consider as the formulaic nature of conventional conflict mediation approaches.[66] The objective of their alternative approach is to transform and empower disputing parties so as to understand and recognise their needs. Similarly John Paul Lederach has attempted to enrich understanding on transformative approaches by articulating sets of guiding principles. He defines conflict transformation as an endeavour 'to envision and respond to the ebb and flow of social conflict as life-giving opportunities for creating constructive change processes that reduce violence, increase justice in direct interaction and social structures, and respond to real-life problems in human relationships'.[67]

Two elements characterise Lederach's definition. The first is that it emphasises the need for constructive changes in social relations in the

[66] R. A. Baruch Bush and J. P. Folger, *The Promise of Mediation: The Transformative Approach to Conflict* (San Francisco: Jossey Bass, 2004).

[67] J. P. Lederach, *The Little Book of Conflict Transformation* (Philadelphia: Good Books, 2003), p. 14.

quest for durable conditions of peace. This is because this type of transformative engagement facilitates 'greater understanding of underlying relational and structural patterns while building creative solutions that improve relations'.[68] Thus the 'key to transformation is a proactive bias towards seeing conflict as a potential catalyst for growth'.[69] Second, it perceives peace as a process centred in structures of relationships that are dynamic and changing. Lederach argues that 'rather than seeing peace as a static "end state," conflict transformation views peace as a simultaneously evolving and developing quality of relationships'.[70] This sense of continuity in Lederach's formulation is 'characterised by intentional efforts to address the natural ebb and flow of human conflict through non-violence'.[71]

The premise of Lederach's construction of transformative approaches to conflicts revolves around the significance of social relations and structures in peacebuilding. Traditional approaches to peacebuilding in Africa correlate with this premise to a considerable degree. However the integrated approaches embedded in the Constitutive Act vary from Lederach's two main propositions. The first is his suggestion that a transformative peacebuilding approach aspires to create change processes through *conflict*, and the second is that a 'transformational approach recognises that conflict is a normal and continuous dynamic within human relationships'.[72] There is a certain supposition or, at least, an implied assumption that because conflict is a natural feature of human relations, transformative approaches can only be pursued through the frames of conflict. In other words, his formulation has the tendency to consign peacebuilding solely within the frames of conflict, relying, in effect, on a negative reaction rather than a positive proactive inclination. This may be problematic given the scale, scope and oscillation of internal conflicts in Africa.

There is need, therefore, for an approach capable of potentially providing an alternative that transcends current limitations. The Constitutive Act embodies an attempt, however limited, at such a recasting. But what is the significance of the normative shift that the Constitutive Act represents? And how might this impact and shape approaches to violence and conflicts in Africa? The Constitutive Act's peacebuilding and transformative approaches are embedded in three distinct but organically interrelated paradigms. These revolve around, first, the 'non-indifference'

---

[68] *Ibid.*, p. 19.   [69] *Ibid.*, p. 15.   [70] *Ibid.*, pp. 20–1.   [71] *Ibid.*, p. 21.
[72] *Ibid.*, pp. 12–15.

concept in Article 4; second, norms formulation; and third, social integration and interdependence. Together, they constitute the African Union's peace and security framework.

Article 4 and the 'non-indifference' concept

Article 4(h) of the Constitutive Act provides the African Union with the 'right to intervene in a Member State pursuant to a decision of the Assembly in respect of grave circumstances namely, war crimes, genocide and crimes against humanity'. A subsequent protocol amending the Constitutive Act expanded the scope of Article 4, specifically providing that the circumstances conditioning the Union's intervention mandate would also include a 'serious threat to legitimate order to restore peace and stability to a Member State upon the recommendation of the [AU's] Peace and Security Council'.[73] Article 4(j), on the other hand, provides the right of member states to request intervention for the restoration of peace and order. Two preliminary observations are worth making here. First, Article 4(h) does not require consent from the member state in whose territory intervention is being invoked. In effect a state's adoption and subsequent ratification of the Constitutive Act amounts to a willingness to surrender certain sovereign powers to an organisation established by a multilateral treaty. By extension, this includes granting consent to the type of intervention anticipated under Article 4. Second, Article 4(h) falls short on specifics as regards means and methods of intervention.

However, the incorporation of the Panel of the Wise and the African Standby Force into the African Union's institutional structures are perhaps grounds to suggest that the type of intervention so conceived, encompasses military countermeasures and non-violent initiatives. Beyond this, the Constitutive Act can be viewed as an attempt to recharacterise international law's engagement with internal conflicts in Africa. Thus the genesis of Article 4 is linked to the reticence of the OAU to deal with the scale of conflicts that have pervaded African postcoloniality. The codification of Article 4 as a template in the 'law' of the African Union is, in this sense, a reflection of past institutional and normative inadequacies and an expressed intention to depart from them. Perhaps nothing less could have been expected from an organisation that envisions an integrated Africa,

---

[73] See Protocol on the Amendment to the Constitutive Act of the African Union, Maputo, Mozambique, 11 July 2003, www.africa-union.org/root/au/Documents/Treaties/ (last visited July 2010).

driven by its people and characterised by peace and stability.[74] As Tiyanjana Maluwa notes, 'in an era in which post-independent Africa had witnessed the horrors of genocide and ethnic cleansing on its own soil against its own kind, it would have been absolutely amiss for the Constitutive Act to remain silent on the question of the right to intervene in respect of grave circumstances'.[75]

In another major departure from the OAU Charter, the Constitutive Act puts in place an enforcement mechanism intended to facilitate compliance with African Union policies and decisions. Article 23(2) provides that 'any Member State that fails to comply with the decisions and policies of the AU may be subjected to other sanctions, such as the denial of transport and communication links with other Member States, and other measures of a political and economic nature to be determined by the Assembly'. The significance of the enforcement regime is clearly predicated on a non-indifference doctrine, an expression of a will to act so as to avert violence and impunity. Ambassador Said Djinnit, a former African Union Peace and Security Commissioner, formulates this as a duty to act, one that imposes a duty to remain proactive in confronting Africa's tragedies. This implies moving away from the practice of non-interference to non-indifference.[76]

Since its promulgation, there have been suggestions that Article 4 would contravene the UN Charter if recourse to military action occurred that was not authorised by the UN Security Council. Contemporary international *jus ad bellum*, as noted in Chapter 4, is outlined in Articles 2(4), 53(1) and 103 of the UN Charter. The regulatory regime renders the threat or use of force as amounting to *jus cogens*, which is a peremptory norm of international law. *Jus cogens* norms do not provide room for derogation occasioned by contingent circumstances or obligations arising from treaty law. Article 53 of the Vienna Convention on the Law of Treaties (VCLT) also reinforces this.[77] However, the legal basis for the Constitutive Act could be situated in Article 52 of the UN Charter. The provision empowers regional organisations to perform functions of a peace enforcement nature. To the extent that the Constitutive Act is a product of a

---

[74] African Union Commission, *Strategic Framework of the African Union Commission 2004–2007*, www.uni-muenster.de/Politikwissenschaft/Doppeldiplom/docs/Strategic.pdf (last visited July 2010).

[75] T. Maluwa, 'Reimagining African Unity: Some Preliminary Reflections on the Constitutive Act of the African Union', *African Yearbook of International Law*, 9 (2001), 3–38 at 38.

[76] See quote at start of chapter and n. 1 above.

[77] See Vienna Convention on the Law of Treaties, 23 May 1969, 1155 UNTS 331.

multilateral treaty, with Article 4 intervention seeking the kind of regional peace and stability alluded to in the UN Charter, it falls outside the remit of Article 53(1) of the Charter.[78] This prevails so far as the pertinent multilateral treaty was freely negotiated and adopted by state parties as the International Court of Justice held in the *Lotus* case.[79]

There have also been interpretations of the UN Charter's *jus ad bellum* regime in a way that departs from conventional legal readings. The focus of such perspectives has been the desire to make the Charter relevant and accessible by 'reproducing' its peacebuilding anatomy in regional organisations. For instance in 1992 the UN Secretary General, Boutros Boutros-Ghali, reaffirmed the peacebuilding connections between the Charter and regional organisations.[80] In a subsequent sequel presented to the Security Council in 1995, he argued that:

> The founders of the United Nations, in Chapter VIII of the Charter of the United Nations, envisaged an important role for regional organisations in the maintenance of international peace and security. It is increasingly apparent that the United Nations cannot address every potential and actual conflict troubling the world. Regional or sub-regional organisations sometimes have a comparative advantage in taking the lead role in the prevention and settlement of conflicts and to assist the United Nations in containing them.[81]

The scope of Article 4 of the Constitutive Act was extended in 2003 with the threshold of the original right to intervene in grave circumstances lowered to also include serious threat to legitimate order so as to restore peace and security in the member states of the Union. The amendment was perhaps a further reflection on the fragility of the African postcolonial state, and so the underlying rationale for lowering the threshold for intervention was therefore to accommodate situations that are serious enough to potentially threaten peace and security where some kind of engagement would otherwise have been logically considered.[82]

---

[78] See also D. Kuwali, *The Responsibility to Protect: Implementation of Article 4(h) Intervention* (The Hague: Martinus Nijhoff, 2010).

[79] SS *Lotus* (*France* v. *Turkey*).

[80] See B. Boutros-Ghali, *Agenda for Peace, Preventive Diplomacy, Peace Making and Peace Keeping* (New York: United Nations, 1992), para. 64.

[81] Report of the Secretary General: *Improving Preparedness for Conflict Prevention and Peace-keeping in Africa*, UN Document S/1995/911, 1 November 1995, para. 4.

[82] See B. Kioko, 'The Right of Intervention under the African Union's Constitutive Act: From Non-interference to Non-intervention', *International Review of the Red Cross*, 85:852 (2003), 807–25 at 811.

The amendment has, however, been criticised for being too elastic in scope, going well beyond the initial provisions on intervention. Everest Baimu and Kathryn Sturman warn that the amendment not only appears to be inconsistent with the foundational values of the Constitutive Act, but poses the danger of being interpreted to give precedence to regime security over human security. They argue that 'in many instances, the perceived or authentic threat to legitimate order is used as a pretext to violate human rights', and so 'its inclusion as one of the grounds for intervention could be viewed as a step backward in the efforts to secure better protection of individual rights in Africa'.[83] Kristina Powell has similarly argued that the amendment could be invoked to satisfy the political whims of certain African leaders, adding that 'if not properly delimited, the concept of threats to legitimate order is sufficiently elastic to encompass even peaceful protests for more accountable government as grounds for intervention on the part of the AU'.[84] Credible as these concerns are they do, however, adopt an overtly teleological reading of the substance of the amendment. The amendment could alternatively be read with the circumstances and nature of internal conflicts in mind. This is particularly so considering that internal conflicts have continued to defy the conventional classification ascribed to them by international law.

With the applicability of international law to internal conflicts largely limited, the amendment captures a whole set of jurisdictional applicabilities. Internal disturbances, tensions, sporadic violence and related acts are often considered not grave enough to warrant the level of engagement espoused in the Constitutive Act's non-indifference conception. But these patterns of violence cannot be discounted as marginal to internal conflicts. It was therefore imperative for the Constitutive Act's peacebuilding framework to acquire the flexibility to configure and retain the elements of what Peter Fitzpatrick regards as the concept of law-making as a living process that must be transformative to meet contingent problems. In the changing nature of Africa's postcolonial condition, 'law cannot simply secure certainty and predictability' unless it can 'change in response to the illimitable unpredictability and uncertainty which ever confronts it'. For 'should

---

[83] E. Baimu and K. Sturman, 'Amendment to the African Union's Right to Intervene: A Shift from Human Security to Regime Security', *African Security Review*, 12:2 (2003), 37–45 at 42.

[84] K. Powell, 'The African Union's Emerging Peace and Security Regime: Opportunities and Challenges for Delivering on the Responsibility to Protect', ISS Monograph Series, 119 (2005), at 12.

it fail to do so', Fitzpatrick warns, 'it will cease to rule situations changing around it or be unable to extend to them'.[85]

The amended provision ought to be seen as fulfilling this transformative formulation by lowering the original high threshold of Article 4(h). Its primary function appears to be an attempt to address the genesis of conflicts and not consolidate rogue regimes. The provision was adopted to enable the African Union to resolve conflicts more effectively without the obstacles of non-interference coming in the way.[86] The lack of faith in the *status quo ante* was also located in 'frustration with the slow pace of reform of the international order and with instances in which the international community tended to focus attention on other parts of the world at the expense of more pressing problems in Africa'.[87] It is perhaps in this sense, that the African Union's non-indifference conception could have an impact in confronting internal conflicts more seriously, especially 'where a weak state is unable to protect its citizens, as when a repressive state is unwilling to do so or itself the cause of abuse'.[88]

Criticism has also been directed at the semantic construct of the intervention provision, with suggestions that it has a weak impulse since the use of 'right' implies that the African Union could *exercise discretion* whether to intervene or not.[89] Kithure Kindiki contends that the language of the provision should have made the requirement to intervene a matter of 'duty' considering that 'the sense of obligation to intervene is more likely to move the AU into action'.[90] There is some logic here. The *Oxford Dictionary of Law* defines 'duty' as 'a legal requirement to carry out or refrain from carrying out any act'.[91] 'Right' on the other hand implies the 'freedom to exercise any power conferred by law'.[92] Thus the performance of a duty appears to place a higher onus than the exercise of a right, which, it appears, opens up possibilities for discretion. It is unlikely, however, that the need for intervention would be evaluated on

---

[85] P. Fitzpatrick, 'The Triumph of a Departed World: Law, Modernity and the Sacred', paper presented at the Warwick University Law Seminar Series, 2005, at 29.

[86] Kioko, 'The Right of Intervention under the African Union's Constitutive Act', at 817.

[87] *Ibid.*, at 821.

[88] J. Cilliers and K. Sturman, 'The Right of Intervention: Enforcement Challenges for the African Union', *African Security Review*, 11:3 (2002), 1–5 at 3.

[89] K. Kindiki, 'The Normative and Institutional Framework of the African Union Relating to the Protection of Human Rights and the Maintenance of International Peace and Security: A Critical Appraisal', *African Human Rights Law Journal*, 13:1 (2003), 97–117.

[90] *Ibid.* [91] *Oxford Dictionary of Law* (Oxford University Press, 1997), p. 155.

[92] *Ibid.*, p. 409.

these legal nuances, for 'at the end of the day what matters is whether states have the political will to undertake what they committed themselves to do'.[93] Nevertheless, the absence of a definition or consensus as to the true meaning of 'serious threat to legitimate order' could invariably lead to dilemmas, more perhaps of uncertainty than of a blanket licence for individual abuse. Equally, it would be ill-advised to frame a definition given that the nature and circumstances of internal conflicts in Africa have always been dynamic in character.

Beyond its primary function as an instrument of first instance in the maintenance of order, Article 4 might also be interpreted as an African perspective on the *Responsibility to Protect*. The notion is a middle-ground engagement between the necessity to confront impunity and the dictates and imperatives of sovereignty. The African Union's percipience on the philosophical orientations of Responsibility to Protect bears considerable resonance in the dynamics of internal conflicts in Africa. The capacity of international law in confronting internal conflicts has largely been hampered by state sovereignty or factors associated with it. This generates two paradoxes. The first is that in view of its ambiguous and artificial character the postcolonial African state leaves much to be desired. Its crisis of legitimacy, structure and anatomy disrupts the traditional platform necessary for the protection and promotion of peace. The second aspect of this paradox is that the history of international law has been shaped by interstate relations, and its progression has been defined by, and dependent on, the willingness and capacity of states to enforce its norms. States are also sustained by, and operate on, the principle of sovereign equality.

But of course state sovereignty has been a problematic phenomenon in Africa, not least because 'the concept of state sovereignty, on which the international system and the OAU were founded, presumes that each state has the power, authority and competence to govern its territory'. But of course 'for many African States, however, sovereignty is a legal fiction that is not matched by governance and administrative capacity'.[94] In this respect, the enunciation of sovereignty as responsibility in the African Union's normative framework was most certainly inescapable. What the Constitutive Act has done, however, is to induce an innovation through Article 4 that allows a recharacterisation of state sovereignty so as to consolidate an ethos of non-indifference.

---

[93] Baimu and Sturman, 'Amendment to the African Union's Right to Intervene', at 3.
[94] Cilliers and Sturman, 'Enforcement Challenges', at 3.

The right to intervene through Article 4(h) can be perceived as a milestone in the evolution of a continental normative framework that could provide the parameters through which a genuine peacebuilding culture may emerge. Most importantly, perhaps, is its potential as an additional impetus to the long quest for a credible framework for an African solution to African problems. It is imperative to note, however, that pivotal as Article 4 remains to the African Union's integrated framework, it does not totalise the Constitutive Act's transformative approaches to conflicts and peacebuilding architecture. The right to intervene is *only* a contingent provisional approach to arresting the scourge of violence and internal conflicts. And so read in conjunction with the other provisions of the Constitutive Act, Article 4 is provisional and not intended to be a definitive, permanent fixture in the law, philosophy and practices of the African Union. This is because its rationale is, fundamentally, to provide an expedient approach to confronting volatile situations pending the deepening of some of the more durable peacebuilding approaches. Thus the interventionist features of Article 4 are mainly intended to constitute a short-term measure to maintain order whilst other aspects of the peace and security framework are envisaged to cultivate conditions of durable peace.

Integrated norms formulation and localisation

Peacebuilding is not merely the absence of violence, but also a process and a social aspiration that encompass a strong intercourse of normative values. Consolidating normative values in peacebuilding is to ascribe relevance and continuity to transformative approaches. The Constitutive Act appears to provide a reference point for this, located in two foundational epochs that informed the transition from the OAU to the African Union. These have been identified as Pan-Africanism and the Kampala CSSDCA process. In whatever way perceived, the African Union is largely a Pan-African institution that feeds from that ideology's transformative character. Its continuing relevance relates to the fact that the ideology is no longer fixated on its early reactive rhetoric. In the post-Cold War global political order, Pan-Africanism has acquired an organised ideal that attempts to distil new modes of neo-liberal dominance whilst also providing empowering sources of reference for the formulation of an African institutional and normative order. This unfolds in two interrelated tiers.

The first pertains to the advancement of a narrative that envisions an Africa driven by its people with the object of making the continent and its institutions dynamic forces in global politics.[95] The narrative draws from the strength in common identity and the imperative of advancing collective mutual interests. Through organised Pan-Africanism, it becomes an ascribed outlet for the continent's political leadership and institutional structures. Whether it is conscientious activism necessitated by global transformations or enforced reaction to postcolonial turbulence, this force has potential in formulating norms and recasting Africa's interfaces with the world. Some of the norms embedded in the Constitutive Act are aimed at promoting unity and cohesion, whilst others have a focus specific to the quest for a viable peaceful order. In its 2004 Strategic Framework Report, the African Union Commission elaborates on the rationale of these norms. The Report notes that the Constitutive Act envisions an Africa that:

> will be united and integrated; an Africa imbued with justice and peace; an interdependent and virile Africa determined to map for itself an ambitious strategy; an Africa backstopped by political, economic, social and cultural integration which will restore to Pan-Africanism its full meaning ... an Africa capable of promoting its own values.[96]

What this appears to point to is the promise to deepen normative values relevant to the African context and sensitive to its course. The interconnected nature of these values also suggests an approach to peacebuilding that leans on a social process that attempts a reorientation of the very way Africa's social order is constructed. It must be recognised, though, that whilst this vision is possible, the rhetoric in which it is couched remains at the moment largely aspirational. Its fulfilment will be dependent on how it is translated in practice. From the evidence thus far, much needs doing if this narrative is to garner purchase.

The second tier of Pan-Africanism as facilitator for norms formulation involves the process of institutionalisation. The rhetoric of unity and solidarity that animate Pan-African ideals often translate into the urge for the creation of institutions that serve as embodiments of collective aspirations. The mission of such institutions is to not only help in the realisation of the visions upon which the African Union is conceived, but also provide the support towards achieving them. Three examples are evident: the Pan-African Parliament, the Panel of the Wise and the African Union Commission on International Law (AUCIL).

---

[95] See African Union Commission, *Strategic Framework of the African Union Commission 2004–2007*, www.uni-muenster.de/Politikwissenschaft/Doppeldiplom/docs/Strategic.pdf (last visited July 2010).
[96] *Ibid.*

Although the Pan-African Parliament is yet to be fully functional, its integration into the African Union organs represents a move to further institutionalise Pan-Africanism as a frame of reference for Africa's current and future ambitions. Similarly, the AUCIL signifies intentions to not only reflect the 'laws' of the African Union as important components of international legal development, but also facilitate codification of practices within member states of the Union. It remains to be seen whether the AUCIL will fulfil the reclamation narrative upon which it is founded.

In addition to Pan-Africanism, the Kampala CSSDCA constitutes an important part of the Constitutive Act's norms formulation framework. The CSSDCA functions as a frame of reference for the development and institutionalisation of normative values for Africa. Most of the principles and approaches it embodies, especially those relating to the quest for peace, have been incorporated in the Constitutive Act. For instance, the Constitutive Act's norms formulation suggests a kind of integrated approach that intends to place certain values at the core of peacebuilding approaches. This is an offshoot of the *Report on a Brainstorming Meeting* organised by the ALF on the CSSDCA in November 1990.[97] The meeting recognised the integrated nature of Africa's security and emphasised that lessons from armed conflicts in Africa suggest that 'security must not be conceived in the narrow terms of its physical aspects only but in a dynamic and comprehensive manner embracing among others the more fundamental attributes of enduring security such as political pluralism, economic development, and positive social transformation'.[98]

Thus, given its wide outreach, it is perhaps difficult to conceive a continental normative framework that could be oblivious to the influences of the ethos underpinning the CSSDCA. In fact the African Union's *Memorandum of Understanding on Security, Stability, Development and Co-operation* was merely a restatement of the normative values espoused by the CSSDCA.[99] The MoU recognises that 'a fundamental link exists between stability, human security, development and cooperation in a

---

[97] Africa Leadership Forum, *Report on a Brainstorming Meeting for a Conference on Security, Stability, Development and Co-operation in Africa*, Addis Ababa, 17–18 November 1990, www.africaleadership.org/Finreports/Objectives.pdf (last visited April 2010).

[98] *Ibid.*, para. 8.

[99] African Union, *Memorandum of Understanding on Security, Stability, Development and Cooperation in Africa*, Durban, July 2002, www.dfa.gov.za/foreign/Multilateral/africa/cssdca.htm (last visited April 2010).

manner that each reinforces the other' and aspires to an order that views 'the centrality of security as a multi-dimensional phenomenon that goes beyond military considerations and embraces all aspects of human existence, including economic, political and social dimensions of individual, family, community and national life'.[100] This was acknowledged at the African Union Durban Summit, where African leaders noted that the CSSDCA has 'provided a forum for the progressive development and advancement of common values and a structure that consolidates the constructive implementation of the agendas of the Political and Community Affairs Department by relating activities in the sphere of security, stability, development and cooperation more closely to each other and interfacing their initiatives'.[101]

The framework underpinning the CSSDCA initiative has been given added impetus with the New Partnership for Africa's Development (NEPAD). NEPAD is a product of initiatives from African leaders aimed at addressing impoverishment, underdevelopment and social exclusion in Africa. Although it emerged as an initiative outside the African Union architecture, some of its programmes have found resonance in the quest for peace in Africa. These include the promotion of economic cooperation and the acceleration of integration as a means to tackling social factors that have contributed to the resurgence of conflicts in Africa. However, the initiative is at its embryonic stages and still appears to revolve around issues of interstate socio-economic relations rather than internal domestic engagement. In this sense, the initiative's utility in advancing the African Union's emerging approaches to internal conflicts is limited for now.

Social integration and interdependence

In African postcoloniality, the concepts of integration and interdependence through regional and sub-regional building blocks have been touted as important crucibles in the attainment of closer cooperation and solidarity. The principal objective in most of these so-called 'first generation African integration' pacts has been the promotion of trade through the liberalisation of certain trading areas and the consolidation of specific bilateral political cooperation. For the most part, the

---

[100] *Ibid.*

[101] See African Union Summit, Durban, 2002 at www.au2002.gov.za/docs/dbnsummit/index. html (last visited April 2010).

arrangements were constructed in the wake of fear arising from the volatility of the artificial nature of the postcolonial state and doubts over the viability of some economically weak states. Although their names often suggest some kind of integration of member states' economies, the reality was far from what the labels suggested. In practice, the traditional economic justification for these regional institutions was doubtful simply because their 'economies were structurally disarticulated because they had been developed as aggregations of enclaves, each linked to the metropolitan economy but not necessarily to one another'.[102]

The proliferation of integration arrangements between the 1960s and early 1990s did not yield much practical benefit. The nature of integration schemas has, however, undergone some transformation post-Cold War. Their revitalised imagery possesses certain attributes that are 'home grown, organic development within specific historic, political, economic, regional and global contexts'.[103] These genres of integration have a multi-dimensional character and combine an array of political, economic, social and historical as well as defence and security ambitions. Baylis and Smith define this type of integration 'as the creation and maintenance of intense and diversified patterns of integration among previously autonomous limits. These patterns may be partly economic, social and political in character'.[104] The African Union falls in this category, with two integration schemas that can be identified from the Constitutive Act. Article 3(a) and (c) of the African Union's objectives speak of achieving unity and solidarity, and accelerating the political, social and economic integration of Africa. This theme features prominently in most of the provisions of the Constitutive Act and its related instruments. Also, the organs are delineated and interlinked in a way that attempts to synchronise a sense of integration. This emerging model is based on two integration routes. The first pursues social integration and interdependence, and the second lays emphasis on economic integration.

The Constitutive Act presents the process of social integration and interdependence as a template that institutionalises a kind of peacebuilding approach that aspires to make conflicts both illogical and unattractive.

---

[102] M. Adejo, 'From the OAU to AU: New Wine in Old Bottles?' Paper prepared for CODESRIA's 10th General Assembly on 'Africa in the New Millennium', Kampala, Uganda, 8–12 December 2002.

[103] A. Van Nieuwkerk, 'Regionalism into Globalism? War into Peace? SADEC and ECOWAS Compared', African Security Review, 10 (2001), at 7.

[104] See R. J. Baylis and S. Smith, The Globalisation of World Politics: An Introduction to International Relations (New York: Oxford University Press, 1997), p. 411.

As the African Union's peacebuilding formulation is still evolving, there is a lack of detail in the mechanism of achieving this. It is possible, nonetheless, to outline what may be termed the binary of social integration and interdependence as mechanism of peacebuilding. The binary embodies a process of enhancing common values and shared identity as entities for mutual engagement in constructing spaces of peace. Its primary essence is to harness the constitutive elements that anchor peacebuilding dispositions embedded in social integration and interdependence. Social integration could mean different things depending on the context and utility. It thrives on the premise that promoting harmony and spaces of interaction may provide an antidote to the recourse to conflict as means of redressing disputes.

Integration is not, however, self-sustaining. It is complemented by interdependence, a factor that enhances shared goals and ideals whilst accommodating the possibilities or existence of diversity. Interdependence implies an act and the recognition of mutual reliance, interaction and support amongst members of a community or group. Its cornerstone hinges on the sociological dimension of *solidarity*. Solidarity denotes both cooperation and the application of values towards the common good. The realisation of the 'common good' radiates on the assumption that there is an existence of values and shared identity whose preservation and consolidation are a source of strength and a symbol of collective necessity. The binary's basic formation is preoccupied with the provision of a platform of reference for both the individual and community. This is often manifested through social networks which function as templates that animate communal sense of purpose.

The potential of social integration and interdependence in peacebuilding is a strong one. The focus of analyses and articulation of peace theories tend to disproportionately dilate on differences – actual or imagined – that exist in a given state or community. This has the tendency to limit the ability and spaces for alternatives, especially those that emanate from the capabilities and promises of social institutions. In contrast, the binary of social integration and interdependence is driven by the possibilities in the human potential for peace.[105] Its focus is on the social ties, cultural patterns and structural relationships that animate a people's heritage and means of existence. Its utility in peacebuilding is to help propel the strength of social linkages by tapping into the

---

[105] See D. Fry, *Beyond War: The Human Potential for Peace* (Oxford University Press, 2007).

overtures of integration and interdependence in a way that would render conflicts unattractive and illogical. The temptations to the recourse to conflicts could be exponentially reduced where integration and interdependence are well rooted.

Janna Thompson has attempted to situate the reflexes of the binary in the context of cooperative relations drawn within political and socio-economic frames.[106] She asserts that cooperative relations help communities 'motivated by self-interest ... [to] develop institutions and the habit of co-operation with the appreciation of each other's needs making mutual satisfaction of those needs possible'.[107] She notes that 'since all are better off because of the existence of this system than they would be without it, they are predisposed to do what they can to ensure its effective operation. In the course of doing so, they will police and control each other's behaviour.'[108] Mutual self-containment finds resonance in the African conception of *ubuntu*. The notion of *ubuntu* encompasses collective personhood, which according to Lovemore Mbigi 'involves images of group support, acceptance, co-operation, care, sharing and solidarity'.[109] In this sense, *ubuntu* 'moves away from the thinking of social relations in dualistic oppositions' by seeking 'a balance between self and other'.[110] The social intersections found in *ubuntu* resonate with the binary of integration and interdependence.

Anthropological studies have shown that where social integration and interdependence exist as bases for social relations, the prospects of conflict are not only considerably diffused, but their underlying causes may be confronted through non-juridical social processes of dialogue, reconciliation and mutual reaffirmation. In this sense, Margaret Mead has spoken of the object and capabilities of this binary as 'reducing the strength of all mutually exclusive loyalties ... and constructing some quite different form of organisation in which the memories of these loyalties and the organisation residues of these former exclusive loyalties cannot threaten the total structure'.[111]

---

[106] J. Thompson, *Justice and World Order: A Philosophical Inquiry* (London: Routledge, 1992), p. 40.

[107] *Ibid.*, p. 41.   [108] *Ibid.*

[109] L. Mbigi, *Ubuntu: The Spirit of African Transformation Management* (Randburg: Knowledge Resources Ltd, 1994), p. 2.

[110] N. Masina, 'Xhosa Practices of Ubuntu for South Africa' in I. W. Zartman (ed.), *Traditional Cures for Modern Conflicts: African Conflict 'Medicine'* (Boulder, Colo.: Lynne Rienner, 2000), p. 169.

[111] M. Mead, 'Alternatives to War' in M. Fried, M. Harris and R. Murphy (eds.), *War: The Anthropology of Armed Conflict and Aggression* (New York: Natural History Press, 1967), p. 224.

Although harnessing the potential of integration and interdependence often presupposes the existence of certain commonalities, it is not entirely contingent on it. Kwame Anthony Appiah, for instance, extols the virtues of this binary even across societies with very little common ground. His 'cross-cultural conversation' theory maximises the social benefits of what a particular people have in common.[112] Once they find enough they share, he explains, 'there is the possibility that [they] will be able to enjoy discovering things [they] do not yet share'.[113] Others, such as Ulrich Beck, have spoken of a cosmopolitan vision of the actuality of interdependence expanded by emotional imagination from the local, national and international. In Beck's view, it is not necessary to isolate and organise human beings into antagonistic groups, not even within the broad expanse of the nation, for them to become self-aware and capable of political action that is framed within a durable peaceful order.[114]

The focus of integration and interdependence on the interrelation and consolidation of collective interest so that the recourse to force becomes unattractive, may well give rise to concern that it might impact on individual autonomy and choices. But the character of communal life in a political community is not so adverse to individual choices. Ronald Dworkin, the American legal philosopher, has argued that integration and interdependence do not necessarily suppose that a good citizen or member of a community will be concerned for the wellbeing of fellow citizens.[115] What the binary encompasses, he explains, is that a citizen 'must be concerned for his own well-being, and that, just in virtue of that concern, he must take an interest in the moral life of the community of which he is a member'.[116] The position of the individual is built around what Dworkin calls a 'unit of agency' whose effectiveness depends on the depths of social practices and attitudes. Three elements constitute *unit of agency*.

The first element presupposes the existence of 'acts socially denominated as collective'. According to Dworkin, these are 'acts identified and individuated as those of a community as a whole rather than of members of the community as individuals'.[117] Second, the individual acts are concerted and performed self-consciously, which means that they contribute

---

[112] K. A. Appiah, *Cosmopolitanism: Ethics in a World of Strangers* (London: Penguin Group, 2006), p. 96.
[113] *Ibid.*, p. 97.   [114] U. Beck, *Cosmopolitan Vision* (Cambridge: Polity Press, 2006), p. 6.
[115] R. Dworkin, *Sovereign Virtue: The Theory and Practice of Equality* (Cambridge, Mass: Harvard University Press, 2002), p. 224.
[116] *Ibid.*, p. 224.   [117] *Ibid.*, p. 227.

'to the collective act, rather than as isolated acts that happen to coincide in some way'.[118] Third, the composition of the community is tailored to its collective acts. There appears to be a correlation with the balancing act that underpins *ubuntu*. This is so because *ubuntu*'s 'orientation to life is opposed to individualism and insensitive competitiveness, neither is it comfortable with collectivism where collectivism stresses the importance of the social unit to the point of depersonalising the individual'.[119] Dworkin's formulation provides an understanding of not only the position and role of an individual in an integrated community, but how this could potentially promote solidarity and cohesion that envisions a mutual coexistence capable of rendering the recourse to force unattractive.

Subsets of the Constitutive Act's peacebuilding approaches

The peacebuilding and transformative approaches to conflict embedded in the Constitutive Act correspond to each of the three outlets of the African Union's peace and security framework. The three outlets – Article 4 non-indifference, norms formulation, and social integration and interdependence – embody respectively, what could be labelled as constitutive subsets of peacebuilding. These subsets are *Restorative, Corrective* and *Preventive.*

The Restorative subset

The Restorative subset functions as a transformative agent seeking to arrest intervening factors which provide the frames through which group identity is shaped and also violence and conflicts often tend to manifest. It tackles the underlying origin, contingent dynamics and potential source(s) of conflicts. Restorative is often the first serious engagement following the outbreak of a conflict. This may involve a kind of inter-vention through consensual dialogue where parties caught up in a conflict are encouraged to partake in a process that seeks to address not only the underlying causes of the conflict, but also how their concerns may envision a collective beneficial interest in an inclusive non-violent approach.

[118] *Ibid.*, p. 227.
[119] P. Christie, R. Lessem and L. Mbigi, *African Management Philosophies, Concepts and Applications* (Randburg: Knowledge Resources Ltd, 1993), pp. 122–3.

Unlike contemporary international law approaches to peacebuilding, the Restorative subset pursues the restoration of peace through the social structures that serve as the focal point of identity amongst communities and social groups. Quite often, where social tension is imminent, engagement may be either too slow or limited. In such situations, conditions could degenerate into violence occasioning harm and grave breaches of rights and values. In this instance, the Restorative dimension advances to countermeasures that may include protection forces whose function is to halt violence and facilitate the gradual deepening of the two other constitutive subsets. In the Constitutive Act, the Restorative subset appears in the form of Article 4, where the African Union acquires the right of consensual and non-consensual intervention through military and non-military countermeasures. Once fully functional, the African Standby Force would comprise the military element whilst the Panel of the Wise and other components of the African Union Commission are anticipated to constitute the non-military dimension.

The Corrective subset

The gains in the Restorative stages are built on and consolidated by the Corrective subset. In literary terms, 'corrective' implies the intention 'to correct or counteract something undesirable'.[120] This involves instituting remedies or facilitating restitution by constructing spaces of dialogue capable of building trust, initiating healing and repairing social and structural embodiments of injustice. The objective is to ensure fairness by limiting dominance in the social and political realm, whilst also consolidating values that may promote alternative frameworks for social justice and community cohesion. This would almost inevitably require the recasting of social and political structures, especially those entrapped in historical legacies and uneven hierarchies that thrive on division. The Corrective subset is not wholly homogeneous. It can take different forms and habitats ranging from mediation, conciliation and power-sharing. In post-Cold War peacebuilding, the Corrective subset has assumed a more transformative feature in the form of comprehensive peace agreements. Of course peace agreements as mechanisms for confronting conflicts are not new. They had long been utilised in interstate conflicts in Africa, especially where the security

---

[120] *Concise Oxford English Dictionary* (Oxford University Press, 2006), p. 321.

and stability of a particular region was at risk. However, their use in internal conflicts has been on the rise. But their viability has often been a concern especially in recent times when they have been violated more than they have been respected.

Virginia Page Fortna has offered perspectives on the viability of peace agreements as transformative elements of the Corrective subset. Fortna argues that far from being mere rhetoric or statements of intent, peace agreements have potential in providing institutional and normative frameworks that could end and prevent the resurgence of conflicts.[121] This is because the probability of violent conflicts recurring is significantly reduced when peace agreements make the resort to violence a costly option.[122] Fortna identifies two variables she considers crucial in the transformation of conflicts. The first pertains to what she calls the situational variable that includes cost and outcome of war, historical context and capabilities of belligerents.[123] The second variable emerges in ceasefire agreements, arms control and third party involvement.[124]

But the utility of the Corrective subset lies in its potential in providing space for a coherent interaction between law, social institutions and the state. When configured to reflect the needs and structures of a given society, legal frameworks can play a vital role in the transformation of social imbalances that are often sources of tension and violence.[125] One way of achieving this is through national constitutional instruments. Although internal conflicts in Africa are caused by numerous factors, social and structural imbalances in a society play a central part. The function of the Corrective subset is to attempt to reverse these sources of conflict through genuine reconfiguration in the social and political realms. Thus what the Corrective dimension can potentially do is to enable legal frameworks to assume some associational forms of social bargaining, mediation and negotiation in the quest to reversing injustice and structural imbalance.[126] The Corrective subset is represented in the Constitutive Act through norms formulation and localisation. This encompasses Pan-African ideas and visions, the CSSDCA process and the AUCIL.

---

[121] V. P. Fortna, *Peace Time: Ceasefire Agreements and the Durability of Peace* (Princeton University Press, 2004), p. 24.

[122] *Ibid.*   [123] *Ibid.*, pp. 77–82.   [124] *Ibid.*, pp. 25–9.

[125] V. Tismaneanu, *Fantasies of Salvation: Democracy, Nationalism, and Myth in Post-Communist Europe* (Princeton University Press, 1998), p. 157.

[126] T. E. Paupp, *Achieving Inclusionary Governance: Advancing Peace and Development in First and Third World Nations* (New York: Transnational Publishers, 2000), p. 194.

The Preventive subset

Whilst Corrective and Restorative subsets are preoccupied with past and contingent concerns, the Preventive dimension focuses on imagining futures. The Preventive subset functions as a mechanism through which conflicts could be prevented from occurring. There are two possible ways in which this could be achieved. First, a preventive approach deepens engagement and seeks a proactive construction of structural patterns that envision a kind of social order where armed conflict becomes an unattractive vocation or means of interaction. Second, there is an emerging consensus that although the underlying causes of internal conflicts are multifaceted, the suppression and erosion of frameworks capable of advancing normative values, shared purpose and commonality of interests are often major factors. It is therefore imperative that the Preventive subset provides space for the consolidation of social cohesion through communal solidarity, promotes interdependence, espouses positive peacebuilding as a collective endeavour within, and amongst, communities as well as being a point of reference for a just social order.

However, for the Preventive subset to be effectively realised, traditional social institutions must be incorporated into peacebuilding initiatives. This is because in African postcolonial statehood where there have been recurring problems of weak state structures, social institutions often provide a sense of identity, security and patronage to individuals and social groups. Most of this role has, however, been considerably distilled by the incoherent nature of nation-building in postcolonial statecraft.[127] The new post-independence political order that emerged in Africa attempted to distance itself from the traditional social institutions on the basis that their existence as emblems of identity formation was antithetical to the social homogeneity of modern statehood.[128] What it did was to render the postcolonial state neither able to fulfil neutrality, nor capable of maintaining convivial relationships with traditional social institutions. This tension trivialised the value of social institutions and alienated their capabilities and potential.

The possible role of the Preventive subset, in this context, is to help discard exclusion by granting agency to social institutions perceived as

---

[127] For insights into the nature and contradictions of post-independence nation-building in Africa, see B. Davidson, *The Black Man's Burden: Africa and the Curse of the Nation-State* (New York: Time Books, 1992).

[128] See L. Vail (ed.), *The Creation of Tribalism in Southern Africa* (Berkeley: University of California Press, 1989).

sources of security and identity. It is also in these social constructions that the 'ideological self-assurance' of an individual is espoused creating spaces for interaction and engagement. This is often sustained by a continuity of purpose that blends communal interests with individual aspirations. Such a delicate preservation remains a cornerstone of African cultural philosophy to the extent that contemporary African human rights and human security instruments, particularly the African Charter and the African Union's Constitutive Act, may appear alien when analysed outside the boundary of this social construction. The Preventive subset emerges in the Constitutive Act in the form of the binary of social integration and interdependence. This allows for a possibility through which social patterns, structures and institutions could be drawn as collective consociational avenues for the realisation of durable conditions of peace.

Conclusion

This chapter has set out to examine the scope, capacity and dynamics of the Constitutive Act's normative order and institutional structures, and the extent to which they represent a renewed perspective in confronting violence and conflicts in Africa. It is argued that the integrated framework provides a window of opportunity, howsoever limited, in confronting internal conflicts in Africa in a way that transcends the inadequacies of contemporary international law approaches. This potential is encapsulated in three interrelated pillars. The first relates to the intervention mechanism of Article 4, which typifies an approach, albeit provisional, that is intended to confront internal conflicts as a right of the African Union. This mechanism represents the Restorative subset of the Constitutive Act's peacebuilding framework.

The second pillar concerns the norms formulation and localisation framework that engenders values considered crucial in the advancement of individual and collective mutual interests. It functions as the Corrective subset of peacebuilding. The third takes shape in the binary of integration and interdependence, whose objective is to deepen integration in a way that makes the recourse to conflict both unattractive and illogical. This equates to the Preventive subset. Taken together, the approaches potentially constitute parameters of an African-inspired recharacterisation of responses to internal conflicts.

The Constitutive Act has significantly departed from, and reconfigured, some of the defining ethos that underlined Africa's postcolonial normative architecture. The evolving normative shift implies that strict reverence to the doctrines of state sovereignty and territorial integrity that characterised and inhibited the OAU no longer hold. In the Constitutive Act, sovereignty is conditional, not total, and it must be exercised in a way that shows responsibility and value for human life. It draws from the wisdom that the political, social and economic integration of Africa could provide a framework capable of confronting the enigma of armed conflicts by adopting a multidimensional approach of prevention, preparedness, response, mitigation and recovery. That, at least, is the theory. But as Douglas Fry notes, peace cannot solely be achieved 'simply through modifying beliefs, attitudes, and values, but rather that such modification is one ingredient in a complex recipe for abolishing war'.[129] And so in the next two chapters this theory is put to the test.

[129] Fry, *Beyond War*, p. 223.

7

The African Union peacebuilding travails
in Burundi

> In the absence of the AU Mission, Burundi would have been left to its own
> devices, which probably would have resulted in an escalation of violent conflict.
> AMIB was therefore engaged in peace building through preventing violent
> conflict and trying to lay the foundations for reconciliation and reconstruction.
>
> Tim Murithi[1]

Introduction

In the previous chapter, an argument was made that the integrated
nature of the Constitutive Act of the African Union provides a *tabula
rasa* through which approaches to internal conflicts in Africa could be
conceived and pursued. The potential, it was noted, emerges with the
backdrop of the African Union's departure from, and attempted recharacterisation of, some of international law's defining principles, ideas
that quintessentially shaped Africa's post-independence normative order
under the OAU and its conflict management approaches. The objective
in this chapter is to test the extent to which the basis of that argument –
the strength of perspectives on transformative approaches to conflicts
enunciated in the Constitutive Act and its normative framework – is
capable of confronting conflicts in ways that signify potential remedies
to the inadequacies of international law approaches to internal conflicts.
Representing the first of two case studies, the chapter focuses on Burundi,
an old African enclave in the Great Lakes region of central Africa, whose
post-independence history has been largely characterised by considerable
violence and social upheaval.

---

[1] T. Murithi, 'The African Union's Evolving Role in Peace Operations: The African Union
Mission in Burundi, the African Union Mission in Sudan and the African Union Mission
in Somalia', *African Security Review*, 17:1 (2008), 71–82 at 75.

The choice of Burundi is influenced by three factors. First, like most of Africa, Burundi displays patterns of colonial residues, and has gone through social disarray and political challenges that have dogged a large part of African postcolonial statehood. This burden of inheritance has the tendency to render the African postcolonial state an ambiguous entity almost condemned to perpetual struggles, forcing it to compete for spaces of legitimacy. Second, Burundi's struggles with the legal fiction of its sovereignty and postcolonial crises have, as elsewhere in Africa, resulted in the institutionalisation of social conditions that make violence and conflicts enduring. This has brought international law and regional mechanisms into the equation, with the proposition of a number of approaches to confront Burundi's post-independence crises. Third, and perhaps most important, Burundi was the first country where, in 2003, the African Union invoked provisions of its Constitutive Act's peacebuilding framework. The aim was to utilise the restorative and stabilisation mechanism under Article 4 with the view to halting the cycle of violence so as to facilitate the implementation of the other components of the African Union's peace and security framework.

The invocation of Article 4(h) came in the wake of continuous dithering and abdication of international responsibility, particularly from a United Nations that showed limited interest in providing leadership in confronting the Burundi crisis. What this situation did, in effect, was to provide space for the African Union to assert its presence by attempting to invoke its peacebuilding framework in Burundi through the African Union Mission in Burundi (AMIB). It is imperative, therefore, to examine AMIB, under whose auspices approaches to the Burundi conflict had been conceptualised. This analysis will provide insights into not only the operational functionality of the mission, but also the potential, challenges and future direction of the philosophy underpinning the Constitutive Act's peacebuilding framework.

Burundi – a historical overview

Burundi is one of Africa's oldest 'nation states'. In a continent where the overwhelming majority of territorial boundaries are the product of colonial social engineering, it is one of only a few countries in Africa whose geographic layout has remained virtually unchanged.[2] Thus the

---

[2] R. Lemarchand, *Burundi: Ethnic Conflict and Genocide* (Cambridge University Press, 1994), p. 1.

country occupies a territorial identity similar to that defined by its pre-colonial boundaries. Similarly, Burundi's precolonial demographic profile had four group stratifications that continue to inhabit its postcolonial nationhood. These are the Hutu, Tutsi and Twa. Another group, the *ganwa*, was a kind of social group associated with Burundi's royalty, but has ceased to exist following the abolition of the monarchy in 1966. The sense of commonality amongst the groups was striking as they shared the same language, culture and customs, traditional political institutions and spiritual beliefs.[3] In addition to these common traits, the social groups had maintained, prior to Burundi's postcolonial cycle of violence, what has been described as 'a life rich in inter-group relations ... marked by a keen sense of solidarity'.[4] This was enhanced through the consolidation of trade relations, interdependence and social integration through inter-group marriages.

Precolonial Burundi was governed by a monarchy – a *mwami* (king) who was perceived as a father figure and held in considerable reverence, possessing, in effect, 'near-divine powers and [functioning as] a symbol of national unity'.[5] The *mwami*'s role was primarily to ensure stability and social cohesion, promote prosperity and provide a conducive environment for the harnessing of individual aspirations. In achieving these goals, the *mwami* delegated authority to the *ganwa* (administrative chiefs) and *bashingantahe* (council of elders).[6] This had the benefit of promoting individual and collective worth, facilitating interpersonal interaction, harmony and consultative decision-making in the interest of the common good. The strength in the monarchy's distribution of authority and maintenance of peaceful coexistence could be located in what Joseph Gahama calls a 'subtle interplay of alliances' with the main social groups.[7] According to Peter Uvin 'the system displayed a fair degree of legitimacy and was capable of addressing social conflicts'.[8] Some even claim that Burundi's

---

[3] See generally R. Lemarchand, *Burundi: Ethnocide as Theory and Practice* (Cambridge University Press, 1994).

[4] J. Gahama *et al.*, 'Burundi' in A. Adedeji (ed.), *Comprehending and Mastering African Conflicts: The Search for Sustainable Peace and Good Governance* (London: Zed Books, 1999), p. 81.

[5] R. Kay, 'Burundi Since the Genocide', *Minority Rights Group*, 20 (1995), at 3.

[6] See R. Lemarchand, *Rwanda and Burundi* (London: Pall Mall, 1970).

[7] J. Gahama, 'Conflict Prevention, Management and Resolution in Burundi', http://unpan1.un.org/intradoc/groups/public/documents/CAFRAD/UNPAN009002.pdf.

[8] P. Uvin, *Life After Violence: A People's Story of Burundi* (London: Zed Books, 2009), p. 9.

relatively orderly precolonial political structure was responsible for the near absence of intergroup armed conflicts.[9]

Although this claim may be overstated, it is worth noting that even where conflicts were apparent, they arose from power struggles within the royal household motivated by factors that transcended identity.[10] The political structure also reveals the level of decentralisation that characterised precolonial Burundi. Integral to this was the influence of two distinct but broadly complementary social determinants: chiefdom and clientage.[11] Their role was seen as multidimensional, especially given that at the very least they bound individuals, primordial groups and institutional structures that defined them.[12] By so doing, they accelerated the composition of group identities and the mobilisation of individual loyalties towards a particular social objective. Precolonial identity, it is worth noting, had no particular ethnic affiliation. Status in society was determined by a patron–client relationship, which opened up opportunities.[13] At the heart of it, Rene Lemarchand explains, was a kind of relationship that facilitated exchange between individuals of unequal status.[14]

Burundi's highly driven decentralised political system remained in place until the late nineteenth century. But by 1889, Burundi's internal cohesion had been disrupted by a series of natural and social episodes. A drought devastated its flora and fauna, followed by an outbreak of disease that killed two-thirds of the population.[15] Food insecurity and the grief that followed the deaths dampened the communal spirits of a people whose unity was dependent on this social resource. The political leadership was not immune from this turbulence either. The reigning king at the time, *mwami* Mwezi Gisabo, had seen his leadership challenged by sustained and sometimes violent opposition to his power and ambitions. Old age, coupled with an inability to contain recurrent resistance from aggrieved social groups such as the *ganwa*, weakened and eroded trust in the *mwami*'s capacity to assert authority or reclaim past (and increasingly fading) glories of the monarchy.

---

[9] R. P. Herisse, 'Development on a Theatre: Democracy, Governance and the Socio-political Conflict in Burundi', *Agriculture and Human Values*, 18:3 (2001), 295–304 at 296.

[10] See G. Prunier, *The Rwandan Crisis 1959–1994: History of a Genocide* (London: Hurst & Company, 1995).

[11] D. J. Eller, *From Culture to Ethnicity to Conflict* (Ann Arbor: University of Michigan Press, 2002), p. 203.

[12] *Ibid.*   [13] Lemarchand, *Burundi: Ethnic Conflict*, p. 13.   [14] *Ibid.*, p. 12.

[15] Eller, *From Culture*, p. 210.

Rene Lemarchand has described this internal turmoil as 'a situation bordering on chaos'.[16] The internal chaos was perhaps the final straw in the monarchy's attempts to salvage a crumbling dynasty. It changed Burundi forever. First, it dislodged the distribution of power and chain of alliances that maintained a sense of amity amongst the respective social groups.

Second, with the authority of the *mwami* almost gone, it created the material conditions for colonial penetration. Social structures that would ordinarily have challenged imperial expansion were muzzled, with little prospect of recovery. Unsurprisingly, these structures gradually resigned to the dominance of the new colonial political dispensation. The social turmoil of 1889–91 unfolded with the backdrop of increasing colonial activity. The Berlin Conference on the partition of Africa had taken place a few years earlier, and consolidation of colonies followed almost immediately. Expansionism and territorial consolidation in and around central and eastern Africa soon materialised. Burundi and its sister state, Rwanda, were seen as essential geopolitical entities for both German and British imperial ambitions in the region.[17] Through a strategy of so-called 'explorations of possessions', Germany consolidated its grip on the region and held the two territories as the joint colony of Ruanda-Urundi from 1892.[18] However, German occupation was short-lived, ending almost immediately after World War I. During the brief occupation, Burundi's social order experienced patterns of disruption, designed to not only reconstitute its social configuration, but also to introduce certain attitudes and mindsets that would entrench the various habitats of the colonial project.[19]

In the aftermath of World War I, Burundi's social dynamics experienced profound transformation. German colonial rule was replaced by that of Belgium in 1923, through the institution of the League of Nations mandate.[20] Belgian colonial policies held remarkable implications for Ruanda-Urundi. In many ways, they orchestrated some of the deeper patterns of postcolonial statehood that sowed the seeds of the subsequent violence and conflicts. The mandate policy, framed under the blessing of the League of Nations Mandate (and later UN Trusteeship Council) also exposed the complicity of international

---

[16] Lemarchand, *Rwanda and Burundi*, p. 49.   [17] Eller, *From Culture*.
[18] See Lemarchand, *Rwanda and Burundi*.   [19] Uvin, *Life After Violence*, p. 8.
[20] S. R. Weissman, *Preventing Genocide in Burundi* (Washington, DC: United States Institute of Peace, 1998), p. 5.

law.[21] The Belgians essentially consolidated Germany's earlier attempt in creating material and physical distinctions amongst social groups. In strengthening identities and social differences, a certain ethnography reinforcing variations in physique between the social groups was not only seen as necessary, but also a policy central to the realisation of the colonial reform agenda. Joseph Gahama explains that this ethno-graphic narrative, and the manner in which it was promoted, had the objective of projecting the Tutsi as a social group with aristocratic appearances, intelligent and capable of leading and making sound judgements.[22] According to Mahmood Mamdani, the Hutu–Tutsi dif-ferentiation created 'political identities that changed with the changing history of the [Ruandan-Burundi] state'.[23]

Social distinction, though, was more than just symbolic. It enhanced social standing, influence and privileges. For example, Tutsi 'fine bearing alone guarantee[d] them considerable prestige'.[24] Individual ethnic neutrality was seen by colonial authorities as an obstacle to the reorganisation of Burundi's political structure. The priority was to determine the fulcrum of social group cohesion and then introduce an isolationist policy tailored to conform to colonial ambitions. Thus ethnic identity, relatively alien to precolonial Burundi, was gradually introduced as a method to ascribe identity to the main social groups.[25] By delineating such identities, colonial authorities created imbalances in Burundi's social structure. The Tutsi emerged from this as the dominant group enjoined with power and colonial favour.[26] In particular, missionary education was made readily available to Tutsi traditional rulers with the aim of converting them to Christianity and consolidating their standing as 'qualified operatives in the colonial system'.[27] And as Jack Eller explains, this kind of colonial favour towards the Tutsi, and 'discrimination against [the] Hutu ... could only serve to widen the gulf, and inflame the resentment, between the two groups'.[28]

---

[21] See A. Anghie, *Imperialism, Sovereignty and the Making of International Law* (Cambridge University Press, 2005).

[22] Gahama, 'Conflict Prevention', at 4.

[23] M. Mamdani, *When Victims Become Killers: Colonialism, Nativism, and the Genocide in Rwanda* (Princeton University Press, 2002), p. 73.

[24] *Ibid.*, p. 4.   [25] Uvin, *Life After Violence*, pp. 8–9.

[26] P. Daley, *Gender and Genocide in Burundi: The Search for Spaces of Peace* (Oxford: James Curry, 2008), p. 49.

[27] Eller, *From Culture*, p. 211.   [28] *Ibid.*

The medium of implementation of colonial policies was the system of indirect rule.[29] This entailed the cooptation of traditional rulers into the colonial administration machinery, and was subsequently used to great effect. On the surface, it provided a deceptive presumption of indigenous participation in the colonial reform agenda. But indirect rule, whether in its original form in Northern Nigeria or its reincarnation in Burundi, was essentially a manipulation of existing traditional institutional structures and was meant to provide a platform from which a substantial part of colonial reform could be enforced with minimal resistance. The use of existing traditional structures was premised on the idea of exploiting, to the fullest extent, the loyalty and patronage enjoyed by chiefs. The weakening of the social system facilitated sweeping reorganisation and introduction of economic reforms in rapid succession.[30] By the dawn of World War II, the Belgian colonial reform agenda had been firmly constituted. New identities had been 'invented', and traditional institutions that had for many centuries undergirded social relationships now saw their feudal characteristics stripped away and replaced with a bureaucratic machinery based on exploitation and dominance.[31]

The depths and impact of exploitation degenerated into considerable waves of resentment. Disenchantment was not just a verdict on colonial reforms, but also a prelude to agitation for independence.[32] Demands for self-rule intensified following minor political reforms in 1948 allowing for the formation of political parties. But given the divisive character of Belgian colonial policies, especially the premise of inequality they engendered, party formation became a mere reflection of the inherent imbalances in Burundi's social system.[33]

Yet if there was anything that rallied unity amongst the otherwise divided political elites, it was the desire to return to the *status quo ante* of separate polities that had existed prior to imperial rule. To this end, in January 1959 Burundi's *mwami*, Mwambutsa IV, submitted a request to

---

[29] Indirect rule as an administrative system was largely associated with Lord Lugard, who pioneered its introduction in Northern Nigeria. For more on this see M. Perham, *Native Administration in Nigeria* (Oxford University Press, 1937).

[30] Between 1926 and 1930 differentiation amongst social groups became even more pronounced and access to facilities highly restricted. For example, a specialist institution, the *L'Ecole Astrida*, was established to provide training to the children of Ganwa and Tutsi families with the view to providing them with skills to occupy administrative positions in the colonial set-up. Furthermore, in 1930 a decree made it a requirement for a person's ethnicity to be inserted in national identity cards. See Eller, *From Culture*, p. 212.

[31] Eller, *From Culture*, p. 215.   [32] *Ibid.*   [33] Eller, *From Culture*.

the Belgian Minister of Colonies demanding the dissolution of the Ruanda-Urundi joint colony.[34] Soon after, two political parties emerged: the Union for National Progress (UPRONA) and the Christian Democratic Party (PDC). In July 1962, Burundi declared independence. It retained the monarchy as the head of state.[35]

Civil war and the cycle of violence

Ever since decolonisation in the 1950s, most of the Great Lake region has been a flashpoint of seemingly unending chaos and disorder.[36] Wars have been fought, assassinations carried out, countries ravaged and millions of people displaced. Burundi's postcolonial experience in particular has been punctuated with political turbulence and ethnic strife, the magnitude of which has essentially made all Burundians into vulnerable targets.[37] Rene Lemarchand asserted powerfully in a 1988 testimony to the United States Congress that 'nowhere else in Africa have human rights been violated on a more massive scale, and with more brutal consistency, than in Burundi'.[38] Lemarchand's assertion was informed by the scale and almost enduring nature of the cycle of violence and the rights abuses that became a fundamental part of the methods and consequences of the crises. Burundi's cycle of violence shows a certain gradation that has been both intense and total. Four periods are evident: eve of independence transitional disorder; the 1972 genocide; 1988 ethnic tensions; and the violence and uncertainty that followed the 1993 multi-party democratisation initiatives.

Burundi's transition from a colony to self-rule was anything but smooth. In 1961, just a year shy of independence, parliamentary elections were held as part of the political transition process. UPRONA emerged with 84 per cent of overall votes and its leader, Prince Rwagasore, was sworn in as Prime Minister.[39] Two weeks later he was assassinated in what was deemed a politically motivated act. Reaction to his murder was swift and bloody. Opponents from the PDC party were identified for blame and a dozen

---

[34] *Ibid.*   [35] Uvin, *Life After Violence*, p. 8.

[36] See J. P. Chritien, *The Great Lakes of Africa: Two Thousand Years of History* (New York: Zone Books, 2003).

[37] N. Alusala, 'Disarmament and the Transition in Burundi: How Soon?', *Institute for Security Studies*, Occasional Paper, 97 (2005), 1–16 at 1.

[38] R. Lemarchand, 'Burundi: The Killing Fields Revisited', *Journal of Opinion*, 18:1 (1989), 22–8 at 22.

[39] See Lemarchand, *Rwanda and Burundi*.

of its senior hierarchy executed.[40] Instability further ensued with the assassination in 1965 of a Hutu Prime Minister, Pierre Ngendumwe. A *ganwa* replacement appointed by the *mwami* was interpreted as an act of royal nepotism, insensitive to, and unmoved by, previous disenchantments.[41] Hutu army officers attempted an abortive coup to rectify the unfolding political crisis. The Tutsi-dominated army reacted with brutal reprisals, summarily executing the coupists and nearly purging the military of Hutus.[42] The *mwami* fled, and the line of succession fell to his nineteen-year-old nephew, whose inexperience made it possible for Michel Micombero to stage a coup in 1966.[43]

If the transition to independence epitomised chaos, the second period in the gradation of violence was monumental and tragic in its scale and effects. Micombero oversaw massive breaches of fundamental freedoms. The excluded Hutu majority were severely prejudiced. In many ways, his regime was a symphony of disorder with rumours, plots and counterplots, often culminating in violent state reprisals.[44] The last straw was in April 1972, when a Hutu rebellion broke out in the south, unleashing terror on the Tutsi population. Eyewitness accounts spoke of indiscriminate killing on a large scale.[45] The government response 'was not so much a repression as a hideous slaughter of Hutu civilians'.[46] At a conservative estimate, 200,000 Hutus were killed with thousands more forced to flee to neighbouring Tanzania. There is even a suggestion that 'by August of 1972, almost every educated Hutu element was either dead or in exile'.[47] There is consensus that these killings amounted to genocide.[48]

---

[40] The killing of Rwagasore was seen as the turning point in Burundi's domestic politics. The Prince was hugely popular, and was able to mobilise people from all groups, especially in the march to independence. The killing hardened Tutsi and Hutu, laying seeds for identity politics. See Eller, *From Culture*.

[41] *Ibid.*, p. 231.   [42] *Ibid.*

[43] R. Krueger and K. Krueger, *From Bloodshed to Hope in Burundi: Our Embassy Years during Genocide* (Austin: University of Texas Press, 2007), p. 28.

[44] R. Lemarchand, 'The Burundi Genocide', (1994), http://migs.concordia.ca/documents/Burundi.doc, at 3.

[45] *Ibid.*, at 4.   [46] *Ibid.*   [47] *Ibid.*

[48] According to Article II of the Genocide Convention of 1948, an act becomes genocide when 'committed with intent to destroy, in whole or in part, a national, ethnical, racial or religious group', and done by '(i) killing members of the group; (ii) causing serious bodily or mental harm to members of the group; (iii) deliberately inflicting on the group conditions of life calculated to bring about its physical destruction in whole or in part; (iv) imposing measures intended to prevent births within the group; forcibly transferring children of the group to another group'. The targeted killing of the Hutus, imposition of conditions of hardship and the evisceration of pregnant women have been widely viewed as fulfilling all the elements of Article II.

The 1972 genocide had enduring effects, with consequences that for long remained engraved in the collective minds of the social groups, determining individual attitudes and daily behaviour.[49] This was evident in Burundi's third wave of violence in 1988. A few years after the genocide, Micombero was overthrown by his cousin, Colonel Jean-Baptiste Bagaza, in 1976. The new government, lasting until 1987, had the rare merit of not having known any major intercommunity conflict.[50] But Bagaza was no saint: religious freedom was curtailed, intimidation by security forces continued and state policy of exclusion intensified.[51] Unpopular at home and shunned by the international community, his fate was sealed when in September 1987 another military coup installed Major Pierre Buyoya as head of state. The new regime started promisingly and its compass was set on a path to reconciliation.[52] But little changed as ethnic fissures and a culture of impunity continued. Ethnic tension flared in the northern town of Marangara in 1988 with a dozen Tutsis reportedly killed by Hutu extremists.[53] Once again, the Burundi army used heavy weaponry, killing almost 20,000 Hutus.[54]

The fourth period of violence followed the 1993 democratisation initiative and its aftermath. The 1988 wave of violence had triggered a more robust international response, with the European Community and US Congress condemning gross violations of human rights.[55] The pressure persuaded the Burundi government to introduce constitutional reforms. In June 1993, presidential and legislative elections were finally held, which the predominantly Hutu Front pour la Démocratie au Burundi (FRODEBU) won overwhelmingly and its leader, Melchoir Ndadaye, was installed as president. However in October 1993 Ndadaye and half a dozen of his cabinet were killed by Tutsi soldiers. The ensuing violence claimed the lives of over 300,000 people.[56] Political turmoil and disorder continued in the streets of Bujumbura until 1994, when

---

[49] Gahama, 'Conflict Prevention', at 6.
[50] Ibid.   [51] Krueger and Krueger, From Bloodshed to Hope, p. 29.
[52] For example, Buyoya appointed a Hutu Prime Minister and a few more Hutus to his cabinet. His diplomatic tact enticed the international community, bringing in the large disbursements of International Development Association (IDA) loans. See Krueger and Krueger, From Bloodshed to Hope, p. 31.
[53] Krueger and Krueger, ibid.   [54] Ibid.
[55] In the 1988 Congressional hearing, leading scholars on Burundi such as Rene Lemarchand were invited to make presentations on the killings and social transformations unfolding at the time.
[56] See Institute for Policy Research, 'Burundi and the Crisis in Central Africa', Foreign Policy in Focus, 2:13 (1997), at 1.

Cyprien Ntaryamira assumed the presidency. A few months later, whilst returning from a peace summit in Tanzania, Ntaryamira and his Rwandan counterpart, Juvenal Habyarimana, were both killed when their aeroplane was rocketed at Kigali airport. The event led to the Rwandan genocide, but also triggered violence in Burundi. The search for peace had become even more complicated. A transitional administration installed under a so-called Convention of Government collapsed. Violence resumed and in 1996 Major Pierre Buyoya staged his second military coup.[57]

It is clear that Burundi's gradation of violence has been greatly disruptive, not only to its postcolonial statehood but also to the Great Lakes' regional security. Although the causes of internal conflicts in Africa are many and varied, there are, however, patterns of commonalities that bind them. These include residual colonial effects and burden of inheritance – elements that Burundi has suffered its share of. There are also factors that may be relatively country-specific. In Burundi, the political landscape had been mapped using lenses of ethnicity so thick that the capacity of social institutions in advancing qualities of humanity and forgiveness had been greatly limited. What this did, however, was to project a false impression that no credible alternative existed beyond ethnic identity. Rene Lemarchand even suggests that this perceived absolutism of ethnicity has drawn Burundians to act solely in the name of this identity.[58] 'What is being remembered by many Hutu', he writes, 'is an apocalypse that has forever altered their perceptions of the Tutsi, now seen as the historic incarnation of evil'.[59]

A psychological dimension may also be evident, according to Ahmedou Ould-Abdallah, a former UN Special Envoy to Burundi. This, he explains, departs from the premise that Burundians are entrapped in 'a self-enforced psychological ghetto surrounded by high walls of fear, rumour, and death'.[60] This mindset, Ould-Abdallah suggests, is exacerbated by impoverishment, overpopulation and a certain hysteria and paranoia accentuating fears for individual and collective ethnic survival.[61] Notwithstanding this theorisation, the centrality of the postcolonial state in Burundi's cycle of violence is more than evident. From the outset, the state was besieged by a colonially altered social order. Historically

---

[57] Krueger and Krueger, *From Bloodshed to Hope*, p. 268.
[58] R. Lemarchand, 'Genocide in the Great Lakes: Which Genocide? Whose Genocide?', *African Studies Review*, 41:1 (1998), 3–16 at 7.
[59] *Ibid.*
[60] A. Ould-Abdallah, *Burundi on the Brink 1993–95 – A UN Special Envoy Reflects on Preventive Diplomacy* (Washington, DC: United States Institute of Peace, 2000), p. 15.
[61] *Ibid.*

functional social institutions that had played a major role in the diffusion of tension and prevention of systemic violence became marginalised. But the social balance of communities and social groups drastically meta-morphosed through colonial encounters. The outcome was a disjointed political system lacking the capacity to transform the social system in which the potential for violence was embedded.

Rene Lemarchand has attempted to situate this in the state's struggle for relevance and legitimacy. The Burundi state, Lemarchand explains, has been an instrument that facilitates group domination as well as 'an arena where segments of the dominant group compete amongst them-selves to gain maximum control over patronage resources'.[62] The deeper the competition became, the more pronounced was the gap between those who succeeded in appropriating the sources of reward and others who became embattled adherents of deprivation.[63] Eventually, neither the state, nor its military custodians, could reverse these sources of tension. In fact, what subsequently emerged bore striking parallels to most of Africa's postcolonial statehood. Thus Burundi's independence mobilisation rhetoric could not conceal, let alone heal, the trauma emanating from both the legacy of colonial social engineering, in which international law played a devastating part, and the inadequacy of the state as the focal institution for the organisation of social life. The state's constant struggle for legitimacy pitted it against a disenchanted social system whose faith in the agencies of state had long gone. This sense of bifurcation created a kind of social inversion so deep that structures ordinarily capable of diffusing conflicts had atrophied. The absence of social harmony strengthened the divisive character of ethnic stratifi-cation. This paved the way for violence and chaos. It was this that eventually produced some international response.

International response to Burundi's crises

International engagement with Burundi was largely constrained throughout most of the periods documented above. The sequence of assassinations attracted little concern and military dictatorship was tolerated if not actively supported. Even the reaction to the 1972 geno-cide was hesitant, and in some instances, bordering on complicity. The UN was remarkably passive. Its Secretary General at the time, Kurt

[62] Lemarchand, *Burundi: Ethnic Conflict*, p. 77.   [63] *Ibid.*

Waldheim, simply expressed 'fervent hopes that peace, harmony and stability can be brought about successfully and speedily, that Burundi will thereby achieve the goals of social progress, better standards of living and other ideals and principles set forth in the UN Charter'.[64] Similarly, the OAU did little, opting instead to adopt a non-confrontational, largely passive and almost indifferent stance to the plight of victims and their futures. Its Secretary General at the time, Diallo Telli, remarked during a visit to Bujumbura that 'the OAU being essentially an organisation based on solidarity, my presence here signifies the total solidarity of the Secretariat with the President of Burundi, with the government and the fraternal people of Burundi'.[65]

These levels of international passivity amounted to an abdication of responsibility in light of the existence of collective legal obligations under the 1948 Genocide Convention.[66] Such indifference left Burundi at the mercy of state impunity. Reginald Kay writes that 'the virtual absence of international protest at the time ... encouraged the government to pursue its discriminatory policies'.[67] Nor were Burundi's bilateral and multilateral relations affected.[68] The reasons for the lack of adequate engagement are not difficult to discern. First, as discussed in Chapter 4, international law had precluded jurisdiction regarding internal conflicts. Second, it operated on a presumption that the responsibility for human protection is the prerogative of the state. But as already shown in Chapters 3 and 4, the postcolonial African state in many ways embodies an entity in crisis, struggling for the most part to contain excessive expansion of social institutions through violence and other modes of coercion. It was only following the events of 1993 that a relatively proactive international approach began to emerge. The UN Security Council approved the appointment of Ahmedou Ould-Abdallah as the special envoy to Burundi of the Secretary General in November 1993.[69]

---

[64] See Lemarchand, 'The Burundi Genocide', at 7–8.   [65] *Ibid.*, at 7.

[66] State and international obligations under the Genocide Convention of 1948 are fairly broad. Article 8 of the Convention provides that 'any contracting party may call upon the competent organs of the United Nations to take such action under the Charter of the United Nations as they consider appropriate for the prevention and suppression of acts of genocide or any of the other acts enumerated in Article 3'. See Convention on the Prevention and Punishment of the Crime of Genocide, 1948, www.un.org/millennium/law/iv-1.htm (last visited August 2010).

[67] Kay, 'Burundi Since the Genocide', at 6.   [68] *Ibid.*

[69] Security Council Statement on the Appointment of Ahmedou Ould-Abdallah, 16 November 1993.

The envoy's objectives were spelt out as follows: (i) restore democratic institutions overthrown by the military in October 1993; (ii) facilitate dialogue between parties to the crisis; (iii) work towards the establishment of a Commission of Enquiry into the events of October and subsequent massacres; and (iv) work in collaboration with the OAU.[70]

On the first objective, Ould-Abdallah rallied support from the largely isolated *bashingantahe*, and a few political parties and personalities. Following protracted negotiations and compromises, consensus was reached to amend Burundi's constitution so as to empower parliament to elect an interim president. Cyprien Ntaryamira was subsequently elected interim president and a so-called Convention Government was formed in September 1994.[71] Further initiatives were undertaken by Ould-Abdallah and some foreign diplomatic representatives in Burundi to promote dialogue and enhance the survival of the transitional government. But these international responses, though providing some reprieve from the general sense of insecurity, could not fundamentally alter the country's increasingly violent landscape. The transitional government became entrapped in a culture of suspicion, indecision and constant internal power struggles. It was not long before the very limited window of dialogue vanished, culminating in a vacuum at the governmental level. Violence was soon to return to Burundi as the resurgence of Hutu uprisings provided space for the creation of a number of insurgent groups with a determination to wrestle the balance of power from the Tutsi-dominated military.

Despite these initiatives in international responses, faultlines pervaded the entirety of UN-led multilateral engagement in Burundi. The indifference was in particular also a manifestation of the historically restrictive principles and focus of international law approaches to peacebuilding in the domestic sphere. Most crucially, the UN Security Council Resolution framing the legal basis for these engagements was flawed in a number of respects. First, it adopted an essentially neo-liberal peace dispensation to sets of circumstances whose genus was defined by intricate social dynamics that often remain invisible to the radar of such approaches. The significance of incorporating endogenous social structures as constituents of peacebuilding initiatives cannot be overstated. Postcolonial Africa is largely a mosaic of communities entangled in contradictions. Its political structures are fairly recent, being products of colonial social engineering, and locked in an almost perpetual struggle for legitimacy

---

[70] See Ould-Abdallah, *Burundi on the Brink*, p. 38.   [71] *Ibid.*, p. 73.

against indigenous institutions and their constituencies. To negate the role and increasing practical relevance of these is to overlook what is clearly an influential social phenomenon, more so at a time when their resurgence is on the increase.

Corollary to this negation is the primacy of the neo-liberal international law approach to conflict – the consolidation of state institutions or their restoration in the event of state collapse is a *sine qua non* in the advancement of durable peace. And so for the most part, international approaches expended considerable time and resources in consolidating an agenda that was neither suitable for, nor relevant to, Burundi's recurrent conflict. For example, the series of transitional power-sharing agreements were shallow, and their precursor, the so-called Convention of Government, was not leaning towards peace, but mainly installed as a political device.[72] The process, for all its good intent, was merely resuscitating institutions that had been mediums of violence and impunity in postcolonial Burundi. Traditional institutions and social networks, through which community cohesion and individual loyalties and sanctuaries of security are often framed, were treated as alien structures lacking relevance. Fillip Reyntjens observes that 'rather than attempting to tackle the real problems of the country, these negotiations dealt with the distribution of offices and functions'.[73] Unable to address the escalation of violence, the Convention of Government collapsed.

The nature of these approaches also exposes the tension symptomatic of contemporary international engagement with the quest for peace. But peace is not a condition achieved through spontaneous reflexes of international diplomacy, nor is it attainable as mere absence of violence. All these faultlines occurred with the backdrop of an apparent lack of understanding of Burundi's internal sociological dynamics. The level of ignorance was, in some instances, difficult to fathom. For instance, despite evidence to the contrary, Ould-Abdallah noted in a publication that 'all Burundi at a given moment are extremists'.[74] As one of the focal custodians of international peacebuilding initiatives in Burundi, Ould-Abdallah was adamant that 'in the context of African conflicts, the most effective sticks include temporarily denying visas to some extremists and scholarships to their children, and threatening to freeze their bank

---

[72] F. Reyntjens, *Burundi: Breaking the Cycle of Violence* (London: Minority Rights Group, 1995).

[73] *Ibid.*, pp. 18–19.

[74] A. Ould-Abdallah, 'La diplomatie pyromane', cited in R. Weisman, 'Preventing Genocide in Burundi: Lessons from International Diplomacy', *Peaceworks*, (1998), at 5.

accounts'.[75] This isolationist approach is largely reactive and is unable to view conflicts as dynamic processes that are sustained by complex variables whose nuances transcend the simplicities of the special envoy's neo-liberal approaches. As Christopher Mitchell notes, an effective mediation ought to be seen as a 'process to which many entities might contribute, simultaneously or consecutively, rather than as the behaviour of a single, intermediary actor'.[76]

Although the international community and the special envoy's poor sense of appreciation of Burundi's social dynamics could also be attributed to international law's long-standing reluctance in engaging internal conflicts, the association of peace with cease-fires and imposition of sanctions on individuals suggested that the only way out of Burundi's labyrinth of violence was through the limited classical approach of statist diplomacy. Yet this approach relies heavily on formal institutions that are identifiable with international law. Whilst this may be useful in interstate warfare, it is less so in postcolonial internal conflicts. Unlike interstate conflicts where the decision to wage war is an exclusive remit of the centralised state, internal violence can flare from numerous non-state actors whose incentive is often not driven by the adherence to international legality or the enforcement of cease-fire agreements. No wonder, then, that the peacebuilding approach in Burundi pioneered by the UN had 'little impact and its capacity to influence events was therefore tenuous, and trickled away bit by bit, day by day'.[77]

The African Union and the Burundi conflict

The approaches to the Burundi crises entered another phase once the African Union came into being. In April 2003, the African Mission in Burundi (AMIB) was constituted, and the African Union's Article 4 Restorative subset and intervention mechanism were accordingly invoked. This provided the legal basis for the mission's deployment. To further realise Article 4 objectives, the mission was also mandated with the implementation of the Arusha Peace and Reconciliation Agreement signed at a regional summit held in Arusha, Tanzania, in August 2000.

---

[75] Ould-Abdallah, *Burundi on the Brink*, p. 143.

[76] C. Mitchell, 'External Peace-making Initiatives and Intra-national Conflict' in M. I. Midlarsky (ed.), *The Internationalisation of Communal Strife* (London: Routledge, 1992), p. 140.

[77] Krueger and Krueger, *From Bloodshed to Hope*, p. 42.

It is important to note that at the time of AMIB's deployment the African Union's Peace and Security Council was yet to be in operation. The deployment was therefore mandated by the Central Organ of the Mechanism for Conflict Prevention, Management and Resolution (MCPMR), the last remaining organ of the OAU.[78] As the first African Union mission conceived through Article 4, how important a step was AMIB in translating the Constitutive Act's rhetoric on peace and security into action? And to what extent did it represent a kind of learning curve in the African Union's quest for durable approaches to conflict and peacebuilding in Africa? To assess the capability of this framework, it is worth considering four factors vis-à-vis the engagement of AMIB. First, the Arusha Peace Process which formed part of AMIB's objectives; second, the structures and operations of AMIB; third, its contribution to the Burundi peace process; and fourth, AMIB's challenges and shortcomings.

Arusha Peace and Reconciliation Agreement for Burundi

As already seen above, most of Burundi's post-independence politics has been a telling of violence and disorder. Whilst this state of affairs continued, little was done to address it. The failure of international efforts culminated in regional initiatives 'concerned about the protracted nature of the conflict and its destabilising impact on the region'.[79] The initiatives also came in the wake of the 1996 military coup, which, it was feared, had the tendency to further aggravate Burundi's history of violence and state complicity in it. The regional efforts were led by Tanzania with endorsement from the OAU[80] and the United Nations.[81] The regional initiatives began with a summit in the Tanzanian town of Arusha on 25 June 1996. A communiqué on the summit's proceedings reiterated the need for national reconciliation through a comprehensive solution to Burundi's crisis.[82] It also called for the restoration of constitutional order in Burundi.

---

[78] See 'Communique of the Ninety-first Ordinary Session of the Central Organ of the Mechanism for Conflict Prevention, Management and Resolution at Ambassadorial Level', Addis Ababa, Ethiopia, 2 April 2003, Central Organ/MEC/AMB/Comm. (XCI).

[79] Daley, *Gender and Genocide in Burundi*, p. 195.

[80] Between November 1995 and March 1996, the OAU made two declarations to express support with the initiatives. These were the Cairo Declaration and the Tunis Declaration.

[81] The UN's support came in the form of the UN Security Council Resolutions 1049, 5 March 1996, and 1072, 30 August 1996.

[82] See 'Press Communique of the Arusha Regional Summit on Burundi', 26 June 1996, www.africa.upenn.edu/Urgent_Action/apic_7596.html (last visited October 2010).

What was significant about the summit was that there was almost unanimous condemnation of the military regime, as the leaders declared rather unequivocally that they 'would no longer accept an individual who came to power through a *coup d'état* as a legitimate Head of State'.[83] This was soon followed by sanctions aimed at putting pressure on the military administration of Pierre Buyoya. However these preliminary regional actions, especially those relating to sanctions, had very little effect. Burundi's key allies – the USA, Canada and some EU countries – objected to the regional actions and even threatened to withdraw support for the peace process. Nyerere refused to bow to pressure arguing that it was imperative to 'balance the significance of their financial contribution, the power of the governments and multilateral organisations they represent and the amount of damage the pursuit of their own parochial interests can cause to the process'.[84]

The campaign against regional initiatives had widened by 1997 with the World Bank, UNDP and other international NGOs adopting a critical position on aspects of the peacebuilding process. Encouraged by these developments, Pierre Buyoya showed little regard for Nyerere's efforts and even sought to undermine them by initiating internal peace talks with his adversaries.[85] In subsequent months, he entered into negotiations with FRODEBU and began resuscitating key political institutions such as the national assembly. But not much came from this. Suspicion over his ambitions grew, and with the absence of prominent exiled Hutu politicians the internal peace process largely failed.[86] The failure of the internal peace negotiations reactivated regional initiatives. In 2000, Nelson Mandela took over as facilitator following the death of Nyerere. He identified his main task as ensuring an all-inclusive peace process. Within a short time, negotiations on the proposals that began under Nyerere were finalised and signed in 2000.

The Arusha Agreement consisted of a number of provisions that reflected the fluidity of the Burundi crisis and the need to advance durable peace through transformative approaches. To achieve this, Articles 1–4 of the agreement provided for a reflection of the nature and historical causes of the conflict.[87] Protocol I defined the conflict as 'fundamentally political

---

[83] I. Bunting, B. Mwansasu and W. Bagoya, *Overview of the Burundi Peace Process* (1999), cited in Daley, *Gender and Genocide in Burundi*, p. 195.

[84] Burundi Peace Negotiations, Report of the First Session of the Burundi Peace Negotiations, Arusha, Tanzania, 15–21 June 1998, pp. 14–15.

[85] Daley, *Gender and Genocide in Burundi*, p. 200.   [86] *Ibid.*

[87] Arusha Peace and Reconciliation Agreement for Burundi, 28 August 2000, www.usip.org (last visited September 2010).

with extremely important ethnic dimensions'.[88] Solutions were also provided. These included the 'institution of a new political, economic, social and judicial order' and the 'reorganisation of the State institutions to make them capable of integrating and reassuring all the ethnic components of Burundian society'.[89] The agreement proposed a new constitutional instrument inspired by the realities of Burundi. Under Article 7, the rectification of ethnic imbalances was proposed so as to combat ethnic-based violence. To this end, the agreement noted the importance of indigenous social structures in the quest for spaces of peace and proposed the rehabilitation of the institution of *ubushingantehe*.[90]

Protocol II addressed issues of governance, transitional power-sharing and judicial and executive functions.[91] Other aspects of peace and security were contained in Protocol III, whilst issues relating to defence and the conduct of the security forces were the subject of Protocol IV. Clearly the Arusha Agreement had a broad provision which in many respects tried to proffer an alternative approach to conventional approaches to conflict. Two important observations are worth making. First, it is plausible to suggest that the Arusha process was perhaps the most comprehensive peace agreement of an internal conflict in Africa. Although the dynamism of, and reverence for, Tanzania's Julius Nyerere and South Africa's Nelson Mandela were key influencing factors, the timing of the peacebuilding process was also crucial. It was concluded at around the same time that major developments were taking place to transform the OAU and thereby create a new and vibrant organisation capable of advancing viable spaces of peace. One such result was the adoption of the Constitutive Act.

Second, the transformations helped to produce a peace process that not only aimed at tackling the crisis, but also attempted to use constitutional instruments to address the ethnic divide that had been at the centre of Burundi's cycle of violence. It was perhaps in this context that the peace agreement incorporated unique approaches that reflected an urge to break from the past. Once the OAU was disbanded and the African Union created, the new organisation sought to engage the Burundi conflict through the implementation of the Arusha Peace and Reconciliation Agreement as well as the Constitutive Act's peace and security initiatives. It was in this light that AMIB was created.

---

[88] Arusha Agreement, Protocol I, Chapter I, Article 4(a).
[89] *Ibid.*, Chapter II, Article 5(1) and (2).   [90] *Ibid.*, Chapter II, Article 7(27).
[91] *Ibid.*, Protocol II, Articles 1–22.

Structures and operations of AMIB

The creation of AMIB was the first conflict transformation mission undertaken by the African Union. The desire to actualise the mission was motivated by the fact that Burundi had suffered from protracted conflicts with considerable implications for its neighbours. Securing peace in Burundi was considered essential in tackling the inter-connected violence of the Great Lakes region. AMIB was constituted within the framework of Article 4(h) of the Constitutive Act, whose purpose is premised on the recognition of the vicissitudes of the ambiguous character of the postcolonial African state and the desire of the African Union to pursue an African solution to African problems.[92] Underpinning this sense of *African ownership*, Kristina Powell explains, was also the perception of AMIB 'as a crucial opportunity for the [AU] to demonstrate its departure from the OAU and to assign itself a prominent role in delivering on a peace and security agenda in Africa'.[93]

AMIB was deployed in April 2003 and assigned a set of objectives that included the creation of a secure and conducive environment, disarmament, demobilisation and reintegration of combatants.[94] The most challenging objective, however, was to contribute to the political and economic stability of Burundi by providing overall logistic and security support to members of the transitional administration. This required proactive engagement with relevant parties and social institutions for the implementation of cease-fire agreements.[95] To achieve these, specific tasks critical to AMIB's Article 4 stabilisation mission and its underlying transformative qualities were also outlined. These were to maintain liaison between parties; monitor and verify the implementation of cease-fire agreements; facilitate access to and movement of parties to designated assembly areas; facilitate and provide technical assistance to the disarmament, demobilisation and reintegration (DDR) processes; facilitate the delivery of humanitarian assistance, including to refugees

---

[92] See AMIB, 'An Explanatory Memorandum, Bujumbura, Burundi', October 2003, p. 4.

[93] K. Powell, 'The African Union's Emerging Peace and Security Regime: Opportunities and Challenges for Delivering on the Responsibility to Protect', ISS Monograph Series, 119 (2005), at 35.

[94] See 'Communiqué of the Ninety-first Ordinary Session of the Central Organ of the Mechanism for Conflict Prevention, Management and Resolution at Ambassadorial Level', www.africa-union.org/News_Events/Communique (last visited April 2010).

[95] *Ibid.*

and internally displaced persons; and coordinate mission activities.[96] The mission was mandated for an initial period of one year.[97]

The institutional arrangement of AMIB was structured as an integrated mission with both civilian and military components. The civilian component consisted of diplomatic and technical support staff that provided logistic and administrative support.[98] Its other functions included the promotion of a cohesive understanding between AMIB, Burundi's transitional government and the ordinary people the mission encountered during its operation. Both components were headed by the Special Representative of the African Union Commission.[99] At its full capacity, AMIB consisted of 3,335 military personnel from South Africa, Ethiopia and Mozambique.[100] Further contributions from Burkina Faso, Gabon, Mali, Togo and Tunisia constituted the observer element of the mission with a capacity of forty-three personnel. Deployment was not devoid of hitches. Although South Africa was able to fulfil its promises given that its troops, under the aegis of the South African Protection Support Detachment (SAPSD), were already on the ground, contributions from Ethiopia and Mozambique arrived as late as October 2003. The delay was largely attributed to lack of adequate funding and ground preparation at the time. Even with this hiatus, fragility in cease-fire agreements meant that further negotiations with some of the warring parties had to be undertaken to facilitate deployment.[101]

The operational conception of AMIB was outlined in three strategic components. The first component assigned South African and Ethiopian contingents with the task of establishing two demobilisation centres in the Bubanza and Buhinga provinces respectively. Its main focus was to harness the inclusionary approaches generated through AMIB's political engagement by accelerating disarmament, demobilisation and reintegration of combatants.[102] Disarmament essentially involves the collection of weapons to reduce the threat of fear and violence. Demobilisation takes

[96] Ibid.

[97] See the Ninety-first Ordinary Session of the Central Organ of the Mechanism for Conflict Prevention, Management and Resolution, April 2003, Central Organ/MEC/AMB/Comm.(XCI).

[98] See F. Agoagye, 'The African Mission in Burundi: Lessons from the First African Union Peacekeeping Operation', www.issafrica.org, at 11.

[99] Ibid.   [100] Powell, 'The African Union's Emerging Peace and Security Regime', at 34.

[101] See A. J. Bellamy and P. D. Williams, 'Who's Keeping the Peace: Regionalisation and Contemporary Peace Operations', International Security, 29:4 (2005), 157–95 at 191.

[102] Agoagye, 'The African Mission in Burundi', at 11.

the form of transition of ex-combatants from a military mindset to a civilian life. This transition, however, hinges on the success of reintegration. Given the protracted violence in Burundi's postcolonial statehood, the disarmament, demobilisation and reintegration component was considered an important step in advancing the Restorative dimension of transformative peacebuilding approaches. According to Tim Murithi, the demobilisation centres registered progress in reintegrating combatants despite the difficulties presented by the prevailing environment.[103]

AMIB's second strategic component related to the provision of security to officials, NGOs and institutions involved in the actualising of the transition process. The objective of this component was to provide sufficient security to facilitate the smooth implementation of the Arusha Peace Process as well as to assert presence in the country and facilitate dialogue with the people. It was also crucial that parties to the conflict who had expressed the intention to collectively shape Burundi's future be able to fulfil their undertakings without resorting to violence. Once they realised that their security was largely guaranteed, it spurred others to join the peace process.[104]

The third component was the first part of a long healing process that involved encouraging internally displaced persons and those living in refugee camps in Tanzania to return home. Although the situation was still precarious, it was believed that for reintegration as a mechanism for reconciliation and peace to take effect the dignity of people must be restored through the preservation of the notion of *ubuntu*. AMIB's role in helping facilitate this was to provide improved security conditions in Burundi as an incentive to persuade the return of refugees and the settlement of internally displaced persons. In the process of doing so, the civilian component of the mission intensified its engagement with some of the visible indigenous social institutions.

Normative and institutional assessment of AMIB

The African Mission in Burundi was the first intervention mission by the African Union in pursuance of the peacebuilding mandate of the Constitutive Act. It was conceived on the backdrop of mounting optimism in

---

[103] Murithi, 'The African Union's Evolving Role in Peace Operations', at 75.

[104] H. Boshoff and W. Vrey, 'Disarmament, Demobilisation and Reintegration During the Transition in Burundi: A Technical Analysis', *Institute for Security Studies Monograph Series*, 125 (2006), 32.

the continent's revamped political institutions. The mission was in many respects a bold one, not least because African-led interventions conceptualised through a continental peacebuilding framework had been rare prior to the Constitutive Act of the African Union. The determination to deploy was both a fulfilment of a legal obligation under the Constitutive Act and broader African philosophical persuasion – you're your brother's/sister's keeper – intrinsic to Pan-African ideals and culture.[105] In this sense, AMIB was as symbolic as it was a venture into uncharted territory. Deployed amidst sporadic violence and tension, its main focus was to implement the Restorative dimension of the Constitutive Act's conflict transformation approaches, which were anticipated to be inclusive and cognisant of the capacity and sensibilities of social institutions.

From the outset, AMIB sought to put in place mechanisms for the creation of an environment that was capable of advancing peace and stability, 'without which progress toward other goals would have been much more difficult'.[106] There is no doubt that AMIB's mere presence in Burundi served as some kind of deterrence to the further escalation of violence.[107] The mission's initiatives, and in some instances, departure from conventional neo-liberal approaches, were particularly helpful in this regard. Whilst confronting some of the agencies of violence, AMIB made attempts to pursue an inclusionary engagement by courting the proactive involvement of non-state armed groups that would ordinarily be classified as outlaws under international law approaches. By so doing, the social networks providing the support bases of these armed groups, which are also often invisible to the radar of international legality, were brought on board as legitimate entities to the peacebuilding process. Through these initiatives, the armed group CNDD-FDD Nkurunziza, which had constantly eluded international statist diplomacy, found AMIB's initiatives sufficiently inclusionary and trustworthy to warrant their formal participation in the peacebuilding process.

With most of these groups engaged, AMIB could operate without coming across as hostile. This had practical benefits. With the exception of Agathon Rwasa's PALIPEHUTU-FNL faction, the mission registered considerable success in ensuring that cease-fire agreements were not only honoured, but that the relative sense of cordiality they ushered in was

---

[105] See K. Wiredu, *Cultural Universals and Particulars: An African Perspective* (Bloomington: Indiana University Press, 1997).

[106] Boshoff and Vrey, 'Disarmament, Demobilisation and Reintegration', at 32.

[107] Murithi, 'The African Union's Evolving Role in Peace Operations', at 75.

utilised to optimise community cohesion as an agency of transformative peacebuilding. This was attempted through the involvement of communities and local actors. The degree of stability also allowed AMIB to facilitate delivery of humanitarian assistance as well as establish coordination networks with civil society groups and the remnants of the UN mission in Bujumbura.[108]

Particularly helpful to AMIB's peacebuilding endeavours was that custodians of traditional institutions and communities could genuinely identify with the mission, and even acquire a sense of ownership over some of the peace initiatives. In some instances, the institution of *bashingantahe*, sidelined during colonial rule, played a small but significant role in mobilising local elders to complement AMIB. The *bashingantahe* is an old institution that predates Burundi's postcolonial state. But it was largely consigned to irrelevance during the country's colonial encounters. It had been traditionally composed of men selected from a community on the basis of their wisdom and sense of justice.[109] According to Peter Uvin, their function 'was to give advice in local conflicts and to propose judgments'.[110] Their status as embodiments of peace and fairness in Burundi society is well documented. It was this role that perhaps motivated the incorporation of Article 7 of the Arusha Peace Agreement, which called for its rehabilitation. In 2005, the Burundi government passed an ordinance creating the National Council of the Bashingantahe in pursuance of durable peace and reconciliation. Of course, the institution requires some modernisation to make it more gender sensitive as well as reflective of the demands of modernity.

The collaborative approaches AMIB created with the *bashingantahe*, agencies and parties to the conflict were credited for the stabilisation of about 95 per cent of Burundi.[111] This level of stabilisation was the first in decades. An obvious beneficiary was Burundi's civilian population, in particular vulnerable groups such as women and children. Civilians bear the brunt of the human cost that arises from Africa's internal conflicts. It is a concern that is reflected in the objectives and principles of the Constitutive Act as well as its related security instruments. And so for AMIB to garner any purchase in this regard, its mandate had inevitably to be reflective of this responsibility. At the time of deployment, protection of civilians was not part of the mission's mandate. This was,

---

[108] See also Boshoff and Vrey, 'Disarmament, Demobilisation and Reintegration'.
[109] See Uvin, *Life After Violence*, p. 62.   [110] *Ibid.*
[111] Agoagye, 'The African Mission in Burundi', at 14.

however, rectified with the adoption of Rules of Engagement that specifically granted AMIB's troops the mandate to apply force to protect civilians in 'imminent danger of serious injury or death', with prior authorisation from military officers.[112]

Given that Article 4 intervention provided relative stability for the other peacebuilding provisions of the Constitutive Act to take effect, AMIB could be said to have succeeded on that front. In fact Henri Boshoff and Waldemar Vrey are adamant 'that AMIB has been one of the AU's success stories'.[113] The success in the face of challenges perhaps demonstrates that with the requisite international support and political will, the ascription of African ownership to the integrated peacebuilding framework embedded in the Constitutive Act could become more of a reality than an aspiration. The mission's innovative methodology, framed within the Constitutive Act's transformative approaches to conflict, was seen as a model for the ascription of a coherent meaning to the quest for an 'African solution to African problems'. A 2003 joint communiqué issued by the African Union and regional leaders on peace initiatives on Burundi concluded that AMIB represents a 'shining example and model of African solutions to continental security challenges'.[114] Although the leaders are expected to say exactly that, the contribution of AMIB to the stabilisation of Burundi has been increasingly acknowledged.

Peter Uvin's *Life After Violence* provides not only an overview of the vision of peace from the perspectives of ordinary Burundians, but also affirms the contribution of AMIB and the Arusha Peace Process in the gradual transformation of what were otherwise highly polarised social conditions.[115] A study commissioned by the Centre for the Prevention of Conflict (CENAP) and the North-South Institute (NSI) has established a strong link between the implementation of the Arusha Peace Process by AMIB and the subsequent restoration of improved conditions of peace in Burundi.[116] Similarly, Tim Murithi argues that AMIB's role

---

[112] See Human Rights Watch, 'Everyday Victims: Civilians in the Burundi War', *Human Rights Watch Report*, 15:20 (2003), at 10.

[113] Boshoff and Vrey, 'Disarmament, Demobilisation and Reintegration', at 31.

[114] See 'Communiqué of the 20th Summit of the Great Lakes Regional Peace Initiative on Burundi', November 2003, www.issafrica.org/AF/profiles/Burundi/sumcomnov03.pdf (last visited June 2010).

[115] Uvin, *Life After Violence*, p. 52.

[116] See CENAP and NSI: *Rapport du Sondage sur les Perceptions de l'Etat de la Sécurité et le Rôle des Corps de Défence et Sécurité au Burundi* (Bujumbura: CENAP and NSI, 2006).

in Burundi 'demonstrates that the continental body can in fact make useful peacebuilding interventions on the continent'.[117] He notes that 'by the end of its mission AMIB had succeeded in establishing relative peace to most provinces in Burundi, with the exception of the region outside Bujumbura where armed resistance, in the form of the Forces Nationales de Libération (FNL), remained a problem'.[118] He concludes that 'in the absence of the AU Mission Burundi would have been left to its own devices, which probably would have resulted in an escalation of violent conflict'.[119] The UN has also recognised the contribution of AMIB. In Resolution 1545 of 2004, the Security Council paid tribute to the efforts AMIB made in implementing the Arusha Peace Process culminating in the gradual improvement of conditions.[120] It was this considerable improvement of the situation in Burundi that encouraged the UN to absorb AMIB into the United Nations Operation in Burundi (ONUB), having earlier refused to lead.[121]

Challenges and shortcomings of AMIB

Despite the generous endorsements of the African Union Mission in Burundi, the kind of peacebuilding espoused by the Constitutive Act is a long and arduous process, open to challenges and difficulties. Perhaps nowhere is this more true than in Africa's recent history, where its political landscape imposes *sui generis* conditions of a particularly challenging nature. From its inception, AMIB was faced with an enormous task with severe limitations in the capacity of the African Union institutions. At the time of deployment the African Union's key institutions, central to its peace and security architecture – the Peace and Security Council and the Peace and Security Department – had just been constituted. Of course, given that these structures were just evolving, there was a lamentable absence of managerial capacity and technical knowhow to facilitate the financial and organisational components of the mission. This meant that some of the stronger nations like South Africa had to assume a dominant part of the mission's leadership responsibilities.[122]

Moreover, limitations in capacity had constraining effects on the operation of AMIB, particularly in respect of fulfilling the totality of

---

[117] Murithi, 'The African Union's Evolving Role in Peace Operations', at 75.   [118] *Ibid.*
[119] *Ibid.*   [120] UN Security Council Resolution 1545, S/RES/1545, 21 March 2004.
[121] *Ibid.*, para. 22.
[122] See also Powell, 'The African Union's Emerging Peace and Security Regime', at 38.

its mandate. For instance, when the mission was first conceived, the provision of a security protection mechanism for civilians was largely a peripheral one. The initial exclusion was clearly conditioned by the restricted ability of the evolving African Union institutions to provide both the conceptual and material support for AMIB. Without the requisite equipment, the mission was for the most part confined to the urban communes. Some of the concerns created an environment of fear. The relatively small size of the mission was also a problem. In fact it has been suggested that with its very broad mandate and highly limited military and civilian personnel, AMIB was given a 'nearly impossible mission'.[123] At its fullest capacity the mission had just under 4,000 military personnel, assigned a task of disarming about 20,000 combatants.

The limited military and civilian personnel of AMIB hinged largely on the lack of adequate funds. The agreement in principle reached by the African Union was that the accrued costs and incidental expenses of initial deployment were to be borne by contributing nations. Both Mozambique and Ethiopia had to source funding from the United Kingdom and the United States respectively. As Festus Agoagye writes, 'the mission's logistical sustainment and funding was particularly problematic, owing to the lack of substantive support from within Africa, as well as from the UN and the international community to provide requisite assistance'.[124] This concern resonated in a number of preliminary reports on AMIB. The UN Secretary General lamented in one of his country reports on Burundi, that 'the mission suffered from a serious lack of funds and logistic support' and that these 'constraints under which AMIB is operating prevent the force from fully implementing its mandate'.[125] What this shows is a potential for what Bogland et al. call a triangular tension between 'the AU ambitions, the organisation's resources, and the capacity and the member states' political will'.[126] Such patterns of challenges and financial constraints often associated with

---

[123] International Crisis Group, 'End of Transition in Burundi: The Home Stretch', *Africa Report*, 81 (2004), 10.

[124] F. Agoagye, *The African Mission in Burundi: Lessons from the First African Union Peacekeeping Operation*, Swedish Defence Research Agency, (2008), 14, www.foi.se/upload/projects/Africa/foir2475.pdf.

[125] *Report of the Secretary General on Burundi*, 16 March 2004, S/2004/210, at p. 13, http://daccessdds.un.org/doc/UNDOC/GEN/N04/269/25/IMG/N0426925.pdf?OpenElement (last visited 2010).

[126] K. Bogland, R. Egnell and M. Lagerstrom, 'The African Union – A Study Focusing on Conflict Management', *Swedish Defence Research Agency Report*, (2008), 1–52 at 44.

African peace missions have even lured some to conclude that 'from a funding perspective, the only viable peacekeeping operations in Africa are UN peace operations'.[127]

Perhaps AMIB's challenges and shortcomings are more than a reminder that although collective political will is an essential building-block for a successful Article 4 undertaking, it is not on its own sufficient. Institutional capacity, material resources and operational competence are just as important. But instructive as this may appear, AMIB's logistical and operational shortcomings were not a representation of normative limitations in the Constitutive Act's peacebuilding framework. On the contrary, most of them were largely reflective of operational inadequacies that sprung from paucity in international support and the African Union's novice credentials in undertaking a mission of this nature. The expectations for AMIB in some quarters as regards the construction of durable peace within the framework of its mandate amounted to clear misreading of the functions of Article 4. For example, Festus Agoagye has lamented that in spite of its achievements, 'the contribution of the mission to political and economic stability in Burundi was limited'.[128]

There seems to be inadequate understanding of the rationale of Article 4. The provision is only meant to serve as a restorative or emergency instrument of stabilisation so as to facilitate the application of the constitutive subsets of peacebuilding such as norms formulation, social integration and interdependence. It is these two social phenomena that could be utilised to engender a kind of social cohesion that would reduce the recourse to conflict. Indeed, deepening integration and inter-dependence hinge on a number of factors. The primacy of the state has to be recharacterised to grant agency to people and the social institutions through which they conduct a substantial part of daily life and business. What this means is that indigenous social institutions must not be seen as dysfunctional or anachronistic, but as viable and necessary compositions of social order.[129] Legal and constitutional instruments must be used to address imbalances in a country's social order. Where legal frameworks are used in postconflict situations as agents of social change, inclusion and rectification, they could provide a *modus vivendi* to help

---

[127] C. De-Coning, 'Towards a Common Southern African Peacekeeping System', *CIPS Electronic Briefing Paper*, 16 (2004), 6.

[128] Agoagye, 'The African Mission in Burundi', at 14.

[129] See H. Wiarda, *Ethnocentrism in Foreign Policy: Can We Understand the Third World?* (Washington, DC: American Enterprise Institute for Public Policy, 1985), p. 60.

construct peace. In this sense, legal frameworks expand spaces of toleration which can serve as an antidote to tension. This is crucial in ethnically diverse societies, not least because 'law understood as a framework of restraint and coexistence among those pursuing divergent purposes presupposes diversity and the toleration of this diversity'.[130]

Since the completion of AMIB's mandate, Burundi has made some progress towards consolidating peace. The relative success of AMIB was as symbolic as it was instructive. The mission's primary function was to help in the sufficient stabilisation of Burundi so that broader peace cultivation approaches could be enforced. The significance of the mission lies in its ability to provide preliminary assessment of the efficacy and futures of the Constitutive Act's peacebuilding framework. This is especially important considering that the UN Security Council repeatedly rejected earlier calls for a UN peacekeeping mission in the wake of Melchoir Ndadaye's assassination in 1993. The unwillingness of the UN to take charge, coupled with the limitations in its peacebuilding approaches, are the very reasons that make the emergency stabilisation function of Article 4 of the Constitutive Act an especially important element. It was this imperative to stabilise that also informed the basis on which the success of AMIB could be gauged. At the time of deployment, African leaders emphasised that the 'African Mission would have fulfilled its mandate after it has facilitated the implementation of the Ceasefire Agreements and the defence and security situation in Burundi is stable and well-managed by newly created national defence and security structures'.[131]

In some ways, AMIB also demonstrates that with the integrated nature of the Constitutive Act's peace and security architecture, a small mission can make considerable impact in the pursuit of stability and the advancement of broader peacebuilding initiatives. Of further help to its course was the mission's departure from the regimented nature of international law peacebuilding efforts. Despite its resource constraints and the circumstances in which deployment was carried out, AMIB's engagement with Burundi's social institutions helped to restore a stable order in the country. What is evident here is a gradual transformative

---

[130] T. Nardin, *Law, Morality and the Relations of States* (Princeton University Press, 1983), p. 324.

[131] See 'Communique of the Ninety-first Ordinary Session of the Central Organ of the Mechanism for Conflict Prevention, Management and Resolution at Ambassadorial Level', Addis Ababa, Ethiopia, 2 April 2003, Central Organ/MEC/AMB/Comm. (XCI).

process initiated first through the Arusha Peace Plan and subsequently consolidated by state and traditional institutions. All this has since culminated in the installation of a 'system of co-optation and consociationalism [in the minds of Burundians] that is uniquely theirs, and they have implemented it beyond what many thought was possible'.[132]

Of course it would be naïve to assume that Burundi's cycle of violence and conflict is now consigned to the past. The past has not entirely vanished. The longevity of the country's collective social trauma implies that colonially crafted ethnic stratifications have not shed their salience, for there still remain a lot of pain and memory.[133] But there is also hope. The approaches to conflict appear to ignite a kind of transformation that is inclusive in many respects. Integration has deepened more than ever and there seems to be an emergence of a collective mindset that perceives this process as indispensable if peace must prevail.[134] This is also being reflected in the social order, where some attempts have been made to promote social integration. What is perhaps needed is the deepening of normative values to help in the opening up of political spaces so as to increase participation and fairness in Burundi. The tension and uncertainties generated by the 2010 presidential elections showed that the consolidation of normative values is imperative.

There are three epochs that account for the relative success of approaches to conflict in Burundi. The Arusha Peace Process, which coincided with the transformations from the OAU to African Union, represented a paradigmatic shift in the perception of, and approach to, internal conflicts. Its broadly inclusionary formulations culminated in the reflection of social identity in the constitutional order of Burundi. The benefit has been encouraging. Thus under the present political dispensation, social inclusion is both a constitutional requirement and moral imperative in the relation between state and society. In addition, the Arusha Peace Process provided the foundation upon which AMIB departed in the aftermath of the creation of the African Union. AMIB played a significant role in stabilising Burundi so as to facilitate transformation from conflict to peace. Third, and perhaps vitally important, the deepening of social integration and interdependence restored trust amongst adversaries and provided space for the pursuit of collective ambitions.

---

[132] Uvin, *Life After Violence*, p. 24.   [133] *Ibid.*, p. 78.
[134] FAST Update: *Burundi: Semi-annual Risk Assessment, November 2005 to May 2006* (Berne: Swisspeace, 2006).

Conclusion

Like in most of Africa, the impact of colonialism on Burundi has been profound, ranging from exploitation and the reconstitution of social relationships to the creation of new forms of structures and ethnic stratification. These imbalances conditioned the direction of Burundi's post-independence politics, mostly manifested in violence and a recurrent civil war. During this time, violence intensified with virtually no significant response from both the OAU and the United Nations Security Council. The former's passivity was conditioned by the restrictive nature of its Charter, whilst the latter suffered from a historically conditioned reluctance to extend its jurisdiction to internal violence. But even where international law engages the fissures of postcolonial violence, the approaches often adopted do little to advance durable conflict-transformation and peace-cultivation initiatives. Their limited success often displays an inability to institute or articulate a typology of conflict transformation that is capable of engaging the social system from which violence emanates. Neo-liberal peacebuilding often focuses on the agency of the state as the medium through which advances to peace and security are conceived. In the process, social institutions and traditional structures from which individuals and communities seek sanctuary when faced with conditions of violence are pretty much consigned to irrelevance.

But the dynamics of vulnerability of the African postcolonial state make any reliance on its institutions for the construction of spaces of peace untenable. The recharacterisation of some of international law's foundational precepts by the Constitutive Act, however, opened up a window of opportunity for the reformulation of dialogue between the continental body and African states. This culminated in the African Mission in Burundi. AMIB's contribution to the stabilisation of Burundi created the environment conducive for the advancement of the other equally relevant components of the Constitutive Act's peace-cultivation framework. These include the promotion of social integration and interdependence through the reintegration of displaced persons and the constitution of legal instruments to essentially reflect adequate representation of social groups and networks often invisible to the state-centric focus of international law.

As the first mission to be set up under an Article 4 mandate, AMIB was faced with challenges and logistical difficulties. But through a collective will to engage and actualise African solutions to African problems, the mission generally averted further escalation of large-scale violence. To this end, it played a crucial role in helping in the transformation of the agencies of violence and overseeing sufficient stability for the advancement of durable peace. In part the transformation in Burundi took shape in the form of the *Restorative, Corrective* and *Preventive* subsets of transformative peacebuilding. It is from this perspective that the invocation of the Constitutive Act in Burundi, notwithstanding its related challenges, shows patterns of hope and promise in the African Union interfaces with internal conflicts in Africa.

8

The African Union and peacebuilding in Somalia

Expatriates in Somalia misunderstood Somalis, Somalis misunderstood one another, the West misperceived the 'State' of Somalia, the regime in Somalia misunderstood its exact place in the world, and all sides mistook the extent to which they could or could not influence events and each other. And the compounded result of all this misunderstanding has been singular disaster.

Anna Simons[1]

Introduction

In the last chapter an attempt was made to illustrate the utility of the Constitutive Act's peacebuilding framework and how it may constitute some promise in securing a progressive outcome in conflict and postconflict situations. The focus in this chapter is to examine the second study, regarding the case of Somalia. The state of Somalia is located in the Horn of Africa with the Arabian Peninsula to the north, Djibouti to the northwest, Ethiopia to the west and Kenya to the southwest. The choice of Somalia is influenced by two main factors. First, it has been beset by violence and conflicts for the most part of its post-independence existence, culminating in the collapse of the formal state in 1991. Second, its gradation of violence led the African Union to invoke an Article 4 intervention in 2006 under the African Union Mission in Somalia (AMISOM) following endorsement from the UN Security Council. The chapter assesses the viability of transformative approaches to conflict in Somalia within the framework of the Constitutive Act and its affiliated instruments. It considers the extent to which the Constitutive Act constitutes an evolving functional duality capable of confronting not only 'orthodox' types of internal conflicts, but also those that emerge from situations where there is virtual collapse of state institutional apparatuses.

---

[1] A. Simons, *Network of Dissolution: Somalia Undone* (Boulder, Colo.: Westview Press, 1995), p. 4.

The chapter also undertakes a comparative analysis of the conditions in southern Somalia and the self-declared state of Somaliland in the north. It specifically asks, what factors have been responsible for the restoration of peaceful order in Somaliland, when southern Somalia, which had considerable international engagement, continues to encounter problems in the quest for peace? What is it about these models that has transformed threats of armed violence into opportunities for peace? And what may current international law approaches learn from these experiences? In order to engage these questions, the chapter first undertakes a historical overview of modern Somali statehood, showing the influence of social structures as well as the struggles and disorder that have afflicted it. The genesis of violence and conflict are considered as are international responses to Somali poststate conflict. Further, the African Union engagement with the Somali conflict is assessed, and there is a comparative analysis with the transformative indigenous peacebuilding approaches initiated in the breakaway region of Somaliland.

The modern Somali state – an overview

Precolonial Somalia was constituted of nomadic groups structured along kinship lines.[2] A family clan structure existed, mainly composed of the Isaaq, Dir, Hawiye, Digil and Darod social groups.[3] The internal composition was a mixture of settled and nomadic communities conditioning a social order that has been labelled as a 'pastoral democracy'.[4] Power distribution and decision-making processes suggested a stateless society lacking the strictures and rigours of centralised and formalised institutions.[5] According to I. M. Lewis, this structure owed its dynamics to the Somali social lineage.[6] Lineage as a system of social order frames the identity of individuals and defines the loyalties of social networks. It reproduces normative values and sets out a cycle of existence underlined

[2] M. H. Brons, *Society, Security, Sovereignty and the State in Somalia: From Statelessness to Statelessness?* (Utrecht: International Books, 2001), p. 115.
[3] See I. M. Lewis, *Understanding Somalia: Guide to Culture, History and Social Institutions* (London: Haan Associates, 1993); I. M. Lewis, *Blood and Bone: The Call of Kinship in Somali Society* (Lawrenceville: Red Sea Press, 1994).
[4] I. M. Lewis, *A Pastoral Democracy* (Oxford University Press, 1961), p. 2.
[5] On the nature of stateless societies, see J. Middleton and D. Tait, *Tribes Without Rulers: Studies in African Segmentary Systems* (London: Routledge, 1970).
[6] Lewis, *Blood and Bone*, p. 58.

by individual autonomy. In this sense, the absence of an institutional-ised hierarchy provided a sense of egalitarianism.[7] Given its depths and scope, clan lineage served as a source of security on a broad spectrum of social issues. The strength and vibrancy of the lineage system is perhaps best exemplified by its ability to survive despite the constantly changing nature of the political landscape in Somalia. Since 1991 there has not been an effective formal government in Somalia and condi-tions have worsened over the years. But amidst the scale of Somali postcolonial chaos, kinship lineage has retained its primacy and con-tinues to offer, for good or bad, an alternative to the absence of state institutions.

In its precolonial and postcolonial dispositions, lineage performs certain social security functions that begin with the empowerment of the individual. Empowerment confers a feeling of certainty and psychological comfort of belonging and identity.[8] Through its subsidiary networks, a support base emerges whose focus is to strengthen solidarity as well as ensure the material and social survival of people.[9] This was secured through the sustenance of what the philosopher Kwame Anthony Appiah describes in a different context as a social structure with 'a sense of family and tribe that was multiple and overlapping'.[10] Beyond this, the lineage structure assumed some conflict resolution functions. For instance, where conflict was imminent at the domestic level, clan elders constituted an ad hoc committee known as the *shir* council, whose task was to adjudicate between individual disputants. And in the event of armed conflict involving rival social groups, the *shir* performed duties of a generally peacebuilding nature.[11] The resolution of conflict through clan elders filtered through the postcolonial era and became an important part of the Somali judicial culture. As Amina Mahamoud Warsame notes,

> a large percentage of conflicts never passed the local police station and were never referred to courts. When cases ended up in the courts, it was common for these cases to be 'taken out' of the court by elders of the two conflicting parties and solved according to tradition. In fact, in some

---

[7] A. A. Mohamoud, *State Collapse and Post-Conflict Development in Africa: The Case of Somalia (1960–2001)* (Lafayette: Purdue University Press, 2006), p. 38.

[8] Brons, *Society, Security, Sovereignty*, p. 122.   [9] *Ibid.*

[10] A. K. Appiah, *Cosmopolitanism: Ethics in a World of Strangers* (London: Penguin, 2006), p. xviii.

[11] See Lewis, *A Pastoral Democracy*, p. 198.

instances, like family cases, Somalis prefer to settle them through traditional methods. It can cause embarrassment to the 'elders' and the other
family members when such cases are taken to law courts.[12]

Despite its pervasiveness, primordial kinship experienced considerable
external disruption during the early nineteenth century.[13] Somalia could
not withstand this wave of imperial expansionism nor could it entirely
preserve the established layout of its society. Ultimately, its territory was
subject to foreign dominance on a large scale. By the middle half of
the nineteenth century, Somalia was rapidly drawn into the political
interplay of colonial rivalry between Britain, France, Italy, and to a lesser
extent, Egypt and Ethiopia.[14] Before long its predictable kinship culture
witnessed some structural and normative transformations. One such
effect was that the precolonial political formations were considerably
disrupted. The partition of Somalia was almost complete towards the
end of the nineteenth century. By this time the presence of foreign rule
had been substantially consolidated. Imperial expansion combined
forceful seizure with diplomatic engagement and the use of treaties
and concessions as political bargaining tools. The intensification of
expansionism resulted in Somali frontiers undergoing some tinkering
to cater for specific needs of colonialists.[15] It was this fixation on
the protection of individual interest that made imperial rivalry fierce,
competitive and enduring to the Somali nation. Imperial rivalry also
brought distinct approaches, interpretations and understandings of
Somali society. The disparity in vision and identity was to play a
significant role in the formation and eventual disintegration of the
modern Somali state.

Like elsewhere in Africa, colonial impact on the Somali social order
did not go unchallenged. In northern Somalia, British rule inspired a
subaltern anti-colonial movement spearheaded by local cleric Sayyed

---

[12] See A. M. Warsame, *The Civil War in Northern Somalia (Somaliland): Its Impact on Pastoralists, Especially Women and Children* (The Hague: Institute of Social Studies Research, 1997), p. 48, cited by Brons, *Society, Security, Sovereignty and the State in Somalia.*

[13] The intrusion came with the expansion of Empire and the rapid construction of the colonial state. Due to space considerations and the specific focus of this chapter, the nature of imperial expansion cannot be discussed in detail.

[14] I. M. Lewis, *A Modern History of the Somali*, 4th edn (Ohio University Press, 2002), p. 40.

[15] For example Britain's goal was to protect its interest in Aden as a safe supply route, which it acquired in 1839. See L. V. Casanelli, *The Shaping of Somali Society: Restructuring the History of a Pastoral People 1600–1900* (University of Philadelphia Press, 1982).

Mohammed Abdulle Hassan in 1895 under an umbrella movement called the *daraawiish*.[16] Sayyed Mohammed became a formidable figure who could not be ignored by British and Italian colonial authorities. In 1905, the *daraawiish* anti-colonial movement culminated in a concession that ceded some territory in northeastern Somalia to its leadership.[17] But that rise to prominence ended soon after World War I, when the movement and its hierarchy were toppled by colonial military expeditions.[18] The complexion of colonial presence in Somalia changed considerably in the aftermath of World War II. The period saw a wave of Somali nationalism whose underlying aim was to foster the unification of captured Somali territories.[19] In 1949, the former Italian Somalia was placed under an international trusteeship system by a United Nations General Assembly Resolution for a period of ten years under the Italian Trust Administration.[20] On 26 June 1960 the British colony of Somaliland gained its independence. Five days later, on 1 July 1960, the Italian Somali colony also achieved independence. On the same day, an Act of Union was signed between the two states creating a unitary independent state of the Somali Republic.[21] The union remained operative until 1991 when Somaliland proclaimed independence in the aftermath of the collapse of the Somali Republic.

At independence Somalia was faced with significant challenges. Its encounters with colonialism had introduced a particular mindset, culture and social pattern alien to its people and the social lineage that had defined their existence. Buoyed by newly won political freedom, its leadership embarked on nation-building initiatives that to some degree

---

[16] See S. Touval, *Somali Nationalism* (Cambridge, Mass: Harvard University Press, 1963), pp. 53–6.

[17] Drawing support from different clan groups, he governed this region with an institutional framework that combined religious codes and political authority. See S. Samatar, *Oral Poetry and Somali Nationalism: The Case of Sayyid Mahammad Abdille Hasan* (Cambridge University Press, 1982).

[18] Lewis, *Modern History*, pp. 112–16.   [19] *Ibid.*, p. 116.

[20] United Nations General Assembly Resolution on the Question of the Disposal of the Former Italian Colonies, 21 November 1949, www.un.org/documents/ga/res/4/ares4.htm (last visited December 2010). The mandate required the trusteeship to 'foster the development of free political institutions and to promote the development of the inhabitants of the territory towards independence'. Further, the inhabitants were to be given a 'progressively increasing participation in the various organs of government'. (See UN General Assembly Resolution, 21 November 1949.)

[21] For first-hand account and analysis on this see P. Contini, *The Somali Republic – An Experiment in Legal Integration* (London: Routledge, 1969).

embraced neo-liberal values and a democratic system of governance.[22] Core freedoms and social organisations were allowed to proliferate and a semblance of order and bureaucratic efficiency had begun to crystallise amidst the presence of contrasting colonial legacies.[23] But postindependence euphoria was short-lived. Clan conflicts coupled with personal ambitions of political elites sowed seeds for social discord. Differences in vision soon began to overshadow the collective good resulting in marginalisation and social ostracism of communities and minority groups.[24] Increasingly during this period, ordinary Somalis saw themselves detached from the state apparatus and its networks of governance.[25] What emerged was the resurgence of non-state structures that challenged the legitimacy of postcolonial statehood.[26] Parliamentary democracy such as it was had clearly started to recede. And so a few years into self-rule, Somalia was edging ever closer to a de facto one-party state.[27]

The democratisation process and its representations had turned sour giving rise to a constituency of discontents.[28] A series of events unfolded that had severe impact on Somali social order.[29] First, national disaffection cascaded into wider grievances and sporadic and organised violence, the culmination of which was the killing of President Abdirashid Ali Sharmake in 1969. Subsequent succession disputes and power struggles

---

[22] A. M. Abdulahi, 'Perspectives on the State Collapse in Somalia' in A. A. Osman and I. K. Souare (eds.), *Somalia at the Crossroads: Challenges and Perspectives on Reconstituting a Failed State* (London: Adonis and Abbey Publishers Ltd, 2007), p. 43.

[23] From 1960 to 1969, two successful presidential and parliamentary elections were held that tested the governance credentials of newly independent Somalia. On this and some of the problems that emerged subsequently, see A. A. Jimale (ed.), *The Invention of Somalia* (Lawrenceville: Red Sea Press, 1995).

[24] Brons, *Society, Security, Sovereignty.*   [25] See Abdulahi, 'Perspectives', pp. 43–4.

[26] *Ibid.*, p. 45.

[27] See D. Laitin and S. S. Samatar, *Somalia: Nation in Search of a State* (Boulder, Colo.: Westview Press, 1987), p. 47.

[28] A. O. Mansur, 'Contrary to a Nation: The Cancer of Somali State' in Jimale (ed.), *The Invention of Somalia*, p. 114.

[29] The weakening democratic culture that followed the progression of self-rule experienced a major dent in the 1969 elections. Clan considerations infiltrated the political process with most of the political parties that participated virtually based on or driven by clan ideology and regional politics. The remaining credibility was tainted by widespread vote-rigging as the ruling Somali Youth League party clinched desperately to power. In a further move towards autocracy, the ruling party absorbed the opposition members of parliament effectively entrenching a one-party dictatorship, often seen as a turning point in Somali post-independence political history. See Abdulahi, 'Perspectives', p. 43. See also Lewis, *Modern History.*

within the ruling elites led to the intervention of the military through a coup d'état on 21 October 1969. The coup was initially received with considerable popular support because of widespread 'disenchantment with the clannishness and gridlock that plagued politics under civilian rule'.[30] The military administration under Siad Barre ruled Somalia from 1969 until its disintegration in 1991. During that period Somalis endured fear, chaos and anarchy. Barre ruled with ruthlessness, continued the divisiveness of clan politics and exploited Cold War superpower rivalry, the proceeds of which he utilised to prosecute the Ogaden War with Ethiopia and subsequent terror campaigns against those who defied him.[31] By 1991 Somalia was in total disarray. State institutions had completely collapsed.[32]

Opinions as to the reasons for the collapse of the Somali state are diverse. At the core of the arguments is what is seen as the final triumph of primordial lineage segmentation. This theory points to the status of clanship as framing the bedrock of the Somali social order. The clan system's depths and continued influence, it is argued, transcend the ordinary rhetoric of distinction, and that the overbearance, or rather superimposition, of kinship ties over national collective identity foreshadows a prioritisation of the self over the collective.[33] Subsequent state disintegration could therefore be seen as a manifestation of this tension. I. M. Lewis insists that Somali state collapse symbolises a more nuanced meaning. It 'represents technically a triumph for the segmentary lineage system and the political power of kinship'. And so 'for better or worse', Lewis notes, 'clanship has certainly prevailed, and the assertions of some Somali and non-Somali ideologues that clanship was an atavistic force doomed to oblivion in the modern world seem rather dated'.[34]

---

[30] World Bank Report, *Conflict in Somalia: Drivers and Dynamics*, http://siteresources .worldbank.org, p. 10.

[31] See A. Samatar, *Socialist Somalia: Rhetoric and Reality* (London: Zed Books, 1998).

[32] See Brons, *Society, Security, Sovereignty*, p. 4.

[33] A number of scholars have subscribed to this theory; see for example Lewis, *Blood and Bone*; O. Yohannes, *The United States and the Horn of Africa: An Analytical Study of Pattern and Process* (Boulder, Colo.: Westview Press, 1997); S. Samatar, *Unhappy Masses and the Challenges of Political Islam in the Horn of Africa* (2005), www.wardheernews .com (last visited December 2010); A. Simons, *Network of Dissolution: Somalia Undone* (Boulder, Colo.: Westview Press, 1995); V. Luling, 'Come Back Somalia? Questioning a Collapsed State', *Third World Quarterly*, 18:2 (1997), 287; J. Stevenson, *Losing Mogadishu: Testing US Policy in Somalia* (Annapolis: Naval Institute Press, 1995); J. Herbst and W. Clarke (eds.), *Learning from Somalia: The Lessons of Armed Humanitarian Intervention* (Boulder, Colo.: Westview Press, 1997).

[34] Lewis, *Blood and Bone*, p. 233.

In view of this contention, clan identity was set against symbols of state and nationhood, often resulting in violence and social division. The implication, then, for Somalia has been a kind of persistent struggle between state survival and clan supremacy. But Okbazghi Yohannes contends that primordial kinship has always been the defining factor in Somali social institutions.[35] He argues that 'there has never been a state in Somalia in the strictest sense of the term'. Thus Somalia, Yohannes concludes, has historically been 'a country of clans where the beginnings of a modern state have been only in the making in the midst of capricious forces of history within the context of a unitary capitalist order and yet politically compartmentalised system'.[36] But the strength of lineage kinship surpasses the simplicity of the identity thesis. It has, as a consequence, also given rise to the validation of Somali irredentism. This involved a quest for the return of territories that formally were part of Somalia.

As a people scattered across four main international boundaries – the Ogaden region of Ethiopia, Djibouti, Chad and Kenya – postindependence Somali national politics leans on a near obsession with the ultimate unification of its people. David Laitin and Said Samatar locate this yearning for unification in the very factors that source the Somalis as a people from the same genealogical tree. They argue that 'this fervent sense of belonging to a distinct national community with a common heritage and a common destiny is rooted in a widespread Somali belief that all Somalis descend from a common founding father, the mythical Samaale to whom the overwhelming majority of Somalis trace their genealogical origin'.[37] This aspiration has often scripted an ambitious foreign policy that has placed Somali engagement with its neighbours on the margins of tension and war.[38] Somalia had always contested the principle of retaining inherited colonial boundaries. Its leadership had always argued that political boundaries were artificial and arbitrary, and

---

[35] O Yohannes, *The United States and the Horn of Africa*, p. 225.   [36] *Ibid.*

[37] See Laitin and Samatar, *Somalia*, p. 29.

[38] It was also in sharp contrast to the foundational principles of the OAU, which, among others, called for the sanctity of state sovereignty and respect for the territorial integrity of states. See J. A. Lefebvre, *Arms for the Horn: US Security Policy in Ethiopia and Somalia 1953–1991* (University of Pittsburgh Press, 1991); T. Lyons, 'Crises on Multiple Levels: Somalia and the Horn of Africa' in A. Samatar (ed.), *The Somali Challenge: From Catastrophe to Renewal?* (Boulder, Colo.: Lynne Rienner Publishers, 1994); T. Lyons and A. Samatar, *Somalia: State Collapse, Multilateral Intervention, and Strategies for Political Reconstruction* (Washington, DC: The Brookings Institution Occasional Paper, 1995).

so were determined to promote the self-determination of Somali ethnic ancestry scattered across international territories. In 1978, after constant threats by Somalia to annex the Somali-speaking Ogaden region of Ethiopia in pursuance of its irredentist policies, Somalia and Ethiopia entered into a war lasting longer than both countries could afford. Since then, Somalia has not been able to fully recover from the trauma and destruction of that war. This national political obsession with unification was even given constitutional legality. Article 6(4) of the first republican constitution of Somalia provides that: 'the Somali Republic shall promote, by legal and peaceful means, the union of Somali territories'.

Irredentist foreign policy found an abiding template in the Cold War: a divisive ideology often referenced as a contributory factor to Somali state collapse.[39] In fact throughout its colonial and postcolonial history, as Alice Hashim notes, Somalia has found itself to be a pawn in the hands of more powerful states and their allies.[40] Its strategic position lends it to the competing politics of superpower rivalry, played out in the form of a regular supply of external support, military hardware and technical and financial assistance. Once such dependence heightened, the Somali state slowly abdicated its social responsibility to provide the most basic of services. Though conceding that 'it may be an exaggeration to claim that the Somali state is a creation of external assistance', Ken Menkhaus emphasises nonetheless that it is almost a given that 'the state has never been remotely sustainable by domestic sources of revenue'.[41] Substantial amounts of funding came from Cold War-driven foreign aid leading to what Menkhaus calls 'a bloated and artificial structure' whose final disintegration materialised the moment aid was frozen in the late 1980s.[42]

What this suggests is that Somali state collapse was not a historical accident. Some of the very colonial policies that shaped modern Somali statehood created circumstances that thrived on the politicisation of

---

[39] See especially Lyons and Samatar, *ibid.*, W. Clarke and R. Gosende, 'Somalia: Can a Collapsed State Reconstitute Itself?' in R. Rotberg (ed.), *State Failure and State Weakness in a Time of Terror* (Washington, DC: Brookings Institution Press, 2003); A. B. Hashim, *The Fallen State: Dictatorship, Social Cleavage and Dissonance in Somalia* (Virginia: UMI Dissertation Service, University of Virginia, 1995).

[40] Hashim, *The Fallen State*, p. 219.

[41] K. Menkhaus, 'US Foreign Assistance to Somalia: Phoenix from the Ashes?', *Middle East Policy*, 5:1 (1997), 124.

[42] K. Menkhaus and J. Prendergast, 'Governance and Economic Survival in Post-intervention Somalia', *CISS Africa Notes*, 172 (1995).

lineage structures and institutionalisation of collective clan acquiescence. These turned out to be avenues of contestation to the survival of the postcolonial state. The Somali state was therefore a deficient hybrid of other Somali historical precolonial social entities and an imposed colonial system inadequate for governance.[43] In this sense, the successor postcolonial state neither succeeded in totally suppressing the traditional system nor was it able to willingly accommodate it within a new hybrid.[44]

Genesis of violence and conflict in Somalia

The Horn of Africa – a geographical appellation that straddles the peninsula in East Africa and constitutes four territories, namely Somalia, Ethiopia, Eritrea and Djibouti – has been almost continuously afflicted with violence and armed conflicts since the 1960s. Reasons for the Horn's volatility are diverse and are exacerbated by internal and external factors.[45] Somalia's turbulent political history accounts for a considerable portion of this regional profile.[46] Its struggles since independence have been characterised by violence, hardship, disorder and a crisis of identity.[47] Hundreds of thousands of people, civilians and combatants, have been killed and a lot more internally displaced in what is one of the most enduring humanitarian catastrophes. The conditions of the internally displaced and refugees in the Horn of Africa are considered by the United Nations as some of the most desperate in the world. Similarly, the United States Committee for Refugees has reported an estimate of over 4.5 million internally displaced people in four of the region's most

---

[43] Abdulahi, 'Perspectives', p. 56.   [44] *Ibid.*

[45] C. Clapham, 'The Horn of Africa: A Conflict Zone' in O. Furley (ed), *Conflict in Africa* (London: Tauris Academic Studies, 1995), p. 72.

[46] For perspectives on the volatility of the Horn of Africa, particularly the turbulence of the statehood of Somalia, see generally J. Markakis, *National and Class Conflict in the Horn of Africa* (Cambridge University Press, 1987); P. B. Henze, *The Horn of Africa: From War to Peace* (London: Macmillan, 1991); I. M. Lewis, 'The Ogaden and the Fragility of Somali Segmentary Nationalism', *African Affairs*, 88 (1989); Samatar, *Socialist Somalia*; C. Besteman, *Unravelling Somalia: Race, Violence and the Legacy of Slavery* (University of Pennsylvania Press, 1999); Laitin and Samatar, *Somalia*.

[47] See H. A. Dualeh, *From Barre to Aideed – Somalia: The Agony of a Nation* (Nairobi: Stellagraphics, 1994); Africa Watch, *Somalia: A Government at War with its Own People: Testimonies about the Killings and the Conflict in the North* (New York: Africa Watch Committee, 1990); H. M. Adam, 'Somalia: A Terrible Beauty Being Born?' in I. W. Zartman (ed.), *Collapsed States: The Disintegration and Restoration of Legitimate Authority* (Boulder, Colo.: Lynne Rienner, 1995).

unstable countries: Somalia, Sudan, Ethiopia and Eritrea.[48] The situation has been further aggravated by the 2011–12 Somali famine. The violence in Somalia has occurred in four main periods: the Ogaden war, battles for the control of the northwest, the chaos and lawlessness of the 1990s and the anarchy that pervaded efforts at state reconstitution at the turn of the millennium.

The 1977–78 Ogaden war with Ethiopia was the first of the sequence of conflicts that challenged the capacity of the state to cope with conflict-induced disorder. The conflict was caused by state ambitions of complementing efforts of rebel groups attempting to liberate the Somali-inhabited region of Ogaden from Ethiopian control.[49] Ogaden was ceded to Ethiopia by the United Nations in 1948, but the dispute surrounding its ownership was never settled. Since independence the desire to reunite the region with mainland Somalia has been ever growing. In 1977, Siad Barre deployed sections of the Somali armed forces in pursuit of this aim. A conflict with Ethiopia soon ensued, accounting for the deaths of over 25,000 people.[50] This encounter overstretched the Somali armed forces who suffered heavy material and human losses.[51] Unable to fulfil this ambition, the abortive military campaign sowed seeds of discord that thereafter had a permanent bearing on Somali society. It is, however, ironic that the same nationalist sentiments that helped justify the conflict also shaped opposition to the Somali leadership, especially on its failings to deliver the promise to salvage Ogaden. The fragile political order that emerged therefore instigated internal agitation and the proliferation of open and underground movements whose primary aim was to topple Siad Barre's government.[52]

The second period pertains to an uprising in northern Somalia in May and June 1988. The conflict pitted the Somali military against the Somali National Movement, a splinter group that was created in 1981 by members of the Isaaq clan who harboured grievances in the wake of the

---

[48] See United States Refugee Committee at www.refugees.org. See also Amnesty International, *Somalia: A Human Rights Disaster* (London: Amnesty International, 1992); Human Rights Watch, *So Much to Fear: War Crimes and the Devastation of Somalia* (New York: Human Rights Watch, 2008).

[49] Word Bank, *Conflict in Somalia*, p. 10.   [50] See Brons, *Society, Security, Sovereignty.*

[51] It is reported that about 25,000 lives perished during the war. See Samatar, *Socialist Somalia*, p. 137.

[52] One of the movements that really stood out was the Somali Salvation Democratic Front (SSDF), created in 1978 under the leadership of Abdullahi Yusuf. Comprising mainly recruits from the Mejerten clan, the SSDF engaged in sporadic combat with the Barre regime that translated into a wave of violence and disorder mainly in the northeast. See World Bank, *Conflict in Somalia*, p. 9.

Ogaden war.[53] It was also fuelled by clan rivalry aggravated by widespread social injustice. Once their region was placed under military administration, the Isaaq clan became targets for persecution from the Barre regime. Local Isaaq personalities were jailed, with some disappearing in mysterious circumstances, whilst others had their properties vandalised and businesses expropriated.[54] In response, the northwest took up arms in a bloody civil war that began in May 1988. The challenge to the Barre regime was not taken lightly. Government forces unleashed atrocities that terrified civilians and brought an estimated killing of 60,000 Isaaq.[55] The regional capital, Hargeysa, and most of its vital infrastructure, were destroyed.[56] With the Somali state collapsing in 1991 the northwest region seceded from the ruins of southern Somalia and became the self-declared state of Somaliland.[57]

The third episode, in the 1990s, saw Somali society's divisive politics becoming particularly self-destructive. Between 1989 and 1990, Barre's embattled government was further weakened by attacks from multiple armed groups. State institutions had then virtually collapsed with the government unable to extend its jurisdictional competence beyond the fringes of Mogadishu. Increasingly, from 1990 and 1991, violence intensified to the point of general lawlessness; targeted killings escalated, looting and vandalism became commonplace. In January 1991, President Barre vacated power and left Mogadishu. The Somali state officially ceased to exist. The phenomenon of 'warlords' then replaced traditional state authority. In due course the social cohesion and collective consciousness of Somalia as a nation was fragmented into numerous competing fiefdoms governed by anarchy and social disarray.[58]

---

[53] Brons, *Society, Security, Sovereignty*, p. 157.

[54] For accounts of some of the levels of impunity meted out on Isaaq civilians, see Africa Watch, *Somalia: A Government at War with its Own People*.

[55] *Ibid.* See also M. Sahnoun, *Somalia: The Missed Opportunities* (Washington, DC: United States Institute of Peace, 1994).

[56] P. Schraeder, 'The Horn of Africa: US Foreign Policy in an Altered Cold War Environment', *Middle East Journal*, 46:4 (1992), 571–93 at 571.

[57] It ought to be noted that Somaliland is yet to succeed in its efforts to gain international recognition despite making considerable strides in building peace and experimenting with an indigenous democracy. For arguments supporting state recognition see F. Henwood, 'A Contribution to the Case for Somaliland's Recognition' in Osman and Souare (eds.), *Somalia at the Crossroads*.

[58] Mohamoud, *State Collapse*, p. 16. Situations were dire and according to Terrence Lyons and Ahmed Samatar, the Somali people, as a consequence of this complete fragmentation, 'suffered the horrible brutality of living in a Hobbesian world without law or

Fourth, since 2000 both organised and guerrilla-style fighting has been prevalent. In 2004 international re-engagement with the Somali crisis was reactivated after the fiasco that characterised previous UN missions. Diplomatic endeavours through trans-state initiatives spearheaded by the Intergovernmental Authority on Development (IGAD) resulted in the creation of a Transitional Federal Government (TFG). The government consisted of exiled Somali politicians and former warlords. Its institutions were anticipated at the time to revive the Somali state and chart a way for a peaceful order. But this ambition was never actualised. An amalgam of militia groups, constituting the Union of Islamic Courts (UIC), launched a massive assault to dislodge any entrenchment or representation of the TFG. The UIC comprised warlords and Islamic clerics aspiring to create a political order based on strict interpretations of Sharia law. Their combined presence culminated in a reign of terror that brought misery to most of southern Somalia.[59]

To help consolidate its faltering grip, the TFG tried to take on the Islamists with military support from Ethiopia. From 2006 until the withdrawal of Ethiopian troops in December 2008, tales of atrocities re-emerged. Renewed hostilities led to an escalation of the humanitarian catastrophe. An African Union peacekeeping force was then despatched with a mandate to restore order and formulate peacebuilding initiatives. Violence has occasionally intensified, and although progress has been intermittently registered, conditions in southern Somalia are far from orderly, aggravated by a devastating famine which not only claimed thousands of lives, but also overstretched what was already a fragile political and social structure.

The complexities of the political landscape have remained precarious. Battlegrounds are sometimes indeterminate and, as Human Rights Watch reports, the 'grim reality of widespread impunity for serious crimes is compounded by the fact that both TFG and insurgent forces are fragmented into multiple sets of largely autonomous actors'.[60] Although the Ethiopian forces withdrew from Somalia soon after helping dislodge the UIC insurgents from most parts of Mogadishu in 2007,

institutions to regulate relations among groups or to protect the most vulnerable from the most vicious'. Lyons and Samatar, *Somalia: State Collapse*, p. 7.

[59] See International Crisis Group, 'Can the Somali Crisis be Contained?', *Africa Report*, 116 (2006).

[60] Human Rights Watch, *So Much to Fear: War Crimes and the Devastation of Somalia* (2008), www.hrw.org/node/76419, at 10 (last visited February 2009).

the battle for the control of Somalia continued unabated. A section of the UIC mutated into a hardline group, the Al-Shabaab. With weapons at its disposal, and coupled with the inability of the TFG to expand beyond Mogadishu, the Al-Shabaab has been in effective control of large swathes of southern Somalia, including Mogadishu which was only recaptured by the TFG and AMISOM in August 2011.

The gradation of the Somali conflict evokes a set of intriguing paradoxes and confusing conundrums. Its protracted nature also appears to challenge some underlying assumptions on causality of postcolonial internal conflicts in Africa. This Somali paradox has attracted considerable debate amongst commentators and scholars. Ahmed Samatar, for example, enquires, 'why and how could this society, one of the few nations in the continent with one ethnic group, one culture, one language and one religion, find itself in such parlous circumstances – verging on self destruction?'[61] Like elsewhere in Africa, answers to this query do not come easily, especially given that some of the factors that may be identified as key drivers in the sequence of armed conflicts have also contributed to preventing conflicts – and in some instances, playing a part in ending them.[62]

The Somali conflict could be explained from a multi-causality perspective that encompasses a combination of factors.[63] During Siad Barre's reign a divide-and-rule state policy was crafted to consolidate authoritarianism and diffuse challenges to his leadership. The regime's autocratic 'strength' was made possible not only by a weak civil society, but also by the dysfunctional structures of bourgeoisie class formations. As Alice Hashim explains, the 'absence of a hegemonic bourgeoisie, capable of addressing issues on a national level and of cutting across clan lines created a vacuum into which an authoritarian ruler stepped'.[64] Once class formations were reconfigured, a useful social template for resistance was replaced with fear and indifference, forcing formal institutions to sink into atrophy. Fear of dictatorial reprisals implied that resistance movements had to go underground, inadvertently creating space for vigilante groups to occasionally take on the regime.

---

[61] A. Samatar, 'Under Siege: Blood, Power, and the Somali State' in P. Anyang' Nyong'o (ed.), *Arms and Daggers in the Hearts of Africa* (Nairobi: Academic Science Publishers, 1993), p. 23.

[62] World Bank, *Conflict in Somalia*, p. 9.

[63] Adam, 'Somalia: A Terrible Beauty Being Born?' in Zartman (ed.), *Collapsed States*, p. 69.

[64] A. B. Hashim, *The Fallen State: Dissonance, Dictatorship and Death in Somalia* (Lanham: University of America Press, 1997), p. 7.

It is worth noting that although the Somali conflict has certain unique particularities, it nonetheless shares patterns of commonalities with most other conflicts in Africa. Ethnicity has often formed part of the analytical framework that tries to deconstruct the primary, if not central, causalities of internal conflicts. The predominant theoretical approaches on ethnicity are premised, to a certain degree, on the proposition that conflicts in Africa have certain ethnic derivatives compounded by colonial boundaries that arbitrarily forced distinct communities with a history of animosity to live under an artificial ethnic patchwork. This is not to say that ethnicity by *itself* causes conflicts. But once it is associated with social uncertainty or material dispute, it becomes a prism through which society fractures. Going by this traditional stereotypical ethnic assertion, Somalia may not, at a glance, fit into such classification. Its ethnographic composition is homogenous. That is to say its people share the same religion, language and cultural heritage. There is a fair amount of consensus on the homogeneity of the Somali nation. Some scholars have, however, begged to differ. Anna Simons, in particular, has argued that the premise upon which Somali homogeneity is constructed remains contested. She contends that Somalia:

> is a container of people whose lines were drawn from the outside; in this sense, it is no different from any other African country, despite irredentist rhetoric to the contrary. There is nothing ethnically, linguistically, or culturally homogenous about all of the people occupying Somalia.[65]

It may follow that the divisive dimension of ethnicity could not be manifestly rooted in Somali society. But in primordial kinship lineage both the strengths and weaknesses of a homogenous Somali society are displayed with sometimes fundamental contradictions. The depths and impact of Somali kinship can be as engrained in the psyche of a member of a group as in other, non-homogenous societies. It has been suggested that in kinship an individual's identity and loyalty are not only shaped by clan structures and ideology, but that by virtue of birth, a person's membership is perceived as axiomatic in the same way as membership is often determined by ethnic groups elsewhere.[66] In the aftermath of state collapse, Somali clan groups became repositories of social relation and

---

[65] A. Simons, 'Somalia: A Regional Security Dilemma' in E. J. Keller and D. Rothchild (eds.), *Africa in the New International Order* (Boulder, Colo.: Lynne Rienner Publishers, 1996), pp. 71–3.

[66] J. Chipman, 'Managing the Politics of Parochialism' in M. E. Brown (ed.), *Ethnic Conflict and International Security* (Princeton University Press, 1993), p. 240.

providers of security and protection. Protection of the individual and the cohesion of the clan arise from a social institutional obligation which, once pursued to the end, may often conflict or clash with either state structures or entities not sharing the same clientele or objectives with opposing subclans. Thus as an entity representing the collective, the clan emanates a dimension of violence which emerges from a social structuring that imposes duties and obligations over which individuals seldom have control.

From that perspective, as Donald Rothchild and David Lake explain, it is the 'social system that breeds violent social conflict, not individuals, and it is the socially constructed nature of ethnicity that can cause conflict, once begun, to spin rapidly out of control'.[67] But given its history, the state's role in the prolongation of the Somali conflict cannot be underestimated. Beyond the burden bequeathed to it by imperial legacies of colonialism, the Somali state had breached its social contract with society so deeply that it became a symbol of despair and a source of violence. For most of its post-independence life, the state had fought battles with itself and against what has constantly emerged as its parallel rival – kinship social structures. The influence of kinship has subjected the state to a condition of perpetual conflict. In this context, John Markakis notes that 'the target of the attack is the state: the custodian of wealth and protector of privilege. The state is both the goal of the contest and the primary means through which the contest is waged.'[68]

International response to the Somali crisis

Somalia has posed considerable challenges to international legal institutions. The slow and often half-hearted engagement has reinforced the charge that international law, and the precepts that underpin it, operate only when there is an emergence of 'an unusually propitious constellation of political factors'.[69] The succession of violence that followed state collapse in 1991 led to an exodus of diplomatic missions accredited to Somalia.

---

[67] D. Lake and D. Rothchild, *The International Spread of Ethnic Conflict: Fear, Diffusion and Escalation* (Princeton University Press, 1998), p. 6.

[68] J. Markakis, *National and Class Conflict in the Horn of Africa* (Cambridge University Press, 1987), p. xvi.

[69] R. H. Jackson, 'The Nuremberg Case, as Presented by Robert H. Jackson 1947', at 8, cited by C. Booth, 'Prospects and Issues for the International Criminal Court: Lessons from Yugoslavia and Rwanda' in P. Sands (ed.), *From Nuremberg to the Hague: The Future of International Criminal Justice* (Cambridge University Press, 2003).

Mogadishu's political vacuum was quickly occupied by competing militias seeking to establish clan territorial dominance in areas controlled and inhabited by their affiliates and social networks. Two personalities who emerged from the poststate crisis – Muhammad Farah Aideed and Ali Mahdi Muhammad – fought fierce battles to capture what little was left of Somali political capital and power bases. Local efforts at reconciling them led to a joint alliance of the United Somali Congress (USC)/Hawiye subclans, whose intention was to facilitate reconciliatory dialogue between factional groups and provide an accessible alternative dispute resolution process. This could not sufficiently contain the feud between Aideed and Muhammad, whose mutual antagonism eventually dislodged the fragile alliance.

Meanwhile, the human tragedy continued unabated. In early 1992, the United Nations estimated that about 4.5 million people were at risk of starvation, malnutrition and other famine-related diseases. Alarmed by the deplorable conditions, the Security Council passed Resolution 733 on 23 January 1992, imposing an arms embargo on the supply of weapons to Somalia and calling on warring parties to cease hostilities for the delivery of humanitarian assistance.[70] This opened up a door for a cease-fire negotiated by UN Special Envoy, James Jonah. But the cessation did not hold for long; clan feuds had already crystallised into full-blown armed conflict. Secretary General Boutros-Ghali presented two reports to the Security Council, on 21 and 24 April 1992, on the deteriorating conditions in Somalia. The Council responded with Resolution 751, which provided the legal framework for the United Nations Operation in Somalia (UNOSOM) as well as an agreement for the immediate deployment of a limited contingent of fifty UN observers.[71]

Hostilities continued nonetheless, and the observer mission found itself entangled in a deadlock with no sign of readiness for dialogue from the feuding clans. A decision was then taken by the Secretary General to appoint Mohamed Sahnoun, an Algerian diplomat, as the UN Special Representative to Somalia.[72] It was hoped that with his input

---

[70] United Nations Security Council Resolution S/RES/733, 1992.

[71] United Nations Security Council Resolution 751, available at www.un.org/sc/committees/751/. The deployment was shrouded in bureaucratic incompetence, and could only be effected in July and September 1992 when military observers and security personnel arrived in Mogadishu. See I. K. Souare, 'The United Nations Intervention in Somalia: A Retrospective Look and Lessons for Future Africa-UN Partnership in Conflict Resolution' in Osman and Souare (eds.), *Somalia at the Crossroads*, p. 159.

[72] D. J. Williams, *UN Peacekeeping, American Policies and the Uncivil Wars of the 1990s* (New York: St Martin's Press, 1996), p. 316.

and personality, an identifiable authority would be on the ground to facilitate a cease-fire. Of course, Sahnoun's task was far from easy. The conditions in Somalia were worsening, and by the time the UN observer mission arrived hostilities had already outgrown the mission's capacity to register immediate impact. On Sahnoun's recommendations, the Secretary General advised the Security Council to enlarge both the mandate and capacity of UNOSOM. In August 1992 Resolution 775 was passed authorising the expansion of UNOSOM to a standing strength of 4,219 personnel.[73]

It soon became clear that despite the increment in strength, UNOSOM could not make much difference to the crisis; the mission lacked an integrated strategy and understanding of the complexities of Somali social order.[74] With sound knowledge of the region's politics, Sahnoun initiated an inclusionary engagement with local community elders and clan structures with the view to harnessing their transformative peacebuilding potentials. He remained an advocate for a gradual approach and rejected the UN's insistence on a quick fix as both myopic and a misreading of the conflict.[75] But the conceptual disagreement with the UN was growing in the face of mounting challenges that exposed the inadequacies of a narrowly defined UNOSOM. Sahnoun became increasingly frustrated, not only by bureaucratic institutionalism of UN operations, but also that the Secretary General was not so keen on the transformative peacebuilding approaches Sahnoun advocated. In October 1992 Sahnoun resigned, citing excessive bureaucracy and unwillingness and ignorance on the part of the UN hierarchy to address the crisis.[76] Ismat Kittani was named as a replacement, but lasted for five months after which the mandate of UNOSOM was revised to cater for military intervention.

In December 1992 approaches of the UN to the conflict were significantly transformed by Security Council Resolution 794. First, it effected a shift in the legal apparatus of the UN's approach and strategy. The

---

[73] United Nations Security Council Resolution S/RES/775, 28 August 1992.

[74] See Souare, 'The United Nations Intervention in Somalia' in Osman and Souare (eds.), *Somalia at the Crossroads*, p. 160.

[75] See Sahnoun, *Somalia*.

[76] Sahnoun was clearly frustrated not only by the rigmarole of bureaucratic institutionalism of UN operations, but also that the Secretary General was not so keen on the inclusionary peacebuilding approach adopted by himself. All this was further aggravated by a personality clash between Sahnoun and Boutros Boutros-Ghali. See M. Bryden, 'New Hope for Somalia? The Building Block Approach', *Review of African Political Economy*, 26:79 (1999), 134–40 at 135.

initial peacekeeping mission under Chapter VI was now replaced by enforcement provisions of Chapter VII. It meant that there was now a legal basis for military force to be used to contain the violence, protect civilians and possibly change the course of the conflict. Second, the shift was important to the extent that it signalled an admission that the UN's fixation with the restoration of order by a quick fix approach was clearly flawed. The approach conceptualised peace as the absence of violence. Resolution 794 was endorsed by the Security Council on 3 December 1992. It provided that 'action under Chapter VII of the Charter of the United Nations should be taken in order to establish a secure environment for humanitarian relief operations in Somalia as soon as possible'.[77] The Resolution authorised the creation of the Unified Task Force (UNITAF), under American command, with a mandate to use all necessary means to establish a secure environment in Somalia.

Yet despite earlier failings in the UN's approach, UNITAF's mandate was very narrowly defined. Its primary objective, according to the then US President George Bush (Senior), was to 'open the supply routes, to get the food moving, and prepare the way for a UN peace-keeping force'.[78] That goal was echoed in a subsequent visit to Somalia when he told an assembly of Somali locals that 'we come to your country with one reason only: to enable the starving to be fed. Once the food flows freely, the US will go home.'[79] By this and the Resolution's omission to incorporate Somali indigenous institutions, international engagement was merely interpreting the Somali conflict as mainly a humanitarian problem. The implication was that the underlying causes of the conflict and the social dynamics that fed into it were neglected and consigned to irrelevance.

UNITAF made some modest strides in securing vital supply routes for humanitarian relief. The civil composition of the mission also embarked on a number of projects that had some momentary benefits, such as undertaking vital engineering works that brought to life some of the long-disused infrastructure.[80] However, UNITAF's operational vision was challenged by a conceptual disparity between the UN and policymakers in

---

[77] United Nations Security Council Resolution 794, S/RES/794, 1992.

[78] Africa Report, 'US Commits Force to Somalia, but for How Long?', (1993), cited by Mohamoud, *State Collapse*, pp. 139–40.

[79] 'Bush Addresses Somalis', *Time Magazine*, 14 December 1992, 25.

[80] See W. S. Clarke, 'Testing the World's Resolve in Somalia', *Parameters*, 23 (1993–94), 42–58 at 48.

Washington. The Americans wanted to pursue the humanitarian focus of the mission as a temporary measure.[81] The Secretary General emphasised that the UN was pursuing 'the cause of security, humanitarian relief and political reconciliation', which included a fair amount of civil institution-building and the restoration of state authority.[82] The disagreement brought considerable unease in the international response to the crisis. A compromise was initiated as an attempt to harmonise policy directions and advance a collective international approach.

In March 1993 UNITAF was absorbed by UNOSOM II. Its legal basis was derived from the peace enforcement provision of Chapter VII.[83] The objectives of UNOSOM II were to facilitate an orderly humanitarian relief programme, initiate a comprehensive disarmament of militia factions, enforce a durable cease-fire and promote national reconciliation. In comparison with previous missions, these constituted an expanded mandate that were to be tested by events. The first came in June 1993 when the Pakistani contingent came under sustained artillery attack suffering serious casualties.[84] Shortly after, eighteen American soldiers were killed by forces loyal to Farah Aideed. The Americans expressed dismay at the events, charging the UN with incompetence and thereafter withdrew their troops from Somalia. The remaining contingents under UNOSOM II completed their withdrawal in March 1995. The international forces left Somalia pretty much the same as they found it: in a state of violence, anarchy and disorder.

So, what then went wrong with these international approaches? Why was the UN-led international engagement conceptualised through the frame of international law unable to neither appreciate nor adequately confront the Somali crisis? And what does this say about international law in relation to postcolonial internal conflicts? From the foregoing, it is clear that international approaches to the Somali crisis have been characterised by a multitude of sins. These range from neglect, poor understanding of the genesis of the crisis, burden of inheritance and the limitations of international law identified in the previous chapters.

---

[81] See *Time Magazine*, 21 December 1992, 20.

[82] *Newsweek International*, 21 December 1992, 8.

[83] United Nations Security Council Resolution 814, S/RES/814, 1993.

[84] Despite the need to confront the challenges posed by the violence, the UN announced a sudden U-turn. In August 1993, barely five months after the creation of UNOSOM, the UN reached a decision to reduce the size of the mission to 17,200, effective September 1994. See Souare, 'The United Nations Intervention in Somalia' in Osman and Souare (eds.), *Somalia at the Crossroads*, p. 162.

Corollary to these is the fact that almost the entire international involvement was dedicated to reviving state institutions as preconditions to peace. The consequence has been disaster.

It took the UN and the international community almost a year to begin a process of engagement with the conflict in Somalia. By ignoring the desperate calls of Somalis the institution was in effect doing what amounted to prioritising the conflict in former Yugoslavia over the Somali tragedy. The considerable delay demonstrated further the often poor margin of appreciation of and increasing sense of alienation fostered by the UN and instruments of international legal order, especially when they pertain to the plight of the African condition. In fact the same margin of appreciation shapes the legal limitations of the extent to which international law applies to postcolonial internal conflicts. In a book published shortly after his resignation, Mohamed Sahnoun was unequivocal about the effects of the collective failure to act. He argues that 'if the international community had intervened earlier and more effectively in Somalia, much of the catastrophe that had unfolded could have been avoided'.[85]

It has been suggested that although the delay was as a result of the difficulties and unprecedented circumstances of Somalia, the UN was resource constrained as it was preoccupied with the conflict in the former Yugoslavia.[86] Whilst it is true that the Yugoslav conflict had taken some time from the organisation and possibly stretched its resources, this is not sufficient ground for the level of institutional ineptitude that characterised prolonged international neglect. The reluctance to intervene early shows that the UN as an international institution, and international law as its guiding frame, appear far removed and often alienated from the realities of postcolonial social conditions. It also meant that an opportunity was forfeited to support crumbling institutional structures and those indigenous Somalis trying to prevent disintegration of a society whose social structures are instrumental to the survival of its people and national identity.[87]

Once formal institutions collapsed and social disintegration deepened there was virtually no framework upon which an international approach

[85] See Sahnoun, *Somalia*, p. xiii.
[86] See Souare, 'The United Nations Intervention in Somalia' in Osman and Souare (eds.), *Somalia at the Crossroads*, p. 159.
[87] A. Zacarias, *The United Nations and International Peacekeeping* (London: I. B. Tauris, 1996), pp. 67–8.

could be built, the reason being that international peace initiatives in the form of neo-liberal approaches cannot work in the absence of formal structures because of their organically state-centric focus. And even when engagement with the crisis finally began, it was within a state-centric paradigm. For the particular circumstances of postcolonial African internal conflicts this approach runs the risk of marginalising crucial parties and indigenous factors to a conflict. Take for example the Secretary General's recital to Resolution 794 contained in a letter dated 29 November 1992. In it he writes that Somalia's militia leaders 'do not exercise effective authority over all the armed elements in the areas which they claim to control'.[88] As a result, he concludes that the 'reality is there are ... very few authorities in Somalia with whom a peace-keeping force can safely negotiate an agreed basis for its operation'.[89] Clearly, traditional social structures were not considered relevant in the Secretary General's assessment of what constituted 'authority'. This was surprising, especially noting that the structures were the only thing of substance left in the aftermath of state collapse.

Reliance on statehood and its presumed functions as indispensable variables in conditioning peacebuilding is often unrealistic in postcolonial Africa. As an unstable artificial variable, the capability of the postcolonial African state is not a given and its fragility often transforms it into an outlet of resource extraction. In the context of Somalia, this has culminated in a tendency to institutionalise a clash of interest between the state and its subordinate constituents. As Menkhaus notes, for the most part of their country's post-independence history, Somalis have seen the state and its formalised institutions as nothing more than 'an instrument of accumulation and domination, enriching and empowering those who control it and exploiting and harassing the rest of the population'.[90] This then rendered international approaches inadequate, because the constituents of peace are not necessarily conjoined with postcolonial statehood or its affiliated apparatuses. Institution-building and the art of peacebuilding 'are two separate and, in some respects, mutually antagonistic enterprises in Somalia'.[91]

---

[88] See letter dated 29 November from the Secretary General to the President of the Security Council of the United Nations, S/24868, 30 November 1992.

[89] *Ibid.*

[90] K. Menkhaus, 'Reassessing Protracted State Collapse in Somalia', *Adelphi Series*, 44:364 (2004), 15–35 at 19.

[91] K. Menkhaus, 'State Collapse in Somalia: Second Thoughts', *Review of Africa Political Economy*, 97 (2003), 405–22 at 407–8.

But the failure of international law in Somalia also demonstrates that confronting internal conflicts is still alien to the international legal order. The UN's disagreement with Sahnoun exposes this. Besides casting aspersions on Sahnoun's personal abilities and intellectual competence, the disagreement revealed the extent to which international law and its agencies are often incapable of appreciating the socialised hierarchies of postcolonial societies. Somali society is a complex configuration of subsidiary clan structures driven by layers of local entities. These entities wield enormous power, influence and control, especially in respect of key determinants of social relations and the hierarchy upon which they mediate. Sahnoun understood this and recognised the importance of social networks whose continued challenge to state instruments brought about the collapse of the Somali Republic in the first place. Thus his initial focus was to gain the trust and confidence of clan leaders by adopting transformative approaches which required subordinating state-centric international approaches. The positive disposition of kinship was then used as a negotiating tool to initiate reconciliatory dialogue.

Indeed, Sahnoun's approach was a logical reflex of the Somali social condition and its continued resistance to contemporary international law approaches. Contemporary TWAIL scholars would embrace Sahnoun's approach as an attempt to actualise the legitimate participation, recognition and validation of indigenous voices in matters relating to their coexistence and destiny. It also accords with the notion of peace cultivation and the binary of integration and interdependence. In this sense, Sahnoun's refusal to impose on local Somalis mindsets conceived from international approaches that are founded on precepts of particular Western origin, represented a counteracting challenge to international law's approach to postcolonial internal conflicts.

Beyond these variables, international engagement also assumed problems of an operational nature. Like the poverty of strategy that characterised UNOSOM, the US and UN partnership was far from ideal. For the most part, the conflict was being viewed from the perspective of 'innocent humanitarians bringing much needed aid and succour to Somalia.'[92] This understanding exhibited what I. M. Lewis calls 'mutually incompatible expectations' exacerbated by ignorance of Somali culture.[93] Further operational failures were highlighted in a Comprehensive Report of the UN Department of Peacekeeping Operations (DPKO). The Report

---

[92] Lewis, *Modern History*, p. 277.   [93] *Ibid.*

criticised the formulation of the successive UN missions as 'vague, changing frequently during the process and ... open to myriad of interpretations'. It also noted the lack of preparation, indicating that 'integrated planning was limited to two short visits to Somalia by interdepartmental technical teams'. All these unfolded in the backdrop of internal bureaucratic wrangling that not only hampered the operational efficiency of the UN, but also made it unable to appreciate the exigencies of the social and human challenges in Somalia.[94]

So in sum, the failures and faultlines are symptomatic of the internalisation of ethnocentrism in conflict and peacebuilding, often culminating in sets of dilemmas described by Howard Wiarda as 'an inability to understand the third world on its own terms, an insistence of viewing it through the lenses of ... western experience, and the condescending and patronizing attitudes that such ethnocentrism implies'.[95] Like international law-driven approaches in Burundi, multilateral engagements in Somalia have been profoundly flawed. And even in cases where such engagements appeared genuine and sustained, they have been characterised by the patterns and pathologies of neo-liberal international law conceptions. Corollary to this has also been an obsession with the idea that *only* international law approaches to conflicts can make a difference. Amongst others, the initiatives fell short of drawing from the strength of Somali indigenous social institutions and the politics that propel them. Sahnoun's attempt to initiate transformative peacebuilding was interpreted as alien to the ethos and approaches of the UN. In its place, international engagement pursued a quick fix approach relying on the fading Somali state structures and an inadequate international legal architecture.

The African Union and the Somali conflict

The departure of UNOSOM abandoned Somalia to the competing whims of warlords and vigilante groups. Violent armed conflicts imploded and the human tragedy of death and disease escalated. A few trans-state bodies remained with the Somali cause. Amongst them were the United

---

[94] See United Nations Department for Peacekeeping Operations, *The Comprehensive Report on Lessons Learned from United Nations Operation in Somalia (UNOSOM), April 1992–March 1995* (New York: UN Department of Public Information, 1995).

[95] H. Wiarda, *Ethnocentrism in US Foreign Policy: Can We Understand the Third World?* (Washington, DC: American Enterprise Institute for Public Policy, 1985), p. 1.

Nations Development Office for Somalia (UNDOS), Somalia Aid Coordination Body (SACB), Intergovernmental Authority on Development (IGAD) and the European Union. These institutions assumed a range of functions that are traditionally the jurisdictional domain of state authorities. To facilitate operational clarity, a working understanding was drawn to formulate 'joint policy and act as the primary forum for the exchange of information on developments in the country'.[96] Although a few services dedicated to the internally displaced have improved with occasional exposure of the scale of the humanitarian challenge, these have been generally modest. It was this realisation that led IGAD to attempt initiatives aimed at revitalising both the Somali peace process and political institutions. The outcome was the creation of the Transitional Federal Government (TFG) in 2005.[97]

Background to the African Union involvement

The formation of the TFG was besieged by tension and power struggles between rival clans. Peace initiatives resulted in a series of reconciliatory conferences held in Kenya, Djibouti and Ethiopia. But these generally failed because they tended to fuel tensions and conflicts and encouraged divisive lobbying for positions in a proposed state.[98] The Arta Peace Conference of 2000 managed to forge an agreement that led to the creation of a Transitional National Government (TNG). The TNG had a short lifespan. A string of corruption scandals, misguided priorities and inter-clan wrangling eroded its legitimacy and threatened to restore the chaotic *status quo ante*. The TNG subsequently degenerated into disarray and was replaced by the TFG. Initially based outside Mogadishu, the TFG has demonstrated an inability to facilitate the restoration of order in southern Somalia. This and other factors led to the rise of the

---

[96] UNHCR/USAID/EUE, *Somalia: Humanitarian Assistance and Development in Support of Peace and Stability*, Draft Proceedings of an Informal Meeting held in Addis Ababa, 11 June 1996.

[97] Abdillahi Yusuf was elected President by the Transitional Federal Government. The election was surrounded by controversy amidst allegations of vote-buying. The main institutions of the TFG are the Transitional Federal Parliament (TFP) and the Transitional Federal Charter (TFC). For a detailed account of the negotiations and politicking surrounding the creation of the TFG and the circumstances leading to the rise of the Islamists, see International Crisis Group, 'Can the Somali Crisis be Contained?', *Africa Report*, 116 (2006).

[98] World Bank Report, *Conflict in Somalia*, p. 13.

Islamist Union of Courts, who launched a campaign to battle for the control of Mogadishu in 2006. A chaotic situation ensued involving an Ethiopian invasion and US anti-terror activities degenerating into full-scale conflict.

The uncertainty over Somalia's future galvanised renewed interest in regional peace initiatives. The UN Security Council adopted Resolution 1725 in December 2006 endorsing the sub-regional peace support mission (IGASOM) and therein lifting the arms embargo earlier imposed on Somalia.[99] The Resolution asserted that the TFG offers 'the only route to achieving peace and stability in Somalia' and emphasised the need for a political process that could culminate in the 'conditions for the withdrawal of all foreign forces from Somalia'.[100] It also authorised the mission to protect the free passage of personnel involved in the peace process, ensure the safety of TFG officials and institutional structures as well as facilitate the re-establishment of a national security force for Somalia. Despite renewed interest, the Resolution was hardly a departure from earlier neo-liberal rhetoric. It was problematic on two fronts.

First, by proclaiming that the TFG offered the *only* solution to Somali poststate crisis, the Resolution was placing unrealistic faith in a fragile institution lacking attributes of empirical statehood or support from its social constituencies. The TFG is a product of political bargaining and alliances between people and factions who have a history of animosity. Internal rivalry makes it weak and constantly on the precipice. Its survival is not a certainty. What has been certain since is the fragility that the TFG has always struggled to contain. Second, the Resolution was repeating past mistakes of prioritising the formation of state political institutions as precondition to peacebuilding. This state-centric approach overlooks the importance of traditional social institutions, which have had a central role in Somali history. In this regard, the Resolution and its prescriptions amount to imposing a structure that has failed to deliver a realistic political system in an environment that is constantly held captive by social institutions feeding from the residual effects of primordial kinship. Any genuine engagement 'should

---

[99] IGAD Peace Support Mission to Somalia (IGASOM) was a regional proposal for a protection and peace-support mission to Somalia. It was approved by both the African Union and the UN Security Council. It was originally meant to be a peacekeeping mission to help bolster the TFG. But by 2006 the situation in Mogadishu had rapidly changed with the consolidation of Islamist militias. IGASOM was abandoned to give way for the African Union Mission in Somalia (AMISOM).

[100] United Nations Security Council Resolution 1725, S/RES/1725, 2006.

endeavour to understand how progress in Somaliland and Puntland has been achieved and how their successes might be replicated in the troubled south'.[101]

Uncertainty continues to engulf Somalia, and its changing political dynamics have raised doubts over the survival of the TFG. There are still a fair amount of threats emanating from the contestation between social structures and representations of the juridical dynamics of the state. Regional factors have also been at play. Since 2004, Ethiopian interference in Somalia appears less than discreet. Its public backing of the TFG has been supplemented by military and material support, often justified on grounds of national security concerns about the rise of Islamist militarism.[102] Between May and July 2006 both the Ethiopian rhetoric and the military build-up had intensified, with an intervention that violated both the Constitutive Act of the African Union and Resolution 1725 which imposed an arms embargo on Somalia. On 28 December 2006 Ethiopian and TFG forces took control of Mogadishu.[103] Ethiopia then fought alongside the TFG until early December 2008 when it began withdrawing its troops from Somalia.

Despite continued conferment of juridical statehood and international support for the TFG, the disorder in southern Somalia has remained critical. In January 2009, the TFG consented to a broadening of its governance structures with the creation of a government of national unity. This is composed of TFG representatives and members of the opposition group, the Alliance for Re-liberation of Somalia (ARS). Whilst advances on the political front show signs of progress, this is yet to translate into safety for civilians and access to humanitarian relief.[104]

---

[101] I. M. Lewis, 'New UN Adventures in Somalia', *Horn of Africa Bulletin*, 3 (2000), 19–20 at 19.

[102] The Ethiopian Parliament articulated this fear by labelling the Islamist Courts as an instrument of 'clear and present danger' and in effect granting a carte blanche mandate to Prime Minister Menes Zenawi to defend the interest of Ethiopia and support the TFG. See Chatham House, 'The Rise and Fall of Mogadishu's Islamic Courts', *Africa Program*, AFPBP/07/02 (2007), 5.

[103] The Ethiopian determination in consolidating the authority of the TFG in Mogadishu had led to an all-out war. Heavy fighting was reported in which Ethiopian troops were alleged to have used heavy weaponry in densely populated neighbourhoods, indiscriminately killing hundreds of civilians and with injuries amounting to thousands. Their activities created a humanitarian catastrophe, forcing almost 500,000 people to flee the degrading conditions of Mogadishu. See Human Rights Watch, *Shell Shock* (New York: Human Rights Watch, 2006).

[104] Refugee International Field Report, *Somalia: Political Progress, Humanitarian Stalemate* (3 April 2009), www.refugeesinternational.org/policy/field-report/somalia-political-progress-humanitarian-stalemate (last visited March 2010).

It was in the backdrop of these prolonged security conditions that the African Union concluded that circumstances in southern Somalia required the invocation of an Article 4 mandate with the aim of providing space for the implementation of the Constitutive Act's peacebuilding framework. The UN Security Council agreed. Enter the African Union.

The AU mission in Somalia (AMISOM)

The African Union's active engagement with the Somali conflict came in the wake of the slow pace of IGASOM and the rapidly degenerating conditions in southern Somalia. Situations were complicated by the Ethiopian intervention and the resistance it generated from factional militias determined to dislodge the TFG. The series of battles for Mogadishu had devastating consequences: disproportionate use of heavy weaponry; indiscriminate killing of civilians; destruction of property and shelling of essential services such as hospitals; commission of acts of rape, torture and other serious sexual violence on women; conscription and enlisting of children in hostilities; and blockade of aid and humanitarian assistance.[105] The gruesome nature of the hostilities outraged the international community, particularly African leaders. In January 2007 the African Union, in conjunction with the UN, granted approval for the deployment of troops to southern Somalia for an initial period of six months. The terms of reference were defined under the framework of the African Union Mission in Somalia (AMISOM). Its legal basis was sourced from Article 52 of the UN Charter and Article 4(h) and (j) of the Constitutive Act. The mission was mandated to offer security support to the transitional federal institutions for the stabilisation of Somalia and the furtherance of dialogue and reconciliation. It was also tasked with facilitating the flow of humanitarian assistance and initiating realistic foundations for reconstruction and development.

The first contingent of Ugandan troops arrived in the Somali town of Baidoa on 1 March 2007. The deployment had initially been fraught with difficulties. Once in Mogadishu, the contingent occupied the two positions most sought after by militias: Villa Somalia (Presidential Palace) and the Mogadishu International Airport. The idea was to use the airport to secure access for humanitarian relief, whilst the palace was to provide safe sanctuary for members of the besieged transitional

---

[105] See Human Rights Watch, *So Much to Fear: War Crimes and the Devastation of Somalia* (New York: Human Rights Watch, 2008).

government. But this was overshadowed by hostilities in March and April 2007. The TFG-Ethiopian alliance used the Mogadishu International Airport to launch helicopter gunships on densely populated neighbourhoods killing hundreds of civilians. It used the presidential compound as a storage facility for heavy artillery, most of which was used for bombardment and a campaign of terror on civilians and essential services like hospitals, private property and infrastructure.[106] Aid agencies expressed outrage at the degenerating security conditions, accusing the military alliance and AMISOM of jeopardising humanitarian access to Mogadishu and its satellite regions.

For the most part, the Ugandan contingent appeared almost oblivious of the gravity of the alliance's military campaign and the repercussions of allowing their bases to be used for purposes that were antithetical to the ethos of the Constitutive Act. Although its deployment was rushed and its mandate initially appeared vague, Article 4 of the Status of Mission Agreement (SOMA) clearly enjoins AMISOM to refrain from any action or activity incompatible with the impartial and international nature of its duties.[107] Similarly, Article 9 of SOMA stipulates that AMISOM must conduct its operations in full respect for principles and rules of international conventions such as the Geneva Conventions of 1949, the 1977 Additional Protocols and the UNESCO Convention on the Protection of Cultural Property. These provisions reiterate the protection of civilians and civilian-related infrastructure during armed conflicts as an established principle of customary international law. To the extent that AMISOM forces were initially negligent or even complicit in the hostilities implies that the objective of the mission was being undermined.[108]

---

[106] Ibid.

[107] Status of Mission Agreement between the Transitional Federal Government of the Somali Republic and the African Union on the African Union Mission in Somalia, Addis Ababa, March 2007, www.africa-union.org/root/AU/AUC/Departments/PSC/AMISOM/amisom.htm (last visited April 2009).

[108] The extent of the AU's complicity was subsequently expressed in a letter from the European Union Security Adviser for the Horn of Africa leaked to the British-based Guardian newspaper. In the email, addressed to Eric van der Linden, EU Representative in Kenya, the Security Adviser wrote that 'I need to advise you that there are strong grounds to believe that the Ethiopian government and the transitional federal government of Somalia and the AMISOM force commander ... have through commission or omission violated the Rome Statute of the international criminal court.' See details of story at www.guardian.co.uk/world/2007/apr/07/eu.warcrimes (last visited January 2009).

The role of AMISOM has improved over time. First, Burundi, a country that benefitted from earlier African Union peace initiatives following a devastating civil war, was stable enough to reciprocate by contributing troops in January 2008. The additional troops, though insufficient in number to fulfil AMISOM's mandated strength of nine infantry battalions, provided nonetheless a boost to the overstretched Ugandan contingent and facilitated the provision of security to the weak transitional federal institutions including vital infrastructure and international entry points.[109] Improvement in the mission's security mandate has also allowed a steady flow in the provision of humanitarian assistance, with the AMISOM field hospital providing lifesaving medical supplies to weak, vulnerable and displaced civilians. Disarmament of militia groups has also seen stockpiles of weapons deposited with the mission.[110]

Most important perhaps is the shift in the mission's focus, seemingly necessitated by the imperative to untangle itself from the burden of the legacy of successive international failures and the neo-liberal approaches that underlined them. The shift includes attempts to broaden reconciliatory dialogue and peace-cultivation initiatives. In August 2007 the mission facilitated a national reconciliation conference which was attended by over 2,000 delegates. The agenda and the amity that emerged from it were built on by a follow-up meeting held in Mogadishu in March 2008. The meeting was attended by government and opposition figures as well as local clan leaders.[111] In February 2009, another peace conference was convened attended by Islamic clerics, TFG officials and clan elders. AMISOM emphasised that its focus was to help initiate inclusionary peacebuilding by creating conditions to enable Somalis to formulate their own indigenous programme of peacebuilding. Lineage participation is seen as an important turnaround and may well open up a new front in confronting southern Somalia's crisis. It also symbolises the recognition of indigenous social institutions whose inputs are imperative in peace initiatives, a crucial factor international structures often find hard to accommodate. This is a significant element that has been missing in decades of international engagement in Somalia.

Prospects and challenges of AMISOM

Neo-liberal international peace approaches have been perceived to have complicated and prolonged the conflict in southern Somalia. Such

[109] See 'For Peace, Stability and Development in Somalia', *AMISOM Newsletter*, 1 (2008), 5.
[110] *Ibid.*   [111] *Ibid.*

concerns continue to grow and successive UN failure has served as a reference point for factional groups and their sympathisers. Further, hostility to international engagement has been fanned by clan sentiments that perceive state and trans-state institutions as axes of contestation with Somali kinship structures. In fact on a number of occasions AMISOM bore the brunt of this local hostility with targeted attacks on its forces which brought about the deaths of many of its peacekeepers.[112] The presence of international military forces, therefore, has always had critical consequences in Somalia. This legacy of discontent not only prejudices the average Somali's receptiveness to the idea and actuality of international engagement, but also influences the trajectory of externally perceived initiatives in Somalia.

Unlike in Burundi, the African Union intervened in southern Somalia almost twenty years after state collapse and well after the fiasco of successive international missions. During the period of multilateral engagement, approaches to the Somali conflict were theorised from a mindset that ignored the capability and relevance of indigenous social structures. Clan and sub-clan entities were perceived by the UN and sections of the international community as fundamentally violent and disorderly. It was believed that recognising and incorporating them into peacebuilding initiatives would inadvertently amount to granting legitimacy to a whole network of social undesirables. At the protestation of Sahnoun, Boutros-Ghali pursued an agenda that dismembered the trust of the very social structures that held the key to unlocking the deadlock that pervaded international engagement. Even when the UN finally pulled out in 1995, the vestiges of its legacy had consolidated a distasteful memory amongst Somalis.[113]

AMISOM found southern Somalia in a messy state, still nursing the failures of multilateral engagement conceptualised through international law approaches. The legacy and public disillusionment they generated were inherited by AMISOM. The prioritisation of the reconstruction of state political institutions over the initiation of peace cultivation is still very much an obsession of trans-state actors occupied with the conflict. Even in the shadows of its failure, the UN continues to believe that *only* the TFG could provide a route to peace and stability in Somalia. Such an insistence on the supremacy of the TFG in the search for peace could

---

[112] See 'For Peace, Stability and Development in Somalia'.

[113] See M. Angeloni, 'Somalia: The Tortuga of the 21st Century', *Transitional Studies Review*, 16 (2009), 755–67 at 760.

shut down other possible alternatives. Despite its fragile composition, jurisdictional limitations and administrative incompetence, the TFG represents, through endorsement and acquiescence by UN instruments, the only internationally recognised authority in Somalia. It is as if nothing else matters. This mindset shows no sign of waning, and its centrality to the international order provides glimpses into the collective faultlines of peacebuilding initiatives in Somalia.

The UN is not expected to conceive otherwise because, as Balakrishnan Rajagopal asserts, 'international law remains trapped in a version of politics that is narrowly focused on institutional practice, and an understanding of the social that accepts the unity of the agent as a given'.[114] Ahmedou Ould-Abdallah, the former Special Representative of the UN Secretary General to Somalia, who had also served in a similar capacity during the Burundi crisis, is reported to have castigated aid agencies and trans-state institutions for negotiating with armed opposition groups, local authorities and clan networks, arguing that doing so undermines the authority of the federal government and grants legitimacy to opposition entities.[115] He has even suggested that aid agencies must define their operations with the view to consolidating the transitional federal institutions.[116] Ould-Abdallah's approaches are a replica of the neo-liberal approaches pursued earlier in Burundi. Unfortunately, AMISOM was for the most part of its early engagement caught up in the genus of this restrictive mindset. And so before it could find its ground, the mission expended considerable time and resources inadvertently validating a process that epitomised the inadequacy of international law approaches.

In Burundi, AMIB's Article 4 stabilisation mandate was complemented by a deepening process of courtship and engagement with traditional social institutions such as the *bashingantahe*. Even when the mission handed over to the UN, the foundations of peacebuilding from below had already been laid. The UN had to merely follow and build on the process formulated by the African Union initiatives. The Somali challenge is that unlike in Burundi, where the African Union attempted to invoke the Constitutive Act's transformation initiatives before a UN mission, AMISOM entered the fray long after international neo-liberal engagement. The implication is that once the burden of inheritance is engraved in a country's peace process, even institutions with a more inclusionary

---

[114] B. Rajagopal, 'International Law and Social Movements: Challenges of Theorising Resistance', *Columbia Journal of Transnational Law*, 41 (2003), 397–434 at 406.
[115] See Refugee International Field Report, p. 3.   [116] *Ibid.*

peacebuilding dispensation may run the risk of being entangled in a messy legacy which they neither created, nor are able to completely shed.

Challenges for the mission also resulted from circumstances that were self-made. From the beginning, the mission was beset with uncertainty and lack of clarity as regards its mandate and modus operandi. Whereas the African Union's expectations are broadly construed to include the creation of conditions conducive for peace and stability, President Museveni appears to view the role of the Ugandan contingent in a slightly different light. He emphasised:

> We will not go to Somalia to impose peace on the Somalis, because we shouldn't do that and we can't do it. What we are going to do in Somalia is to empower our Somali brothers to rebuild their state.[117]

The Ugandan formulation is, at least in theory, based on a peacebuilding approach that seeks to reverse classical and neo-liberal approaches adopted by successive UN missions to Somalia. Of initial concern was the absence of coordination and a detailed operational concept for the mission at the time of deployment. This meant that the contingent had to generally operate within its command structures using considerable discretion and moral suasion. There has been convergence, however, and despite its limitations the mission has attempted to embrace aspects of the Constitutive Act's transformative approaches. From a logistical perspective, AMISOM still remains largely understaffed, operating on a shoestring budget and without adequate troops, basic systems and equipment.

It will be difficult for the African Union, as an evolving organisation, to address these logistical problems on its own. It is still faced by institutional weakness, compounded by lack of political will from some member states. And for the Constitutive Act to be a living instrument that espouses normative values capable of shaping a renewed Africa, confidence in, and support for, the African Union are both critical and essential. Transformative peacebuilding approaches are unpredictable, cumbersome and often exorbitantly expensive. As the only remaining international force in southern Somalia, AMISOM carries both the burden and hope of international society, and its conscience would depend on the extent to which the mission's approaches serve as a springboard for the consolidation of integrated security frameworks

---

[117] Statement by Yuweri Museveni, President of Uganda, in a farewell address to his troops at Jinja, Uganda, news.bbc.co.uk/1/hi/world/africa/6409167.stm (last visited May 2010).

capable of advancing the Constitutive Act's peacebuilding philosophy. International support to make that happen has generally been uncoordinated and inconsistent.

The UN and sections of the international community appear encouraged by AMISOM. In January 2009, the Security Council passed Resolution 1863 authorising the use of UN peacekeeping funds to provide a support package for the Somali peace process.[118] But this ought to be viewed with caution as the underlying intent of Resolution 1863 is fundamentally flawed. The Resolution aims to establish a UN peacekeeping mission to Somalia whose tasks would be 'to assist in the delivery of humanitarian aid; protect political actors and Government buildings and staff, and United Nations staff; monitor implementation of the Djibouti Peace Agreement and any subsequent ceasefires and joint security arrangements; and build Somali security forces'.[119] There is still lack of a genuine intention to engage the real movers of Somali social structures. What is striking is the Resolution's affirmation of resuscitating previously failed neo-liberal approaches. Take, for instance, its conclusion that 'if the international community placed the acknowledged priority of a comprehensive peace on the ground ahead of its efforts to help the Somali Government promote and ensure stability and political progress in the meantime, it might take another 10 years' and that Somalia 'will miss the boat'.[120] Similarly, the Resolution's flirtation with a grand UN peacekeeping force may be counterproductive. Further, it may well be a recipe for disaster and undo the little that has been done so far, especially in courting traditional social institutions. And perhaps if history is anything to go by, a UN deployment would be seen by Somalis as a 'polarising and destabilising symbol of foreign meddling on Somali soil'.[121]

The initial mixed result from the African Union engagement presents neither a total failure nor does it augur well for its institutional image and narrative of hope and promise. Its intervention amidst international indifference is a commitment to the transformative peacebuilding that underpins the Constitutive Act's evolving peace and security architecture. But continuing the process of peace indigenisation will, for a while, remain challenging. Over the decades, the Somali political terrain has been subjected to a confusing mix of contradictory and competing

---

[118] United Nations Security Council Resolution 1863, S/RES/1863, 2009.
[119] *Ibid.*, para. 3.   [120] *Ibid.*, para.11.
[121] Refugee International Field Report, p. 4.

forces. Despite its flaws, AMISOM remains a better option, with a sense of African ownership. It may not, realistically, make significant progress if it reverts to working within a defined framework unpredisposed and insensitive to social structures and clan networks critical in the advancement of peace in Somalia. Its scale of fragmentation implies that southern Somalia needs sound social rehabilitation from the inside. For that to happen, inclusionary peace cultivation must be given a chance. It had some impact in Burundi and it appears to be working well in Somaliland. It is this latter area that is worth examining in such a context.

Transformative peacebuilding in Somaliland

Poststate Somalia is synonymous with chaos and successive international failures. But this has been largely confined to southern Somalia. In the breakaway northwestern region of Somaliland, situations have, comparatively, been far more orderly. The relative peace has emerged from a gradual process that has been in the making since the collapse of the Somali postcolonial state. So, what has been responsible for the restoration of peaceful order in northwestern Somalia when southern Somalia, which had considerable international engagement, has remained in precarious conditions for over two decades? And what is it about the models for northwestern Somalia that has transformed threats and recurrence of conflict to opportunities for peacebuilding?

It is important to note that AMISOM's mandate had been largely confined to southern Somalia. And so peacebuilding approaches in the breakaway state of Somaliland are not pursued under the framework of the Constitutive Act. However, Somaliland is relevant on three fronts. First, without international recognition, support and a functional state apparatus, Somaliland has been able to initiate and pursue transformative peacebuilding that has significantly helped in instituting peace and order. Its relevance is that transformative peacebuilding shows potential. Second, the process utilised social institutions and network groups as essential parts of the peace-formulation process. This supports aspects of the Constitutive Act's peace and security framework. Third, the success of the Somaliland model may provide valuable insights into the possible trajectory of peacebuilding in Africa.

Somali state collapse generated opposing outcomes for the two former colonies constituting the Somali Republic. Whereas the former Italian Somalia imploded in chaos, former British Somaliland leapt towards 'impoverished independence with only a limited modicum of political turbulence'.[122] Somaliland's success lies in the collective initiation by traditional elders and the Somali National Movement (SNM) political group to begin a process of *shir* reconciliatory peacemaking. On 16 May 1991, a diverse gathering in the northwestern town of Burao discussed and reached a decision to repeal the Act of Union that created the Somali Republic in 1960. Two days later, Somaliland proclaimed independence.[123] The proclamation emerged from what could be viewed as a postmodern institution-building, one that integrates traditional social structures into political decision-making.

Somaliland's new institutional order comprises: an executive branch leaning towards a presidential democracy; a judiciary, which incorporates customary law; and an elected parliament of two chambers, which fuses modern legislative structures with traditional social institutions. An important part of the parliament is the *golaha guurtida*, or Upper House of Elders. It is composed of representatives from clan networks with a broad range of peacebuilding capabilities. The composition is carefully constructed to ensure balance of power, stability, social integration and interdependence.[124] The evolving institutional structures resemble a kind of home-grown hybrid democratic state driven by participatory consultation and consensus. Although still without international recognition, Somaliland has managed to utilise traditional structures to oversee the restoration of peace, demobilisation of former militias and a gradual social rehabilitation with some form of participatory governance and social contract with its civil society.[125]

Several factors have been offered to explain the difference in the approaches and conditions of peace between southern Somalia and the northwestern region of Somaliland. These range from the monopoly on the means and methods of violence to the resuscitation of indigenous peacebuilding processes. During UN engagement, humanitarian relief

---

[122] G. Prunier, 'Somaliland: Birth of a New Country?' in C. Gurdon (ed.), *The Horn of Africa* (University College London Press, 1994), p. 61.

[123] Somaliland remains unrecognised as a state. However the AU has been engaging the country's leadership with the view to offering support. See African Union Commission, *Resume: African Union Fact-finding Mission to Somaliland 30th April to 4th May 2005* (Addis Ababa: African Union Commission, 2006).

[124] S. Kibble, 'Somaliland: Surviving Without Recognition; Somalia: Recognised but Failing?', *International Relations*, 15 (2001), 5–25 at 14.

[125] Since ratifying the UDHR, Somaliland has adopted a new constitution and successive elections have been held, bolstering its emerging democratic credentials. See Kibble, *ibid.*

barely reached Somaliland, and even when it did vigilante groups attacked relief convoys and looted their contents. Aid agencies reacted by terminating their operations and evacuating their staff. According to Yusuf Farah, the cessation of humanitarian operations meant that militia groups that thrived on looting relief supplies had their main incentive curtailed, ultimately denying them a major cause for contention.[126] Farah further notes that whereas in southern Somalia competition for political dominance involved multiple armed groups who could not individually exert undue influence on others, in Somaliland the Isaaq remained the dominant military group with strength sufficiently capable of counteracting potential threats from rival groups.[127] This presence has translated, with great effect, into an opportunity to repel clan skirmishes, banditry and vigilantism.

But the most influential factor pertains to Somaliland's adoption of transformative peacebuilding capable of consolidating peace from below. Confinement of international engagement to southern Somalia opened up space for Somaliland to chart its own course. Lineage structures were placed at the centre of social affairs. Clan leaders occupied the vacuum left by the collapsed state and initiated intensive reconciliation processes. Central to this has also been the utilisation of local structures of govern-ance that place emphasis on dialogue, arbitration and restitution. Whilst the process depends, to some degree, on the functionality of individual local institutions, it is not, like neo-liberal international law approaches to conflicts, a stand-alone entity with a hegemonic persuasion. The process is a socially driven chain of interconnected and interdependent variables with each stage representative of matters of significant social concern, embodying a collective sense of cohesiveness. Somaliland's peace-cultivation processes evolve in three critical stages: they are shaped at the local community councils, reaffirmed at regional authority level and 'constitutionally' validated at the *guurti* national conference level.

The *shir* process of peacebuilding begins at the lowest stratum of social organisation where clan elders are constituted into community committees at the village level. Their task is to serve as first port of call in mediating local clan disputes, enforcing community peace contracts, regulating pastoral and commercial activity as well as responding to

---

[126] Y. A. Farah, *Somalia: The Roots of Reconciliation – Peace-making Endeavours of Contemporary Lineage Leaders: A Survey of Grassroots Peace Conferences in Somaliland* (London: Action Aid, 1993), p. 10.

[127] *Ibid.*

immediate threats to legitimate public order.[128] Local peace frameworks run into regional structures, complementing and reinforcing the village-level *shir* process. The functions of networks of personalities and structures converge to enhance continuity, integration and interdependence. Inter-clan violence and banditry is taken seriously and the notion of collective responsibility is introduced, implying that a whole sub-clan is held accountable for the undesirable conduct of its members. What is evident here is a construction of a collective accountability framework that maximises the value of deterrence whilst promoting accountability. Matters arising at the regional level are often products of normative values underpinning grassroots structures and given 'constitutional' validation at the highest level.

Other important actors include the *akils*, spiritual leaders and regional elders. The *akil* is an old institution that predates the postcolonial era. Its function is mainly maintenance of order and the dispensation of justice. But occasionally the institution runs into the difficulty of delicately balancing competing interests of clan lineage against the compelling obligation to generally maintain order.[129] Spiritual leaders have always remained central to Somaliland's domestic affairs. In most cases, their functions are identical to those of local authorities and clan elders. Even though these functions have a primarily religious disposition, interpretations and rulings are done in 'light of their segmentary lineage principles'.[130] In theory, these leaders see peacebuilding as a role they ought to fulfil. In this sense, religious figures are not merely spiritual leaders.[131]

Critical to the success of these initiatives is the *guurti*, which is composed of spiritual leaders, clan and sub-clan elders and local authorities. As the highest political and jural body of traditional authority, the *guurti* is viewed as composed of the 'most enlightened and judicious persons that are found in a group or a nation at large'.[132] Its functions are broad but mainly hover around reconciliatory dialogue. The *guurti's* approaches to peace are many and varied, often depending on the people involved in a dispute and the prevailing context. For example, in less serious conflicts, proverbs, poems and indigenous peacemaking skills are utilised to ease tension with the help of ad hoc committees of the *guurti*. Mutual trust, transparency and fairness are guiding principles that underpin the *shir* process. And in its attempt to consolidate peace, the *guurti* attaches no specific time limits or ultimatums to peacebuilding

---

[128] *Ibid.*, p. 20.   [129] *Ibid.*, p. 26.   [130] Lewis, *A Pastoral Democracy*, p. 29.
[131] *Ibid.*, pp. 29–31.   [132] Farah, *Somalia: The Roots of Reconciliation*, p. 17.

processes. It is not uncommon for conflicting parties to live together for prolonged periods for the purposes of subsiding prejudice, allaying fears and deflecting psychological barriers between them.[133]

Somaliland's peace initiatives have been a gradual process. The first of its constitutive sessions was held in the town of Berbera in February 1991. Its aim was to initiate reconciliatory dialogue amongst feuding sub-clan groups. The amity it created provided a springboard from which the subsequent May 1991 Burao *shir* culminated in the collective proclamation for independence. Similar peace cultivation conferences took place in Beer, Ainabo and Lasanod. Their successes have been astounding. In 1992, conflict erupted in Berbera following a series of government initiatives that were interpreted by clan leaders as moves towards centralisation of authority. The *sheikh* conferences were convened to tackle the causes of the conflict and normalcy was thereafter restored. These processes are intense, cumbersome and often involve patience and attention to detail, a luxury neo-liberal approaches do not have.

Perhaps the most important of these peacebuilding assemblies is the Borama conference of 5 March 1991. It was convened in the backdrop of the resurgence of rivalry amongst Somaliland's political leadership. Failure to resolve their differences led traditional elders and religious leaders to take on the initiatives to deepen the peacebuilding process. One of its main tasks was to negotiate a comprehensive peace deal and set institutional frameworks for political transition.[134] The elders saw the conference as another way of restoring the traditional role of indigenous peacebuilding structures.[135] Differences were settled in many forms, using methods that concurred with the concept of *heer*, the compensation of honour, central to Somali culture.[136] Once reconciliation was achieved the conference ended with the election of a transitional civilian administration.

The Borama conference epitomised the practical functionality of transformative peacebuilding and its potential in confronting postcolonial conflicts. As Mark Bradbury notes, it was an impressive exemplification of the 'Somali reconciliation process, in which the role of lineage elders

---

[133] See Lewis, *A Pastoral Democracy*.

[134] R. Omaar, 'The Best Chance for Peace', *Africa Report*, (1993), 44–8 at 44.

[135] The chairman of the council of elders, Sheikh Ibrahim, emphasised that 'our task [as traditional leaders] is to ensure security and reconciliation. The government's responsibility is management, administration and development.' Cited by Omaar, *ibid.*, at 48.

[136] Prunier, 'Somaliland: Birth of a New Country?' in C. Gurdon (ed.), *The Horn of Africa*, p. 67.

as mediators in the internal affairs of the communities were clearly displayed', providing in the process 'an alternative model to the [failed] reconciliation process promoted by the United Nations in Somalia after the resignation of Ambassador Sahnoun'.[137] The conference generated three significant outcomes. First, it produced a peace charter, or national contract, that sought to consolidate security frameworks by institutionalising the process, entities and normativity upon which peace cultivation percolates. Second, a transitional charter was adopted with a grace period of two years to facilitate the constitutional operation of the interim government. Third, and perhaps most important, was the formulation of a bicameral legislative system that incorporated and integrated a traditional council of elders into an upper House of Guurti, whilst also catering for an elected lower House of Representatives.

Integrating social structures into Somaliland's peacebuilding initiatives amounts to resuscitating an important aspect of precolonial African social order. Postcolonial internal conflicts are multifaceted and engage issues relating to legitimacy and identity. Once these are on a collision course, the nature of conflicts often takes a certain character that displaces the dynamics of social coherence. Africa still retains certain characteristics that make indigenous structures the embodiment of social security and moral cohesion. But the main influences of these social structures and their abiding hierarchies are concealed by the language of domination central to the heritage of international law. As a result, 'much of what occurs in the extra-institutional spaces in the Third World remains invisible to international law'.[138] In conceptualising inclusionary peacebuilding initiatives, regard must be had to how identity relates to power and to the broader systems and structures that organise and govern their relationships.[139] The importance of this has a particular resonance for postcolonial societies, whose 'people feel their identity has historically been eroded, marginalised, or under deep threat'.[140]

But the assumption of peacebuilding functions by lineage structures in repairing Somaliland's broken social order is not wholly accidental. Throughout its history, the establishment of central authority in Somalia

---

[137] M. Bradbury, *Somaliland CIIR Country Report* (London: Catholic Institute for International Relations, 1997), p. 29.

[138] Rajagopal, 'International Law and Social Movements', at 406.

[139] J. P. Lederach, *The Little Book of Conflict Transformation* (Philadelphia: Good Books, 2003), p. 60.

[140] *Ibid.*

has generally been received with trepidation. Its kinship lineage creates a remarkable sense of individual autonomy that makes the centralisation of authority at great risk of disintegration. Somali hostility towards the notion of central authority is rooted in the capacity of kinship lineage to localise loyalties. For as Bradbury notes, 'the political constitution of Somali society lies not in the centralised political institutions of a European model, but in a particular social system where the notion of a social contract has more to do with regulating political and economic relationships between pastoral kinship groups, than with delegating responsibility to a central polity'.[141]

To conclude, it is plausible to suggest that the Somaliland peacebuilding model provides reason to believe that transformative approaches are better suited to the intricate nature of internal conflicts than are neo-liberal international law approaches. The model demonstrates a remarkable ability to tap into peacebuilding dispositions of traditional social institutions in ways that international law and its implementation agencies cannot. Above all, as it is a practical crisis-responsive initiative seeking to confront the underlying causes of social tension, internal violence and their imprimatur, the Somaliland approach encourages greater understanding and recognition of complex structural patterns that are imperative in shaping mutual coexistence. Fundamentally, this model of peacebuilding from below fits well with the key aspects of the transformative peacebuilding embedded in the Constitutive Act. For instance the *shir* process, which has been central to Somaliland peacebuilding initiatives, equates to the *Restorative* subset, whilst the *guurti* and integrationist features constitute *Corrective* and *Preventive* mechanisms. Thus the Somaliland experience could potentially help in enriching perspectives on the Constitutive Act's peacebuilding approaches.

Conclusion

The experience of southern Somalia since the collapse of the Somali Democratic Republic in 1991 has shown that successive neo-liberal approaches conceptualised through the frame of international law have failed. More than once, the rebuilding of state institutions has been interpreted as a prerequisite condition for the consolidation of peace. And more than once, these state-centric perceptions have appeared to

---

[141] Bradbury, *Somaliland CIIR Country Report*, p. 43.

provide no meaningful solution to a conflict whose multitudinous actors and complex outlook continue to challenge some of the foundational ethos of contemporary international law. The reasons relate not only to the absence of collective political will, logistical support and leadership assiduity, but also to a context in which approaches have been conceptualised, defined and enforced by a certain framework and mindset rooted primarily in an international law that displaces, contradicts and expurgates indigenous social institutions and the philosophies that underpin their modes of existence.

It has also been established that the desire for the indigenisation of transformative peacebuilding led to the invocation of Article 4(h) of the Constitutive Act and the deployment of AMISOM in southern Somalia. Achieving only a modest impact, the mission has been dogged by challenges, most of which are a culmination of the legacy of successive international failures. It has been argued that this lingering legacy has constrained AMISOM's ability to chart its own path. However, a gradual departure from this legacy in the northwestern region of Somaliland appears to temper violence and offer valuable insights into the mechanics and potentials of transformative peacebuilding. Somaliland's success lies in its exploitation of peacebuilding strengths of local structures to restore order and embark on installing social institutions in the shadows of the ruins of the postcolonial state. There are three lessons from these experiences.

The first is that the continued dysfunctional state of southern Somalia in the face of international engagement and the triumph of Somaliland under indigenous initiatives show quite clearly that confronting internal violence in Africa requires a strong engagement with traditional social structures and institutions. Social institutions are the conduits of communities and the entities from which individuals source sanctuary in times of need. Second, the success of transformative peacebuilding approaches is not entirely dependent on the primacy of the modern state. The state as an entity for the organisation of social life is merely one of several possible options. The Somaliland model amply demonstrates that for Somalis – and indeed African postcolonial societies in general – the state is nothing more than an organised expression of the people's aspirations and way of life. This is partly driven by a community's shared values, commonality of interests and desire to create conditions that have the potential of fostering mutual coexistence, peace and social justice. Third, Somaliland's integration of modern institutions with traditional social structures appears to drift away from the strict Westphalian model to one that moves towards a people-centred interpretation of security. This may well represent a kind of postmodern recharacterisation of the structures and normative composition of the postcolonial African state and its perception of peace and security.

But considering the depth of disintegration propelled by the sequence of violence and the history of contestation between modernity and Somali lineage structures, it would be remiss to definitively conclude that armed conflict on a grand scale will be less probable in Somaliland. Construction of frameworks for peace is a continuously evolving process with its every stage critical. As Farah notes, in the medium and long term, 'the most that can be hoped for is that [social] institutions capable of resolving conflict should be in place and functioning'.[142] This is not to say that Africa is better off without the state. The state and international law will still remain important elements of international society. What is needed, however, is a certain conceptualisation that incorporates the intricate nature of the social dynamics of indigenous structures into the functions of the state and outlay of international law. At least for now, transformative peacebuilding framed around normative values, social integration and interdependence provides grounds for hope.

[142] Farah, *Somalia: The Roots of Reconciliation*, p. 8.

9

Towards an African Union philosophy on peacebuilding?

In any case, until it is acknowledged that orthodox conceptions of warfare more closely reflect a particular theoretical orientation than any empirical reality, the search for explanations will fail to advance beyond their present embryonic condition. What is needed are theoretical conceptions of Africa's wars that more closely resemble the reality on the ground.

Richard Jackson[1]

Introduction

The social and political historiography of postcolonial Africa has been largely a telling of violence and conflicts. The conflicts have culminated in the deaths of millions of people, large-scale destruction of property and considerable disruption to economic and political spheres. In fact, the disruptions in the past decades have been so widespread as to almost consume the totality of the continent with virtually every region affected or susceptible to the vestiges of conflicts. Even in some of the countries that escaped the scourge of conflicts, there emerged within their domestic spheres coercive regimes that thrived on authoritarianism, holding hostage their countries and peoples. Taken together, these episodes muzzled, for far too long, the capacity and potential of a continent with enormous prospects. Although there are fewer conflicts now as there were two decades ago, the legacy and remnants of conflicts continue to produce contrasting paradoxes. And aside from the human cost, the most visible ramifications of conflicts in Africa have been the challenges and dilemmas they have posed to international society by exposing the

---

[1] R. Jackson, 'Africa's Wars: Overview, Causes and the Challenges of Conflict Transformation' in O. Furley and R. May (eds.), *Ending Africa's Wars: Progressing to Peace* (Aldershot: Ashgate, 2006), p. 21.

inadequacy of international legal frameworks and mechanisms in confronting conflicts, especially those of an internal character.

The focus of this book, then, has been to gauge the relevance and applicability of international law in confronting postcolonial internal conflicts in Africa. It has examined the perceived limitations in the philosophy and structural configuration of international law in the context of peacebuilding, and considered whether this necessitates a conceptual recasting, one that may potentially be carried out through the window of opportunity offered by the integrated normative and institutional framework of the Constitutive Act of the African Union. It has been argued in three ways that international law fails in its application to postcolonial internal conflicts: first, in relation to the principles underpinning action vis-à-vis internal conflicts; second, in relation to international law's ambiguous position regarding the postcolonial condition; and third, by using case studies to gauge the capacity of the Constitutive Act's peace and security framework and its utility in ascribing alternative thinking to peacebuilding approaches in Africa.

Frames of the book's arguments

The principal claim of this book is that international law in its normative and institutional configuration is incapable of advancing innovative approaches to confronting internal conflicts in postcolonial Africa. A major reason for this is that despite the rhetorical claims and emancipatory dispositions of international law, it is still overwhelmingly entrapped in dialogues of historical contradictions and controversies. In so far as approaches to internal conflicts and peacebuilding are concerned, the nature of the contradictions has been manifested in a crisis of method and dispute about the contextual basis, legitimacy and relevance of international law. Integral to this is the nature and source of the development of international law and the particular ethos that has emerged from it over different historical timeframes. To mitigate this, it is proposed that the transformative peacebuilding approaches embedded in the Constitutive Act could enunciate forms of approaches that may enhance a more appropriate engagement with internal conflicts in Africa. In an attempt to consolidate this argument, an analytic framework that undergirds the book is outlined in Chapter 2. Its focus and purpose are twofold.

First, the analyses provide the framework upon which approaches to peacebuilding conceived through international law can be contextualised. This is done by offering a brief exploration of the development and purpose of international law and stemming from this the founding norms that animate the discipline's points of reference as well as the inadequacies that characterise its peacebuilding approaches. The context also offers a prism through which a postmodern critique of the identity and identification of international law can be understood. Second, the analytic framework offers an articulation – through Third World Approaches to International Law – which makes a case for a purposeful interrogation of international law with the view to provoking a re-imagination of approaches to conflicts so as to make them sensitive to the quest for postcolonial peace as well as reflective of the imperative for institutionalising endogenous structures into peacebuilding processes. The claim is not that alternative propositions be regarded as the absolute elixir that provides answers to all inadequacies besetting international law and its approaches to internal conflicts. Rather, the analytic framework opens up the door for the formulation of potential alternatives capable of engaging constituencies largely invisible to the past and current outlay of international law.

The reflection of Third World perspectives and contestation of the disempowering dimension of hegemonic international law has been mediated through TWAIL. There is relevance and symbolism in this, not least because the conventional international law influences on and approaches to conflicts have been so dominant that alternatives conceptualised with a Third World perspective have often been perceived as merely representing the *other*. And of course irrespective of the increasing outlets of toleration of international legal scholarship to Third World issues, writing about *otherness*, as Peter Mason asserts, is still pretty much writing *otherwise*.[2] That is to say, perspectives from the 'other' are largely considered as possible alternatives *only* when everything else fails, rather than as equal parallels to the dominant. With the analytic framework formulated, the subsequent task has been to determine the nature and limitations of international law in peacebuilding. How is international law applicable to internal conflicts? And to what extent are this tension and the faultlines in international law responsible for the recurrence of postcolonial internal conflicts?

In engaging these questions, the neo-liberal framework which constitutes a dominant part of international law's approach to conflicts is examined. Early incarnations of the neo-liberal approach generally hinged on statist

---

[2] P. Mason, *Deconstructing America: Representations of the Other* (London: Routledge, 1990), p. 4.

diplomacy as a mechanism and approach to conflicts. The thrust of the approach was anchored on, and fixated by, the idea of a negotiated settlement to conflicts through conciliation, mediation, resolution and compromise. Contemporary neo-liberal approaches, on the other hand, imply a modification of liberal values to advance normatively induced conflict resolution frameworks. The utility of this as an approach to conflict perhaps lies in the fact that it encompasses a kind of process that advocates for norms that could diffuse some of the underlying social causes of conflicts. Some of these norms entail enhancing human freedom by empowering individual rights and spaces of autonomy. It has, however, been illustrated that the efficacy of the neo-liberal approach has been hampered by both the Eurocentric persuasion of international law and the continued reliance on the state as the medium through which such an approach is organised. Eurocentrism generally refers to what Upendra Baxi calls 'settled habits of thoughts which have led to the acceptance, mostly uncritical, of European intellectual and socio-cultural traditions, as the invariable, if not superior, frameworks for enquiry'.[3] Eurocentricism has been a powerful concept, language of communication, political movement and jurisprudential methodology. What its elements tend to do is to impose limits on approaches to conflicts based on international law by subjecting them to a mindset that is alien to the social conditions and cultural settings of those to whom they are meant to engage.

The disproportionate reliance on the state, on the other hand, is fundamentally problematic. The state as an entity for organising social life derives part of its power and authority from the notion of sovereignty. Sovereignty provides the state with the instruments to exercise supremacy and competence within a given territorial space. The supremacy of the state is framed within a perspective of international law predicated on the assumption that the maintenance of domestic order is a function over which the state has an unrestricted *monopoly*. And thus its engagement with entities outside its jurisdiction is often determined by the goodwill and willingness of state actors. As a result, the extent to which approaches based on international law garner purchase is to a great degree dependent on the nature and strengths of possible incentives for the state apparatus. In postcolonial Africa, however, the state is an artificial creation, a progeny of colonial tinkering. It is neither strongly constituted nor sufficiently capable of appreciating the elements that undergird classical and neo-

---

[3] U. Baxi, 'Some Remarks on Eurocentrism and the Law of Nations' in R. P. Anand (ed.), *Asian States and the Development of International Law* (Delhi: Vikas Publications, 1972), p. 3.

liberal international law approaches. And to the extent that the postcolonial state is a major source of violence, it is hardly the primary reference point for conceptualising approaches to conflicts.

Thus an alternative proposition is imperative. This is so particularly in light of the recurrence and mutating nature of conflicts in Africa as shown in Chapter 3, which examines the causes and dynamics of internal conflicts, assessing in particular the reasons for their recurrence and continued resilience to approaches conceptualised through international law and its regulatory regimes. Given that the causes of conflicts are as varied as the theoretical strands that set out to engage them, a TWAIL perspective is sketched to articulate its distinctive way of thinking with the view to provoking recuperation of the narrative of internal conflicts. But the pervasiveness of conflicts, and the limitations that characterise neo-liberal approaches, cannot be entirely detached from the question regarding the extent of applicability of international law to internal conflicts. In other words, the limitations in the approaches have a strong correlation with the jurisdictional competence of international law. And so in Chapter 4, the capacity and relevance of international law approaches to internal conflicts are assessed. First, an overview of the evolution of international law responses to conflicts is undertaken to illustrate their particularities and limited utility. The objective was to reinforce the argument of the inadequacy of international law's treatment of internal conflicts and the extent to which it influenced perceptions.

The query in this regard is approached by examining the UN Charter and academic legal perspectives on the jurisdiction of international law in internal conflicts. The Charter is not, *expressis verbis*, helpful in this regard. For instance, its lack of clarity, arising from a balancing act of sovereignty and international legality, has given rise to a near consensus amongst legal scholars that international law's engagement with internal conflicts is limited by virtue of the state's traditional monopoly of domestic jurisdiction. This implies that the legal frames that provide the space for the conceptualisation of international law's approaches to conflicts are incoherent and incapable of appreciating, let alone confronting, postcolonial peace dilemmas. This is further accentuated by the fact that internal conflicts appear neither justified nor outlawed by international law. In the context of Africa, the inherited particularities of international law were transfused into the institutional culture of the OAU, whose attempts to confront internal conflicts remained largely unsuccessful. It is also argued that the principal factors attributable to the failures of the OAU relate to the very overlay of international legal order.

From this perspective, the shortcomings of the OAU's approaches to internal conflicts reflected the broader inadequacies of international law.

Indeed, the ultimate paralysis of the OAU exposed the false premises that undergird Africa's institutional and normative order. As regards international law, this represented a paradox in that for its structures and normative orientations to generate a sense of relevance to the African peace and conflict problematic, they would have to be reconfigured, at the very least. On its own, though, international law has largely struggled to do so partly because it constitutes, as TWAIL scholars assert, a fundamental part of Third World problems. This necessitated a compelling need for normative recasting, which culminated in the formulation of a new continental instrument and the launch of the African Union in July 2002. The journey to the launch was, however, far from smooth. Compromises were reached and setbacks were mediated. In Chapter 5, the genesis of the African Union is accounted for, a major part of which is attributed to a combination of external and internal factors. The end of the Cold War and the resurgence of Pan-African ideals provided the catalyst that inspired Thabo Mbeki, Olusegun Obasanjo and Muammar Ghaddaffi to spearhead the transition to the African Union. Pan-Africanism provided the historical context and the collective spirit that made it possible for the reorientation of Africa's institutional order. The capacity of Pan-Africanism to self-invent has triggered a paradigmatic shift towards an engagement process that generates values and their localisation. This is partly embodied in the Constitutive Act.

Emerging in the backdrop of an ineffectual OAU, the Constitutive Act and the ethos underpinning its institutional and normative framework have been viewed as constituting a significant development in the evolution of the continent's security architecture and the possible beginning of a narrative in Africa's norms formulation initiatives. This growing optimism is predicated on the perceived potential of the Constitutive Act to not only actualise the aspirations of the people of Africa, but also provide a window of opportunity in confronting internal conflicts. In Chapter 6, the focus shifts to the Constitutive Act and its attempts to depart from the crisis and burden of inheritance that constrained the OAU. It examines the distinction between the new dispensation and the old order, and the former's capabilities of advancing possible solutions to problems that afflicted its predecessor. In particular, key questions are engaged: in what ways could the Constitutive Act and its normative framework enunciate viable approaches to postcolonial internal conflicts beyond the patterns of current international law inadequacies? And could this constitute parameters of an African-induced reinvention of international law? The questions are approached by examining the philosophy that underpins this normative and institutional architecture, showing first the expanded ambits of the organisation's principles and objectives in comparison to the defunct OAU.

Three components of the Constitutive Act deemed central to peace-building in ways that the *status quo ante* could not be are particularly examined. Its Article 4 provision on the right of the African Union to intervene – with or without the consent of a member state, in circumstances of grave breaches as well as legitimate threat to public order – to restore peace and stability is a novelty in the continent's approaches to internal conflicts. Although this *Restorative* subset of Article 4 is an important provision, it does not, however, totalise the Constitutive Act's peace and security architecture as the emerging literature tends to suggest. Indeed, Article 4 is provisional to the extent that the broader objective of the African Union is to advance towards a continental social order that makes conflicts both unattractive and illogical. To achieve this, it is argued that the two other components of the Constitutive Act's normative architecture are as vitally important as they are integral to it. These are the norms formulation framework and the concept of social integration and interdependence. The framework engenders a set of values considered crucial in the advancement of individual and collective mutual interests. Comprising the *Corrective* subset, the framework involves strengthening platforms of social justice, deepening participation in governance structures and promoting avenues of redress through conscientious non-violent reflexes.

Social integration and interdependence, on the other hand, embody the *Preventive* subset and are motivated by an urge to grant agency to people and the social institutions they identify with so as to deepen integration. The aim is to consolidate shared heritage and commonalities sufficient to neutralise temptation to the recourse to conflicts. The approaches to conflicts and peacebuilding espoused in Article 4, the norms formulation and localisation framework, and the binary of integration and interdependence suggest a feature in the Constitutive Act to recharacterise some of international law's principles that shaped Africa's institutional order under the erstwhile OAU. The evolving normative shift implies that strict reverence to the doctrine of state sovereignty and territorial integrity that characterised and inhibited the functionality of the OAU no longer holds. In the image of the Constitutive Act, sovereignty is conditional, not total, and it must be exercised in a way that shows responsibility and value for human life and social justice. It draws from the wisdom that a political, social and economic integration of Africa would provide a framework that confronts the recurrence of armed conflicts.

As the Constitutive Act cannot operate in a vacuum, two case studies – Somalia and Burundi – are used to test the extent to which the framework's approaches to conflicts have been translated into practical relevance. The choice of Burundi as one of the case studies is based on the fact that it was the first country where the peacebuilding dimensions of the Constitutive Act were invoked, in 2003. This came in the wake of international failure in resolving Burundi's crises. To provide context, an attempt is made to offer a historical overview into the disintegration of precolonial social institutions and their subsequent replacement with first, German colonial rule, and later Belgian through the Mandate System. The narrative illustrates the defining impact of colonialism on Burundi and how the imbalances created through ethnic stratification conditioned the trajectory of the country's post-independence chaos and violence. The analyses periodise the country's history of conflicts, assessing the international responses and their shortfalls. It is argued that where international law engaged the fissures of postcolonial violence, the approaches often adopted have been limited and largely ineffectual.

International law failure and the subsequent resurgence of violence in Burundi coincided with the creation of the African Union. In 2003, AMIB was despatched to Burundi under the framework of the Constitutive Act's Article 4. The case study illustrates AMIB's contribution to the stabilisation efforts in Burundi. The mission created the environment for the advancement of the other equally relevant components of the Constitutive Act's peacebuilding framework, which included the promotion of social integration and interdependence through the reintegration of displaced persons. The integration components of the Arusha Peace Plan were also reflected in the constitution and legal instruments of Burundi. Further, AMIB played a major role in helping in the transformation of the agencies of violence across Burundi. From this perspective, the invocation of the Constitutive Act in Burundi provided patterns of hope and promise in the African Union's peace and security architecture. Of course, there were limitations and obstacles. But most of these were logistical in nature rather than normative flaws in the instruments of the Constitutive Act. But the challenges AMIB faced also show that implementing the transformative approaches embedded in the new order would require considerable cooperation and collective will from African states.

The second case study relates to Somalia. Its objective is to further interrogate the viability of the Constitutive Act's peacebuilding approaches. The Somali case study also considers the extent to which the philosophy underpinning the Constitutive Act constitutes a functional duality able to confront 'orthodox' types of internal conflicts as well as those that emerge from situations where there is virtual collapse of formal state institutions. The case study examines the historical evolution of the modern Somali state showing its colonial residues and how they have impacted on postcolonial crises. Also explored are the gradation and causes of conflicts and eventual state collapse. Like Burundi, international approaches to the Somali conflict have been based on successive neo-liberal international law approaches conceptualised through the frame of international law. And again like Burundi, these approaches failed, throwing Somalia into turmoil. For the most part too, the approaches adopted an overwhelming state-centric focus which turned out to provide no meaningful solutions.

In the wake of these failures and the slow pace of regional initiatives, the African Union invoked its Article 4 to establish AMISOM. The mission entered the Somali crisis almost two decades after failed UN missions. AMISOM's initial attempts at restoring a semblance of order in southern Somalia have been patchy. Although it has registered some intermittent advances, these have been in the main beset by challenges most of which are a culmination of the legacy of successive international failures. This legacy has constrained AMISOM's ability to chart its own path. Unlike Burundi where AMIB went in first, established its authority and then the kind of peace cultivation 'mindset' enunciated in the Constitutive Act, AMISOM's deployment followed the heel of a UN mission that essentially 'destroyed' most of the social structures needed for durable peace in Somalia. But the chaos that is Somalia has been largely confined to southern Somalia, where international engagement has been focused. In the breakaway northwestern region of Somaliland, conditions are very different. Somaliland appears to temper violence and offer insights into the mechanics of peacebuilding through indigenous social institutions. In many ways, Somaliland's success is attributed to its exploration of peacebuilding capabilities of local structures to restore order and embark on installing social institutions in the shadows of the collapse of the Somali Republic in 1991. Although Somaliland's success had little to do with the Constitutive Act, it bears relevance for three main reasons.

First, that the continued dysfunctional state of southern Somalia despite international engagement and the triumph of Somaliland under indigenous initiatives illustrate strongly that confronting internal conflicts in Africa requires an engagement with traditional social structures and institutions. The process involves creating spaces that can trigger transformative changes in the social and structural patterns of relationships in a given community or state. The significance of constructing the foundations for peace in these social structures cannot be overemphasised, for it is through them that conflicts often tend to manifest themselves. And it is also through them that individuals and communities often source their identities and security needs. Second, to realise the benefits of transformative approaches is not entirely dependent on the primacy or existence of the structures of the modern state. The state as an entity for the organisation of social life is merely one possible option. In this sense, the Somaliland experience demonstrates that the postcolonial African state is largely an 'organised expression' of the social aspirations and ways of life of people. This is partly driven by a community's shared values, commonality of interest and the desire to create conditions that have the potential of fostering a bond of mutual coexistence that embodies aspirations for peace and social justice. Third, Somaliland's integration of modern institutions with traditional social structures drifts away from the regimented Westphalian model to some kind of hybrid institution focusing on a people-centred interpretation of peace and security. This affirms an interpretation of internal conflicts and their aftermaths as attempts to 're-traditionalise' the 'non-emancipated' state. All these conjure, to some degree, the forms of peacebuilding approaches embedded in the integrated framework of the Constitutive Act.

The Constitutive Act as an alternative proposition

In a volume seeking to underscore the meaning, impact and relevance of international law to Africa, Jeremy Levitt notes that 'Africa is a legal marketplace, not a lawless basket case'.[4] Levitt's assertion is perhaps rooted on the premise that beneath the melancholy associated with Africa, there are outlets of normative formulation that often go unnoticed. The reason may also be that even where such frameworks are known to exist, their perpetual non-functionality occasioned by the disjoint between theory and practice consolidates a pessimistic telling.

---

[4] J. Levitt, 'Introduction – Africa: A Marker of International Law' in J. Levitt (ed.), *Africa: Mapping New Boundaries in International Law* (Oxford and Portland: Hart Publishing, 2010), p. 1.

In this book, the aim has been to examine the encounters between international law approaches to peacebuilding and the social conditions of postcolonial Africa, enquiring in the process as to the potential of the Constitutive Act in serving as an alternative outlet for the recasting of these approaches. The book's overall argument has been that approaches to conflicts conceptualised through the frame of international law are neither adequate nor capable of confronting the complex nature of internal conflicts in Africa. The historical determinants of international law ascribe it a kind of orientation that perceives internal conflicts from very narrow parameters. This is further aggravated by the fact that postcolonial conflicts have variously acquired a multitude of defining attributes that impose a disproportionate burden on the capacity of international institutions, and as a result, ostensibly defy conventional approaches of international law.

Glimmers of hope and promise

The challenges of internal conflicts in Africa have been defining in methods and outcome. Thus given their nature and probability of reoccurrence, confronting them requires the introduction of concepts and approaches that depart from the state-centric nature of current international law limitations. As Claude Bruderlein notes, the inadequacies of conventional peacebuilding approaches necessitate international society 'to detach itself from state-centred perceptions of security stakeholders, and move toward a more systemic role for communities, not only as bystanders and collateral victims of conflicts, but core actors of the conflicts'.[5] It is the inability of institutions and structures of the international order (and regional bodies such as the OAU) to do exactly that which culminated in the formulation of the Constitutive Act.

The novelty of the Constitutive Act lies in its integrated approach seeking to formulate constructive responses to internal conflicts in Africa. Its provisions make the African Union the first international organisation to have the *right* to intervene (with or without consent) in the internal affairs of member countries with the view to protecting vulnerable populations from serious threats to legitimate order, violence, war crimes, crimes against humanity and genocide. The incorporation of a strong norms-creation agenda and the emphasis on the binary of social

---

[5] C. Bruderlein, 'People Security as New Measure of Global Security'. Paper presented to the International Security Forum, Geneva, 15–17 November 2000.

integration and interdependence elevate the Constitutive Act's orientation of the peace problematic in an entirely new dimension. This transformation has potentially far-reaching implications.

From an international law perspective, it constitutes a departure from the tepid responses to, and reception of, conflicts and the modes of approaches to their transformation in Africa. And from an African standpoint, it ushers in a potentially new dawn in the functional dynamics of endogenous institutions 'driven by an Africa which cannot afford to wait until tomorrow to have its problems resolved'.[6] In this sense, the philosophy of the Constitutive Act symbolises a milestone in the political and social history of the continent. Such a symbolism implies that the African Union 'can be said not to be a child of an impetuous inspiration but the offspring of a gradual but dedicated progression of ideals and commitments'.[7] It is a project personifying hope and promise in the reconstitution of a proactive political, economic, institutional and legal order for Africa.

Although recognising the limitations of approaches to conflicts based on international law, the Constitutive Act does not disregard the latter's relevance to Africa. As Anthony Anghie reiterates,

> the Third World cannot abandon international law because law now plays such a vital role in the public realm in the interpretation of virtually all international events. It is through the vocabulary of international law, concepts of 'self-defence', 'human rights' and 'humanitarian intervention' that issues of cause, responsibility and fault are being discussed and analysed, and interpretations of these doctrines which reproduce imperial relations must be contested.[8]

The recasting in the Constitutive Act of some of the ethos of international law is mainly an attempt to make the latter reflective of the African postcolonial condition. The recent creation of the African Union Commission on International Law may well be a useful outlet through which the norms-creation dimensions of the African Union could be harnessed and codified. Of course, the philosophy of the Constitutive Act and the institutions it formulates will equally undergo transformation over time.

---

[6] AU Commission, *Strategic Plan of the African Union Commission, Volume 1: Vision and Mission of the African Union* (Addis Ababa: AU Commission, 2004), p. 3.

[7] *Ibid.*, p. 15.

[8] A. Anghie, *Imperialism, Sovereignty and the Making of International Law* (Cambridge University Press, 2005), p. 318.

Challenges and disjunctures

Despite the glimmers of hope and promise, the challenges faced by the African Union are numerous, complex and desperate. To tackle them would require considerable resilience and political will from member countries. The diversity of Africa and its intricate socio-political config-uration means that the African Union will continue to be confronted with challenges to overcome. It must, to invoke Olufemi Babarinde, eventually 'chart its own course, travel at its own pace, find its own rhythm, and write its own history'.[9] The fundamental issue is not so much an exercise in recounting the benefits but that of developing the political will amongst African states and their readiness to bear the costs that are required to produce and sustain an effective union.[10] Beyond its idealised depiction as a Pan-African ideology, it must 'take suffering seriously' and use as well as bolster its existing institutions and instruments in realising the peace and security ambitions of Africa. The Constitutive Act at least provides the principled basis for achieving these ambitions. But the nature of the challenges is such that an awful lot needs to be done if the promises of the Constitutive Act are to be actualised. A few are worthy of note.

The success of any institution requires the existence of faith in its work, progressive ambition in its focus, and the appropriate moral and financial support from the states that constitute it. The initial excitement embodied by the OAU during the first decade of its founding was driven by the faith invested in it by those who saw it as central to Africa's future. By the 1980s and 90s the attitudes towards the OAU were a far cry from what it used to be. The withdrawal of faith in the body contributed to its demise. The creation of the African Union was partly meant to recuper-ate the significance – both symbolic and actual – of a continental body and draw a line between the past and the future. So for the African Union to succeed it must be allowed to effectively utilise the authority and values of the Constitutive Act. Doing so, however, requires that member states provide the necessary support through their political will and readiness to share the burden of the organisation. Since the fanfare that surrounded its launch, the African Union has occasionally

---

[9] O. Babarinde, 'The EU as a Model for the African Union: The Limits of Imitation'. Paper presented at conference 'The European Union: Fifty Years after the Treaty of Rome', University of Miami, 26 March 2007, 1–12 at 4.

[10] *Ibid.*

struggled to exert its authority and visibility where the 'African voice' is most needed. Two examples stand out.

First, despite the AU creating AMISOM, the mission has been in a constant state of desperation where neither the resources nor sufficient troops have been forthcoming. This is not only a serious setback to the people of Somalia who have suffered greatly, but also betrays the promises of the Constitutive Act. Second, the neglect suffered by Somalia since 1991 has resulted in the creation of a situation that meanders between what Judith Shklar describes as the dilemma of misfortune and injustice.[10a] During the course of 2010–12, a devastating famine swept across Somalia resulting in the deaths of thousands of people with close to a million more displaced internally and like numbers crossing the border to Kenya. The principles espoused in the Constitutive Act would have triggered a massive operation to confront what is the world's most desperate humanitarian crisis. However, the response from the African Union has been both passive and disappointing. Whilst occasionally highlighting the need for international action, not much has come from member states. For the African Union to distance itself from the OAU, it must move away from some of the rhetoric and diplomatic niceties that animate it and endeavour to give effect to the Constitutive Act. Similar instances of dithering occurred during the so-called Arab spring, where as with the Somalia famine, proactive engagement came more from outside Africa than from within it. Thus beyond its idealised internalities as a product of Pan-African ideology, the African Union must 'take suffering seriously', and use as well as bolster its existing institutions and instruments and thereby be able to fulfil key strengths of the Constitutive Act.

The norms-creation dimension of the Constitutive Act is a major departure from the OAU. The creation of institutions like the Pan-African Parliament, PSC and the AUCIL are positive developments. The principles upon which the institutions are founded speak of the creation of a dynamic Africa that promotes rights articulation and constitutional governance, individual freedom and progress, the sanctity of human life, social justice, interdependence and development. The realisation of these objectives would require a synergy between theory and practice. However, the level of dithering and sometimes inaction that pervades the African Union has created a disjunction between the

---

[10a] J. Shklar, *The Faces of Injustice*, p. 2.

principles and objectives espoused in the Constitutive Act and the actual practice of both the African Union Commission and African leaders. In the case of rights violations in Zimbabwe, for instance, the African Union kept virtually mute. In regard to Côte d'Ivoire, the confusion and shifting positions from the Commission and member states meant that, in actual fact, there was no position. Had it not been for the dogged engagement of the Economic Community of West African States (ECOWAS), there would have been no principled position from an African organisation.

Of course, these silences are in stark contradiction to the proactive inclinations of the ethos of the Constitutive Act. What this shows, then, is that the future of the African Union will be dependent on its ability to seriously mediate the dynamism of its Constitutive Act with the practices of its Commission and member states. There is also a need to more effectively integrate the African Commission on Human and Peoples' Rights and the now slowly functioning African Court of Justice and Human Rights into the Constitutive Act's peacebuilding and security architecture. This is particularly important given that since the inauguration of the African Union in 2002, the organisation has remained largely disengaged from both the Commission and the Court, functioning in an almost stand-alone manner. This level of disconnect needs to be corrected if the rights dimensions of peacebuilding are to be effectively incorporated into the continent's peacebuilding framework.

Finally, the claim in this book has been that the approaches to conflict and peacebuilding embedded in the Constitutive Act offer a window of opportunity through which a more peaceful Africa could be envisioned. Whilst there is potential in the framework, it cannot function in a vacuum. Its utility would undoubtedly be dependent on the extent to which the African Union and its member states are prepared to give effect to the Constitutive Act. The mystery of peace which has eluded most of the history of postcolonial Africa must be unlocked. But as Richard Jackson puts it:

> In the final analysis, solutions to Africa's wars lie not in external intervention, but in internal transformation; the people and nations of Africa have to reconstruct their own realities. This is not to deny a role for external actors, nor is it an excuse to continue in studied indifference to Africa's plight or to evade the ethical responsibility to alleviate human suffering wherever it may occur; rather, it is a call for genuine partnership with Africa's local peacemakers.[11]

---

[11] Jackson, 'Africa's Wars' in Furley and May (eds.), *Ending Africa's Wars*, p. 26.

For Africa to be in a position to reconstruct its own realities and initiate social advancement, its encounters with international law approaches to peacebuilding need to be reassessed and a way forward charted out. The Constitutive Act provides the principled basis upon which this could be done. In this sense, it may embody what could be termed an African-induced recharacterisation of international law approaches to internal conflicts. This constitutes patterns of hope and promise.

GLOSSARY OF TERMS

akil	a title of an elder or venerable person
bashingantahe	traditional tribunals with judicial and peacebuilding functions
daraawiish	followers of Somali anti-colonial activist, Sayyed Mohammed Abdulle Hassan
ganwa	an aristocratic lineage
golaha guurtida	Upper House of Elders in Somaliland composed of clan representatives
guurti	a committee constituted for purposes of the resolution of conflict
heer	an obligation arising from an understanding or contract
mwami	king or monarch
Sayyed	title given to a religious leader
Sharia	laws and regulations derived from Islamic teachings
Sheikh	title given to an accomplished religious teacher
shir	an indigenous process of peace cultivation
ubuntu	an act or expression of humanity

BIBLIOGRAPHY

Abdulahi, A. M., 'Perspectives on the State Collapse in Somalia' in A. A. Osman and I. K. Souare (eds.), *Somalia at the Crossroads: Challenges and Perspectives on Reconstituting a Failed State* (London: Adonis and Abbey Publishers Ltd, 2007).

Abi-Saab, G., 'The Development of International Law by the United Nations' in F. Snyder and S. Sathirathai (eds.), *Third World Attitudes to International Law* (Dordrecht: Martinus Nijhoff, 1987).

Acharya, A., 'How Ideas Spread: Whose Norms Matter? Norms Localisation and Institutional Change in Asian Regionalism', *International Organisation*, 58 (2004), 239–75.

Adam, H., 'Somalia: A Terrible Beauty Being Born?' in I. W. Zartman (ed.), *Collapsed States: The Disintegration and Restoration of Legitimate Authority* (Boulder, Colo.: Lynne Rienner Publishers, 1995).

Adebajo, A. and Scanlon, H. (eds.), *A Dialogue of the Deaf: Essays on Africa and the United Nations* (Johannesburg: Fanele, 2006).

Adedeji, A., *Africa Within the World: Beyond Dispossession and Dependence* (London: Zed Books, 1993).

(ed.), *Comprehending and Mastering African Conflicts: The Search for Sustainable Peace and Good Governance* (London: Zed Books, 1999).

Adejo, A. M., 'From the OAU to AU: New Wine in Old Bottles?' Paper prepared for CODESRIA's 10th General Assembly on 'Africa in the New Millennium', Kampala, Uganda, 8–12 December 2002.

Adi, H. and Sherwood, M., *Pan-African History: Political Figures from Africa and the Diaspora Since 1787* (London: Routledge, 2003).

Adogamhe, P. G., 'Pan-Africanism Revisited: Vision and Reality of African Unity and Development', *African Review of Integration*, 2:2 (2008), 1–34.

Africa Leadership Forum, 'Origins of the Conference on Security, Stability, Development and Cooperation in Africa', www.africaleadership.org/CSSDCA.htm.

Africa Watch Committee, *Somalia: A Government at War with its Own People: Testimonies about the Killings and the Conflict in the North* (New York: Africa Watch Committee, 1990).

Agoagye, F., *The African Mission in Burundi: Lessons from the First African Union Peacekeeping Operation* (Stockholm: Swedish Defence Research Agency, 2008).

Ake, C., 'The Future of the State in Africa', *International Political Science Review*, 6:1 (1985), 105–14.

Akehurst, M., *A Modern Introduction to International Law*, 6th edn (London: Routledge, 1992).

Alao, A. and Olonisakin, F., 'Post Cold War Africa: Ethnicity, Ethnic Conflict and Security' in A. Oyebade and A. Alao (eds.), *Africa After the Cold War* (Asmara, Eritrea: Africa World Press, 1998).

Ali, T. M. and Mathews, R. O. (eds.), *Civil Wars in Africa: Roots and Resolutions* (Montreal: Queens University Press, 1999).

Alusala, N., 'Disarmament and the Transition in Burundi: How Soon?', *Institute for Security Studies*, Occasional Paper, 97 (2005), 1–16.

Amate, O. C., *Inside the OAU: Pan-Africanism in Practice* (New York: St Martin's Press, 1986).

Anand, R. P., 'Role of the "New" Asian-African Countries in the Present International Legal Order', *American Journal of International Law*, 56 (1962), 383–406.

International Law and the Developing Countries: Confrontation or Cooperation? (Dordrecht: Martinus Nijhoff Publishers, 1987).

Andemicael, B., *The OAU and the UN: Relations Between the Organisation of African Unity and the United Nations* (New York: Africana, 1976).

Angeloni, M., 'Somalia: The Tortuga of the 21st Century', *Transitional Studies Review*, 16 (2009), 755–67.

Anghie, A., 'Time Present and Time Past: Globalisation, International Financial Institutions, and the Third World', *New York University Journal of International Law and Policy*, 32 (2000), 243–90.

Imperialism, Sovereignty and the Making of International Law (Cambridge University Press, 2005).

Anghie, A. and Chimni, B. S., 'Third World Approaches to International Law and Individual Responsibility in Internal Conflicts', *Chinese Journal of International Law*, (2003), 78–103.

et al. (eds.), *The Third World and International Order: Law, Politics and Globalisation* (Leiden: Martinus Nijhoff, 2003).

Annan, K., 'Two Concepts of Sovereignty', *The Economist*, 18 September 1999.

We the Peoples: The Role of the United Nations in the 21st Century, The Secretary General's Millennium Report to the General Assembly of the United Nations, 3 April 2000.

'Ten Years After: A Farewell Statement to the UN General Assembly', 19 September 2006.

Appiah, K. A., *Cosmopolitanism: Ethics in a World of Strangers* (London: Penguin, 2006).

Arnold, G., *The End of the Third World* (New York: St Martin's Press, 1993).

Arthur, P., 'The Anglo-Irish Peace Process: Obstacles to Reconciliation' in R. Rothstein (ed.), *After the Peace: Resistance and Reconciliation* (London: Lynne Rienner Publishers, 1999).

Assefa, H., 'Crucible of Civilisation and Conflicts: Ethiopia' in P. Anyang' Nyong'o (ed.), *Arms and Daggers in the Heart of Africa* (Nairobi: African Academy of Sciences, 1993).

AU Commission, *Strategic Plan of the African Union Commission, Volume I: Vision and Mission of the African Union* (Addis Ababa: AU Commission, 2004).

Avari, B., *India: The Ancient Past* (London: Routledge, 2007).

Babarinde, O., 'The EU as a Model for the African Union: The Limits of Imitation'. Paper presented at 'The European Union: Fifty Years after the Treaty of Rome' conference, University of Miami, 26 March 2007.

Badie, B. and Birnbaum, P., *The Sociology of the State* (The University of Chicago Press, 1983).

Baimu, E., 'The African Union: Hope for Better Protection of Human Rights in Africa?', *African Human Rights Law Journal*, 1 (2001), 299–314.

Baimu, E. and Sturman, K., 'Amendment to the African Union's Right to Intervene: A Shift from Human Security to Regime Security', 12:2 (2003), *African Security Review*, 37–45.

Baruch Bush, R. A. and Folger, J., *The Promise of Mediation: The Transformative Approach to Conflict* (San Francisco: Jossey Bass, 2004).

Baxi, U. 'Some Remarks on Eurocentrism and the Law of Nations' in R. P. Anand (ed.), *Asian States and the Development of Universal International Law* (Delhi: Vikas Publications, 1972).

'Geographies of Injustice: Human Rights at the Altar of Convenience' in C. Scot (ed.), *Torture as Tort: Comparative Perspectives on the Development of Transnational Human Rights Litigation* (Oxford: Hart Publishing, 2001).

The Future of Human Rights (Delhi: Oxford University Press, 2006).

'What May the "Third World" Expect from International Law?' in R. Falk, B. Rajagopal and J. Stevens (eds.), *The Third World and International Law: Reshaping Justice* (Abingdon: Routledge-Cavendish, 2008).

'Epilogue: Whom May We Speak For, With, and After? Re-Silencing Human Rights' in G. Bhambra and R. Shilliam (eds.), *Silencing Human Rights: Critical Engagements with a Contested Project* (London: Palgrave Macmillan, 2009).

Bayart, J. F., *The State in Africa: The Politics of the Belly* (London: Longman Group, 1993).

et al., *The Criminalization of the State in Africa* (London: James Currey, 1999).

Baylis, R. J. and Smith, S., *The Globalisation of World Politics: An Introduction to International Relations* (New York: Oxford University Press, 1997).

Beck, U., *Cosmopolitan Vision* (Cambridge: Polity Press, 2006).

Bedjaoui, M., *Towards a New International Economic Order* (New York: United Nations Educational, Scientific and Cultural Organisation, 1979).

'General Introduction' in M. Bedjaoui (ed.), *International Law: Achievements and Prospects* (Boston: Martinus Nijhoff, 1991).

Bellamy, A. J. and Williams, P. D., 'Who's Keeping the Peace: Regionalisation and Contemporary Peace Operations', *International Security*, 29:4 (2005), 157–95.

Berger, M. T., 'After the Third World? History, Destiny and the Fate of Third Worldism', *Third World Quarterly*, 25:1 (2004), 9–39.

'The End of the "Third World"?', *Third World Quarterly*, 15:2 (1994), 257–75.

Berman, N., 'Privileging Combat? Contemporary Conflict and the Legal Construction of War', *Columbia Journal of Transnational Law*, 43 (2004), 1–72.

Bernard, M., *A Historical Account of the Neutrality of Great Britain during the American Civil War* (Massachusetts: Applewood Books, 1870).

Besson, S. and Tasioulas, J. (eds.), 'Introduction', *The Philosophy of International Law* (Oxford University Press, 2010).

Bienen, H., 'The State and Ethnicity: Integrative Formulas in Africa' in D. Rothchild and V. A. Olorunsola (eds.), *State Versus Ethnic Claims: African Policy Dilemmas* (Boulder, Colo.: Westview Press, 1983).

Boege, V., 'Traditional Approaches to Conflict Transformation – Potentials and Limits', Berghof Research Center for Constructive Conflict Management (2006), www.berghof-handbook.net/documents/publications/boege_handbook.pdf.

Boone, C., *Merchant Capital and the Roots of State Power in Senegal 1930–1985* (Cambridge University Press, 1992).

Booth, C., 'Prospects and Issues for the International Criminal Court: Lessons from Yugoslavia and Rwanda' in P. Sands (ed.), *From Nuremberg to the Hague: The Future of International Criminal Justice* (Cambridge University Press, 2003).

Borchard, E., 'The Multilateral Treaty for the Renunciation of War', *American Journal of International Law*, 23 (1929), 116–20.

Boutros-Ghali, B., *Agenda for Peace, Preventive Diplomacy, Peace Making and Peace Keeping* (New York: United Nations, 1992).

Boyd, J. B., 'African Boundary Conflict: An Empirical Study', *African Studies Review*, 22:3 (1979), 1–14.

Boyle, J., 'Natural Law and International Ethics' in T. Nadine and D. Mapel (eds.), *Traditions of International Ethics* (Cambridge University Press, 1992).

Bradbury, M., *Somaliland CIIR Country Report* (London: Catholic Institute for International Relations, 1997).

Brons, M. H., *Society, Security, Sovereignty and the State in Somalia: From Statelessness to Statelessness?* (Utrecht: International Books, 2001).

Brown, S., *The Causes and Prevention of War*, 2nd edn (Basingstoke: Macmillan Press, 1994).

Brownlie, I., *Principles of Public International Law*, 7th edn (Oxford University Press, 2008).

Bryden, M., 'New Hope for Somalia? The Building Block Approach', *Review of African Political Economy*, 26:79 (1999), 134–40.

Buchanan, A., 'The Legitimacy of International Law' in S. Besson and J. Tasioulas (eds.), *The Philosophy of International Law* (Oxford University Press, 2010).

Bugnion, F., '*Jus ad Bellum, Jus in Bello* and Non-International Armed Conflicts', *Yearbook of International Humanitarian Law*, 6 (2003), 168–98.

'The International Committee of the Red Cross and the Development of International Humanitarian Law', *Chicago Journal of International Law*, 5 (2004), 191–215.

Bull, H., Kingsbury, B. and Roberts, A. (eds.), *Hugo Grotius and International Relations* (Oxford: Clarendon Press, 1990).

Burgess, M. E., 'The Resurgence of Ethnicity: Myth or Reality?', *Ethnic and Racial Studies*, 1 (1978), 265–85.

Burgess, S. F., 'African Security in the Twenty-first Century: The Challenges of Indigenisation and Multilateralism', *African Studies Review*, 41:2 (1998), 37–61.

Burrows, E., *Flower in My Ear: Arts and Ethos on Ifaluk Atoll* (Seattle: University of Washington Press, 1963).

Burundi Peace Negotiations, Report of the First Session of the Burundi Peace Negotiations, Arusha, Tanzania, 15–21 June 1998.

Busia, K. A., *Africa in Search of Democracy* (New York: Frederick A. Praeger, 1967).

Camilleri, J. and Falk, J., *The End of Sovereignty? The Politics of a Shrinking and Fragmenting World* (Aldershot: Edward Elgar, 1992).

Campbell, H. G., 'Walter Rodney and Pan-Africanism Today'. Paper presented at the Africana Studies Research Centre, Cornell University, Ithaca, New York. Africa Colloquium Series, 28 September 2005.

Camus, A., *The Rebel* (London: Penguin Books Ltd, 1978).

Carey, H. F., 'The Postcolonial State and the Protection of Human Rights', *Comparative Studies of South Asia, Africa and the Middle East*, 22:1 (2002), 59–75.

Carnegie Commission, *Carnegie Commission on Preventing Deadly Conflict* (Carnegie Corporation of New York, 1997).

Carty, A., *The Decay of International Law: A Reappraisal of the Limits of Legal Imagination in International Affairs* (Manchester University Press, 1986).

'The Implosion of the Legal Subject and the Unravelling of the Law on the Use of Force: American Identity and New American Doctrines of Collective Security' in H. Kochler (ed.), *The Use of Force in International Relations: Challenges to Collective Security* (Vienna: International Progress Organization, 2006).

Cassese, A., '*Ex iniuria ius oritur*: Are We Moving towards International Legitimation of Forcible Humanitarian Countermeasures in the World Community?', *European Journal of International Law*, 10 (1999), 23–30.

International Law, 2nd edn (Oxford University Press, 2005).

Chabal, P. and Daloz, J. P., *Africa Works: Disorder as Political Instrument* (Oxford: James Currey, 1999).

Chakrabarty, D., 'Postcoloniality and the Artifice of History: Who Speaks for "Indian" Pasts?' in B. Aschcroft, G. Griffiths and H. Tiffin (eds.), *The Postcolonial Studies Reader* (London: Routledge, 1992).

Chege, M., 'Conflict in the Horn of Africa' in E. Hansen (ed.), *Africa: Perspectives on Peace and Development* (London: Zed Books, 1987).

Chimni, B. S., *International Law and World Order: A Critique of Contemporary Approaches* (Delhi: SAGE Publications Ltd, 1993).

'Third World Approaches to International Law: A Manifesto', *International Community Law Review*, 8 (2006), 3–27.

'The Past, Present and Future of International Law: A Critical Third World Approach', *Melbourne Journal of International Law*, 8 (2007), 1–17.

Chinkin, C. and Sadurska, R., 'The Anatomy of International Dispute Resolution', *Ohio State Journal of Dispute Resolution*, 7 (1991), 39–81.

Chipman, J., 'Managing the Politics of Parochialism' in M. E. Brown (ed.), *Ethnic Conflict and International Security* (Princeton University Press, 1993).

Chopra, J. and Weiss, T., 'Sovereignty is No Longer Sacrosanct: Codifying Humanitarian Intervention', *Ethics and International Affairs*, 6 (1992), 95–117.

Christie, P., Lessem, R. and Mbigi, L., *African Management Philosophies, Concepts and Applications* (Randburg: Knowledge Resources Ltd, 1993).

Cilliers, J. and Sturman, K., 'The Right of Intervention: Enforcement Challenges for the African Union', *African Security Review*, 11:3 (2002), 1–5.

'Challenges Facing the AU's Peace and Security Council', *African Security Review*, 13:1(2004), 97–104.

Clapham, C., 'The Horn of Africa: A Conflict Zone' in O. Furley (ed.), *Conflict in Africa* (London: Tauris Academic Studies, 1995).

'Rethinking African States', *African Security Review*, 10:3 (2001), 1–12.

(ed.), *African Guerrillas* (London: James Currey, 1998).

Clark, W. and Herbst, J., *Somalia and the Future of Humanitarian Intervention, Centre of International Studies* (Princeton University Press, 1995).

Clarke, W. S., 'Testing the World's Resolve in Somalia', *Parameters*, 23 (1993–94), 42–58.

Collier, P., *The Bottom Billion: Why the Poorest Countries are Failing and What can be Done About It* (Oxford University Press, 2008).

Colson, E., 'Competence and Incompetence in the Context of Independence', *Current Anthropology*, 8 (1967), 92–111.

Comaroff, J. L. and Comaroff, J., 'Introduction' in J. L. Comaroff and J. Comaroff (eds.), *Civil Society and the Political Imagination in Africa: Critical Perspectives* (Chicago University Press, 1999).

Commey, P., 'African Union – What Next?', *New African*, 1:410 (12–17 September 2002).

Contini, P., *The Somali Republic – An Experiment in Legal Integration* (London: Routledge, 1969).

Cooley, J. W., 'A Classical Approach to Mediation Part II: The Socratic Method and Conflict Reframing in Mediation', *University of Dayton Law Review*, 19:2 (1993–94), 589–632.

Cox, R., *Pan-Africanism in Practice: An Eastern African Study 1958–1964* (Oxford University Press, 1964).

Cryer, R. and White, D. N., 'Unilateral Enforcement of Resolution 687: A Threat Too Far?', *California Western International Law Journal*, 29 (1998–99), 243–82.

Daley, P., *Gender and Genocide in Burundi: The Search for Spaces of Peace in the Great Lakes Region* (Oxford: James Currey, 2007).

D'Amato, A., *International Law: Process and Prospect* (New York: Transnational Publishers, 1987).

'The Invasion of Panama was a Lawful Response to Tyranny', *AJIL*, 84 (1990), 516–24.

Danso, K., 'The African Economic Community: Problems and Prospects', *Africa Today*, 42:4 (1995), 31–5.

Davidson, B., *Modern Africa: A Social and Political History* (London: Longman, 1989).
The Black Man's Burden: Africa and the Curse of the Nation-State (New York: Times Books, 1992).

De-Coning, C., 'Towards a Common Southern African Peacekeeping System', *CIPS Electronic Briefing Paper*, 16 (2004).

Delsol, C., *Unjust Justice: Against the Tyranny of International Law* (Wilmington: ISI Books, 2004).

Deng, F. M. and Zartman, I. W. (eds.), *Conflict Resolution in Africa* (Washington, DC: Brookings Institution, 1991).
A Strategic Vision for Africa: The Kampala Movement (Washington, DC: The Brookings Institution Press, 2002).

Denham, M. E. and Lombardi, M. O., *Perspectives on Third World Sovereignty: The Postmodern Paradox* (Basingstoke: Macmillan, 1996).

DeVos, G. and Romanucci-Ross, L. (eds.), *Ethnic Identity: Cultural Continuities and Change* (University of Chicago Press, 1982).

Dillon, E. J., *The Inside Story of the Peace Conference* (New York: Harper and Brothers, 1920).

Dinstein, Y., *War, Aggression and Self-Defence* (Cambridge University Press, 2005).

Du Bois, W. E. B., *The World and Africa* (New York: International Publishers, 1979).

Duffield, M., *Global Governance and the New Wars* (London: Zed Books, 2001).

Dugard, J., 'The Organisation of African Unity and Colonialism: An Enquiry into the Plea of Self-Defence as a Justification for the Use of Force in the Eradication of Colonialism', *International Comparative Law Quarterly*, 16 (1967), 157–90.

Dworkin, R., *Sovereign Virtue: The Theory and Practice of Equality* (Cambridge, Mass: Harvard University Press, 2002).

El-Ayouty, Y. and Zartman, I. W. (eds.), *The OAU After Twenty Years* (New York: Praeger, 1984).

Elias, T. O., *The Nature of African Customary Laws* (Manchester University Press, 1956).

Government and Politics in Africa (London: Asia Publication House, 1961).

Africa and the Development of International Law (Leiden: A. W. Sijthoff; Kluwer Academic Publishers, 1972).

Eller, J. D., *From Culture to Ethnicity to Conflict: An Anthropological Perspective on International Ethnic Conflict* (Ann Arbor: University of Michigan Press, 2002).

Emerson, R., 'Pan-Africanism', *International Organisation*, 16:2 (1962), 275–90.

Escobar, A., 'Beyond the Third World: Imperial Globality, Global Coloniality and Anti-globalisation Social Movements', *Third World Quarterly*, 25:1 (2004), 207–30.

Esedebe, P. O., *Pan-Africanism: The Idea and the Movement 1776–1963* (Washington, DC: Howard University Press, 1982).

Esman, M. J. and Telhami, S. (eds.), *International Organisations and Ethnic Conflict* (Ithaca: Cornell University Press, 1995).

Evans, G., 'South Africa's Foreign Policy After Mandela: Mbeki and his Concept of an African Renaissance', *The Round Table*, 352 (1999), 621–8.

'The Responsibility to Protect: Revisiting Humanitarian Intervention', *Foreign Affairs*, Nov./Dec., 81 (2002), 100.

Evans, M. D. (ed.), *International Law* (Oxford University Press, 2003).

(ed.), *International Law* (Oxford University Press, 2006).

Falk, R., 'Janus Tormented: The International Law of Internal War' in J. N. Rosenau (ed.), *International Aspects of Civil Strife* (Princeton University Press, 1964).

'New Approaches to the Study of International Law', *The American Journal of International Law*, 61:2 (1967), 477–95.

'A New Paradigm for International Legal Studies: Prospects and Proposals', *Yale Law Journal*, 84 (1974–75), 969–1021.

Falk, R., Rajagopal, B. and Stevens, J. (eds.), *International Law and the Third World: Reshaping Justice* (London: Routledge-Cavendish, 2008).

Farah, Y. A., *Somalia: The Roots of Reconciliation – Peace-making Endeavours of Contemporary Lineage Leaders: A Survey of Grassroots Peace Conferences in Somaliland* (London: Action Aid, 1993).

Farer, T., 'The Laws of War 25 Years After Nuremberg', *International Conciliation*, 583 (1971), 41–3.

'An Inquiry into the Legitimacy of Humanitarian Intervention' in L. Damrosch and D. Scheffer (eds.), *Law and Force in the New International Order* (Boulder, Colo.: Westview Press, (1991).

FAST Update, *Burundi: Semi-annual Risk Assessment, November 2005 to May 2006* (Berne: Swisspeace, 2006).

Fawcett, L. and Sayigh, Y., *The Third World Beyond the Cold War* (Oxford University Press, 1999).

Fidler, P. D., 'Revolt Against or From Within the West? TWAIL, the Developing World, and the Future Direction of International Law', *Chinese Journal of International Law*, (2003), 29–76.

Fitzpatrick, P., 'The Triumph of a Departed World: Law, Modernity and the Sacred'. Paper presented at the Warwick University Law Seminar Series, 2005.

Foltz, W., 'The Organisation of African Unity and Resolution of Africa's Conflicts' in F. M. Deng and I. W. Zartman (eds.), *Conflict Resolution in Africa* (Washington, DC: Brookings Institute, 1991).

Forde, S., 'Hugo Grotius on Ethics and War', *American Political Science Review*, 92:3 (1998), 639–48.

Fortes, M. and Evans-Pritchard, E. E. (eds.), *African Political Systems* (Oxford University Press, 1962).

Foundation for Inter-Ethnic Relations, *The Role of the High Commissioner on National Minorities in OSCE Conflict Prevention: An Introduction* (The Hague: The Foundation for Inter-Ethnic Relations, 1997).

Francis, D., *Uniting Africa – Building Regional Peace and Security Systems* (Aldershot: Ashgate Publishing, 2006).

Franck, T. M., 'Who Killed Article 2(4)? Or Changing Norms Governing the Use of-Force by States', *American Journal of International Law*, 64 (1970), 809–37.

  Recourse to Force: State Action Against Threats and Armed Attacks: The Hersch Lauterpacht Memorial Lectures (Cambridge University Press, 2002).

Franke, B., 'A Pan-African Army: The Evolution of an Idea and its Eventual Realisation in the African Standby Force', *Africa Security Review*, 15:4 (2006), 1–16.

Frey-Wouters, E., 'The Relevance of Regional Arrangements to Internal Conflicts in the Developing World' in J. N. Moore (ed.), *Law and Civil War in the Modern World* (Baltimore: Johns Hopkins University Press, 1974).

Friedmann, W., 'The Position of Underdeveloped Countries and the Universality of International Law', *Columbia Society of International Law Bulletin*, 2 (1963), 5–12.

Friedrich, J. C. (ed.), *The Philosophy of Kant* (New York: Modern Library, 1949).

Fry, D., *Beyond War: The Human Potential For Peace* (Oxford University Press, 2007).

Fukuyama, F., 'The End of History', *The National Interest* (Summer 1989), 1–12.

  The End of History and the Last Man (Michigan: Free Press, 1992).

Furley, O., 'Child Soldiers in Africa' in O. Furley (ed.), *Conflict in Africa* (London: Tauris Academic Studies, 1995).

  (ed.), *Conflict in Africa* (London: Tauris Academic Studies, 1995).

Furley, O. and May, R., 'Introduction' in O. Furley and R. May (eds.), *Ending Africa's Wars: Progressing to Peace* (Aldershot: Ashgate, 2006).

  (eds.), *Ending Africa's Wars: Progressing to Peace* (Aldershot: Ashgate Publishing Ltd, 2006).

Gahama, J., *Conflict Prevention, Management and Resolution in Burundi* (2002), at http://unpan1.un.org/intradoc/groups/public/documents/CAFRAD/UNPAN009002.pdf.

et al., 'Burundi' in A. Adedeji (ed.), *Comprehending and Mastering African Conflicts: The Search for Sustainable Peace and Good Governance* (London: Zed Books, 1999).

Gallie, W. B., *Philosophers of Peace and War* (Cambridge University Press, 1978).

Garner, W. J., *International Law and the World War* (London: Longman, 1920).

Gathii, J. T., 'Alternative and Critical: The Contribution of Research and Scholarship on Developing Countries to International Legal Theory', *Harvard Journal of International Law*, 41 (2000), 263–76.

'Rejoinder: Twailing International Law', *Michigan Law Review*, 98:6 (2000), 2066–71.

'A Critical Appraisal of the International Legal Tradition of Taslim Olawale Elias', *Leiden Journal of International Law*, 21 (2008), 317–49.

Gene, L. and Mastanduno, M., *Beyond Westphalia? State Sovereignty and International Intervention* (Baltimore: Johns Hopkins University Press, 1995).

Giddens, A., *The Consequences of Modernity* (Palo Alto, Calif: Stanford University Press, 1990).

Gilpin, R., *The Political Economy of International Relations* (Princeton University Press, 1987).

Goodrich, P., 'On the Relational Aesthetics of International Law', *Journal of the History of International Law*, 10 (2008), 321–41.

Gordon, A. A. and Gordon, D. L. (eds.), *Understanding Contemporary Africa* (London: Lynne Rienner Publishers, 2001).

Gordon, D. L., 'African Politics' in A. A. Gordon and D. L. Gordon (eds.), *Understanding Contemporary Africa* (London: Lynne Rienner Publishers, 2001).

Gourevitch, P., *We Wish to Inform You that Tomorrow We will be Killed with Our Families: Stories from Rwanda* (New York: Picador, 1999).

Grovogui, S. N., *Sovereignty, Quasi Sovereignty and Africans* (Minneapolis: University of Minnesota Press, 1996).

Guehennoe, J. M., *The End of the Nation-state* (Minnesota: University of Minnesota Press, 1995).

Gurdon, C. (ed.), *The Horn of Africa* (University College London Press, 1994).

Hale, J., 'War and Opinion: War and Public Opinion in the Fifteenth and Sixteenth Centuries', *Past and Present*, 22 (1962), 18–35.

Hansen, E. (ed.), *African Perspective on Peace and Development* (London: Zed Books, 1987).

Hardt, M. and Negri, A., *Empire* (Cambridge, Mass: Harvard University Press, 2000).

Hashim, A. B., *The Fallen State: Dissonance, Dictatorship and Death in Somalia* (Lanham: University Press of America, 1997).

Hegel, G. W. E., *The Philosophy of History* (New York: Dover, 1956).

Heinbecker, P., 'The Way Forward' in P. Heinbecker and P. Goff (eds.), *Irrelevant or Indispensable? The United Nations in the 21st Century* (Waterloo, Ont: CIGI Publications, 2005).

Held, D., *Democracy and Global Order: From the Modern State to Cosmopolitan Governance* (Cambridge: Polity Press, 1995).

Henze, P. B., *The Horn of Africa: From War to Peace* (London: Macmillan, 1991).

Herbst, J., 'War and the State in Africa', *International Security*, 14: 4 (1990), 117–39. 'Responding to State Failure in Africa', *International Society*, 21:3 (1996–97), 120–44.

Herisse, R. P., 'Development on a Theatre: Democracy, Governance and the Socio-political Conflict in Burundi', *Agriculture and Human Values*, 18:3 (2001), 295–304.

Hershey, A. S., 'The History of International Relations and during Antiquity and the Middle Ages', *American Journal of International Law*, 5 (1911), 901–33.

Hilpod, P., 'Humanitarian Intervention: Is there a Need for a Legal Reappraisal?', *European Journal of International Law*, 2 (2001), 437–68.

Hoffman, S., *Chaos and Violence – What Globalisation, Failed States, and Terrorism Mean for US Foreign Policy* (Lanham: Rowman & Littlefield, 2006).

Holland, T. E., *Elements of Jurisprudence* (Oxford University Press, 1880).

Horowitz, D. L., *Ethnic Groups in Conflict* (Berkeley: University of California Press, 1985).

Hoskyns, C., *The Organisation of African Unity and Eastern Africa* (Dar es Salaam: Mimeo, 1966).

Howard, M., Andreopoulos, G. J. and Shulman, M. R. (eds.), *The Law of War: Constraints on Warfare in the Western World* (New Haven: Yale University Press, 1994).

Huliaras, A., 'Qadhafi's Comeback: Libya and Sub-Saharan Africa in the 1990s', *African Affairs*, 100:398 (2001), 5–25.

Human Rights Watch, *So Much to Fear: War Crimes and the Devastation of Somalia* (New York: HRW, 2009).

Hurrell, I. A. and Woods, N., 'Globalization and Inequality', *Millennium*, 25:3 (1995), 447–70.

Hutchful, E., 'The Fall and Rise of the State in Ghana' in A. I. Samatar and A. Samatar (eds.), *The African State: Reconsiderations* (Portsmouth: Heinemann, 2002). 'From Military Security to Human Security' in J. Akokpari, A. Ndinga-Muvumba and T. Murithi (eds.), *The African Union and its Institutions* (Johannesburg: Fanele, 2008).

Huxtable, P., 'The African State Toward the Twenty-first Century: Legacies of the Critical Juncture' in L. Villalon and P. Huxtable (eds.), *The African State at a Critical Juncture – Between Disintegration and Reconfiguration* (Boulder, Colo.: Lynne Rienner Publishers, 1998).

ICISS, *Responsibility to Protect: Report of the International Commission on Intervention and State Sovereignty* (Ottawa: International Development Research Centre, 2001).

ICRC, *Draft Rules for the Limitations of the Dangers Incurred by the Civilian Population in Time of War* (Geneva: ICRC, 1958).

International Crisis Group, *Congo at War: A Briefing of the Internal and External Players in the Central African Conflict.* Africa Report No. 2, 17 November 1998.

'Somaliland: Democratisation and its Discontents', *ICG Africa Report*, 66 (2003), 1–34.

'Can the Somali Crisis be Contained?', *Africa Report*, 116 (2006), 1–31.

Issa-Salwe, A., *The Collapse of the Somali State: The Impact of the Colonial Legacy* (London: Haan, 1996).

Jackson, R. H. and Rosenberg, C. G., 'Why Africa's Weak States Persist: The Empirical and the Juridical in Statehood', *World Politics*, 35:1 (1982), 1–24.

Personal Rule in Black Africa: Prince, Autocrat, Prophet, Tyrant (Berkeley: University of California Press, 1982).

'Sovereignty and Underdevelopment: Juridical Statehood in the African Crisis', *The Journal of Modern African Studies*, 24:1 (1986), 1–31.

Jenkins, K. and Plowden, W., *Governance and Nationbuilding: The Failure of International Intervention* (Cheltenham: Edward Elgar, 2006).

Jenks, C. W., *The Common Law of Mankind* (London: Stevens Publishers, 1958).

Jeong, H. W., *Understanding Conflict and Conflict Analysis* (London: SAGE Ltd, 2008).

Jimale, A. A. (ed.), *The Invention of Somalia* (Lawrenceville: Red Sea Press, 1995).

Johnson J. T., *Just War Tradition and the Restraint of Warfare: A Moral and Historical Inquiry* (Princeton University Press, 1981).

'Historical Tradition and Moral Judgment: The Case of Just War Tradition', *The Journal of Religion*, (1984), 299–317.

Joseph, R., *State, Conflict and Democracy in Africa* (Boulder, Colo.: Lynne Rienner, 1999).

Kant, I., *To Perpetual Peace: A Philosophical Sketch*, trans. Ted Humphrey (Indianapolis: Hackett Publishing Company, 2003).

Kay, R., *Burundi Since the Genocide* (London: Minority Rights Group, 1995).

Kearney, R. D. and Dalton, R. E., 'The Treaty on Treaties', *AJIL*, 64 (1970), 495–561.

Keen, D., 'War and Peace: What's the Difference?' in A. Adebajo and C. L. Sriram (eds.), *Managing Armed Conflicts in the 21st Century* (London: Frank Cass, 2001).

Kelsen, H., *The Law of the United Nations: A Critical Analysis of its Fundamental Problems* (New York: Frederick A. Praeger, 1964).

Kennedy, D., *Of War and Law* (Princeton University Press, 2006).

Keohane, R. O., 'Governance in a Partially Globalized World', *American Political Science Review*, 95:1 (2001), 1–13.

Kibble, S., 'Somaliland: Surviving Without Recognition; Somalia: Recognised but Failing?', *International Relations*, 15:5 (2001), 5–25.

Kindiki, K., 'The Normative and Institutional Framework of the African Union relating to the Protection of Human Rights and the Maintenance of International Peace and Security: A Critical Appraisal', *African Human Rights Law Journal*, 3:1 (2003), 97–123.

Kingsbury, B. and Roberts, A., 'Grotian Thoughts in International Relations' in H. Bull, B. Kingsbury and A. Roberts (eds.), *Hugo Grotius and International Relations* (Oxford: Clarendon Press, 1990).

Kioko, B., 'The Right of Intervention under the African Union's Constitutive Act: From Non-interference to Non-intervention', *International Review of the Red Cross*, 85:852 (2003), 807–25.

Kleingeld, P., 'Kant's Theory of Peace' in P. Guyer (ed.), *The Cambridge Companion to Kant and Modern Philosophy* (Cambridge University Press, 2006).

Knight, W., *The Life and Works of Hugo Grotius* (London: Grotius Society Publications, 1925).

Koskenniemi, M., *From Apology to Utopia: The Structure of International Legal Argument* (Helsinki: Finnish Lawyers Publishing Company, 1989).

'The History of International Law Today', *Rechtsgeschichte*, (2004), 1–9.

'What is International Law For?' in M. D. Evans (ed.), *International Law* (Oxford University Press, 2006).

Kriesberg, L., 'The Evolution of Conflict Resolution' in J. Bercovitch, V. Kreneyuk, and I. W. Zartman (eds.), *The Sage Handbook of Conflict Resolution* (London: SAGE Publications, 2009).

Krueger, R. and Krueger, K., *From Bloodshed to Hope in Burundi: Our Embassy Years during Genocide* (Austin: University of Texas Press, 2007).

Kunz, J., *The Changing Law of Nations: Essays on International Law* (Columbus: The Ohio State University Press, 1968).

LaCroix, W. L., *War and International Ethics – Tradition and Today* (New York: University Press of America, 1988).

Laitin, D., *Politics, Language and Thought: The Somali Experience* (University of Chicago Press, 1977).

Laitin, D. and Samatar, S. S., *Somalia: Nation in Search of a State* (Boulder, Colo.: Westview Press, 1987).

Lake, D. and Rothchild, D. (eds.), *The International Spread of Ethnic Conflict: Fear, Diffusion and Escalation* (Princeton University Press, 1998).

Langley, J. A., *Pan-Africanism and Nationalism in West Africa 1900–1945* (Oxford: Clarendon Press, 1973).

Lansberg, C., 'Promoting Democracy: The Mandela-Mbeki Doctrine', *Journal of Democracy*, 11:3 (2000), 107–21.

Lauterpacht, H., *Recognition in International Law* (Cambridge University Press, 1947).

Lawrence, T. J., *The Principles of International Law* (London: Macmillan, 1923).

Lederach, J. P., *Building Peace – Sustainable Reconciliation in Divided Societies* (Washington, DC: United States Institute of Peace Press, 1997).

The Little Book of Conflict Transformation (Philadelphia: Good Books, 2003).

Leeson, P. T., 'Better Off Stateless: Somalia Before and After Government Collapse', *Journal of Comparative Economics*, 35:4 (2007), 689–710.

Lefebvre, J., 'Post-Cold War Clouds on the Horn of Africa: The Eritrea-Sudan Crisis', *Middle East Policy*, 4:1 (1995), 34–50.

Legum, C., *Pan-Africanism: A Short Political Guide* (London: Pall Mall Press, 1961).

Lemarchand, R., *Rwanda and Burundi* (London: Pall Mall Press, 1970).

'The State and Society in Africa: Ethnic Stratification and Restratification in Historical and Comparative Perspective' in D. Rothchild and V. A. Olorunsola (eds.), *State Versus Ethnic Claims: African Policy Dilemmas* (Boulder, Colo.: Westview Press, 1983).

'The State, the Parallel Economy, and the Changing Structure of Patronage Systems' in D. Rothchild and N. Chazan (eds.), *The Precarious Balance: State and Society in Africa* (Boulder, Colo.: Westview Press, 1988).

'Burundi: The Killing Fields Revisited', *A Journal of Opinion*, 18:1 (1989), 22–8.

Burundi: Ethnic Conflict and Genocide (Cambridge University Press, 1994).

Burundi: Ethnocide as Theory and Practice (Cambridge University Press, 1994).

'Genocide in the Great Lakes: Which Genocide? Whose Genocide?', *African Studies Review*, 41:1 (1998), 3–16.

Levitt, J., 'Introduction – Africa: A Marker of International Law' in J. Levitt (ed.), *Africa: Mapping New Boundaries in International Law* (Oxford and Portland: Hart Publishing, 2010).

Lewis, I. M., *A Pastoral Democracy* (Oxford University Press, 1961).

'Misunderstanding the Somali Crisis', *Anthropology Today*, 9:4 (1993), 1–3.

Blood and Bone: The Call of Kinship in Somali Society (Lawrenceville: Red Sea Press, 1994).

'New UN Adventures in Somalia', *Horn of Africa Bulletin*, 3 (2000)).

A Modern History of the Somali, 4th edn (Columbus: The Ohio University Press, 2002).

Lillich, R., 'Forcible Self-help by States to Protect Human Rights', *Iowa Law Review*, 53 (1967), 325–51.

Lim, C. L., 'Neither Sheep nor Peacocks: T. O. Elias and Post-colonial International Law', *Leiden Journal of International Law*, 21 (2008), 295–315.

Lindley, F. M., *The Acquisition and Government of Backward Territory in International Law* (London: Longmans, 1926).

Linklater, A., 'Community' in A. Danchev (ed.), *Fin de Siecle: The Meaning of the Twentieth Century* (London: I. B. Tauris, 1995).

Lissitzyn, O. J., 'International Law in a Divided World', *International Conciliation*, (1963), 54–5.

Livey, L. (ed.), *The Nation State: The Formation of Modern Politics* (Oxford: Martin Robertson, 1981).

Luard, E., 'Civil Conflicts in Modern International Relations' in E. Luard (ed.), *The International Regulation of Civil Wars* (New York University Press, 1972).

Conflict and Peace in the Modern International System: A Study of the Principles of International Order (State University of New York Press, 1988).

Lyons, T. and Samatar, A., *Somalia: State Collapse, Multilateral Intervention, and Strategies for Political Reconstruction* (Washington, DC: The Brookings Institute, Occasional Paper, 1995).

Mac Ginty, R., *No War, No Peace: The Rejuvenation of Stalled Peace Processes and Peace Accords* (London: Palgrave Macmillan, 2006).

Macalister-Smith, P., *International Humanitarian Assistance – Disaster Relief Actions in International Law and Organisations* (Dordrecht: Martinus Nijhoff, 1985).

MacFarlane, S. N., 'Africa's Decaying Security System and the Rise of Intervention', *International Security*, 8:4 (1984), 127–51.

MacMillan, J., *On Liberal Peace: Democracy, War and the International Order* (New York: Tauris Academic Studies, 1998).

Magliveras, K. and Naldi, G., 'The African Union: A New Dawn for Africa?', *International and Comparative Law Quarterly*, 51 (2002), 415–25.

Makinda, S. M. and Okumu, W. F., *The African Union: Challenges of Globalisation, Security, and Governance* (London: Routledge, 2008).

Maluwa, T., *International Law in Postcolonial Africa* (Leiden: Kluwer Law International, 1999).

'Re-imagining African Unity: Some Preliminary Reflections on the Constitutive Act of the African Union', *African Yearbook of International Law*, (2002), 3–38.

'The Constitutive Act of the African Union and Institution Building in Postcolonial Africa', *Leiden Journal of International Law*, 16 (2003), 157–70.

Mamdani, M., *Citizen and Subject: Contemporary Africa and the Legacy of Late Colonialism* (Princeton University Press, 1996).

When Victims Become Killers: Colonialism, Nativism, and the Genocide in Rwanda (Princeton University Press, 2002).

Manby, B., 'The African Union, NEPAD, and Human Rights: The Missing Agenda', *Human Rights Quarterly*, 26 (2004), 984–1027.

Mandelbaum, M., *The Ideas that Conquered the World: Peace, Democracy, and Free Markets in the Twenty-first Century* (New York: Public Affairs Press, 2004).

Mansur, A. O., 'Contrary to a Nation: The Cancer of Somali State' in A. A. Jimale (ed.), *The Invention of Somalia* (Lawrenceville: Red Sea Press, 1995).

Markakis, J., *National and Class Conflict in the Horn of Africa* (Cambridge University Press, 1987).

Masina, N., 'Xhosa Practices of Ubuntu for South Africa' in I. W. Zartman (ed.), *Traditional Cures for Modern Conflicts: African Conflict Medicine* (Boulder, Colo.: Lynne Rienner, 2000).

Mason, P., *Deconstructing America: Representations of the Other* (New York: Routledge, 1990).

Mayall, J., 'International Society and International Theory' in M. Donelan (ed.), *The Reason of States: A Study in International Political Theory* (London: George Allen and Unwin, 1978).

'The Hopes and Fears of Independence: Africa and the World 1960–1990' in D. Rimmer (ed.), *Africa 30 Years On* (London: James Currey, 1991).

Mazrui, A., *Towards a Pax Africana: A Study of Ideology and Ambition* (London: Weidenfeld Goldbacks, 1967).

'The Anatomy of Violence in Contemporary Black Africa' in H. Kitchen (ed.), *Africa: From Mystery to Maze* (Toronto: Lexington Books, 1977).

The African Condition (The Reith Lectures) (London: Heinemann, 1980).

'Political Engineering in Africa', *International Social Science Journal*, 35:96 (1983), 279–94.

'Conflict as a Retreat from Modernity: A Comparative Overview' in O. Furley (ed.), *Conflict in Africa* (London: Tauris Academic Studies, 1995).

Mazzeo, D. (ed.), *African Regional Organisations* (Cambridge University Press, 1984).

Mbigi, L., *Ubuntu: The Spirit of African Transformation Management* (Randburg: Knowledge Resources Ltd, 1994).

McKeough, C., *Innocent Civilians: the Morality of Killing in War* (Basingstoke: Palgrave, 2002).

Mead, M., 'Alternatives to War' in M. Fried, M. Harris and R. Murphy (eds.), *War: The Anthropology of Armed Conflict and Aggression* (New York: Natural History Press, Garden City, 1967).

Mehta, V. R., *Beyond Marxism: Towards an Alternative Perspective* (New Delhi: Manohar Publications, 1978).

Menkhaus, K., 'US Foreign Assistance to Somalia: Phoenix from the Ashes?', *Middle East Policy*, 5:1 (1997), 124–49.

'State Collapse in Somalia: Second Thoughts', *Review of Africa Political Economy*, (2003), 405–22.

Somalia: State Collapse and the Threat of Terrorism (Oxford University Press, 2004).

Mickelson, K., 'Rhetoric and Rage: Third World Voices in International Legal Discourse', *Wisconsin International Law Journal*, 16 (1997–98), 353–420.

Middleton, J. and Tait, D., *Tribes Without Rulers: Studies in African Segmentary Systems* (London: Routledge, 1970).

Middleton, K. W. B., 'Sovereignty in Theory and Practice' in W. J. Stankiewicz (ed.), *The Defense of Sovereignty* (New York: Oxford University Press, 1969).

Mill, J. S., *On Liberty* (London: Longmans, 1869).

Mitchell, C., 'External Peace-making Initiatives and Intra-national Conflict' in M. I. Midlarsky (ed.), *The Internationalisation of Communal Strife* (London: Routledge, 1992).

Mohamoud, A. A., 'Somalia: The Pitfalls of Drain of Human Resources' in S. M. Lilius (ed.), *Variations of the Theme of Somaliness: Proceedings of the EASS/ SSIA International Congress of Somali Studies, Centre for Continuing Education* (Turku: Abo Akademi University, 2001).

  State Collapse and Post-Conflict Development in Africa: The Case of Somalia (1960–2001) (West Lafayette, Ind: Purdue University Press, 2006).

Moir, L., 'The Historical Development of the Application of Humanitarian Law in Non-International Armed Conflicts to 1949', *International and Comparative Law Quarterly*, 47:2 (1998), 337–61.

Moore, J. N. (ed.), *Law and Civil War in the Modern World* (Baltimore: Johns Hopkins University Press, 1974).

Moskowitz, M., *The Politics and Dynamics of Human Rights* (New York: Oceana, 1968).

Muchie, M. (ed.), *The Making of the African Nation: Pan-Africanism and the African Renaissance* (London: Adonis & Abbey, 2003).

Muggah, R., 'No Magic Bullet: A Critical Perspective on Disarmament, Demobilisation and Reintegration (DDR) and Weapons Reduction in Post-conflict Contexts', *The Commonwealth Journal of International Affairs*, 94:379 (2005), 239–52.

Munya, P. M., 'The Organisation of African Unity and its Role in Regional Conflicts Resolution and Dispute Settlement: A Critical Evaluation', *Boston College Third World Law Journal*, 19 (1998–99), 537–91.

Murithi, T., *The African Union, Pan-Africanism, Peacebuilding and Development* (Aldershot: Ashgate Publishers, 2005).

  'The African Union's Evolving Role in Peace Operations: The African Union Mission in Burundi, the African Union Mission in Sudan and the African Union Mission in Somalia', *African Security Review*, 17:1 (2008), 71–82.

Murray, R., 'Preventing Conflicts in Africa: The Need for a Wider Perspective', *Journal of African Law*, 45:1 (2001), 13–24.

  Human Rights in Africa: From the OAU to the African Union (Cambridge University Press, 2004).

Mutua, M., 'Why Redraw the Map of Africa: A Moral and Legal Inquiry', *Michigan Journal of International Law*, 16 (1994–95), 1113–76.

  'Critical Race Theory and International Law: The View of an Insider-Outsider', *Villanova Law Review*, 45 (2000), 841–53.

  'What is TWAIL?', *American Society of International Law Proceedings*, 94 (2000), 31–40.

  'Savages, Victims and Saviors: The Metaphor of Human Rights', *Harvard International Law Journal*, 36:3 (2001), 201–45.

Mwakikagile, G., *Africa and the West* (New York: Nova Science Publishers Inc., 2000).

Nabulsi, K., *Traditions of War – Occupation, Resistance and the Law* (Oxford University Press, 1999).

Naipaul, V. S., *The Mimic Men* (London: Vintage Books, 1985).

Naldi, G. J., *The Organisation of African Unity: An Analysis of its Role*, 2nd edn (London: Mansell, 1999).

Naldi, G. J. and Magliveras, K. D., 'The African Economic Community: Emancipation for African States or Yet Another Glorious Failure?', *North Carolina Journal of International Law and Commercial Regulation*, 24 (1999), 601–31.

    'Future Trends in Human Rights in Africa: The Increased Role of the OAU' in M. Evans and R. Murray (eds.), *The African Charter on Human and Peoples' Rights: The System in Practice, 1986–2000* (Cambridge University Press, 2002).

Nardin, T., *Law, Morality and the Relations of States* (Princeton University Press, 1983).

Nayar, J., 'Between Hope and Despair: The Iraq War and International Law Futures?' in P. Shiner and A. Williams (eds.), *The Iraq War and International Law* (Oxford: Hart Publishing, 2008).

Ndulo, M., 'Harmonisation of Trade Laws in the African Economic Community', *International and Comparative Law Quarterly*, 42 (1993), 101–18.

Neff, S. C., *War and the Law of Nations: A General History* (Cambridge University Press, 2005).

    'A Short History of International Law' in M. D. Evans (ed.), *International Law* (Oxford University Press, 2006).

Neuman, G. L., 'Humanitarian Law and Counterterrorist Force', *European Journal of International Law*, 14:2 (2003), 283–98.

Newbury, C., 'States at War: Confronting Conflict in Africa', *African Studies Review*, 45 (2002), 1–20.

Nicholls, B., 'Rubber Band Humanitarianism', *Ethics and International Affairs*, 1 (1987), 191–210.

Nkrumah, K., *The Autobiography of Kwame Nkrumah* (Edinburgh University Press, 1957).

    I Speak of Freedom: A Statement of African Ideology (London: Heinemann, 1961).

    Axioms of Kwame Nkrumah (London: PANAF, 1967).

Noble, F. P., *The Chicago Congress on Africa* (Washington: DC, Library of Congress, 1894).

Nolan, C. J., 'Road to the Charter: America, Liberty and the Founding of the United Nations', *Global Society*, 3:1 (1989), 24–37.

Norwine, J. and Gonzalez, A., *The Third World, States of Mind and Being* (Winchester, Mass: Unwin Hyman, 1988).

Nussbaum, A., *A Concise History of the Law of Nations* (New York: Macmillan, 1954).

Nyamnjoh, F. B., 'Reconciling "the Rhetoric of Rights" with Competing Notions of Personhood and Agency in Botswana' in H. Englund and F. B. Nyamnjoh (eds.), *Rights and the Politics of Recognition in Africa* (London: Zed Books, 2004).

Nyerere, J. K., 'South-South Option' in A. Gauhar (ed.), *The Third World Strategy: Economic and Political Cohesion in the South* (Westport: Praeger Publishers, 1983).

Obasanjo, O., Opening Statement at the Brainstorming Meeting on Conference on Security, Stability, Development and Co-operation in Africa, Addis Ababa, 17–18 November 1990.

'Preface' in F. M. Deng and I. W. Zartman (eds.), *Conflict Resolution in Africa* (Washington, DC: The Brookings Institution, 1991).

Obasanjo, O. and Mosha, F. G. N. (eds.), *Africa Rise to the Challenge: Conference Report on the Kampala Forum* (Abeokuta and New York: Africa Leadership Forum, 1992).

O'Donovan, O., *The Just War Revisited* (Cambridge University Press, 2003).

Odunuga, S., 'Achieving Good Governance in Post-Conflict Situations: The Dialectic between Conflict and Good Governance' in A. Adedeji (ed.), *Comprehending and Mastering African Conflicts: The Search for Sustainable Peace and Good Governance* (London: Zed Books, 1999).

Ofuatey-Kodjoe, W., *Pan-Africanism: New Direction in Strategy* (Lanham: University Press of America, 1986).

Ogot, B. A. (ed.), *War and Society in Africa* (London: Frank Cass, 1972).

Ojo, A., 'Inimitable Population Dispersion: The Case of the Somalian Diaspora' in A. A. Osman and I. K. Souare (eds.), *Somalia at the Crossroads: Challenges and Perspectives on Reconstituting a Failed State* (London: Adonis and Abbey Publishers Ltd, 2007).

Okafor, O. C., *Re-defining Legitimate Statehood – International Law and State Fragmentation in Africa* (The Hague: Martinus Nijhoff, 2000).

'Newness, Imperialism, and International Legal Reforms in Our Time: A TWAIL Perspective', *Osgoode Hall Law Journal*, 43:1 (2005), 171–91.

The African Human Rights System: Activist Forces and International Institutions (Cambridge University Press, 2007).

Okere, B. O., 'The Protection of Human Rights in Africa and the African Charter on Human Rights and People's Rights: A Comparative Analysis with the European and American System', *Human Rights Quarterly*, 6 (1984), 141–59.

Okeye, F. C., *International Law and the New African States* (London: Sweet & Maxwell, 1972).

Olmsted, M., 'Are Things Falling Apart? Rethinking the Purpose and Function of International Law', *Loyola of Los Angeles International and Comparative Law Review*, 27 (2005), 401–42.

Omaar, R., 'The Best Chance for Peace', *Africa Report*, (1993), 44–8.

Orford, A. (ed.), *International Law and its Others* (Cambridge University Press, 2006).

Osgood, R. E. and Tucker, R. W., *Force, Order and Justice* (Baltimore: Johns Hopkins University Press, 1967).

Osman, A. A., 'The Somali Internal War and the Role of Inequality, Economic Decline and Access to Weapons' in A. A. Osman and I. K. Souare (eds.), *Somalia at the Crossroads: Challenges and Perspectives on Reconstituting a Failed State* (London: Adonis and Abbey Publishers Ltd, 2007).

Otto, D., 'Subalternity and International Law: The Problems of Global Community and the Incommensurability of Difference', *Soc. & Legal Stud.*, 5 (1996), 337–64.

Ould-Abdallah, A., *Burundi on the Brink 1993–95 – A UN Special Envoy Reflects on Preventive Diplomacy* (Washington, DC: United States Institute of Peace, 2000).

Owen, J. M., 'How Liberalism Produces Democratic Peace' in M. E. Brown, J. Lynn and S. E. Miller (eds.), *Debating the Democratic Peace* (Cambridge, Mass: MIT Press, 1996).

Oyebade, A. and Alao, A. (eds.), *Africa After the Cold War: The Changing Perspective on Security* (Trenton: Africa World Press, 1998).

Ndegwa, P., 'Africa and the World: Africa on its Own' in O. Obasanjo and F. G. N. Mosha (eds.), *Africa: Rise to Challenge* (Otta: Africa Leadership Forum, 1992).

Padmore, G., *Pan-Africanism or Communism? The Coming Struggle for Africa* (London: Dobson, 1956).

Paret, P., *Clausewitz and the State* (Oxford: Clarendon Press, 1976).

Parker, C. A. and Rukare, D., 'The New African Union and its Constitutive Act', *American Journal of International Law*, 96:2 (2002), 365–78.

Paul, T. V., Ikenberry, G. J. and Hall, J. A., *The Nation-state in Question* (Princeton University Press, 2003).

Paulus, A. L., 'International Law After Postmodernism: Towards Renewal or Decline of International Law?', *Leiden Journal of International Law*, 14 (2001), 727–55.

Paupp, T. E., *Achieving Inclusionary Governance: Advancing Peace and Development in First and Third World Nations* (New York: Transnational Publishers, 2000).

Peterson, V. S., 'Security and Sovereign States: What is at Stake in Taking Feminism Seriously?' in V. S. Peterson (ed.), *Gendered States: Feminist (Re)Visions of International Relations Theory* (Boulder, Colo.: Lynne Rienner Publishers, 1992).

Phillipson, C., *The International Law and Custom of Ancient Greece and Rome* (London: MacMillan, 1911).

Piot, C., *Remotely Global: Village Modernity in West Africa* (University of Chicago Press, 1999).

Powell, K., 'The African Union's Emerging Peace and Security Regime: Opportunities and Challenges for Delivering on the Responsibility to Protect'. ISS

Monograph Series, 119 (2005), www.iss.org.za/Pubs/Monographs/No119/
Contents.htm.

Prunier, G., 'Somaliland: Birth of a New Country?' in C. Gurdon (ed.), *The Horn
of Africa* (London: UCL Press, 1994).

The Rwanda Crisis: History of a Genocide (London: Hurst and Company, 1995).

Rajagopal, B., 'Locating the Third World in Cultural Geography', *Third World
Legal Studies*, (1998–99), 1–20.

'From Resistance to Renewal: The Third World, Social Movements and the
Expansion of International Institutions', *American International Law
Journal*, 41:2 (2000), 529–78.

'International Law and Third World Resistance' in A. Anghie *et al.* (eds.), *The
Third World and International Order: Law, Politics and Globalisation*
(Leiden: Martinus Nijhoff, 2003).

*International Law from Below: Development, Social Movements and Third World
Resistance* (Cambridge University Press, 2003).

'Invoking the Rule of Law in Post-Conflict Rebuilding: A Critical Examination',
William and Mary Law Review, 49 (2008), 1346–74.

Ramphul, R. K., 'The Role of International and Regional Organisations in the
Peaceful Settlement of Internal Disputes (With Special Emphasis on the
Organisation of African Unity)', *Georgia Journal of International and Com-
parative Law*, 13 (1983), 371–84.

Ramsbotham, O. and Woodhouse, T., *Humanitarian Intervention in Contemporary
Conflict: A Reconceptualisation* (Cambridge: Polity Press, 1996).

Ramsey, P., *War and the Christian Conscience* (Durham, NC: Duke University
Press, 1961).

Randelzhofer, A., 'Article 2(4)' in B. Simma (ed.), *The Charter of the United
Nations: A Commentary* (Oxford University Press, 2002).

Rawls, J., *The Law of Peoples* (Cambridge, Mass: Harvard University Press,
1999).

Refugee Policy Group, *Hope Restored? Humanitarian Aid in Somalia 1990–1994*
(Washington, DC: RPG, 1994).

Reno, W., *Warlord Politics and African States* (Boulder, Colo.: Lynne Rienner, 1998).

Reychler, L., 'From Conflict to Sustainable Peacebuilding: Concepts and Analytical
Tools' in L. Reychler and T. Paffenholz (eds.), *Peacebuilding: A Field Guide*
(London: Lynne Rienner, 2000).

Reyntjens, F., *Burundi: Breaking the Cycle of Violence* (London: Minority Rights
Group, 1995).

Richards, P., 'New War: An Ethnographic Approach' in P. Richards (ed.), *No Peace,
No War: An Anthropology of Contemporary Armed Conflicts* (Oxford: James
Currey, 2005).

Rimmer, D., 'The Effects of Conflicts, II: Economic Effects' in O. Furley (ed.),
Conflict in Africa (London: Tauris Academic Studies, 1995).

Robert F. Kennedy Memorial Center for Human Rights, *Kenya at the Crossroads: Demands for Constitutional Reforms Intensify* (New York, 1997).

Roberts, A., 'Law, Lawyers, and Nuclear Weapons', *Review of International Studies*, 16:1 (1990), 75–92.

Robertson, G., *Crime Against Humanity: The Struggle for Global Justice* (London: New Press, 2006).

Rodney, W., *Walter Rodney Speaks: The Making of an African Intellectual* (Trenton: Africa World Press, 1990).

'Towards the Sixth Pan-African Congress: Aspects of the International Class Struggle in Africa, the Caribbean, and America', in M. K. Asante and A. S. Abarry (eds.), *African Intellectual Heritage: A Book of Sources* (Philadelphia: Temple University Press, 1996).

Rogers, B. and Laitin, D., 'Ethnic and Nationalist Violence', *Annual Review of Sociology*, 24 (1998), 423–52.

Rosen, E., *Creating Ethnicity: The Process of Ethnogenesis* (London: SAGE Publishers, 1989).

Rothchild, D., 'An Interactive Model for State-Ethnic Relations' in F. M. Deng and I. W. Zartman (eds.), *Conflict Resolution in Africa* (Washington, DC: The Brookings Institution, 1991).

Rothchild, D. and Olorunsola, V. A. (eds.), *State Versus Ethnic Claims: African Policy Dilemmas* (Boulder, Colo.: Westview Press, 1983).

Sahnoun, M., *Somalia: The Missed Opportunities* (Washington, DC: United States Institute of Peace, 1994).

Salim, A. S., *The Political and Socio-economic Situation in Africa and the Fundamental Changes Taking Place in the World* (Addis Ababa: OAU, 1990).

Samatar, A., 'Somali Studies: Towards an Alternative Epistemology', *Northeast African Studies*, 11:1 (1989), 3–17.

The State and Rural Transformations in Northern Somalia (Madison: University of Wisconsin Press, 1989).

'Under Siege: Blood, Power, and the Somali State' in P. Anyang' Nyong'o (ed.), *Arms and Daggers in the Hearts of Africa* (Nairobi: Academy Science Publishers, 1993).

Socialist Somalia: Rhetoric and Reality (London: Zed Books, 1998).

Samatar, A. I., 'Somalia: Statelessness as Homelessness' in A. I. Samatar and A. Samatar (eds.), *The African State: Reconsiderations* (Portsmouth: Heinemann, 2002).

Samatar, A. I. and Samatar, A. (eds.), *The African State: Reconsiderations* (Portsmouth: Heinemann, 2002).

Samatar, S., *Oral Poetry and Somali Nationalism: The Case of Sayyid Mahammad Abdille Hasan* (Cambridge University Press, 1982).

Samuels, K., '*Jus ad Bellum* and Civil Conflicts: A Case Study of the International Community's Approach to Violence in the Conflict in Sierra Leone', *Journal of Conflict and Security Law*, 8:2 (2003), 315–38.

Sands, P., *Lawless World: The Whistle-blowing Account of How Bush and Blair are Taking the Law into their Own Hands* (London: Penguin Books, 2006).

Santos, B. Sousa, *Towards a New Common Sense: Law, Science and Politics in the Paradigmatic Transition* (New York: Routledge, 1995).

'A Critique of Lazy Reason: Against the Waste of Experience' in I. Wallerstein (ed.), *The Modern World-System in the Longue Durée* (Boulder, Colo.: Paradigm Publishers, 2004).

'The Heterogeneous State and Legal Pluralism in Mozambique', *Law and Society Review*, 40:1 (2006), 39–76.

'Beyond Abyssal Thinking: From Global Lines to Ecologies of Knowledges', *Review*, XXX(1) (2007), 45–89.

'Epistemologies of the South: Reinventing Social Imagination'. Paper presented at the Staff-Student Seminar, School of Law, University of Warwick, 12 April 2010.

Santos, B. Sousa, Nunes, J. A. and Meneses, M. P., 'Introduction: Opening Up the Canon of Knowledge and Recognition of Difference' in B. de Sousa Santos (ed.), *Another Knowledge is Possible: Beyond Northern Epistemologies* (London: Verso, 2008).

Schabas, W., 'International Law and Response to Conflict' in C. Crocker, F. Hampson and P. Aall (eds.), *Turbulent Peace: The Challenges of Managing International Conflict* (Washington, DC: United States Institute of Peace, 2001).

Schachter, O., *International Law in Theory and Practice* (Dordrecht: Martinus Nijhoff, 1991).

Schmitt, M. and Pejic, J. (eds.), *International Law and Armed Conflict: Exploring the Faultlines: Essays in Honour of Yoram Dinstein* (Dordrecht: Martinus Nijhoff, 2007).

Scholtz, W., 'The Changing Rules of *Jus ad Bellum*: Conflicts in Kosovo, Iraq and Afghanistan', *Potchefstroom Electronic Law Journal*, 2 (2004), 1–37.

Schraeder, P., 'The Horn of Africa: US Foreign Policy in an Altered Cold War Environment', *Middle East Journal*, 46:4 (1992), 571–93.

Scott, D., *Refashioning Futures: Criticism After Postcoloniality* (Princeton University Press, 1999).

Sen, A., *Development as Freedom* (Oxford University Press, 1999).

Sesay, A., 'The African Union: Forward March or About Face-Turn?', *Clauke Ake Memorial Papers* (Nordic African Institute, Uppsala), 3 (2008).

Shaw, M., *Title to Territory in Africa: International Legal Issues* (Oxford: Clarendon Press, 1986).

International Law, 3rd edn (Cambridge University Press, 1991).

International Law, 5th edn (Cambridge University Press, 2003).

Shepperson, G., 'Notes on Negro American Influences on the Emergence of African Nationalism', *Journal of African History*, 1:2 (1960), 299–31.

Shiner, P. and Williams, A. (eds.), *The Iraq War and International Law* (Oxford: Hart Publishing, 2008).

Shivji, I. G., *The Concept of Human Rights in Africa* (London: CODESRIA Book Series, 1989).

Shklar, J., *The Faces of Injustice* (New Haven and London: Yale University Press, 1990).

Simma, B., 'NATO, the UN and the Use of Force: Legal Aspects', *European Journal of International Law*, 10 (1999), 1–22.

Simons, A., *Network of Dissolution: Somalia Undone* (Boulder, Colo.: Westview Press, 1995).

'Somalia: A Regional Security Dilemma' in E. J. Keller and D. Rothchild (eds.), *Africa in the New International Order: Rethinking State Sovereignty and Regional Security* (London: Lynne Rienner Publishers, 1996).

Slaughter, A., 'Pushing the Limits of the Liberal Peace: Ethnic Conflicts and the "Ideal Polity"' in D. Wippman (ed.), *International Law and Ethnic Conflict* (Ithaca: Cornell University Press, 1998).

Smith, A., 'The Ethnic Source of Nationalism', *Survival*, 35:1 (1993), 48–62.

Sorabji, R. and Rodin, D. (eds.), *The Ethics of War – Shared Problems in Different Traditions* (Oxford University Press, 2007).

Souare, I. K., 'The United Nations Intervention in Somalia: A Retrospective Look and Lessons for Future Africa-UN Partnership in Conflict Resolution' in A. A. Osman and I. K. Souare (eds.), *Somalia at the Crossroads: Challenges and Perspectives on Reconstituting a Failed State* (London: Adonis and Abbey Publishers Ltd, 2007).

Stahn, C., '*Jus ad bellum, jus in bello . . . jus pos bellum*? Rethinking the Conception of the Law of Armed Force', *The European Journal of International Law*, 17:5 (2006), 921–43.

Starke, J. G., *Starke's International Law* (London: Butterworths, 1994).

Stedman, S., 'Conflict and Conflict Resolution in Africa' in F. M. Deng and I. W. Zartman (eds.), *Conflict Resolution in Africa* (Washington, DC: The Brookings Institution, 1991).

Stremlau, J. J., *The International Politics of the Nigeria Civil War 1967–1970* (Princeton University Press, 1977).

Sunter, A. F., 'TWAIL as Naturalised Epistemological Inquiry', *Canadian Journal of Law and Jurisprudence*, 20:2 (2007), 475–507.

Surya, P. S., *Legal Polycentricity and International law* (Chapel Hill, NC: Carolina Academic Press, 1996).

Suter, K., *An International Law of Guerrilla Warfare* (London: Frances Pinter, 1984).

Tansley, D., *Final Report: An Agenda for Red Cross* (Geneva: Henry Dunant Institute, 1975).

Taylor, I., *Stuck in Middle GEAR: South Africa's Post-Apartheid Foreign Relations* (Westport, CT: Praeger Publishing, 2001).

Taylor, M., *Community, Anarchy and Liberty* (Cambridge University Press, 1982).

Tesha, J., 'Addressing the Challenges of Peace and Security in Africa'. Conflict Management Centre, OAU Secretariat, Addis Ababa, Ethiopia, Occasional Paper Series No. 1, 1999.

Teson, F. R., *A Philosophy of International Law* (Boulder, Colo.: Westview Press, 1998).

Thapar, R., *Early India: From the Origins to AD 1300* (Berkeley: University of California Press, 2002).

Tharoor, S., 'The Messy Afterlife of Colonialism', *Global Governance*, 8:1 (2002), 1–5.

The Nordic Africa Institute, 'Somalia: A Nation Without A State'. Reports from Public Seminars on the Conflict in Somalia, October/November 2007.

Thomas, D. C., *The Helsinki Effect, International Norms, Human Rights and the Demise of Communism* (Princeton University Press, 2001).

Tieku, T. K., 'Explaining the Clash and Accommodation of Interests of Major Actors in the Creation of the African Union', *African Affairs*, 103 (2004), 249–67.

'African Union Promotion of Human Security in Africa', *African Security Review*, 16:2 (2007), 26–37.

Tismaneanu, V., *Fantasies of Salvation: Democracy, Nationalism, and Myth in Post-Communist Europe* (Princeton University Press, 1998).

Tomuschat, C., 'International Law: Ensuring the Survival of Mankind on the Eve of a New Century', *Recueil des Cours*, 23 (1999), 1–281.

Tordoff, W., *Government and Politics in Africa* (Bloomington: Indiana University Press, 1984).

Touval, S., *Somali Nationalism* (Cambridge, Mass: Harvard University Press, 1963).

Tshitereke, C., 'On the Origins of War in Africa', *Africa Security Review*, 12:2 (2003), 32–40.

Udombana, N. J., 'Can the Leopard Change its Spots? The African Union Treaty and Human Rights', *American University International Law Review*, 17 (2002), 1177.

UNDP, *Human Development Report* (New York: Oxford University Press, 1990).

Human Development Report: Deepening Democracy in a Fragmented World (Oxford University Press, 2002).

United Nations Department for Peacekeeping Operations, *The Comprehensive Report on Lessons Learned from United Nations Operation in Somalia (UNOSOM), April 1992–March 1995* (New York: UN Department of Public Information, 1995).

Uvin, P., *Life After Violence: A People's Story of Burundi* (London: Zed Books, 2009).

Van Nieuwkerk, A., 'Regionalism into Globalism? War into Peace? SADEC and ECOWAS Compared', *African Security Review*, 10 (2001).

Villa, S. M., 'The Philosophy of International Law: Suarez, Grotius and Epigones', *International Review of the Red Cross*, 320 (1997), 539–52.

Waal, de, A. and Omaar, R., *Somalia: Operation Restore Hope: A Preliminary Assessment* (London: African Rights, 1993).

Walters, A., *My Life and Work* (New York: Fleming H. Revel Company, 1917).

Walzer, M., *Just and Unjust Wars: A Moral Argument with Historical Illustrations*, 4th edn (New York: Basic Books, 2006).

Wang, T., 'The Third World and International Law' in R. Macdonald and D. M. Johnston (eds.), *The Structure and Process of International Law* (Dordrecht: Martinus Nijhoff, 1986).

Warsame, A. M., *The Civil War in Northern Somalia (Somaliland): Its Impact on Pastoralists, especially Women and Children* (The Hague: Institute of Social Studies Research Report, 1997).

Weber, M., *The Theory of Social and Economic Organisation* (Oxford University Press, 1947).

    The Theory of Social and Economic Organisation, trans. A. Henderson and T. Parson (New York: Free Press, 1964).

Wedgwood, R., 'Limiting the Use of Force in Civil Disputes' in D. Wippman (ed.), *International Law and Ethnic Conflict* (Ithaca: Cornell University Press, 1998).

Weeramantry, C. G., 'International Law and the Developing World: A Millennial Analysis – Keynote Address', *Harvard International Law Journal*, 41:2 (2000), 277–86.

Weissman, S. R., *Preventing Genocide in Burundi* (Washington, DC: United States Institute of Peace, 1998).

Welch, D. A., *Justice and the Genesis of War* (Cambridge University Press, 1993).

Wiarda, H., *Ethnocentrism in US Foreign Policy: Can We Understand the Third World?* (Washington, DC: American Enterprise Institute for Public Policy, 1985).

Williams, D. J., *UN Peacekeeping, American Policies and the Uncivil Wars of the 1990s* (New York: St Martin's Press, 1996).

Williams, P. D. and Bellamy, A. J., 'The Responsibility to Protect and the Crisis in Darfur', *Security Dialogue*, 36:1 (2005), 28–47.

Wilson, A. H., *International Law and the Use of Force by National Liberation Movements* (Oxford: Clarendon Press, 1988).

Wiredu, K., *Cultural Universals and Particulars: An African Perspective* (Bloomington: Indiana University Press, 1996).

Wolfers, A. and Martin, L., *The Anglo-American Tradition in Foreign Affairs* (New Haven: Yale University Press, 1956).

Wolff, S., *Ethnic Conflict: A Global Perspective* (New York: Oxford University Press, 2006).

Woodward, P., 'Sudan: War Without End' in O. Furley (ed.), *Conflict in Africa* (London: Tauris Academic Studies, 1995).

World Bank, *Conflict in Somalia: Drivers and Dynamics* (2005), http://siteresources.worldbank.org/INTSOMALIA/Resources/conflictinsomalia.pdf.

Worsley, P., *The Third World* (London: Weidenfeld Goldbacks, 1964).

Wright, Q., *Research in International Law since the War* (Washington, DC: Carnegie Endowment for International Peace, 1930).

The Role of International Law in the Elimination of War (Manchester University Press, 1961).

WSP, *War-torn Societies Project Somalia* (Geneva: UNRISD, 1988).

Yohannes, O., *The United States and the Horn of Africa: An Analytical Study of Pattern and Process* (Boulder, Colo.: Westview Press, 1997).

Young, C., 'Zaire: Is There a State?', *Canadian Journal of African Studies*, 18:1 (1984), 80–2.

Young, I. M., 'The Ideal Community and the Politics of Difference', *Social Theory and Practice*, 12:1 (1986), 1–26.

Zacarias, A., *The United Nations and International Peacekeeping* (London: IB Tauris Publishers, 1996).

Zartman, I. W., 'African Conflict and Resolution: The OAU Role' in N. Obaseki (ed.), *African Regional Security and the OAU's Role in the Next Decade* (New York: International Peace Academy, 1984).

Ripe for Resolution: Conflict and Intervention in Africa (New York: Oxford University Press, 1985).

(ed.), *Traditional Cures for Modern Conflicts: African Conflict 'Medicine'* (Boulder, Colo.: Lynne Rienner, 2000).

INDEX

Printed in Great Britain
by Amazon.co.uk, Ltd.,
Marston Gate.